WHEN THINGS ARE QUIET
Philip R. Goodwin
permanent collection
National Cowboy Hall of Fame

B-345

Schoolwomen
of the
Prairies and Plains

Schoolwomen
of the
Prairies and Plains

Personal Narratives from

Iowa, Kansas, and Nebraska,

1860s–1920s

Mary Hurlbut Cordier

The University of New Mexico Press

Albuquerque

To the schoolwomen of the prairies and plains who lived with traditions to be honored and changed the traditions to be outgrown. May the schoolwomen of today and tomorrow continue to seek to know the difference.

Library of Congress Cataloging-in-Publication Data

Cordier, Mary Hurlbut, 1930–
Schoolwomen of the prairies and plains : personal narratives from Iowa, Kansas, and Nebraska, 1860s–1920s / Mary Hurlbut Cordier.—1st ed.
p.   cm.
With some primary material by Nancy Rebecca Higgins Gaddis, Missouri, 1862– 1942 and others.
Includes bibliographical references (p.   ) and index.
ISBN 0-8263-1384-1
1. Women teachers—Middle West—Social conditions. 2. Education—Middle West—History—19th century. 3. Women teachers—Iowa—Biography. 4. Women teachers—Kansas—Biography. 5. Women teachers—Nebraska—Biography.
I. Title.
LB2837.C66   1992
371.1'0092'2—dc20
92–493 CIP

Designed by
Linda Mae Tratechaud

Portions of chapters 1, 2, and 3 were first published in *Great Plains Quarterly* 8:2 (Spring 1988: 102–19 and *Plainswoman* 10:6 (March 1987): 3–5. A condensed version of chapter 9 was previously published in "The History of Women in Education in Greater Kalamazoo, a Regional History Project Commemorating National Women's History Week, 'Heritage of Strength and Vision,'" Supplement to *The Western Herald* (March 1989): Western Michigan University, Kalamazoo, Michigan, 5. Reprinted by permission.

Contents

Part II.

Seeing the Context, Hearing the Voice
Introduction to Five Lives
143

Chapter 5.

"A Sense of Unity"
Nancy Rebecca Higgins Gaddis, Missouri,
1862–1942; Nebraska, 1875–1942
149

Chapter 6.

"Greater Usefulness in My Calling"
Sarah Jane Price, Ohio, 1841–1843; Indiana, 1843–1874;
Iowa, 1874–1876; Nebraska, 1876–1920
175

Chapter 7.

"To Be a Teacher"
Sarah Gillespie Huftalen, Iowa, 1885–1955
209

Acknowledgments

Western Michigan University has supported the research for this book in part, through two faculty fellowships and research grants, and a sabbatical leave. The Department of Education and Professional Development, College of Education, enabled me to take a one-semester leave of absence in order to complete the manuscript. My thanks to all who made these leaves and grants possible.

My research was aided by the Graduate College, Western Michigan University, in providing Marilyn Branch-Myers as a research assistant for one semester. Marilyn has continued her support and interest far beyond that one semester commitment. Bettina Meyer and Heidi Rawson-Ketchum of the Inter-Library Loan Services of Western Michigan University Libraries have facilitated my research through obtaining the resources of many libraries. Wayne Mann, director, and the staff of the Regional History Collection, Western Michigan University, have assisted me by providing access to documents, obtaining census records, and through their continued interest in the project.

Therese Douville, Faculty Graphics Artist, College of Education, carefully copied old photographs from private sources, in many cases improving the quality of the photos. Her skills and interest are appreciated.

Special gratitude goes to Dr. James Bosco, director, and Ann Erickson, coordinator, and the late Vivian Welke, of the Merze Tate Center for Research and Information Processing, College of Education, Western Michigan University for their technical advice and support in the early stages of the manuscript.

Mary Baker, founder of the Davenport Community School Museum, Davenport, Iowa, and herself a pioneer schoolwoman, enabled me to use the resources of the School Museum and aided me in locating information about Phebe Sudlow and Agnes Samuelson. The staff of the Iowa State Historical Department, Division of the Historical Society, Iowa City, aided me in locating documents and photographs in the Historical Society's collection. Patricia Michaelis and the staff of the Kansas State Historical Society have laid the groundwork for many researchers through their annotated bibliographies of documents, and their prompt mail service. John Carter, curator of photographs, and the manuscript staff of the Nebraska State Historical Society, made my research there especially rewarding. Anne Diffendal, independent archivist, has been of very special help in answering my many questions.

Elizabeth Hampsten, University of North Dakota, and Frances Kaye, editor, *Great Plains Quarterly*, have encouraged me to continue my research and writing. I appreciate their continuing interest in my research and in the paper I presented at the Symposium on Women's Culture on the Great Plains, Center for Great Plains Studies, University of Nebraska, March 1987.

At Western Michigan University, my colleagues and members of the Women's History and Research Network have helped me by critically assessing my findings and interpretations. Special thanks to Dr. Barbara Havira, Dr. Judith Stone, and the late Dr. A. Edythe Mange, Department of History, and Lynn Smith Houghton, independent historian. Dr. Mary Lou Stewart provided valuable insights and guidelines in the organization of the index.

My thanks to the people who, through interviews and photographs, gave me access to their lives and their family documents. Eleanor McKinney and her aunt, the late Ruth Gaddis Wilson, have been generous with their time, information, documents, and photographs of the life of Nancy Higgins Gaddis. Sarah Jane Price's nieces, Goldie Price and Betty Merrill, Lincoln, Nebraska, gave their permission to publish excerpts from Price's diaries. Mrs. Merrill and Price's grand nephew, DeRoss Andrews, shared their recollections of their aunt. Mr. Andrews and his daughter, Jan Pintcke, both of Bridgeman, Michigan, provided photographs of Sarah Jane Price, and helped to fill in missing details of her life. Bessie Tucker Gilmer, Lincoln, Nebraska, has given me her memories on tape, in her photographs, through her diaries, and her letters to me. Robert and Ethel Hale Russel have shared their lives as children and teachers in Kansas, Nebraska, Idaho, Utah, Iowa, and Michigan. Special thanks to my sister, Betty Rowan, who interviewed pioneer schoolwomen and attended the Benedict School reunions in Kansas with her husband, the late Arlie Rowan.

My gratitude to Barbara Guth, editor, University of New Mexico Press, for her guiding hand and thoughtful suggestions and encouragement.

To my husband, Sherwood S. Cordier, my thanks for his loving support, his listening ear, and for encouraging me throughout the project.

Acknowledgments

Schoolwomen
of the
Prairies and Plains

Introduction

Among the women who made their homes in the west were those who taught the children of the settlers on the prairies and the plains. Their stories are largely lost through omission and obscured in the mire of stereotypes of the selfless, lonely but brave schoolmarm, or the ignorant, mean-spirited prude. These images of schoolwomen of the heartland bear few parallels to my life as a long-term teacher and raised the questions: Who were my professional ancestors?[1] What did they really accomplish? How did they blend their personal lives with their work? What were their hopes and fears? How did they contribute to the high levels of literacy in Iowa, Kansas, and Nebraska? Was it possible to recover and share their lives?

While vacationing at Steamboat Springs, Colorado, I visited the intriguing Tread of the Pioneer Museum, where I admired a small framed landscape constructed of bark, twigs, and moss. As I took a closer look, I found that the picture had been constructed by Emma Hull Peck, superintendent of the Routt County Schools, 1896–1926. Her longevity as a county superintendent amazed me! The public library had a few newspaper articles about Peck and her long tenure as a teacher and county superintendent.[2] I felt that I had discovered a payload of women teachers' history in the Colorado mountains, and I wondered if I could locate other narratives and documents about and by women teachers.

When I returned to my home in Kalamazoo, Michigan, I visited the Regional History Collections at Western Michigan University seeking to test the theory that there was evidence about the lives of women teachers that revealed more than the stereotypic views of the schoolma'am as the heroine of democracy or an incompetent fool. The first document I read was the 1840 diary of Rebecca Bullard, an eighteen-year-old teacher in Dedham, Massachusetts, the hometown of Horace Mann. Her family moved west to Michigan, and through some fortunate circumstances, her diary was housed in the Regional History Collections.[3] To open her diary was in essence the opening of a long-term research project centering on the lives of women teachers. Bullard's diary, other than the syntax of the mid-1800s, read like the journals of my undergraduate students in teacher education as they pursued their field experiences in elementary classrooms and echoed the comments and complaints of the inservice teachers in my graduate classes. Bullard complained that the day would have gone well if a certain undisciplined child had stayed home, a comment familiar to any classroom teacher. She also wished for a "a more liberal education" so that she could answer the children's questions.

Encouraged by this and other documents, I focused the parameters of the research about schoolwomen in a region where teachers and public education appeared to be successful. The heartland states of Iowa, Nebraska, and Kansas emerged as the exemplars because of their high rates of literacy between 1870 and 1900.[4] Although the histories of these states are both separate and interrelated, there were similarities in the patterns of emigration, in the values brought by the immigrants, and in the development of their "self-educated society."[5] The evidence of the continued high rates of literacy indicates that the settlers supported public education at least to the degree that schools were built, teachers hired, and children learned to read. Public education in this region was so effective that between 1870 and 1900, "in Kansas, Iowa, and Nebraska it [illiteracy] fell below 3.0 per cent," while in the largely urban population of the North Atlantic section of the United States, the illiteracy rate dropped from 7.6 to 5.9 percent by 1900.[6]

Within this time and place framework, which coincides with the settlement and formation of communities on the prairies and plains, I have sought to recover the lives of schoolwomen through their own narratives, letters, diaries, interviews with living pioneers, memoirs, school reports, photographs, and other documents. My search for schoolwomen's documents, their "stories," and the personal evidence of their lives has been fruitful, although it often has taken the circuitous route of a treasure hunt: one clue led to another; a name in one place led to a picture or a letter in another place; and eventually the connections began to emerge.[7] Although thousands of schoolwomen left no records, there is a substantial body of documents from schoolwomen and their contemporaries. The State Historical Societies of Iowa (Iowa City), Nebraska, and Kansas have made this search increasingly easier through their continuing efforts to specifically catalog women's documents. However, those sources remain scattered throughout many sources, both public and private.

Numerous histories of education document the progression of state and local education, school policies, curriculum development, and educational standards. However, little is heard or regarded of the voices and experiences of the schoolwomen as the practitioners of education.[8]

The women teachers, principals, superintendents, and teacher educators are largely unknown except as "saints' lives," or in terms of quantification, such as, how many teachers graduated from high school and college; numbers of men and women teachers; or average length of teaching career.[9] The "saints' lives" may serve to honor teachers and, in limited ways, are part of both the prescriptive and descriptive literature conveyed in idealized or laudatory accounts of teachers' accomplishments. While the quantification can be an expression of growth and change, the individual schoolwomen, their lives, conflicts, and contributions, are often lost in the process.

This volume, based on the personal narratives and documents of ninety-six heartland schoolwomen, is an account of their multi-dimensional lives: their motivations, purposes, contributions, and opportunities; their complaints, frustrations, and foibles; their initial and continuing education; the role of work in their lives at home, in schools, in communities, and in their life cycles; their working conditions and what they taught; their families, friends, and relationships; their living conditions and involvement in homemaking, farming, and ranching; their religious faith and affiliations; and their leadership in and dedication to social causes. My goal is to link the voices, narratives, and accounts of schoolwomen within the context and environment of late nineteenth and early twentieth centuries and centering in the prairies and plains of Iowa, Kansas, and Nebraska. To that end, all women cited were schoolwomen during some portion of their lives, and the quotes from narratives, letters and documents are the words of schoolwomen unless otherwise noted in the text or the footnotes. I have tried to include sufficient depth to the quotes to give context to the event, opinion, or observation.

I have chosen to use the word *schoolwomen* rather than school-ma'am or schoolmarm in order to broaden and professionalize the term to include teachers, superintendents, principals, and teacher educators. The term *schoolma'am* tends to bring to mind the nostalgia and the folklore of the frontier school. Many accounts of such schooling begin and end with the superficial descriptions of the schoolhouse itself and some reference to the illusive "good ol' days." The term *schoolwomen* identifies the women themselves, not the stereotyped fiction.

In order to modify the stereotype that married women were universally forbidden to teach in the late nineteenth and early twentieth century, I have referred to the schoolwomen by their maiden or married names, according to the time of the event within the woman's life. To refer to seventeen-year-old Bessie as Bessie Tucker Gilmer is to imply that she was a married teacher. As she writes about her family's experiences during the Depression, she is indeed Bessie Tucker Gilmer. The footnotes will give the woman's full name as it is used in the source materials and documents. This approach will aid the reader in differentiating between a woman's experiences while single and when married and will serve to demonstrate that while many women quit teaching when they became married, there were those who continued teaching while married or returned to teaching at another time in their life cycle.

The inclusion of photographs from archival and private collections documents individual lives, the development of the schools, and the importance of the land. The photographs show the early dugout and log schools, and they picture the children and the visitors at the sod schoolhouses and the white frame buildings. We can pick out the brothers and sisters in their matching calico shirts and dresses, lined up, some barefooted, with their teacher. And at one schoolhouse, we find that a dog was a welcomed addition to the school picture. Photographs of school interiors show us that scholars came in all sizes, many larger and perhaps older than the teacher. Pictures and teaching charts decorate the walls along with the flag and children's schoolwork. We can see Sarah Gillespie Huftalen's scholars working diligently with her in rebuilding the schoolyard. Bessie Tucker Gilmer's diaries tell us that she processed and printed her photographs of her pupils and her schools. The photographs of William and Nancy Higgins Gaddis's timber claim, and the rugged canyons of Custer County, Nebraska, show us hiding places for stray cattle and places to pick wild plums. The photographs add the reality of the environment and the people and reveal transitions over time.

"Part One, The Educational and Historical Setting," establishes the educational, social and physical environment, and the geographical and historical context, thus setting the scene for interpreting the role of teaching in the lives of schoolwomen, and the role of schoolwomen within the emerging communities. An examination of the statistical identification of the schoolwomen, their salaries, the increase in number and percentage of women teachers, and the expansion of the school age population establishes the indigenous women as the educators of the heartland. The issues in the lives of schoolwomen then are examined in the states Iowa, Kansas, and Nebraska from the 1860s to the 1920s.

"Part Two, Seeing the Context, Hearing the Voice," examines the narratives of five schoolwomen, who together illustrate the issues in the lives of schoolwomen and the diversity within this group of working women. Of these five women, Nancy Higgins Gaddis, Missouri and Nebraska 1862–1942, and Bessie Tucker Gilmer, Nebraska, 1898–, were short-term teachers who taught for a few years until they were married. Sarah Jane Price, Indiana, Iowa, and Nebraska, 1841–1920, was an unmarried woman who prized the independence she acquired as a long-term teacher and farmer. Sarah Gillespie Huftalen, Iowa, 1865–1955, and Ethel Hale Russel, Nebraska, Idaho, Utah, Iowa, and Michigan, 1895–, were well-educated women who were the exceptional long-term professionals, teacher educators, and community leaders. The stories of their individual lives are based on their diaries, letters, memorabilia, school records, photographs and oral histories.

As I read and digested the diaries and letters, listened once more to the oral histories of the living pioneers, these schoolwomen became my treasured friends and colleagues as we shared gender, profession, and origins. I had begun my teaching career in a small town in my home state of Iowa after completing the two-year elementary curriculum at Iowa State Teachers College (now the University of Northern Iowa). Over the course of my career, I continued my education, became an elementary principal, and then a teacher educator. My life experiences have helped me to know these schoolwomen, their work, their triumphs and disappointments, and their world. I know Nancy Higgins Gaddis through her daughter, the late Ruth Gaddis Wilson, her granddaughter, Eleanor McKinney, and the family memorabilia and photo album. I've met independent Sarah Jane Price, the teacher, farmer, and avid reader, through her diaries and the memories of her niece and grand nephew, Betty Merrill and DeRoss Andrews. The voluminous personal diaries, school notebooks, and scrapbooks of Sarah Gillespie Huftalen have helped me to know this complex thinker and professional leader. Bessie Tucker Gilmer and I spent many hours together taping her oral history. The oral history, her diaries, and our correspondence extended our relationship. Ethel Hale Russel is a friend of many years' standing; however, it is only in recent years that we have specifically discussed and recorded her childhood, her education, her years of teaching and community service.

Through their overlapping lives, the transitions and progress in the education of children and teachers can be seen as well as the diversity of the roles of women. Their personal narratives, while different in form from one another, reveal their motivations and aspirations, not only to teach, but in their lives in general. Their narratives stand to serve for their many unknown colleagues.

Part I.

The Educational
and Historical Setting

CHAPTER
ONE

The Schoolwomen of the Prairies and Plains, 1860s–1920s

If the schools of the West had relied solely on schoolmasters and eastern schoolmarms to educate the children of the settlers, Iowa, Kansas, and Nebraska would not have achieved the highest rates of literacy in the nation during the late nineteenth and early twentieth centuries.[1] The population explosion in the West and the feminization of teaching after the Civil War brought about a demand for teachers that could not be filled by the eastern schoolmarms nor by the dwindling number of men teachers. Romanticized fiction and biased historical accounts of the American West have perpetuated the stock characters of the stern schoolmasters and the genteel eastern schoolmarms while omitting the indigenous schoolwomen as the most numerous educator-participants in the settlement, development, and education of the western society.[2]

To pursue "the profession of teaching [as] second to none in importance, influence and responsibility" in the rapidly developing environment west of the Mississippi in the period from the 1860s to the 1920s, there had to be thousands of schoolwomen such as Elizabeth K. Matthews, a long-term professional in Iowa, who was described by a superintendent as "a western wonder to me.—A genius—Original and successful in her plans and work."[3] Were the schoolwomen of the

9

heartland "western wonders?" On the prairies and plains of Iowa, Kansas, and Nebraska, events came together that pushed women into teaching, who, in another time or place, might not have worked outside of the home: the rapidly expanding but widely dispersed population; educational reform including the support of coeducational public schools and the lengthening school year; economic necessity and lack of employment opportunities for women; the expansion of woman's sphere beyond the home; and the pervasive idealism associated with women's dual role as the preservers and creators of their transplanted and transformed cultures.

The Settlers on the Prairies and Plains

In this subregion of Iowa, Kansas, and Nebraska during the late 1860s to the 1920s, where definitions of Midwest and West, prairies and plains come together, the land itself was the major attraction for the farm families who settled there.[4] The settler families came from New England (especially to Iowa and Kansas), Pennsylvania, Ohio, Indiana, Illinois, Michigan, and other areas east of the Mississippi; in addition there were large immigrant populations from northwestern and central Europe.[5] Encouraged by the Homestead Act of 1862 and the availability of purchasing land on credit from the railroads, the biggest landowners in the West, the settlers as families moved west following the river valleys and later the railroad lines, first to the prairie lands of Iowa, and then on to the prairies and plains of Nebraska and Kansas.[6] They set about the hard work necessary to establish farms, ranches, homes, and communities, in the hope that they would prosper from the potential of the agricultural economy. The families settled in and began to create a society that was reminiscent of but removed from their former homes.[7]

Mary Ward Smith recalled when her parents and their eight children emigrated to the "sparsely settled prairie in Iowa"; they found that the "families forming the settlement where the new home was built were mostly from Ohio, [and were] sturdy, brave, honest people, whose sole ambition was to make homes for themselves and their little ones."[8] Eliza A. Mercer recalled when her family journeyed from Wisconsin to Kansas in 1857: "We were very much surprise when we reached home [Highland, Doniphan County] to find we were the only children in town. . . . The town grew rapidly. Thar were more familys coming every day. Soon we had a happy and contented little town. A School house was built."[9]

Thirteen-year-old Nancy Higgins, her seven brothers and sisters, and her abolitionist parents emigrated from northern Missouri to Nebraska in 1875. With the help of neighbors, her father built a schoolhouse on the family's land where Nancy and her siblings attended school and later where several members of the family taught.[10]

For those who emigrated as children or who were born in the newly settled regions west of the Mississippi, the eastern American or European home sites lived in the memories of their parents.[11] The schoolwomen of the prairies and plains identified themselves as western women through their personal narratives, letters, diaries, and school records where they recorded their attachments to the unadorned plains and rolling prairies as their home country.[12] They realistically described the land with pride in its beauty, respect for the openness, and with the emotional affinity and relationships usually associated with home. For this second generation, the environment of their childhood prairie homes was the long, open vista such as recalled by Nebraskan Isabelle Simmons Stewart, "From my Father's place looking west [in 1869] there was neither house, tree nor cultivated land to arrest the vision. As far as the eye could reach there was nothing but the vast rolling prairie."[13]

For fourteen-year-old Alice Money the view from her family's Iowa farm in the 1860s included the "valley of the Iowa river, skirted on either side by broad belts of timber and numerous little groves in all directions. The farm dwellings, hundred acre corn fields and running brooks are all attractive to the eye." The Money family had immigrated from England to Ohio in 1850, and then to Iowa in 1862.[14]

The settler families brought their values, ideals, and attitudes to their new homes in the West, where the nucleus of their sense of community was the one-room schoolhouse and public education.[15] Indeed, as Malone and Etulain contend: "No social experience involved more westerners than did attendance of elementary and secondary schools, colleges, and universities. Thus schooling lies at the center of western culture and is pivotal to an understanding of that culture."[16]

The resulting character of the region was not unlike other agricultural regions of America.[17] The convergence of various emigrants and immigrants within "new geographic provinces" created, according to Turner, "differing societies in the different sections."[18] Malone and Etulain sum up these diversities of peoples within the American West as the "kaleidoscopic patterns of innovation and replication, of national conformity and regional distinction."[19]

Out of the histories of Iowa, Kansas, and Nebraska emerge the idealistic characteristics that brand this heartland area as the "most representative part of the American nation. . . . with [its] . . . pastoral stability of the region, its traditional moral values, and its down-to-earth veneration of family and hard work."[20] The second generation of native-born Americans and European-born settlers reflects the characteristics of "resilient strength, a self-reliance and sense of worth, and a tested understanding that hard times can be endured."[21] Are these "characteristics" a regional form of "saints' lives?" Turner theorized that these qualities were the result of the frontier shaping the "American intellect" and bringing forth "that practical, inventive turn of mind . . . ; that masterful grasp of material things, lacking in the artistic but powerful to effect great ends; that restless, nervous energy; that dominant individualism . . . which comes with freedom."[22]

Cultural fusion in the Midwest was the foundation of these characteristics of the "clear-eyed, pragmatic folk who had confidence in their own abilities and respect for the land. . . . Friendliness, for example might be expected to flourish where people are spread thin; humility where nature is powerful and capricious; and independence where one is isolated. Coping with life in a severe climate can even produce regional pride."[23] Among these "clear-eyed pragmatic folk" were the indigenous schoolwomen, products of their environment and of their metamorphosed culture.

Many aspects of the settlers' lives and aspirations were, as Earl Pomeroy proposes, the continuation, transfer, or imitation of old institutions, customs, and ideals to the West.[24] This reproduction of the institutions and ideals related to schooling can be seen in the transfer of the school laws from New England to the old Northwest; then particularly from Michigan and Ohio to Iowa and Nebraska.[25] However, by 1850, the midwestern states east of the Mississippi had not yet provided free public education.[26] While many adult prairie settlers grew up with this lack of public education, in the educational and community void of the open country, they sought public education for their own children.

Support for Public Coeducation and Educational Reform

There was a liberating potential in the larger environment and social atmosphere of the prairie frontier and early settlements that encouraged and accepted the development of coeducational public schools. Horace Mann's view that women as teachers brought about "the addition of a new and mighty power to the forces of civilization," was upheld on the prairies and plains where the rapidly increasing population necessitated staffing the schools with available teachers from the region and thus firmly established the social approval of women working outside of the home as teachers.[27] By the 1870s, two-thirds of the teachers in the United States were women; the majority were white and from the lower-middle-class families of farmers, shop-keepers, and artisans.[28] The preponderance of prairie schoolwomen were white women, the wives, mothers, and daughters of the lower-middle-class families who "occupied the rough edge between manual and intellectual labor."[29]

Through "the application of older institutions and ideas to the transforming influences of free land," the heartland settlers established coeducational public schools.[30] According to S. D. Beals, the state superintendent of education in Nebraska in 1869, the settlers were:

> . . . free from the prejudices which grow up amid old associations, that are peculiar to long settled and unchanging communities.
> They are inspired under the influences of a rapid development in physical resources and material wealth, to look for corresponding progress in social, political and religious sentiments and institutions. They have left the old, they expect the new.[31]

Beals further observed that despite the financial hardships the settlers supported universal public education by taxing themselves "to the full limit of the Law, and, in known instances, they have, by common consent, exceeded even that."[32] In Monroe County, Iowa, in 1896, the settlers expressed their support of education by raising money in addition to their taxes in order to hire competent, capable teachers.[33] The settlers apparently believed that teachers who were well qualified both by interest and training would provide education for all children thus aiding the entire community. Sturdy sod school-houses or white frame buildings were constructed as soon as the tax base in a district was adequate to support both the schoolhouse and the teacher's salary.[34] However, until there were enough taxpayers in a school district to build and support a school building, temporary schools were established in settlers' homes, in dugouts, and in sod houses. Amelia Phoneta Bruner, West Point, Nebraska, recalled that in the 1860s, "[for] four or five years school was held in Mrs. Jones' house and one winter in our house."[35] Isabelle Simmons began teaching in Saline County, Nebraska, January 1, 1870, in the Chatman family's log house of two rooms. "They lived in one room and my school [with 16 to 18 pupils] was in the other."[36] School was held in the upstairs of E. Mary Lacy's home in Palo Alto County, Iowa, 1870–1871. She recalled:

> It was hard for mother to have children trooping through her living room which was also dining room and kitchen, eight times a day, for we had recess both forenoon and afternoon as well as the noon hour. But she was willing to put up with any inconvenience for the sake of the children.[37]

Attention was given to establishing schools and obtaining teachers even as the settlers were moving into an area. James Bell, county superintendent, Polk County, Nebraska, reported on the status of seven school districts in 1871. He described the condition of the dugouts and sod schoolhouses in some districts and attested to the swift expansion in others:

> District no. 5. On the Platte River. I was the first settled in the district. Moved here last April. Until then there was not a living habitation to be seen. In six weeks thirty-two families settled here. I set about organizing a school district, which being done, I was elected director. We had our first school meeting on the 21st of June, and on the 1st of November we had a school house built, size 20 x 26, plastered, painted and seated with patent seats from Sterling, Illinois. Total cost $700 beside $64 donated labor from the district. Three months school [term].[38]

Both the leaders and the common folks mandated public education for the prairie children. Iowa governor James W. Grimes identified the significant appeal of education for the ordinary citizens as "the great equalizer of human condition. It places the poor on an equality with the rich. . . . Every consideration . . . impels us to sustain the common schools of the state. . . ."[39]

Ethel Hale Russel recalled the value her family placed on education during the early 1900s in Hardy, Nebraska, near the Kansas border:

> Schooling was very important in our lives. . . . You see the whole attitude in our family was that schooling, a chance to go

to school, to read books: This was the *real* opportunity. This was
generated, largely I think, because my mother had such a strong
feeling about learning, about books and education. . . . And I
think this must have come from her mother. . . . But all of the
time, I remember we knew that schooling, the *chance* to go
to school, the *opportunity* to go to school, was the *paramount*
thing.[40]

Catharine "Cassie" Wiggins's parents as well as other families
moved frequently looking for that elusive but best location. They
wanted Cassie to have a good education,

. . . and mother was still resolved on this, despite the little progress I had made in our moving from place to place. The move to
Lenora [Kansas, 1888] was no exception. The teacher was a miserable excuse. He spent nearly as much time between 9 a.m. and
4 p.m. in the billiard hall as in the school room. There was, of
course, no semblance of order. . . . So again, so far as learning
from books was concerned, the move to Lenora was a failure.[41]

After a move to Fremont, Kansas, Cassie Wiggins was in an over-
crowded school with sixty children taught by Miss Mary Wills. The
Wiggins family moved yet again, this time to Hill City where Cassie
"entered the first really good school I had known since the spring of
1885 when my last year in the Coin [Iowa] school had ended—four
years of school practically lifted out of my life and with which I have
never 'caught up.' "[42]

There were also those parents who kept "their children home to
herd cattle, and to assist them in the various labors on the farm,
thinking that wealth and ignorance constitute a better inheritance to
leave them, than wisdom with the chance of securing wealth after-
wards."[43] There were the "school killers," the "aristocrats," and the
"old fogies" who abided by "the 'cheap plan,' hire[d] the cheapest
teachers, raise[d] as little tax as possible."[44] In the participatory democracy of the rural school districts, the adult men *and* women voters
overruled the "school killers" who did not want public schools and the
"aristocrats" who wanted schools for only the brightest students, the
wealthy, or only for boys. While the fortunes of any given school district deteriorated or flourished depending on the agricultural economy,

the schools were built and maintained, teachers were hired, and the growing population of children learned.

An example of the support for all levels of coeducational public schools appeared in an editorial in *The Iowa Instructor*, a journal of the Iowa State Teachers Association, in response to Dr. Totten, the president of the fledgling University of Iowa. In Totten's plea to the Iowa General Assembly for funds, he advocated educating only bright young men. C. C. Nestlerode, a leader in the development of public coeducation and the editor of *The Iowa Instructor*, reminded the president that the university had been established as a coeducational school in 1857. Nestlerode asserted:

> It is the language of every poor *man* that "All the *fortune* I ever expect to give my children is an *education*, and they shall have that, if I have to work day and night to keep them in school."
>
> . . . the State of Iowa has no institution of learning for young *men* alone, but for the youth of *both sexes*. [45]

The University of Iowa, the first state university to admit women, remained coeducational, as did the precollege and college level public schools throughout the prairies and plains. [46]

The settlers' support for public coeducation was widespread. Nationwide public education had been gradually expanding since the early 1800s, so that by 1900, compulsory attendance laws had been implemented in all but two states outside of the South. [47] By the 1850s, coeducation was taken for granted as "*expedient* and *natural*"; this outstanding gender milestone in American public education had been gradually accomplished throughout the nation with minimal furor. [48] The expediency of coeducation on the prairies and plains was obvious in terms of the costs of hiring a teacher, building and supporting schoolhouses within walking distance of the rural population. By educating girls along with boys, in the same classrooms with the same lessons and rules to be followed, the next generation of teachers was being inculcated with the crude form of rural school democracy. [49] Although the populations of Iowa, Kansas, and Nebraska increased rapidly and were widely dispersed, the settlers expected to have their daughters and sons educated in schools that were nearby and taught by teachers who were affordable and available: hence, the rural school districts on the prairies and plains consisted of one-room coeducational public schools taught principally by women teachers recruited from the region.

In the first schools of the frontier, the school terms were often only two to three months in length (see Table 1). As the school year gradually lengthened from a few months to seven or eight months, it became increasingly more difficult for men to teach school and to maintain a farm or prepare for or pursue a career in law, the ministry, or some other profession. Thus the educational reform of lengthening the school year was a factor in the feminization of teaching. Women became teachers especially in agricultural regions where there were few educated men who would teach.[50]

The standards of education for teachers increased along with the lengthening school terms and demanded continuing education for teachers. Although the first teachers in the newly settled areas of the plains and prairies may have had no other qualifications than literacy and being available, the local and state requirements for teacher certification gradually increased. Teacher examinations for certification, at first composed and administered by the county superintendents, expanded from simple recall tests based on minimal literacy and numeracy, to state-developed tests that examined the content of subjects as well as the teaching methodology. The content of the examinations also reflected the shift from subject-centered instruction toward child-centered methodology, a philosophical shift that deterred some men from seeking teaching positions.[51]

Salaries

Teaching was a seasonal occupation with the periods of unemployment coinciding with the heaviest involvement with farm production, but both men and women had to subsidize their earnings from teaching with support from their families or with a second job if they were to live independently or to provide for a family. Schoolmen were usually paid more than schoolwomen, but this difference was not enough to keep men in the schoolhouses. Although some women and men used teaching as a way to earn money to prepare for another career, most women appear to have combined teaching with unsalaried homemaking and agricultural tasks rather than a second paying job that took them outside of their homes.

While monthly salaries for men and for women increased very little

Table 1
Growth Of Number Of Public Schools And Number Of Teachers

Iowa	1849	1858	1870	1882	1895
Schools					
Schoolhouses	522	2,182	6,888	11,285	13,631
Graded schools	——	——	213	2,359	4,777
Average length of school year	4 months, 4 days	NA	6 months, 4 days	7 months, 2 days	8 months
Value of School property	$68,762	$971,004	$6,191,633	$9,949,243	$15,645,543
Teachers					
Female	245	1,682	7,806	16,037	22,117
Male	336	1,118	4,909	6,044	5,726

Kansas		1861	1870	1882	1894
Schools					
Schoolhouses		NA	1,501	5,555	9,334
Graded schools		NA	NA	NA	NA
Average length of school year		NA	5.2 months	22.8 weeks (4.6 months)	25 weeks (5 months)
Value of school property		NA	$1,520,041	$4,796,368	$11,193,396
Teachers					
Female		NA	1,161	4,808	7,916 *estimate total 11,903
Male		NA	1,079	3,342	3,987 *estimate

Schools					
Schoolhouses	primary	104	298	3,088	6,687
	high schools	4			
Graded schools		——	20	90	393
Average length of school year		——	70 days 3.5 months	NA	NA
Value of school property		——	$177,082	$2,214,474	$8,889,841
Teachers					
Female	primary	74			
	high school	2	269	3,507	6,943
Male	primary	36			
	high school	2	267	1,862	2,548

NA = Data not available
* = Estimated number of women and men
SOURCES: *Twenty-seventh Biennial Report of the Superintendent of Public Instruction of the State of Iowa, November 1, 1895* (Des Moines: 1895), pp. 14–15; *Tenth Annual Report of the Department of Public Instruction of the State of Kansas, 1870* (Topeka: 1870), facing page 52; *Third Biennial Report of the State Superintendent for the School Years Ending July 31, 1881, and July 31, 1882,* Kansas (Topeka: 1882), p. 124; *Ninth Biennial Report of the Department of Public Instruction, State of Kansas, for the School Years Ending July 31, 1893 and 1894* (Topeka: 1894), pp. 5–6; *Second Annual Report of the Commissioner of Common Schools, Territory of Nebraska to the Seventh Legislative Assembly 1860* (Lincoln: 1861), p. 45; *Seventeenth Biennial Report of the State Superintendent of Public Instruction of the State of Nebraska, for the Years 1901–02,* Vol. 2 (Lincoln: 1903), pp. 808–809.

from 1850 to the 1880s, the length of the school year expanded from two months to more than eight months, thus increasing the yearly salaries substantially. This expansion of the school year and the resulting increased salaries for teachers are indicators of the continued support for public education. Table 2 shows these monthly and yearly increases. The statistics, however, do not include such fringe benefits as room and board for the teacher and her horse. In some school districts, the teachers paid room and board out of their salaries, while in others these living expenses were provided in addition to salaries. These variables are not included in the state salary data.

Despite the meager compensation, women, married or unmarried, became teachers because they had few choices for employment, they needed "a paycheck and the challenge and satisfaction of work."[52] While Rury maintains that "saving money by hiring women as teachers may have been more of a consequence of feminization than a cause," the factors of gender in hiring, in determining acceptable salaries, and in defining respect for an occupation must be taken into account.[53] As Clifford points out, "The employment of women would not only open classrooms where none existed, but would make possible longer school terms for the same investment."[54] Thus the low wages of women teachers subsidized the education of children while upholding a canon of womanhood and demeaning the esteem for this "semi-profession."[55]

Although teachers in Iowa in 1860 believed that "females [were] as well capacitated to teach as males; and . . . should receive equivalent wages,"[56] equal pay for equal work and equal qualifications was not to become a reality in public education until the second half of the twentieth century with the unionization of teachers and subsequent collective bargaining. The advent of teachers' associations during the mid 1800s brought endorsements for equal pay, however, few districts paid men and women equally, based on their education and experience.[57] Underlying the inequality of salaries was the "ideal of the nuclear family complete with male breadwinner, dependent wife and two or three school-age children and its opposite, the self-supporting spinster."[58]

Even as the school year lengthened and salaries increased, it is evident that men and women teachers were not among even the more moderately wealthy. By 1900, workers in manufacturing earned 25 percent more than teachers.[59] Men teachers' salaries were roughly

Table 2
Growth In Teachers' Monthly And Yearly Salaries

Iowa

	1849		1858		1870		1882		1895	
	Monthly	Yearly	Monthly	Yearly	Monthly	Yearly	Monthly	Yearly	Monthly	Yearly
Female	$7.64	$32.08	$9.42	$48.98*	$26.80	$166.16	$27.46	$194.97	$31.63	$253.04
Male	14.53	61.03	35.33	131.72*	35.60	220.72	35.20	249.92	37.68	301.44

Kansas

	1861	1870		1882		1894	
		Monthly	Yearly	Monthly	Yearly	Monthly	Yearly
Female	NA	$31.10	$161.72	$24.95	$114.77	$35.01	$175.05
Male	NA	39.60	205.92	31.95	146.97	43.09	215.45

Nebraska

	1860	1870		1882		1895	
		Monthly	Yearly	Monthly	Yearly	Monthly	Yearly
Female	NA primary $24.27 **high school 97.50	$33.00	NA	$28.50	NA	$38.66	NA
Male	NA primary $24.62 **high school 425.50	28.00	NA	37.99	NA	44.18	NA

*Estimated yearly salary
**High school salaries in Nebraska, 1860, appear unaccountably high.
NA = Data not available

SOURCES: *Twenty-seventh Biennial Report, Iowa, 1895*, pp. 14–15; *Tenth Annual Report, Kansas, 1870*, facing page 52; *Third Biennial Report, Kansas, 1881–1882*, p. 124; *Ninth Biennial Report, Kansas, 1893–1894*, pp. 5–6; *Second Annual Report of the Commissioner of Common Schools, Territory of Nebraska, 1860*, p. 45; *Seventeenth Biennial Report, Nebraska, 1901–1902*, vol. 2, pp. 808–9.

equivalent, on a twelve-month basis, to that of a hired farm hand who got his room and board. Women teachers' salaries were similar to those of the hired girl or domestic who got her room and board.[60] The decision whether a woman or teenaged daughter should enter paid employment was based in part on the comparison of her earnings outside of the home with her contribution to the family if she stayed at home.[61] The tangible but small salary of the teacher had to stretch to pay for personal, family, and professional needs. One superintendent thought that teachers would have to steal their clothes if they had to pay for their board, as they would not have enough income to pay for both.[62] From their salaries, any additional income, and supplemental support from their families, teachers paid for "board, clothes (and the public demands taste in the dress of teachers), incidentals, books, magazines, institute expenses, subscriptions, benevolences, and all other expenses."[63]

Among the incidentals for Nancy Higgins were the expenses for her wedding, which she recorded in her school attendance book.[64] In the 1890s, the salary of Kansas teacher, Mary Frances "Frankie" Patton, also paid for her wedding, helped a younger sister attend school at Manhattan, Kansas, for a year, and assisted the farm family.

> I did some few things to help dear daddy finance things in those hard trying days, as well as being on the job most of the time to help him put up feed for the stock, and help him chore in the winter—out of my little $125.00 for my first little 5 mo. school—I payed $45.00 of it on a note for some horses he had bought. The next year I made $180.00 for 6 months teaching. I went to Emporia [State Normal School] for 9 weeks schooling—the most I got was experience, a good dose of enthusiasm that has lasted me thus far through life—did it pay? Oh how I wanted to stay for the next year—but papa said he couldn't see how he could let me stay—had to come home to take care of you [the new baby sister]. . . . I payed $60.00 on that [the new spring wagon] out of my next $180.00. My next $180.00 payed for my wedding dress and most of the things we went to house keeping with—my next $100.00 made after I was married bought our old house cook stove, John some shirts, Alma's baby clothes, etc.[65]

While teachers collectively campaigned for higher salaries, it was through individual negotiations with the school board members that a teacher could achieve a higher salary while staying in the same school district. Sometimes the bargaining for salaries backfired, as when Sadie Smith lost her teaching position to the young woman who underbid her by five dollars.[66] Within the constraints of family needs and ease of transportation, the teachers' route to advancement was through moving to other school districts in order to get better salaries and improved working conditions. Bessie Tucker's four years of teaching began with a poorly equipped run-down schoolhouse with three students. Her next schools had thirty to forty-five children, and her last "brand new schoolhouse" had only twelve. Each move brought better pay and improved working and living conditions.[67] Sarah Gillespie Huftalen was the reluctant cosigner of the bank note for her husband's business. When he went bankrupt, she sought the best-paying teaching position, which required moving to another community.[68] The detrimental effect of teachers moving from district to district for improved salaries and working conditions was that the economically distressed school districts hired only the poorly prepared, ineffectual, and inexperienced teachers who would work for a low salary and tolerate the impoverished working conditions, while the better educated, more effective, and experienced teachers moved onward and upward to more prosperous schools with better salaries, teaching materials, and equipment.

Increase in Number of School-Age Children

The rapid increase in the number of school-age children can be seen in Table 3. In the first decade of Iowa's statehood, and in the thirty-five-year span from 1860 to 1895, both the total number of children and the number of children enrolled in schools increased spectacularly. In Iowa, the total school-age population was eleven times larger in 1858 than in 1847, while the number enrolled increased fifteenfold. By 1895, the school-age population was thirty-four times larger; the number enrolled was 218.9 times larger than in 1847. The percentage of the total number of children enrolled rose from 11.7 percent in 1847, to 75 percent in 1895.

In Kansas, the increases were even more dramatic: the total school-age population was 22.3 times larger in 1870, nine years after statehood; and 101 times larger by 1894. The number of children enrolled in school in Kansas in 1870 was 27 times larger than in 1861; 170

Table 3
Growth In Number Of School Age Children, School Enrollment,
And Average Daily Attendance

Iowa (Statehood 1846)	1849	1858	1870	1882	1895
Pupils					
Total school age children in state	(1847) 20,922 (1849) 50,082	233,927	431,134	604,739	712,941
Number enrolled	(1847) 2,439 (1849) 17,350	36,574	320,803	406,947	533,824
Average daily attendance	NA	NA	202,246	253,688	339,300

Kansas (Statehood 1861)	1861	1870	1882	1894
Pupils				
Total school age children in state	4,901	109,242	357,920	496,139
Number enrolled in school	2,310	63,218	269,945	393,840
Average daily attendance	NA	39,401	162,017	252,215

Nebraska (Statehood 1867)	1860	1870	1882	1895
Pupils				
Total school age children in state	7,041	32,589	165,559	351,846
Number enrolled in school	2,930	12,719	115,546	274,282
Average daily attendance	NA	39%	NA	NA

SOURCES: *Twenty-seventh Biennial Report, Iowa, 1895*, pp. 14–15; *Tenth Annual Report, Kansas, 1870*, facing page 52; *Third Biennial Report, Kansas, 1881–1882*, p. 124; *Ninth Biennial Report, Kansas, 1893–1894*, pp. 5–6; *Second Annual Report of the Commissioner of Common Schools, Territory of Nebraska, 1860*, p. 45; *Seventeenth Biennial Report, Nebraska, 1901–1902*, Vol. 2, pp. 808–809.

times larger in 1894. The percentage of the total number of children enrolled rose from 47 percent in 1861 to 79 percent in 1894.

The number of children in Nebraska showed the same sweeping increases after statehood in 1867. From 1870 to 1882, the school-age population increased five-fold; by 1895, the number had multiplied 10.7 times. The number of children enrolled in 1882 was nine times larger than in 1870; and 21.5 times larger in 1895. The percentage of total number of children enrolled rose from 39 percent in 1870 to 78 percent in 1895.

The increase in numbers of children enrolled and attending school can be seen in the schoolwomen's accounts of their successive schools. Alice Money taught twelve children in her first school in Iowa in 1867, and then lost five during the harvest season. The following summer, she moved to a school closer to her home where she had forty scholars.[69] In the early 1900s in Kansas, Alta Hull had twelve students in her first school and fifty in the second school.[70] Bessie Tucker's experience in Nebraska was similar in 1917, with three students in her first school in the sparsely populated Sandhills of western Nebraska. Her schools during the next two years in eastern Nebraska had enrollments of thirty to forty-five scholars.[71]

The average daily attendance figures, while incomplete, indicate that students attended school sporadically due to illness, inclement weather, and most often because of work at home.[72] While the work of rural children varied seasonally and was essential for the well-being of the family, they were rarely paid a wage for their contributions at home and were not counted by the census reports as being gainfully employed.[73] With the school terms scheduled to avoid the times of heaviest involvement in agricultural tasks, the rural children could attend school and also be involved in the work of the family farm or ranch.

Nationwide, 13 percent of the children were gainfully employed in 1870. Of the total number of children, 19 percent of the boys and 7 percent of the girls were employed. The 1880s showed an increase in the employment of children to 17 percent. Again, of the total number of children, more boys, 24 percent, than girls, 9 percent, were gainfully employed. By 1890 the numbers had dropped to 12 percent of the total number of children employed, which included 17 percent of the boys and 8 percent of the girls working for wages. The proportion of ten- to fifteen-year olds employed for wages gradually diminished below 10 percent by 1901.[74]

Degler reports that after the Civil War most working-class families apparently kept their children out of the work force until they had completed elementary school.[75] More than twice as many boys worked for wages as did girls, possibly affording girls more educational opportunities than boys. However, the opportunity for girls and women to attend school was brought about by the general acceptance of coeducation, the "social decision [which] ranks among the most fateful."[76] As a result of the diminution of child employment and the scheduling of school terms in rural areas to accommodate agricultural work, both boys and girls attended school in great numbers, the teaching force expanded, and the number of schoolhouses increased. In the early 1900s, half of the schoolchildren enrolled attended the nation's 212,000 one-room country schools.[77]

The Feminization of Teaching

The shift from schoolmasters to schoolwomen was not unique to Iowa, Nebraska, and Kansas; however, its evolution in that region was skewed by its historical, social, and environmental context. The nationwide feminization of teaching was based on the changing labor market for men and for women, the increasing demand for teachers brought about by the population growth and educational reforms, and the transitions and increased flexibility in the definitions of woman-hood.[78] The schoolmasters who enlisted during the Civil War were replaced by women teachers, and, apparently, judging from the sharp increase in the number of women teachers after the Civil War as shown in Table 1, Growth of Number of Public Schools and Number of Teachers, p. 18, the veterans and other men lost interest in this "woman's job" with its low salary.[79]

The rapidly growing and widely distributed rural population of Iowa, Kansas, and Nebraska tended to magnify the influence of labor market conditions on the feminization of teaching as the choices of employment for rural women and men outside of the home were limited to agricultural work as a "hired man" or "hired girl" and to whatever industry and commerce the nearest community might offer for employment. The small towns of the heartland offered only limited opportunities for employment often in service occupations such as clerk, domestic, or seamstress. The industrialized cities afforded wider employment options, but relocation in the city required having available money for transportation and while searching for a job. For the rural teenagers whose travel and sophistication had been limited to the open country and occasional trips to a small town for family supplies, the city was indeed daunting. Their Protestant-oriented families were fearful of the corrupting influences of the cities, and because agricultural technology had not eliminated the routine chores, the young people were needed to carry out the tasks of daily farm life.

Education with its promise of increased earning power was available for boys and girls in the coeducational public schools. And, in the areas of widely scattered population, teaching was available as an immediate source of income for those who were literate and willing to work for low salaries in seasonal employment. As the school year lengthened, from two months to six to eight months, teaching became less of a second job option for men whose primary occupations were farming and ranching. Women were educated in accordance with teaching certification requirements, were willing to work with children and youth, were able to combine the demands of teaching, agricultural tasks, and homemaking, and rarely had other opportunities to be employed outside the home for wages in a respected position. Women and teenaged girls who had little experience with salaried positions, accepted low wages for teaching school, an essential occupation that brought positive recognition to the teacher and benefitted the community.

Linked with the labor market and salary concerns were the settlers' definitions of womanhood and domesticity that condoned the employment of women as teachers. Teaching, even with its low salaries, was viewed as an honorable, prestigious occupation for women because nurturing the young was an appropriate, traditional concern for women and girls. The available labor market, the scattered distribution of the population that necessitated numerous one-room schools and numerous teachers, the lengthening school year, and the acceptance of women as teachers were independent and interactive factors leading to the feminization of teaching in the heartland.

With coeducational public schools multiplying to meet the needs of the growing population, the number of teachers tripled nationwide from 1870 to 1900. Nationwide this increase in number of teachers reduced the ratio of teachers to total number of children ages five to nineteen from one teacher to one hundred children, to one teacher to fifty children.[80] Nationwide and in Iowa, Kansas, and Nebraska, where the total number of teachers also tripled, women teachers increased from about two-thirds to three-fourths of the total.[81] While the increase in numbers of both men and women teachers in the heartland was typical of the nation, the ratio of teachers to children was remarkably different in the prairie states than in the nation as a whole. In Iowa, Kansas, and Nebraska, the ratio of teachers to children enrolled in schools decreased from one to twenty-six, to one to twenty-four, an indication of the widely dispersed rural population. The ratio of teachers to total number of school-age children decreased nationally during this same time period from one to thirty-seven in 1870, and one to thirty-two in 1895.[82]

The consequence of the low ratio of teachers to children in Iowa, Kansas, and Nebraska may well be the salient factor in producing the illiteracy rate below 3 percent between 1870 and 1900 for the population ten years old and older.[83] By contrast, in 1880, the illiteracy rate nationally was about 17 percent, falling to 11 percent by 1910, with the national figures including both the well-developed urban school systems and the underdeveloped schools of the South.[84]

The large number of women who had taught and who were teaching school by the 1890s in Iowa, Nebraska, and Kansas, expressed the continuing support for public education. Based on Kansas State Superintendent I. L. Dayoff's 1905 estimate of the average length of teaching career as less than four years, a conservative estimate of the number of women who had taught or who were teaching in the 1890s, is as follows:[85]

Iowa, 72,000 or 12.2 percent of the total female population fifteen years and older; Kansas, 33,400 or 8.2 percent of the total female population fifteen years and older; Nebraska, 26,200 or 8.8 percent of the total female population fifteen years and older.[86]

The percentage of women workers employed as teachers was probably higher than the estimates shown in Table 4. While many beginning teachers were in their middle to late teens, the Census Reports counted ten- to fifteen-year-olds as employed women. There may have been some "teachers" under the age of fifteen, but they would have been rare even in the very first frontier schools. As standards for teacher preparation increased, the minimum age of teachers crept up to eighteen, with twenty-seven as the median age of teachers in 1900 nationwide.[87]

Definitions of Womanhood and the Motivation to Teach

The definitions of womanhood accommodated the burdens of reality of everyday life on the prairies and plains. The environmental demands on the settlers often blurred distinctions between gender-specific jobs, especially when a family worked as a cooperative unit for survival. However, most accounts seem to indicate how women and girls did masculine tasks such as plowing and harvesting with few references to men and boys involved in child care or other feminine roles.[88] The definitions of womanhood included women's paid and unpaid employment as appropriate, particularly when it benefitted the family, the children, and the community. The need for teachers expanded the sphere of womanhood beyond the confines of the home through the gainful employment of women to assure the welfare and education of children in the district schools. In the environment of

Table 4

Women Teachers As Gainfully Employed Workers, 1870–1895

Iowa	1870	1880–82	1890–95
Total gainfully employed female workers, 10 yrs. & older	23,100	44,800	80,400
Total female teachers	7,806	16,037	22,117
% of gainfully employed women workers as teachers	22.1%	35.8%	27.5%

Kansas	1870	1880–82	1890–94
Total gainfully employed female workers, 10 yrs. & older	6,500	19,400	45,500
Total female teachers	1,161	4,808	7,915*
% of gainfully employed women workers as teachers	17.8%	24.7%	17.3%*

Nebraska	1870	1880–82	1890–95
Total gainfully employed female workers, 10 yrs. & older	1,900	10,500	42,600
Total female teachers	269	3,507	6,943
% of gainfully employed women workers as teachers	14%	33.4%	16.2%

*Estimated number of female teachers in Kansas
SOURCES: For total number of female teachers, see Table 1. Population determined from: U.S. Department of Commerce, Bureau of the Census, *Historical Statistics of the United States, Colonial Times to 1970*, Part 1, Series D 26–28; Gainful Workers, by Sex, by State: 1870 to 1950, pp. 129–130. It should be noted that the census records of the 1800s count adult females as 15 years and older, and gainfully employed women workers as 10 years and older.

the new settlements of the western prairies and plains, women found that teaching school was an opportunity for independence and self-direction while fulfilling the expectations of womanhood and being paid a salary that was a cut above unpaid voluntarism.

Women became the preservers and creators of their culture not only at home, but in the schools and the communities where they perpetuated the institutions of the schools, churches, and charities, while establishing their own roles in the development of "a much needed sense of stability, community, and generational continuity in a new region."[89] The irony for women is that they established their roles in the community as unpaid volunteers in the name of betterment of self and community. To have sought payment for services rendered to the development of community institutions would have been regarded as inappropriate, and the projects, schools included, would have died for want of workers and cash to pay them.

The stereotype persists of the unmarried eastern schoolmarm as the missionary who went west to dedicate her life to civilizing the children in the little red schoolhouse. The ideal schoolteacher of the mid-1800s, as characterized by Catherine Beecher, was an educated, unmarried *lady* who was "already qualified intellectually to teach, and possessed of missionary zeal and benevolence," and who was ready to go "to the most ignorant portions of our land to raise up schools, to instruct in morals and piety, and to teach the domestic arts and virtues."[90] In the 1840s, the National Board of Popular Education recruited six hundred teachers from the northeastern United States to be trained, then sent to frontier communities from Ohio to Oregon.[91] Beecher worked with the first two classes of prospective teachers recruited by the National Board of Popular Education before she left to train indigenous teachers in the West. These teachers were indeed pioneers both in terms of their work and where they located in the West. The substance of their motivation to teach was to educate children for the common good as well as to earn a salary. Economic necessity and idealism were also the goals of the indigenous prairie schoolwomen. There was nonetheless, a difference between operating on others as missionaries to the "most ignorant portions of our land" and operating with others as accepted members of the community.[92] Those who were western women by birth, nurture, and choice became a truly new second generation, socialized in the environment replete with the collision of eastern ideals and western realities.

The motivation to teach children in the one-room schoolhouses stemmed from factors in addition to the money earned and the idealism related to educating children. The idealism and aspirations associated with education of children extended the "image of the ideal woman and the ideal mother . . . into the training and work of the ideal teacher."[93] This paradigm plus the lack of employment opportunities for women were perpetuated as justifications for the low salaries for women. Despite the meager income, the schoolwomen apparently believed "That no profession affords greater opportunities for doing *good* than that of teaching; and we consider this as being the highest inducement to influence a person to engage in it."[94] Teachers found they liked the satisfaction of seeing the children learn and the respect they received from their students and the community. Having large blocks of time of unemployment hurt the family budget, but helped the schoolwomen manage their homes and other family concerns.

Sarah Gillespie Huftalen described her "love for my chosen work . . . [as] all but a passion within me."[95] Teaching was Bessie Tucker's "lifelong desire." As she anticipated leaving her second school and moving to another, she wrote in her diary that she would remember

> a little white school house with the beautiful bell . . . [and the] little parsonage which I called home for six months. . . . I shall take the memories of the lives of many people whom I have met and who have made me feel one of them. . . . how I would like to leave something behind me. A memory of a life that might be helpful to someone. I am realizing more and more, little book, the non-importance of things that seem to take up so much of our time. Only as they may be a help to others are they important and I am learning to make that one of the guiding rules of my life.[96]

To be remembered as being helpful to someone, especially to children, was the measure of success and recognition for many of the classroom teachers.

Although the school's finances and maintenance of the school property were managed by the locally elected school board, it was nonetheless, the schoolteacher who was accountable for the day-to-day events within the schoolhouse. It is unknown how many schoolwomen of the nineteenth-century prairies set out to prove their personal independence through teaching school, but the isolation of their working conditions made self-sufficiency imperative. The children and the teacher were neighbors and often part of the same extended family, thus family and community concerns and mores were part of the school setting along with the charge to teach reading, writing, and arithmetic. This sense of community generated in the one-room schoolhouses may have been another factor in promoting the desire to read.[97] In the community-managed institution of the public school, it was individual schoolwoman who received the praise or the blame for the scholars' achievements or failures.

The individual autonomy of each schoolwoman was both attractive and formidable. It was appealing because of the independence and recognition; intimidating because of the professional isolation and the high hopes the settler families vested in education. Every teacher in a one-room schoolhouse had to manage the school building and the daily school events on her own while guiding the education and nurture of the children. Anna Johnson described the job of the rural teacher as "many-faceted":

> I not only taught, but was also an administrator, mother, doctor, nurse, judge and jury, artist, cook, librarian, custodian or janitor, carpenter or fixer, advisor, psychologist, disciplinarian, and humanitarian. I might say that I was a "Jack of all trades and a master of some." In this rural community I was very close to the children and all the parents and many others in the area. Their problems often became my problems, which sometimes made my task even harder.[98]

Depending on the number of schoolhouses in their charge and the distance between them, the county superintendents who visited all the rural schools in their counties were able to offer only minimal supervision and guidance for the beginning teacher. Faced with the full responsibility for the school and for the scholars who may have ranged in age from four to twenty years, the teacher either succeeded on her own or failed, resulting in the abrupt and permanent departure of the schoolmarm. Clara Conron, a beginning teacher in Wakarusa, Kansas, 1884, found after a month of teaching: "I like teaching sometimes and then again I don't. I think it is rather trying to ones nerves and mine are rather 'touchy' I am afraid."[99] By December, Clara wished she could "keep my patience with my scholars, but they are so impudent. . . . Oh my, such a time as I have had with those boys, they nearly drive me wild. I sent a note to Mrs. Forsythe, but don't expect it will do much good. . . . Such a time—I am ashamed of myself and scholars."[100] During the spring term of 1885, Clara Conron found school "amusing" and had "quite a nice time," with no mention of the naughty boys nor of any visits by the county superintendent.

In the rural areas, teaching school allowed women to stay at home, or they boarded in an area similar to their farm homes. While they taught school for only part of the year, they could live and work at their homes when school was not in session. They did not have to move to town in order to teach or to achieve independence, prestige, and the minimal economic autonomy of being a teacher. Those teachers who effectively taught their young scholars how to read, write, and figure gained prestige in the community beyond that of being domestic workers even though their incomes were similar.

Despite inadequate supplies and preparation, the teachers expressed their belief in the value of the education they were providing for the rapidly growing population of school-age prairie children (see Table 3, Growth in Number of School Age Children, p. 23). As a Nebraska teacher and county superintendent, 1888–1914, Genevieve Giddings Richmond found "There were few books, less furniture, but the pupils were eager to learn and we felt the time well spent." She, her husband, F. M., and their children were teachers in Nebraska and South Dakota, demonstrating a generational continuity of both occupation and residence.[101]

After the first day of teaching, Rosa Schreurs knew she had found a job that she "loved and could do. About making the big boys mind? That could wait until winter when they came." Like many teachers, she often stayed late after school to prepare for the following day's work.

> Then on my homeward way there came from newly-plowed fields
> the dewy, earthy smell of early evening, with fireflies flashing
> their lamps above the long, reedy grass in the sloughs. Are diamonds any prettier?[102]

As she looked back on her life, she concluded: "I can think of no better way [to live] than to go back to the country. Would that I could be again a Country Teacher."[103]

The resolutions of the Teachers' Class of Osceola, Clark County, Iowa, 1860, defined the teachers' expectations of idealism and accountability:

3. That a good education to all youth is the surest means of preventing crime, increasing wealth, protecting property, elevating morals, and promoting general happiness.
4. That we believe the profession of teaching to be second to none in importance, influence and responsibility; and that

no person should become a teacher who does not so consider it. . . .

7. That females are as well capacitated to teach as males; and if so, they should receive equivalent wages. . . .

9. That we should hereafter engage in teaching, we will endeavor to be actuated by a desire to do good and from inate [sic] love of knowledge. . . .[104]

The teachers' class charged the parents with the responsibilities of "sending their children regularly and seasonably to school; . . . supplying them with the necessary books and stationary; . . . teaching them to strictly obey the rules and requisitions of the teacher; . . . training them to be orderly and scrupulously regard the right; . . . encouraging them to be studious by taking a personal interest in their studies."[105] How well the parents fulfilled these admonitions varied from district to district. However, with the schoolhouse as the community center, large numbers of parents and other residents attended school programs, political and religious meetings, fund-raisers, and the yearly school meetings.[106] While the parents were generally supportive of the schools, the complaints from county superintendents about unsupportive parents and incompetent school directors appeared in their reports in the early days of a school district and in times of economic depression. Rev. George Graham, superintendent of schools for Butler County, Iowa, observed in 1868–1869: "We have some wide-awake teachers, but far too few wide-awake school boards, and but little general sympathy with real and solid progression as compared with what is needed to place our school system where it should be as to execution."[107]

During the mid to late 1870s, the reports from county superintendents indicated that it was difficult to find support for new schools during the economically distressed times, when corn sold at fifteen cents and wheat at sixty cents.[108] The destruction of crops by grasshoppers resulted in reductions of salaries for teachers in some districts. One superintendent was disgusted to find that the farmers were willing to pay a carpenter $2.00–$2.50 to build a pigpen but were unwilling to pay their teachers.[109] Due to hard times in 1875, Jefferson County, Kansas, lost the "good teachers," and canceled summer school.[110] Even the state normal schools were affected by the depressed economy. In 1876, the State Normal School at Cedar Falls, Iowa, opened with no equipment, no library except for the president's personal books, and held classes in the dormitory due to lack of funds.[111] However, across the prairies and plains, public education in the one-room rural schoolhouses imparted the level of education that the school patrons were willing to support, making the "Middle Border the most literate part of the nation through the years."[112]

Because communities expected teachers to live exemplary lives, they were forbidden to court or to marry in some parts of the United States. In the heartland states, teachers were also expected to lead moral, ethical lives; however, teachers did not universally have to resign when they got married. The viewpoint expressed in the eastern states that most women teachers were or should be unmarried was promoted by Horace Mann and other educational leaders who also believed that women should be paid less than men teachers who might have a family to support.[113] It appears that school districts hired married women when a district was first organized, when the teacher was well known and well liked, and when the need for a teacher was a greater concern than her marital status. Some school districts sought to hire the best qualified teacher, married or single, male or female, thus encouraging schoolwomen to re-enter teaching at various points throughout their life cycles, such as when their children were of school age; when the family needed extra income; when they were widowed, divorced, or abandoned; and when they enjoyed and sought the challenge of teaching.

The ways in which schoolwomen managed their lives became increasingly more dependent not on the conditions of the frontier but on the continuous evolution of community and educational structures. The task of balancing home and work became more complex as the schoolwomen coped with the assumed dichotomy of working outside of the home and homemaking by providing for the well-being of their own and others' children through teaching. In the balance of women teachers' work and their home responsibilities, there was "no time out, no short week, no sabbatical," with teaching usually secondary to "maternal and conjugal responsibilities."[114]

Examples of the home responsibilities of the schoolwomen can be seen among the five lives examined in Part Two of this book. Nancy Higgins Gaddis taught for one term after she was married and then became an active partner in the development of the Golden Rod Stock Farm. Sarah Jane Price combined farming and teaching in much the same manner as a schoolmaster-farmer, in addition to being the homemaker for her widowed father and younger brothers. As a teenager, Jane raised her five younger brothers when their mother died. As an unmarried teacher and farmer in her thirties, she was head of the her household consisting of two younger brothers and her father. In middle age, as she continued to teach and farm, she took her widowed brother and his two young children into her home, and cared for her aging father. Bessie Tucker left teaching after four years at the request of her parents who wanted her at home for a while. She had considered returning to teaching after she was married but fulfilled her husband's wishes that she stay at home. Sarah Gillespie dropped out of teaching to care for her dying mother. She married four years after her mother's death and then returned to teaching. Ethel Hale Russel left her position as teacher educator after the birth of her second child, believing that someone had to be at the center of the home.[115]

The time for their own continuing education and their months of work in their schoolhouses increased for the rural schoolwomen while the hours they spent at home on farm tasks increased seasonally two to three times during the spring, summer, and fall.[116] The time spent with household tasks remained about the same year round for rural and other schoolwomen who were homemakers or assisted with homemaking. Although not all schoolwomen of Iowa, Kansas, and Nebraska were members of rural families, their unpaid labor as homemakers was nonetheless essential to the well-being of their families.[117] In assessments of employment, the unpaid agricultural and homemaking tasks a woman carried out in her own home were not counted as gainful employment by the U. S. Census, even if she was the head of the household.[118]

Opportunities for Advancement

The multiple demands on women as homemakers and working women no doubt prevented many capable women from seeking the better-paying administrative positions. The definitions of teacher and womanhood of the late nineteenth and early twentieth centuries rarely included leadership and administrative ability outside of the home, except in the all-women organizations in the community. Even though teaching was dominated in numbers by women, they were younger and taught for fewer years than did the diminishing number of men who remained in education. Rury describes the "two-tiered system of employment in education" that developed with older men in the administrative roles supervising large numbers of young women teachers.[119]

Obviously the rapid turnover of teachers accounted for the young age of the teachers. A contributing factor of that turnover was the need for teachers to move from school to school in order to achieve better salaries and working conditions. The route to an administrative position required political connections and campaigning for the county superintendency. The position of the county superintendent required traveling by foot, horseback, wagon, sleigh, railroad, and automobile to all the schools in the county. Distance, road, and weather conditions necessitated staying overnight at various homes and communities, while encouraging and educating the teachers, promoting school improvements, and at times dealing with reluctant teachers and parents and with recalcitrant children. For women and men who truly enjoyed the daily contact with children and its observable successes and rewards, the county superintendency was not a prized position.

From 1869, when Iowan Julia Addington became the first woman elected to the position of county superintendent, to 1900, the number of women county superintendents increased nationally to only 276.[120] By 1915, there were close to 3,000 county superintendents in the United States, with 503 of the positions, predominantly west of the Mississippi, filled by women.[121] Close to one-third of the women county superintendents were to be found in the heartland states. In Iowa, 54 of the 99 counties had women superintendents; Nebraska had 93 county superintendents, including 50 women; and Kansas, with 105 county superintendents, listed 54 women in that position.[122] Among these three states, only two women, both in Iowa, were listed as superintendents of public schools in cities and towns of 2,500 population and over.[123] In 1922, Edith Lathrop, rural education specialist in the Office of Education, cited 857 women county superintendents nationwide and determined that women were most likely to be in administrative positions in the West and in places where superintendents were elected and not appointed.[124]

While it was possible for a schoolwoman to become an elected or appointed school administrator, especially in the West, it was not easy. Schoolwomen who ventured into school politics did so with mixed support from their colleagues, their families, and the general public. In some counties the position of the county superintendent who supervised the rural schools was seen as appropriate for women, but the higher-paid appointive positions of superintendent of the schools in town were reserved for men. The increased structure of the educational system brought the benefits of the graded schools, additional instructional equipment, and better educated teachers. It also brought about increased administrative positions for men. Dr. A. E. Winship, editor of the prestigious *Journal of Education* critically observed in 1901, that "more than ninety-five percent of the teaching . . . is done by women, and more than ninety-five percent of the administration and leadership is by men." [125]

Educational leadership by women, except in the normal schools, was not implemented in the late nineteenth century, even though the profession was numerically dominated by women. Teaching had indeed become feminized in the nineteenth century, but administrative positions in education are still dominated by men a hundred years later. Tyack and Hansot conclude:

> The hopes of women leaders at the beginnings of this century
> were not realized, and their temporary gains were reversed. By
> and large, they filled the posts that men did not want, and when
> their jobs became attractive to men, they were displaced. . . .
> the attitudes of the lay decision makers [who hire or appoint administrators] have obviously been a major reason for the scarcity
> of women at the top. [126]

Grumet concludes that the "exclusions [of women] from administrative positions discouraged career planning and encouraged the acceptance of short-range goals and identification with the immediacy of the classroom context." [127]

These assessments, however, tend to emphasize the definition of success as power and authority over others, visibility, public recognition, and material success. The voices of teachers indicate that "the ability to instill in others the joy of discovering things for themselves" was the "very soul of teaching." [128] "The immediacy of the classroom" brought with it the reinforcing human relationships that constitute the core of the teacher-child dyad. Bessie Tucker observed this joy of discovery when one little girl learned to write her numbers so that Bessie could read them. "She cannot get over her amazement and delight and keeps calling me back every five minutes to admire her work." [129] On a rainy Friday with only seven pupils in attendance, when Bessie Tucker's students made little books that they gave to her, she wrote in her diary: "I like them so much. I know they really care and that makes everything worthwhile." [130]

Throughout her diaries, Sarah Jane Price expressed her hopes for "a successful school" and concern for her students. "I feel comfortable and peaceful tonight ready for another week's labor and toil. I trust to make a success of my work and hope to be able to do some good in an humble way." [131]

Sarah Gillespie Huftalen closed her account of graduation day in her Arbor Vitae Summit School, Oneida, Iowa, 1907, as follows, "The Common School graduates from the Rural Schools deserve recognition in a public manner and I want to do my part in behalf of the educational interests and moral benefits [for] our boys and girls." [132]

In her reminiscence of her successful years at the Arbor Vitae Summit School, Huftalen concluded, "To be a resident teacher with community interests at heart places one as a cog in a wheel as an essential factor in matters educational,—possibly cultural, we hope so." [133]

Conclusion

With the professional life of many teachers less than four years by 1905, the schoolwomen were seen as undedicated and unprofessional by their critics. [134] The communities where they taught, however, saw them and their schools as the essential means of educating the children of the prairies and plains. In their diaries and reminiscences, the schoolwomen documented their high regard for educating children by citing their teaching experience as an important part of their personal identity and their *raison d'être*. As members of the community, they were the organizers and members of the professional education associations, the literary societies, churches, schools, and other organizations dedicated to social improvements. [135] During the period from the 1860s to the 1920s, teacher education became professional in substance and mandatory for certification. The schoolwomen continued their own education throughout their years of teaching and maintained their community influence as schoolwomen, homemakers, farmers, and community builders.

Few successful schoolwomen could have identified their personal philosophies of education, but those who made some record of their lives seemed to know what they valued. Their personal writings indicate that they were rarely shaken by the joys, hopes, fears, and labors of each day. These were not the women who lost their hold on reality through fear and loneliness, although they certainly knew trepidation, loss, despair, and failure. Because the teachers were members of the settler families, their motivation to teach was part of the ambience of the time and place as they brought to the schoolhouses the moral, ethical life-styles demanded by their communities "that embrace[d] Protestantism, prohibitionism, McGuffeyism, and Republicanism."[136] The pervading influence of domesticity and the changing definitions of womanhood took form in the personal autonomy of schoolwomen that transcended the walls of conventional domesticity while nurturing the ideals of womanhood. Although they were practical in their day-to-day concerns of earning a living and managing their schoolhouses, they were inspired by an idealistic belief in universal public education as the means of improvement for children, for themselves, and for the community at large.

The involvement of the schoolwomen and other women in community and educational development enabled them to benefit from the social, educational, political, and economic advancements while being part of the social milieu that brought about these achievements. Their activism was largely directed toward their own self-improvement and the betterment of their own homes, families, schools, and communities. The issues in their lives were those of working women: balancing the demands of their homes with the time spent in the schoolhouses, and in the community; improving both their working and living conditions; acquiring, maintaining, and applying the necessary education and skills needed for successful teaching; and sustaining their relationships with their families and friends.

With the schoolhouse as the public social center that gave identity to an area, local men and women as the elected school directors, and the indigenous schoolwomen in charge of the educational events in the schoolhouse, schooling and teaching were fraught with trials and errors, but there were sufficient successes that tax-supported education for the prairie girls and boys became a reality. The schoolwomen during the frontier and early settlement days of the prairies and plains were the ordinary western women who, through the stability of their lives and their belief in the value of education for children and themselves, created extraordinary results in the schoolhouses scattered across the prairies. In an atmosphere of transition, idealism, democratic floundering, ignorance, and hope, the prairies and plains became flourishing farms and ranches, and the fledgling communities became amalgamations of the old, and expectations of the new.

The snow-covered dugout was warmer than a log schoolhouse. District No 48, Kit Carson County, Colorado, near the Kansas state line. (*Report of the State Superintendent of Public Instruction, Colorado, 1895–96,* facing page 1)

A. PIONEER SCHOOL HOUSE

The two scholars brought available books from home. The teacher boarded with the children's families. (Nebraska State Historical Society)

Chapter 1

Ella J. Bruner taught school in the home of Dr. DeBell. This home was unusually well equipped, having student tables, chalkboard, books, and a scenic backdrop tacked to the wall behind the chalkboard. (Nebraska State Historical Society)

The first schoolhouse at Rushville, Nebraska, about 1885. The scholars, their families, and neighbors turned out for the school program. (Nebraska State Historical Society)

Schoolwomen of the Prairies and Plains

Sod schoolhouse, East Custer County, Nebraska, about 1888. The
two oldest students stood in the back row with the teacher.
(Solomon D. Butcher Collection. Nebraska State Historical Society)

Hetty Evans,
her classmates,
and her dog
posed for this
school picture,
District No. 29,
Fillmore
County, north-
west of Grafton,
Nebraska.
(Nebraska State
Historical
Society)

Chapter 1

Owasa School, Iowa, about 1896. In good weather, many children went to school barefooted. The boys' and girls' cloak rooms were inside the two entrances. (State Historical Society of Iowa—Iowa City)

Schoolwomen of the Prairies and Plains

Model schoolhouse. (*Report of the State Superintendent of Public Instruction, Iowa, 1894–95, facing 199*)

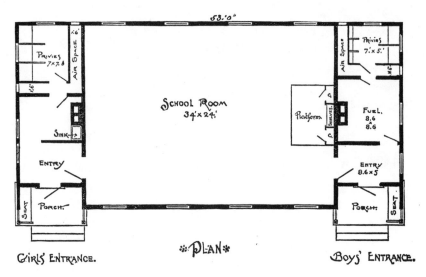

Floor plan of the model schoolhouse. (*Report of the State Superintendent of Public Instruction, Iowa, 1894–95, facing 199*)

CHAPTER
TWO

Educating the Schoolwomen of the Heartland

The idea of educating people specifically to be teachers "was an entirely new thing to many, and there was a spirit of distrust on the part of some as to its usefulness."[1] Education for the children of the prairies had widespread appeal and support, but the education of teachers in state-supported normal schools and institutes remained a lesser priority. Some legislators and tax payers were skeptical about the practicality of educating women teachers who would soon leave teaching for marriage and "who were not expected to become, or to view themselves as, professionals."[2]

Literacy and willingness to attempt teaching may have been the only qualifications of the first teacher in a school district. This was Mary Ward's preparation for teaching in Kansas in 1860. "My dresses dropped from my knees to the floor in a day and I became a woman and a school mam." She had attended the rural school near Centerville, Iowa, in the 1850s. When the family emigrated to Kansas, "There was something for every one to do," and Mary became a teacher.[3]

The state and county requirements for certification to teach increased over the years so that continuing certification gradually became based on ongoing education planned specifically for teachers. An initial teaching certificate could be obtained through passing teachers' examinations given by the county superintendents and passing courses at the teachers' institutes or the normal schools. At age fourteen, E. Mary Lacy attended a four-week teachers' institute in Emmetsburg, Iowa: "New subjects were being introduced, one of which was drawing. It was here that I received my first lessons and though I never became proficient, it was encouraging to know that I had a certain amount of ability."[4] The following spring, 1877, when she was just past fifteen, she started teaching school eight miles from home.

In order to continue teaching, certificates had to be renewed and upgraded, usually yearly through attending and passing a variety of normal education classes and courses offered through teachers' institutes; public, private, and denominational colleges, academies, normal schools, universities; and, in the twentieth century, in many public high schools.[5] In the 1890s in Iowa, Rosa Schreurs Jennings began teaching after completing sixteen weeks at the Iowa State Normal School. She then "acquired some three years of piece-meal normal training, but, as was often then the case with irregular attendance, the work had not been directed toward a degree. I took those courses I felt the need of most in school, or in which I had special interest."[6] Eventually, Jennings completed two degrees in education.

Teachers were required to pay for their own expenses and use their unpaid vacation time while attending the institutes or normal schools. Teachers pursued these avenues of education at one time or another, depending on their financial status, their home responsibilities, and the location, content, and duration of the courses. However, the lengthening school year and increased requirements for teacher education and certification proved "too costly for many men," thus these educational reforms furthered the feminization of teaching.[7]

While literacy was the only prerequisite for teaching on the frontier, the education of the teachers expanded as the schools and communities became increasingly more developed. However, these teachers were not, by and large, among the 5 percent of the nation's teachers who by 1910 had more than a high school education.[8] Tracing the effects of the normal school education upon rural schools in the heartland is difficult because the research available is based on the demographics of the normal school graduates, not upon all those who attended the normal schools, either sporadically or for only a few terms.[9] Histories of the normal schools identify their roles in educational leadership, even though those institutions "failed to make themselves the reliable source of classroom teachers in the country's public elementary schools."[10] While the implication is that 95 percent of the teachers were uneducated and unprepared for teaching, "there was more to minimal training than might appear."[11] The progression from the minimal preparation of teachers on the frontier toward professional continuing education for the schoolwomen of the heartland is an essential chapter in the evolution of national educational reform.

Based on the level of their educational attainment, and their years of employment in classroom teaching, administration, teacher education, and other positions in education, the schoolwomen tend to fall into three consecutive and overlapping groups: short-term teachers, long-term professional teachers, and long-term educational and community leaders. The descriptions of their educational preparation for teaching fills the breach between mere literacy and professional teacher education. Despite the minimal state support for teacher education, the schoolwomen of the prairies and plains continued their educations throughout their professional lives.

The short-term teachers who taught for a few terms to a few years were the largest in number, as documented by the rapid turnover of teachers and their few years of employment. Their educational level in the early years of settlement was generally equivalent to the eighth grade, acquired at the one-room schoolhouses, followed by attendance at the teacher institutes, attempts at self-instruction and correspondence courses, and for some, attendance for a term or two at an academy (the forerunner of the public high school) or a normal school. With the advent of public high schools, short-term teachers' level of education increased especially as teacher education courses became increasingly available as high school electives in the twentieth century.

In the 1870s, Nancy Higgins's preparation for teaching consisted of attendance at the one-room school built on her father's land and a term at an boarding academy. A generation later, her daughter, Elsie Gaddis, attended the one-room rural school, the town school, and then finished high school at a Free Methodist boarding school. She attended the Junior Normal School, geared for high school students, at Alma, Nebraska, for a summer session, then began teaching in a rural school.[12]

As beginners, the short-term teachers were most likely to have the lowest salaries, uncomfortable living conditions, and poorly equipped schoolhouses. If the working conditions didn't squelch the young woman's zeal for teaching, she used the experience as a stepping stone toward obtaining a better-paying teaching position. After the short-term teachers left teaching, most often for marriage, many remained active in school and community affairs through their own children's educational experience and were involved in the development of churches and other community institutions. Nancy Higgins Gaddis taught for only two years, including one term after she was married. Throughout the remainder of her life, she was a leader in her church and a persistent voter in the school elections.[13]

Some of the beginning teachers found that teaching was a person-ally rewarding career and continued attending institutes in nearby towns and summer sessions at the normal schools in order to re-new their teaching certificates. They became the long-term profes-sional teachers who taught school and continued their own education throughout most of their adult lives. In addition to attending the in-stitutes, the long-term professionals were likely to have attended sum-mer sessions at a normal school or college as part of their education for continuing certification. In North Dakota, Enid Bern started teaching after three years of high school. She continued going to school between school terms and eventually earned a degree.[14] Sarah Jane Price was another long-term professional teacher who continued to attend institutes and studied independently during her teaching years in Nebraska from the 1870s to 1890s.[15] The longer women taught, the longer they attended school themselves, but they did not necessarily complete degrees.

Among the long-term professionals were homemakers, both mar-ried and unmarried, who dropped out of teaching from time to time to attend a normal school or college or in order to meet the demands of their families. Because of their years of teaching experience, they held the teaching positions at the most affluent schools that were within easy daily commuting distance from their homes. Catharine Wiggins began teaching at age sixteen after taking the teacher's ex-aminations. She taught one term then returned to high school for a year. She taught at several different locations in Kansas during the next two years, then returned to complete high school when she was almost twenty years old. After teaching two more years and attending the summer teachers' institutes, she had enough money to attend college for the next three years, graduating in 1898. After each in-crease in her own education, her next teaching position was in a bet-ter equipped school; her salary increased from $20.00 a month to

$47.00. She regretted dropping out of teaching when she married in 1902, because she liked teaching and was considered "an excellent teacher."[16] Sadie Smith's high school and normal education, which had been spread over several years while teaching in Nebraska and Colorado, was similar to Wiggins's experience. Smith graduated from Peru State Normal School and continued attending institutes while teaching in various communities. After she married Rollin Trail, she dropped out of teaching for ten years until her husband died, leaving her with young three children and her foster mother to support. Sadie Smith Trail returned to teaching and administrative positions for the rest of her adult working years.[17]

The long-term educational and community leaders, the smallest in number of schoolwomen, may have initially prepared for teaching in the same manner as the short-term teachers and the long-term professionals. Motivated by their interest and success in their work and their personal independence, they pursued education beyond the institutes by attending colleges and universities, subsequently completing degrees. Working throughout their adult lives, they were employed as instructors and administrators at various levels from the elementary grades to the normal schools, colleges, and universities. Their successful teaching experiences and continued education at colleges and universities gave them choices of employment as teachers, as elected or appointed administrators, and as teacher educators. They taught at the teachers' institutes, and as they obtained college or normal school educations, they became teacher educators at the normal schools. Recognition of their achievements put them into positions of prominence as community builders and as the leaders and innovators of educational development at the local, state, and national levels.[18]

In the early 1880s in Iowa, Sarah Gillespie started teaching as a teenager in a one-room school after a few terms at an academy. As a widow in her mid-fifties, she was a teacher educator and community leader, and had completed bachelor's and master's degrees, and had begun work toward a doctorate in education at the University of Iowa.[19] Sarah Gillespie Huftalen's unique school management and instructional strategies plus her leadership in establishing the Rural Section of the Iowa State Teachers Association were her achievements of distinction and renown.

Before Ethel Hale started teaching in 1912 in Nebraska, she had graduated from high school and completed the two-year normal curriculum at Peru [Nebraska] State Normal School. She taught for several years in various western states, then completed her bachelor's and master's degrees while teaching in the experimental school at the University of Iowa. Hale continued as a teacher educator and a teacher in the Campus School of Western State Teachers College, Kalamazoo, Michigan. After her marriage to Robert R. Russel, she taught until the birth of their second child, when she dropped out of teaching because she believed that she needed to be at the center of the home and family. Ethel Hale Russel then became deeply involved in community and state social activism, which may have taken her away from home as much as a salaried position as a teacher educator.[20]

Teacher Examinations

There were substantial changes during the late nineteenth century in the content and purpose of normal education through the institutes and the normal schools. The purpose of normal or teacher education became, "Not merely to learn the lesson of the day, but to learn *how to teach it* to others."[21] The "science and art of teaching" then, ideally, became based on "train[ing] the body for strength and health, the hands to do, the minds to think, and the heart to respond to right motives."[22] The purpose of teacher education shifted: "In place of the former demand that the teacher should know only the three R's, there has grown up the more rational one that he should know the three M's—Matter, Method, and Mind."[23]

This change in the focus of teacher education can be seen in the content of the institute and normal school courses and the questions in the teachers' examinations. The earliest teacher examinations were oral questions determined and administered by the county superintendent, which allowed for many errors in judgment and for more than a little favoritism and nepotism. This practice allowed the superintendent to hire a poor teacher, rather than no teacher at all. "Schools we must have—good schools if we can, poor schools only when we must."[24]

The scarcity of qualified teachers, especially in the early settlement years, and the practice of nepotism, however, drove some school directors and county superintendents to hire their friends, neighbors, and family members regardless of competence or certification.[25] W. E. Parker, superintendent of Buchanan County, Iowa, 1877–1879, reported that a young woman presented a petition "signed by every elector in the district, praying that the bearer be granted a certificate to teach."[26] Her scores on the teachers' examination indicated that "she had not even a respectable acquaintance with the rudiments of the common school branches." The superintendent had no other candidate for the job, so "she did keep school and received the money." Parker indicated that such cases were infrequent, but he stated a superintendent should be "empowered to close all such schools."

County superintendents administered the teacher examinations in the early years of a school district. John and Mary McArdle emigrated to Smith County, Kansas, 1878, after the first term of school had been completed in the district.

> . . . when the school board learned the wife [Mary McArdle] was a 'Wisconsin School Ma'am' they asked her to teach the following three months term, the salary . . . sixteen dollars per month.
>
> The young pioneers journeyed by team and lumber wagon to the County Seat, twenty miles away, where she took the teacher's examination somewhat fearfully, wondering if it would be harder than in her native state.
>
> She evidently answered correctly the *two* questions asked, together with a specimen of her penmanship, for she returned triumphantly with a certificate to teach the second term of school in District 56, White Rock Township, Smith County [Kansas].[27]

By the 1870s, the state departments of public instruction had designed examinations to be administered by the county superintendents to all candidates for certification. The written, state examinations were largely assessments of the teacher's ability to answer specific recall questions based on the content of the common branches of education and to demonstrate some competence in reading, arithmetic, spelling, and grammar. These questions drawn from the 1873 Iowa Questions for Applicants for First Class Certificates, indicating the highest quality of teacher preparation, are representative of the nine sections of the examination. Each section had ten questions, including a few questions on methodology, but primarily assessing the teacher's understanding of the content of each discipline.

Orthography: Give the principle rules for the use of capital letters.
Reading: Name the different kinds of composition.
Writing: What system of penmanship is, in your judgment, the best, and what are its advantages?
Arithmetic: How many cubic feet of stone are required for the wall of a

well; the diameter before being walled, 6 feet; after being walled, 3 feet;
depth, 30 feet?

Geography: Are degrees of latitude of exactly the same length? If they differ
in length, where are they shortest, and why?

Grammar: "To err is human;" parse each word in full.

Physiology: What three kinds of food do we need?

United States History: What causes led to the revolutionary war, and what
were its principal events and results?

Theory and Practice of Teaching: How should a recitation be conducted,
and what are its chief objects? [28]

Within a few years, the examinations included more questions designed to determine the teacher's methods of instruction and school
management. The questions regarding the theory and practice of teaching asked teachers how to determine the grade levels of children, or
classify a school; to compare textbook and lecture methods; and to list
the principles used in asking questions.

Sixteen-year-old Marie Susette [Mari] Sandoz had only four and a
half years of schooling in 1912, when she "sneaked to Rushville [Ne-
braska] the first week in August, and in a pink cross-barred gingham
dress took the teacher's examination in such subjects as arithmetic and
civil government, and the theory of teaching. It seemed impossible
that she could pass. All the other candidates were well-dressed young
ladies and she was a child, but she must get away—peacefully if she
could, because of her mother, but get away." [29] Mari Sandoz taught for
the next seven years in Sheridan and Cheyenne counties, Nebraska. [30]

Although the examinations reflected the expanded curriculum by
including sections on science, history, economics, chemistry, and
Latin, the view of the teacher's role as indicated in the examination
questions was that the teacher was primarily a source of information.
The state courses of study, the normal schools, and institutes accepted
and promoted the view as stated by Sarah Gillespie Huftalen, "Education is the bringing forth and training up of all the faculties and
powers of the mind and body." [31] Nine-tenths of the examination questions, however, remained a test of the candidate's ability to recall specific facts and to demonstrate her own competence in the content of
each area of the school curriculum. Assessments of teacher competence were predominantly based on accuracy in reading, writing, and
arithmetic. Professional knowledge and skills, which were more difficult to assess through testing, were apparently of lesser importance.

The administration of the teachers' examinations gradually became part of the course work at the institutes and the normal schools where teachers, both beginners and experienced, passed the appropriate examinations for first-, second-, or third-class certification. The teachers' continued attendance at the institutes gave them the opportunity to upgrade their certification, the prerequisite of moving to a more affluent school district. Long-term teacher Sarah Jane Price attended institutes, studied on her own, and took teachers' examinations throughout her years of teaching. Her diaries indicate that she lived at her own home and taught at several different schools in the 1870s and 1880s.[32]

The Institutes

As the most common means of teacher education on the prairies and plains of the late 1860s to early 1900s, the institute was readily accessible, acceptable, affordable, and adaptable to the widely ranging populations of the region. Institutes were series of courses in basic content of the school subjects and in teaching methods. They were planned by the county superintendents, met from one to six weeks in centrally located communities such as the county seat, and were taught by outstanding local teachers and administrators and by teacher educators from the normal schools. The term *normal* emanates from "*norm*, or *norma*, meaning rule, pattern, model, or standard, and signified, in general serving the norm or rule of teaching; but whether the name was given because the school was expected formally to teach the norm, to exemplify it in practice, or to do both of these things, history does not inform us."[33] Both the normal schools and the institutes attempted to prepare teachers academically and professionally for the one-room rural schools. Only a minority of the nineteenth-century teachers completed a course of study at a normal school.

The institutes brought beginners and experienced teachers together in a community where they boarded in private homes and attended classes held in school rooms, churches, and public meeting halls for the purpose of becoming competent in the common branches of education (the subjects and content of the curriculum), methods of instruction, and school management. Because many teachers had an eighth-grade education or less, the content and methods instruction of the institute courses or "exercises" were based on the common branches of education: spelling, penmanship, language, grammar, reading, drawing, music, geography, history, civics, arithmetic, physiology and hygiene, agriculture, and practical crafts such as carpentry, sewing, and cooking. In addition to the course work in basic content, there were theoretical and inspirational speeches and lessons in practical application, often taught as demonstrations using the participants or a group of local children as the "scholars." The evening sessions were often public lectures by prominent educators and other speakers, similar to the adult education presentations of the Chautauqua assemblies, and were planned to inform the school patrons and to develop public support for the schools.

When institute classes were not in session, the teachers socialized with those in attendance and with members of the community. Perhaps with the social times in mind, Adda W. Lucas, superintendent of Pierce County Schools, Nebraska, 1872, had specific recommendations about how to have a successful institute:

> First—let the county superintendent so arrange all things as to know what each one is to do. Lectures should be held each evening; one of which should be on the reform needed in Nebraska, one on science, and one on language. Earnest work is the only safe and sure way to success. There should be select readings and singing on the evenings of lectures. Hold it on the "full of the moon;" the moon is more potent in institutes than in potato planting. I have never known it to fail of making the institute more pleasant when the moon shone.[34]

There were widespread views that "teachers [should] take care of themselves . . . and provide for their own special education, as do lawyers, clergymen and other classes."[35] However, starting with the first institutes in Connecticut in 1839, the concept of supplementing the academic education of teachers with specific instruction concerning school management and methods of teaching spread westward quickly, despite the lack of monetary support from the state legislatures. By 1846, there had been institutes in New York, Massachusetts, Ohio, Michigan, and Chicago.[36] In 1849, the first Iowa institute was held in Dubuque, planned by the teachers who were members of the Mining Region Teachers Association.[37]

By 1873, Iowa, Nebraska, and Kansas were struggling to educate a sufficient number of teachers for the expanding population through institutes that were patterned after the older states. H. D. McCarty, state superintendent of public instruction in Kansas, reported to the legislature that other states were using the institutes as the major means to educate teachers and to upgrade the qualifications for certification. He urged the Kansas legislature to "pass one law looking to a more efficient reorganization of our teachers' institutes; for while we cannot do away with them without bringing disgrace upon our State, injury to our schools, and a consequent squandering of our public school fund, yet we should aim to derive the greatest good at the least expense."[38]

Ultimately, most counties in the prairie states held institutes each year, funded in part by small state appropriations of about fifty dollars. The county superintendents were responsible for planning the institutes and encouraging or requiring the teachers to attend. Teachers paid their own registration fees, traveling and living expenses while attending the institutes, even when attendance became a requirement for certification. The enrollment fees were about one dollar per week, a day's pay for the teacher earning twenty dollars a month. Financing their attendance at the institute was within the income of the most teachers because of the low fees, the two- to six-week duration of the institute, the relatively short traveling distance from the teachers' homes, and the generally reasonable room and board expenses.[39] Although some of the institute participants may have aspired to attending a college or university, the costs of travel, room and board, and tuition often made the costs beyond the meager salaries of teachers.[40]

In order to afford the costs of the four-week teachers' institute in Emmetsburg, Iowa, about 1875, fourteen-year-old E. Mary Lacy shared a room with Letty Kettlewell and Florence Bernard. They had

> kitchen privileges for which we paid a dollar a week. We brought our supplies from home and prepared our own meals. I had a new calico dress and a supply of white aprons to last the month. This was the first time I had been away from home for so long and after two weeks mother came to see me. She thought my dress was getting soiled so she loaned me hers and wore mine home. Most of the other girls attending the institute were earning money and could dress better than I. However the lack of raiment did not detract from the pleasure and profit of the experience.[41]

C. C. Nestlerode, a leader in the Iowa State Teachers Association, challenged his teachers to see that the fifty dollars for the county institutes from the State Department of Education "is wisely expended in improving the intellectual and moral qualifications of your teachers; thereby elevating and making honorable the teacher's profession, and increasing the usefulness of our public schools."[42] Teachers expected the institutes to provide "something that would help us get a school and help us to teach it after we had it."[43] One pragmatic teacher wanted the institutes to offer less Shakespeare and elocution and more about the teaching of handwriting and drawing, "practical every-day-school-methods, and . . . something they [the teachers] could teach the children."[44]

The institutes were self-supporting, locally controlled, and were "inspired and promoted by the educators, and . . . the professionals who wrote the course outlines."[45] The local control and lack of sufficient funds often led to hiring local teachers as the instructors, to the chagrin of the normal school instructors who wished to increase the professionalism of the rural teachers.[46] With the success of the institutes based on the quality of the instruction, it was a challenge to obtain competent conductors (organizers) and instructors for little or no pay in the early years of the institutes. In 1874, Nebraska State Superintendent McKenzie stated, "It is useless to expect men of ability to spend their time in working in these institutes . . . without some remuneration."[47] While McKenzie referred to "men of ability," both men and women acted as instructors, leaders, and participants in the institute programs, normal schools, and state teachers' association conferences.[48]

The institutes evolved to differentiate the teachers' institutes from the normal institutes. The teachers' institutes were short in duration, a week or less, and, like today's in-service education workshops, usually related to specific local interests and problems. By comparison, the normal institutes of two to six weeks were highly structured, successive courses leading toward both initial and renewed certification through the organized, sequential two- or three-year programs or courses of study.[49] The courses were sequenced so that passing the lowest level of competence, based largely on the content of the common branches, was the prerequisite for taking more courses. The next level included more difficult content from the school subjects, plus courses in didactics, the methods of teaching, and school management. The approach almost guaranteed success, and, along with the teachers' examinations given at the institutes or through the county superintendents' offices, provided the basis for certification.

Through attending the normal institutes over a period of several years, a prospective teacher could achieve a level of teacher education comparable to normal school preparation. The institutes served as "the rural young people's colleges." [50] The combination of academic courses and the teacher education program can be seen in this 1884 example of the sequential levels of instruction. [51] Note that the institute accommodated the range of students from the experienced teachers with first-class certificates to those students entering the "D Class" who were the uncertified beginners without sufficient education and without teaching experience.

SUGGESTIONS AND GENERAL RULES

I. For admission to the A grade, a teacher should hold a first-class certificate, have done three years' institute work, or had equivalent professional training in normal and high schools or academies, and be a successful teacher.

II. For admission to the B grade, a teacher should hold at least a second-class certificate, have done two years' institute work, or had an equivalent high school training, and have made a success in teaching.

III. For admission to the C grade, a teacher should hold at least a third-class certificate, have done one year's institute work or equivalent.

IV. All those who have not taught and wish to prepare themselves for teaching, should be admitted to the D grade. . . .

THE GRADED COURSE OF FOUR YEARS

FIRST YEAR OR D CLASS.
Orthography [spelling], Penmanship, Language, Geography, Arithmetic, Drawing, School Economy.
SECOND YEAR OR C CLASS.
Orthography, Penmanship and Drawing, Geography, Reading, History, Physiology, Art of Teaching, Science of Teaching.
THIRD YEAR OR B CLASS.
Grammar, Arithmetic, Reading, History, Physiology, Art of Teaching, Science of Teaching, Primary Teaching.
FOURTH YEAR OR A CLASS.
Civil Government, Algebra, Botany, Zoology, Mineralogy, Rhetoric and Literature, Art of Teaching, Science of Teaching, Primary Teaching. [52]

Educating the Schoolwomen

While the teachers saw the institutes as the means to obtain and maintain their teaching certificates, they also relished the social side of the gatherings. For the veteran teacher and beginner alike, the institutes represented a means of renewal of motivation, relief from the professional isolation of the one-room schoolhouse, and a time to have "pleasant times together."[53] Sarah Jane Price, had been teaching at least seven years when she wrote about the institute in her diary:

> Monday, Nov. 2nd 1878
> I have spent today in the schoolroom. I am trying to carry out some of the suggestions of the institute. The pupils seem to be very much interested in their studies and I hope to be able to accomplish some good this season. . . . I feel a slight reaction since the institute closed and a longing for the companionship of those with whom I became acquainted there. I think of Marion Lounsburg, and remember the pleasant communion we had together. I hope I may have done her good. I must close.
> Jane Price, Lincoln Valley Neb.[54]

Price does not describe those suggestions from the institute, but she seems optimistic about the anticipated success of her students. The frequency and purpose of the institutes are shown in Price's expectations and description of the institute the following spring:

> Monday, March 3rd 1879
> Today has been very windy and disagreeable. I washed this morning and it was rather unpleasant work as it was so cold but I finished in good time and scrubbed and got ready to iron tomorrow. . . . I shall be busy tomorrow getting ready for institute next day. I hope we will have a good time and profitable as well.
> Jane Price

> Sat. March 8th 1879
> I have just returned from Aurora where I have been attending Institute week since Wednesday. We had a good institute. I enjoyed it very much, made many new acquaintances and became better acquainted with many others. I hope we shall have pleasant times together hereafter.
> I passed examination, did not need to do so but thought best

to, as I hoped to get a better grade in some of my studies. I think I passed very well and look for a good grade.

Mr. Cass examined us in physiology, he was very good and we would have been glad to have the remainder of the exercises conducted by him, but Mr. Barton came back and gave us a thorough overhauling. I hope the girls will get a good certificate and be able to teach a good school. I am too sleepy to write more tonight as I have not slept good since I went away.

Jane Price[55]

For the experienced teacher like Sarah Jane Price, the institute was a way to upgrade her teaching certificate by taking and passing additional courses and examinations. The teacher with a first-class certificate would be hired by the schools with the best facilities and the highest wages. Sarah Jane Price was concerned and hopeful that "the girls will get a good certificate." These girls were probably her scholars and neighbors.

After her first year of teaching, twenty-year-old Sarah Gillespie attended the normal institute in August of 1884.

Mon. [August] 4. Commence attending the Normal Institute—
138 enrolled. Prof. L. T. Weld of Cresco [Iowa] is Conductor.
We have Arith., Read., Gram., Orthog., Penmanship, Didactics
and Astronomy lectures . . .
Wed. . . . I have missed writing during the normal. The first
week went quickly by. We had such good instructors. Then I am
one of the leaders in my 3rd year Division. Had a discussion in
the reading class every day. . . .
Wed. 13th. Attend Normal—. . . Made the acquaintance of
Miss Fannie Pooley, Primary Teacher of the Earlville school. She
is my intimate friend—if I had any. Mr. Miller is much pleased
with my recitations. Prof. Weld thinks I have grit & pluck and
walked to the little bridge with me one eve. We had a good visit.
He intends to come & see us. All the Profs seem to think I am
just about right.
Thurs. 14th. Attend Normal. Ma came down in afternoon. . . .
We went to the lecture in the evening on "Educate for Citizenship" by Prof. Weld. Fred Patterson offered his fan. Oh! *I don't see how he knew me.* He is nice too. Mrs. Boggs has several boarders. Jessie Heath & Amy are "mashers" as they call themselves.

Educating the Schoolwomen

They flirt & are so boisterous I do not care to associate with
"such". . . .
Fri. 15th. Attend Normal—Last day. 200 . . . enrolled. Good
bye & parting glances.
Sat. 16th. Ma went to town. I study some for examination. Do
not have to be examined in Reading, Writing, Grammar or
Orthography. . . .
Mond. 18. Examination was easy for me. . . .
Tues. 19. Examination closed. I am all right I think.[56]

Sarah Gillespie's experience at this institute included meeting and
socializing with new people, both men and women. Although she
complains about the girls who were flirts, she also enjoyed attention
from the men, both her peers and the institute instructors. She relished receiving recognition for being a well-prepared student. Learning both content and methods of instruction, she had no difficulty
passing the examinations necessary for certification.

The local control of the institutes brought with it the potential for
both isolation from the main stream of educational reform and success in meeting the local educational needs. The majority of the
nineteenth-century teachers received their teacher education and certification through institute attendance. The institutes as the immediate and affordable way to educate teachers were an expression of prairie pragmatism or the cult of the immediately useful and practical.[57]
The consequences of the institutes had the "immediate, practical
utilitarianism" demanded by the taxpayers, through increasing the
number of teachers and promoting morality and literacy. The long-
term benefits of these results were not recognized as a means of financial justification, hence, in accordance with the cult, "teachers,
preachers, and other arts and professions did less well [than the
lawyers, bankers, and doctors], and suffered accordingly" with low
salaries.[58]

Efforts at Self-Instruction

The individual teacher made her personal and professional choices
concerning how and if she would pursue teacher education beyond
passing the teachers' examination and attending the local institute.
While many teachers attended the institutes, normal schools, and colleges, others, especially the beginners, may have had no other choice
than to try to learn on their own, primarily due to lack of funds or

opportunity to attend the institutes or normal schools. Despite their recognition of the need to have more knowledge and skills, an admirable, high-minded motive, the results were often less than successful.

Some teachers enrolled in reading circles in order to read professional books on their own or with other teachers and to pass examinations over the content on a regular schedule. Membership was voluntary, and in some areas carried "one and one-half per cent on the general average of examinations for certificates [to] be given to teachers for each of the . . . books of the year, . . . or three per cent for completing the entire work of the year."[59] The Nebraska Teachers' Reading Circle brochure for 1904–1905 reported that "three-fourths of the counties were interested and two-thirds of all the teachers in the smaller cities, the villages and the rural districts of Nebraska [were] actively engaged in . . . the reading circle work."[60] The reading list and costs for 1902–1903 provide an example of this in-service education project:

Hodge's NATURE STUDY AND LIFE, Ginn & Co., [$1.00]
and one or more of the following:
White's ART OF TEACHING, American Book Co. [95 cents]
Murphy's TURNING POINTS IN TEACHING, A. Flanagan Co. [50 cents]
Sherman's WHAT IS SHAKESPEARE, Macmillan Co. [95 cents]
Shaw's SCHOOL HYGIENE, Macmillan Co. [85 cents]
Wray's Jean Mitchell's School, Public School Pub. Co. [75 cents]
Arnold's Waymarks for Teachers, Silver Burdett & Co. [90 cents][61]

The structure of the reading circles would have been helpful to the isolated teachers such as Clara Conron who taught near Wakarusa, Kansas, 1884–1885, and Anna Webber, Mitchell County, Kansas, 1881. As can be seen in their diaries, they had no professional support for their well-motivated efforts at self-education. They were entirely on their own in the choice of correspondence courses, other self-improvement ventures, and in monitoring their own progress.

In October 1884, Clara Conron was pursuing Spencer's Course of Practical Writing as an independent correspondence course.[62] In January 1885, she "commenced another history," perhaps referring to the "Histories" that her Pa got in Topeka.[63] In February, Conron wrote in her diary that she was "going to study Bookkeeping."[64] In March, she and a friend visited schools in Topeka to observe the teachers.

"Wednesday we visited Clay Street School, I do not see as the city teachers keep any better order than we country ones."[65] Despite her good intentions, her self-education efforts were erratic, with more attention in her diary given to her scholars, the weather, her sewing, her family, and friends.

Anna Webber wrote about her desire to learn more and to be well prepared to teach, but her efforts at self-education didn't always come off according to her plans. Her diary reflects the isolation, indecision, fatigue, and aspirations of the beginning teacher:

> Friday, May 21, 1881
>
> O, Dear! Almost two weeks of my school gone. And how do I like teaching by this time? Well, I hardly know. I think like it. I know I would like it better if things were different. As it is I do not make the progress I had [expected] to. About all I learn is in studying after school is out. And then I am so tired and figety, I can do nothing scarcely, unless it is to walk about, or go to sleep. Perhaps that will wear off tho' as I get more used to teaching. . . . If I can get to Beloit [27 miles away] I will get me a grammar, and some kind of writing system. . . . And I want some ink, yes and something to write on. Before I began school I thought I would write an Essay every day, and I haven't written one yet,—but I must try, it will be a failure I expect, but I can't do more than fail though. I guess I'll take Nature as the subject. It seems as if there is enough to write on that. I am surrounded by nature, about all I see is the hills, and all I hear is the noise of the birds, and a dozen or more of children.[66]

By May 23, Anna Webber had decided to write essays on Tuesdays and Thursday evenings.

> I do not know how to begin now, but I am just going to commence and write any and everything I can think of on the subject, then if I ever have a chance to get any thing that teaches how to place writing under heads and sections, I can learn to do better. . . . I think it will have a tendency to improve my intellect and enlarge my small store of knowledge, if I take the right subject to write on.[67]

She tried to set Saturdays aside for study, "But I studied very little, I did a little sewing, and that was about all I did."[68] On July 26, 1881, the day before school closed, she felt "sad and lonesome . . . one rea-son is that school is so near out and I shall have to leave, and perhaps never see some of my scholars again."[69] The next day, she wrote:

HALF PAST FIVE, P.M.
My school is out. It is all over and done with. And I am just a
little glad and considerable tired. I have been dreading it so long.
It was not so hard afterall. . . . We had a pretty nice time. But I
cannot enjoy myself, or be lively now, it makes little difference
where I am. I am going home tomorrow, and next week to school.
Well school is out.[70]

For those schoolwomen and men who continued to teach beyond the expiration of their first certificate, Anna Webber's "going home tomorrow, and next week to school," meaning the institute or normal school, was indeed part of the teacher's way of life.

The Normal Schools

The normal schools and normal curricula in colleges were in many ways structured extensions of the ungraded common schools inasmuch as they accepted students at whatever level of learning they possessed, encouraged students to go as far as they could, academically and finan-cially, and provided for a variety of social events.[71] The inclusion of normal, commercial, and scientific courses of study at the normal school was typical where "settlers were willing to support normal schools only if they functioned as community colleges or people's uni-versities . . . with the greatest variety of academic and vocational subjects."[72] The Eastern-Iowa Normal School, a private school estab-lished in 1874, Grandview, Iowa, advertised that "Students can enter E.I.N.S. at ANYTIME, but are recommended to try to commence their studies at the beginning of a month or term. January 2d is the opening of the WINTER TERM; and April 1st is the opening of the SPRING TERM."[73] The description of the normal school students published in "Eastern Iowa Normal School, General Statements" characterized the normal school students of the prairies and plains.

Every one desiring a good education is welcomed at this school.
No shoddy aristocracy wanted. No go-easy person asked to come.
No spendthrifts invited here. No dissolute youth tolerated. But
earnest young men and women, possessed of an honest aim in

Educating the Schoolwomen

life—teachers who desire improvement in their vocation, young business men who want to master a commercial course, persons wishing to get a general education, or such as wish to begin the study of Law or Medicine or Teaching, are all invited to come and join our ranks—we will do you good.

"Age need not be considered a hindrance" to prospective students, indeed,

'NONE ARE TOO OLD TO LEARN'
. . . Many teachers, from 25 to 45, have good native ability but have occupied the lower ranks simply because their scholarship was insufficient, or because their

PROFESSIONAL SKILL
was not up to the requirements for the better grade of schools. . . .
Many teachers of large experience, some of them married men and women, have come to perfect their knowledge of their chosen profession, and have increased their proficiency so as to largely enhance their powers of usefulness, and their remuneration as well.[74]

The normal school students, like the institute students, were teen-aged to middle-aged and were obtaining initial or continuing teacher education at an accessible location for a duration that was affordable. The cost of board and tuition at Eastern-Iowa Normal School in 1883 was fourteen dollars a month, comparable to the cost of attending an institute for four weeks. By the year, the costs were eleven dollars a month, giving students options about length of time in attendance.

Although the normal students, both beginners and experienced teachers, were "ardent and faithful," they were also high spirited and enjoyed playing pranks on their professors and on each other.[75] At Cooper Memorial College, Sterling, Kansas, the president's buggy was occasionally found in the chapel.[76] Students' Day was held for a few terms at Iowa State Normal School, during which the students lampooned their professors mercilessly during chapel. When Students' Day was discontinued, the school newspaper carried on the generally good-humored needling.[77]

The development of the sense of community among students and faculty was enhanced through their membership in extracurricular classes, church affiliations, literary societies, drama clubs, and other social groups similar to those found in many communities.[78] The importance of the societies and clubs as social events is evident: their importance as a source of education should not be underrated. For many students, the societies constituted their major exposure to literature, drama, the arts, and the current issues of the day.

A case in point is the education of Catharine "Cassie" Wiggins. For Cassie Wiggins, the greatest benefit of attending Cooper Memorial College in 1895 was derived from the Chrestomatheon Literary Society. Despite her "timidity developed during . . . years of isolation on the northwest Kansas prairie," she participated fully in the society's programs, which included giving readings and recitations, participating in discussions, and, of course, taking part in the social events.[79] Cassie's class of 1898 maintained a class letter among its members for twenty-nine years. Of this class, two members became Presbyterian ministers; one was a college professor; three, including Cassie, were public school teachers; one was an accountant; one was a horticulturist; one got married shortly after graduation; and one student's poor health prevented any career.[80]

For Ethel Hale there was no question that she, her brother, and her sister would attend school beyond high school in the early 1900s in southeastern Nebraska. Cleo, her older sister, had started teaching after finishing tenth grade and passing the teacher's exams. The high school then added grades eleven and twelve, which Ethel and her brother, Russell, completed. Ethel Hale described the situation:

> My sister had taught two or three years by the time Russell and I had graduated from high school. . . . Cleo decided that she had enough money, about $450 that she had saved, to take her through a year at Peru [State Normal School] for training and Mother and Dad decided to send Russell and me, also. So we had three members of the family at Peru that year. . . .
>
> We had good instructors at this Peru State Normal and I remember certain ones of them with real pleasure. I think they put us through excellent classes [such as] how to approach children. I think there was some good psychology. . . . And we had to do practice teaching. . . . [Also] you had to go in the room and sit and watch. . . . So we watched really good people at work. . . . And that training, I expect, was probably what accounted for my being as enthusiastic as I was when I went out to teach. . . .
>
> Anyway, after two years of this, without any question, I was

going to teach. . . . I began when I was [graduated] at 17. I didn't have a very serious outlook. The fact of the matter is, I think, I was having an awfully good time.[81]

Both Ethel Hale and her brother continued their educations while teaching. After several years of teaching in Nebraska, Idaho, and Utah, Ethel completed her B.S. and M.A. in education at the State University of Iowa while teaching in the Experimental School there.[82] Russell Hale taught school, continued his education, and became a superintendent of schools in various Nebraska communities. Cleo Hale taught high school at Waterloo, Nebraska, for several years then continued her education in business, eventually becoming the director of a children's hospital in Omaha until her retirement.[83]

Ethel Hale next taught at the Campus School at Western Michigan Teachers College, where her responsibilities included demonstration teaching, supervising student teachers, and teaching methods courses to in-service teachers through extension courses. In this teacher education position, her colleagues in the Campus School and the college included women from similar backgrounds.[84]

More than half the faculty members of the normal schools in the nineteenth and early twentieth centuries were women, usually with the title of preceptress.[85] Men were given the title of professor. Through successful teaching experience and normal school or college education, both women and men became teacher educators in the normal departments of colleges and universities and in the normal schools. As the state normal schools became recognized as state colleges, there was a significant decline in the number of women faculty members.[86] Feminization of teaching had extended into the normal schools only until they became increasingly more academic, as demanded by the educational professionals.[87] As the role of women in teacher education declined, there were fewer women to serve as role models for the students. This reduction exemplifies the loss of "talent and energy . . . when gender is put ahead of humanity."[88]

Some of the normal school professors had come from eastern normal schools expressly to teach in the western normal schools. Eliza C. Morgan came from New York to become the preceptress of the girls' dormitory at Peru State Normal School. For twenty-six years, Miss Morgan taught rhetoric, literature, and general history in the classroom, and social graces in the dormitory.[89] Many of the teacher educators were life-long residents of the West, such as Susan Frazier and

Sarah Gillespie Huftalen, who had begun their teaching careers in one-room rural schools.[90] After many years of teaching and continuing their own educations, they became administrators and teacher educators through supervising beginning teachers in the schools under their jurisdiction, organizing and providing leadership for the institutes in their counties, and as normal school professors. Becoming a teacher educator was a desirable form of professional advancement and recognition for the long-term educational leader.

For Sarah Gillespie Huftalen, teaching at Upper Iowa University from 1918 to 1923 "was expansive." She taught in four different departments during the regular school year: social science, natural science, physical science, mental science and education. In the summer session Huftalen taught methods courses to classes "being mostly composed of teachers and would-be teachers; the students ranging in age from the teens to that of 73 years."[91] Her students were "largely seniors; few juniors, and fewer Freshmen and preparatory. They were not only pupils but friends and fine in every way." Huftalen next taught at the normal training department, Muscatine [Iowa] High School, 1924–1933, where she had 130 students in her classes daily but found, "All in all these dozen years were like a halo of happiness before retiring."[92]

State-Supported Normal Schools

The private academies, colleges, and state universities were expected to educate the teachers for the common schools of the West, thus following a different pattern from the eastern state normal schools that were dedicated to teacher education.[93] The development of the state-supported normal schools in Kansas, Nebraska, and Iowa took various routes, mostly precarious as in the case of Kansas. Emporia State Normal School was opened in February 1865 with forty-two students taught by Professor L. B. Kellogg, the principal and only teacher.[94] When Leavenworth (Kansas) Normal School was opened in 1870, the prospective students were advised "to bring with them, for reference, any suitable books they may have."[95] Concordia Normal School of Kansas was short-lived, 1874–1876, "owing to the calamity which has befallen our state, in the shape of drouth and grasshoppers."[96] When the ensuing economic problems caused the state of Kansas to withdraw support to all three normal schools, Emporia limped along using the proceeds from its land endowment and fees from the students to pay for operating expenses. Emporia was further endangered in 1878 by an embezzlement through the illegal sale of its lands, followed by severe tornado damage in April and a disastrous fire in October. The board of regents optimistically informed the governor, "The destruction of the Normal School Buildings at Emporia changes in no respect the reasons which establish the vital importance of an efficient system of normal instruction for the state."[97]

The first State Normal School of Nebraska fared somewhat better than did the Kansas Normal Schools. It came into being in 1867, when the state accepted the gift of a building at Peru, Nebraska, with green cottonwood floors and unplastered walls that the Methodist Conference had refused to accept as a contribution. By the fall of 1871, the staff had increased to five, with ninety-one students registered and an additional thirty-eight students in the model school.[98] The purpose of the Peru State Normal School was seen as teaching students who would "either from desire, or necessity, remain there a comparatively short time, and spend whatever time they devote to teaching, in the country districts. The wants of this class of students are kept constantly in mind, and in a quiet way the school is elevating the standard of common school teaching."[99]

In an effort to cope with educating teachers, Nebraska funded three additional normal schools and five junior normal schools early in the twentieth century. At the junior normal schools, three summer sessions of eight to ten weeks were equivalent to one year at a state normal school.[100] The junior normals phased out as normal training became readily available through the public high schools.

State support for a normal school in Iowa was erratic, and slow in being implemented. In 1848, the Second General Assembly of Iowa provided for normal schools at Andrew, Oskaloosa, and Mount Pleasant with appropriations of only $500 for each school.[101] Failure was unavoidable with virtually no operational funds. By 1855, the assembly established a normal department at the newly established co-educational State University of Iowa. During the next seventeen years of rapid population growth in Iowa, the normal department graduated a total of only 185 teachers.[102]

Bills for the establishment of a state normal school were repeatedly introduced in the Iowa General Assembly from 1866 on and finally passed with a one-vote margin in 1876, as a way to utilize the soon-to-be-vacant Iowa Soldiers' Orphans Home at Cedar Falls.[103] Under the leadership of the first two presidents, James C. Gilchrist and

Homer Seerley, the school at Cedar Falls attained the status of a teachers' college, including instruction in the sciences and languages beyond the level being taught in the high schools and academies. Teaching at Iowa State Normal in 1894, according to Sara Riggs, newly appointed professor of history was "Work, work, work; yes, and plenty of it" for faculty and students alike.[104]

By 1902, the president of Columbia University ranked "Seerley's school" second only to Teachers College of Columbia.[105] By 1909, the Iowa State Normal School officially became Iowa State Teachers College.[106]

While the generally recognized mission of the state normal schools was to produce teachers for the public schools, the number of teachers who had graduated from the normals was few. In 1895, 5,726 men and 22,117 women were teaching in the 17,294 schools in Iowa.[107] Of the total of 1,254 graduates of the Iowa State Normal School from 1876 to 1897, only 514 were teaching in Iowa. Eighty-one graduates were teaching in other states; 95 were students in other colleges and universities but would return to teaching; 98 had left teaching to do other work; and 117 had retired or married.[108] At the turn of the century, Nebraska had 9,400 teachers, 6,400 of whom taught in the rural schools. Even with the evident interest and support of normal education in Nebraska, less than 16 percent of the teachers had professional training beyond the institutes; 40 percent had high school education; 29 percent had less than three years of high school or equivalent; 15 percent had no high school education; and only 5.5 percent had college or university education.[109]

The numbers of graduates from the state-supported and other normal schools do not adequately convey the role of the normal schools in the prairie states in the late nineteenth and early twentieth centuries. There was an on-going network of leadership and contacts among teachers and the professional teacher educators through the institutes, the state, county and local teachers' associations, and through the education journals. The institutes and intermittent attendance at the normal schools continued as the principal sources of teacher education for the prairie schoolteachers.

Normal Education for Nonwhite Teachers

The Kansas law in 1866 indicated that the legal voters of a school district "shall have power to make such order as they deem proper, for the education of white and colored children separately, or otherwise, securing to them equal educational advantages."[110] Because areas of large black populations were also those areas of least taxable property, the separate but equal approach doomed the black children to inferior schools and teachers with little professional training.[111] The irony of the segregated schools was that black women teachers had positions in schools that were segregated and in school districts that had predominantly black enrollments. When schools were no longer segregated, the numbers of black women teachers in the West declined.[112]

There were some efforts to educate Native American and African American teachers in Kansas and Nebraska. In 1867, three years before the first black student was admitted to the University of Kansas, the Colored Normal School at Quindaro was established as an effort to provide teachers for the children of freed slaves.[113] A staff of two African Americans was hired; Mrs. J. T. Blachly taught the students, and Dr. Eben Blachly became the president of the "Freedman's University."[114] By 1872, the Colored Normal School had an enrollment of fifty students whose "Want of home culture and means, renders our work peculiarly difficult."[115] By 1873, two of the students taught by Dr. Blachly and Mrs. J. T. Blachly received teaching certificates and were teaching, most likely in "colored" schools.[116] Information from Quindaro as the Colored Normal School then disappeared from the state superintendent's reports.

In 1891, this "Freedman's University" at Quindaro became Western University under the auspices of the African Methodist Episcopal Church. The AME Church continued to operate Western University through World War I and in the 1990s retained ownership of part of the land.[117] Normal and college preparatory courses were offered as well as industrial arts and domestic science.[118] About one-third of the 110 students in 1891 were enrolled in the normal program.[119] The irony of the history of this school appeared in the late 1980s, as the site at Quindaro was being considered for a landfill for the Kansas City area. The archaeological survey of the rugged gully at Quindaro put the landfill project on hold while this noble chapter in the education of African Americans was uncovered. The Historic Preservation Board of the State of Kansas found the site of significant historic importance and determined that it should be preserved. While the questions of the landfill company's claims, ownership of the artifacts, and state acquisition of the site are being resolved slowly, the ruins are exposed and deteriorating rapidly.[120]

Other attempts to educate nonwhite teachers were found at the Santee Normal Training School, Santee Reservation, Knox County in northeastern Nebraska, and the Haskell Indian School, in Lawrence, Kansas. Santee Normal School was founded in 1870 by the American Board of Commissioners for Foreign Missions to educate through religious and industrial training, the teachers, preachers, interpreters, and businessmen who would "regenerate" the Sioux Nation.[121] According to several assessments, the graduates of Santee Normal School accounted for almost half of the educated leaders of the Sioux.[122] The unique aspect of the Santee Normal School was its insistence on teaching Indians in the Dakota language, with English as the second language, while most schools for Native Americans forbade the use of Indian languages.[123]

The Haskell Indian School, a federally supported, off-reservation industrial boarding school founded in 1884, had a normal department, plus kindergarten, and grades one through nine. Where the Santee Normal School drew its day and boarding students from the Santee Reservation and other nearby Sioux, the Haskell Indian School was a boarding school with students from all over the Southwest.[124] By 1900, twenty-five off-reservation industrial boarding schools had been established based on the ineffectual policy of assimilation that required the Native American students to become "white" Indians, without any blending of cultures. These attempts to assimilate and educate Native Americans as teachers and leaders through the mission schools and the boarding schools are linked with the white population's definitions of civilization and salvation, with indeterminate value for the Native American populations.[125] Indeed, efforts for Indian-directed education such as the Cherokee schools of Oklahoma begun in 1841 were abolished by Congress in 1906.[126]

Conclusion

Despite the professional ideals and the gradually increasing stability of state support for teacher education, the problem remained as to how adequately to educate enough teachers for the expanding populations of the West. The National Education Association's Committee of Twelve on Rural Education, chaired by Henry Sabin, Iowa State Superintendent of Public Instruction, presented its findings at the 1895 meeting of the National Council on Education in Denver, Colorado. Those conclusions cited two- and four-year normal training programs as presenting economic and transportation problems for many rural teachers nationwide:

> (1) A large proportion of the teachers of rural schools cannot afford the time and expense of two-years' course in a normal school. (2) The receipts from employment in the rural school under present conditions do not remunerate one for the expense of a normal-school course. This is a matter of business, and sentiment will not change the facts. (3) Other conditions remaining the same, attendance at a school is in an inverse ratio to the distance between school and home.[127]

The recommendations of the Committee of Twelve called for professional supervision in the rural schools; rural school sections in the state teachers' associations; summer school sessions of several weeks' duration; teachers' institutes; reading circles for teachers; establishment and expansion of town libraries; normal school courses specifically for rural teachers; and a short course of normal training offered in every county.[128] The state and local teachers' associations of the prairie states were involved in each of these recommendations as their organized influence extended from the state superintendent to the isolated rural school through the institutes and other forms of normal education, through the educational periodicals, the development of county and state courses of study, and in shaping school legislation.

In the early twentieth century, the frontier conditions in the prairie states had vanished; instead settlers faced the challenges of community development. The affluence of a rural or town school district determined the quality and maintenance of schoolhouses, teachers' salaries, and the value of the teaching supplies and textbooks, but a sense of community was developed with the schoolhouse as its center. The professional education of teachers in its many forms resulted in a range of competencies from imperceptible literacy to four years at a teachers' college or university. The loss of women teachers to marriage and other employment remained high; the motivation to teach continued to be based in the desire to help the children of the community and fulfilling economic needs through socially acceptable employment for women. With all of the large failures and the many small triumphs, there was sufficient progress in educating teachers to lead W. T. Harris, U. S. commissioner of education, 1891–1906, to observe:

> The most important item of improvement that belongs to the re-
> cent history of education is the introduction of professionally
> trained teachers. . . . [who] continue to improve in skill and effi-
> ciency for many years. Such a teacher is constantly increasing his
> number of successful devices to secure good behavior without
> harsh measures, and to secure industry and critical attention to
> study. [129]

Professional teacher education had become a legitimate course of study at the institutes, the normal schools, and at colleges and universities. The schoolwomen had become counted among the educated citizens of the heartland states.

Normal Institute, Johnson County, Iowa, 1896. The few men in attendance stood in the back rows. One African-American woman was enrolled in this institute. (Young Collection, State Historical Society of Iowa—Iowa City)

Summer School for the teachers of Lincoln County, Nebraska, 1901. (Photograph by Broach, North Platte, Nebraska. Nebraska State Historical Society)

Chapter 2

Central Hall, Iowa State Normal School, Cedar Falls, Iowa, erected 1895. (*Report of the State Superintendent of Public Instruction, Iowa, 1894–95,* facing page 12)

University of Nebraska co-eds, early 1900s. Agnes Samuelson, center, became a rural teacher, county superintendent, and state superintendent of public instruction in Iowa, and the president of the National Education Association. (Agnes Samuelson Collection, State Historical Society of Iowa—Iowa City)

CHAPTER
THREE

The Social and Physical Landscape of the
Schoolwomen's Living and Working Conditions

Living Conditions

As nineteen-year-old Bessie Tucker opened her diary in 1918, she described herself and her position as a teacher.

> I will begin by giving you some valuable information about myself . . . then you will have an idea of my importance in the community where I now reside. . . . This is my second year, jumping from an enrollment of three to thirty-three. And from the extreme part of western Nebraska to the extreme eastern part. I am quite sure these thirty-three boys and girls are the cream of the crop and we are good friends.[1]

Tucker and other schoolwomen of the heartland found the circumstances of the homes, schoolhouses, and surroundings were variable from one school district to another, based on the richness of the soil, the annual rainfall, the markets, the state of community development, the stability of the settlers, and the level of their continued support of the local schools. In the more densely populated eastern portions of Iowa, Kansas, and Nebraska, where there were as many as nine schoolhouses within a township of six square miles, those schoolwomen who lived at home had choices of employment among the several schools that were within easy daily commuting distance.[2] The school districts that offered the lowest salaries, poorly equipped schoolhouses, and with boarding conditions often lacking in comforts hired the short-term and inexperienced teachers, those with minimal education, and those who were unable to move to more affluent school districts because of family responsibilities. For the short-term and beginning teachers, these conditions were temporary as the teachers moved from school to school, seeking personal advancements. While teachers were criticized by the school patrons and the educational professionals because they did not stay in a school for any length of time, they were generally hired for only one term at a time, and a longer tenure offered few opportunities of obtaining improved salaries and working conditions.[3]

The living and working conditions of the schoolwomen of the prairies and plains were inexorably intertwined. The schoolwomen were part of the social, religious, political, and educational development, and the camaraderie of the community. They were in the public eye both in school and in the community. They lived in close proximity to their schools, either with their own parents, their spouses, or alone, or they boarded near the schoolhouse with families whose living conditions were similar to the teachers' own homes.[4] They taught the children of their own extended families and their neighbors' children in the one-room schoolhouse that served as "a democratic community institution, representing the *whole* community. In this respect the school stands alone, and in sharp contrast with all other rural institutions. . . . With the school, . . . every individual in the neighborhood has a vital connection, owing to the taxes it necessitates, if for no other reason."[5]

Boarding

The schoolwomen who boarded with families near to their schools, found that the living conditions ranged from intolerable for some beginning teachers to a real "home away from home." The underlying influences on their lives came then not only from their families but also from the people whose children they taught, the people with whom they boarded, and other members of the community. Agnes Briggs Olmstead found that "the people were kind and did their best for me and that was good enough."[6] Rosa Schreurs Jennings knew from her experience that "Teacher" was a respectable and respected title.[7] But a generation earlier in Nebraska Territory, Mollie Dorsey entered teaching during the summer of 1859. In this undeveloped frontier setting, she boarded for just two weeks before she wrote in her journal, "At this place I slept upon the floor, and festive bedbugs held high carnival over my weary frame the night through."[8] As an early example of employment negotiations, she refused to teach another day until her school director found her a comfortable, clean home in which to board. She moved to a pleasant home where she lived for the rest of the summer term. Dorsey was offered the school for the fall term but declined because "I believe I prefer sewing unless I could be a first-class teacher."[9] She found that school was not "a paying affair. The people are too poor. Besides, Father says I cannot teach again. It is too trying on me."[10]

In the twentieth century, seventeen-year-old Phoebe Athey found that the normal training didn't prepare her to deal with the

> . . . kooks, sons of the families at the boarding homes, or neigh-
> borhood boys pestering about. What do you do when you find a
> dead lizard in your bed? How to cope with sand rubbed into your
> bed sheets. Sand burrs hidden under the bottom sheet of your
> bed. A dead snake placed by the door of your bedroom and then
> what to say or do at the table when the food was [passed] around
> the table with "Let's skip the Teach."
>
> How could a person rid themselves of the callers who stopped
> by the schoolhouse with their dreamy eyes? They came to shoot
> the breeze, however. Some were car salesmen, others had bright
> ideas about spending the weekend in Grand Island and you could
> get the car for a song.[11]

On one occasion when Phoebe Athey was working late at the schoolhouse, she fought off a man who attacked her. She ran and hid under a bridge until he left. For fear of hurting her reputation, she never told anyone, and she never stayed alone after school to get her work done.[12]

In the early 1890s, in Butler County, Iowa, long-term professional teacher Rosa Schreurs Jennings found that farmers' wives didn't take in boarders unless they needed money. She referred to her landladies as "Aunts" and described the homes where she boarded with

The Social and Physical Landscape

affection and admiration for her pleasant and well-informed surrogate families.

> Aunt Minnie, my landlady, fed her family sulphur and molasses every spring, and insisted that I join them in the practice, which I did. We took a dose every day for nine days, then interrupted the treatment for nine days, and repeated it for another nine. She was a marvelous cook, had cooked in her father's half-way house in Illinois, as a girl, in stage-coach days. A soft, ginger-molasses cookie of hers was a steady blue-ribbon winner at the county fair. Her breakfast consisted of graham pancakes, light, thick, fluffy, served hot from a wood range; oatmeal, cooked for an hour, served with cream; and one of those ginger cookies. For special, there was sausage or steak in butchering season; and fried chicken in the fall.[13]
>
> I taught seven years in rural one-room schools, and always had a pleasant place to board. Aunt Emma was a widow, versed in good literature which she and her husband had read together through many years. She recited from memory line after line from Shakespeare, Tennyson, Scott, Byron, and our own poets of the Concord group. She had lived in Ontario, Canada and in Wisconsin as a girl, and could tell stories of earlier pioneer days than Iowa knew.[14]

High school teacher Sadie Smith, another long-term professional schoolwoman, enjoyed being indulged while boarding with Mrs. Fraser in North Bend, Nebraska, in 1897. Sadie wrote to her future husband, Rollin Trail: "Mrs. F. is lonesome without her daughter and I kind of come in as one of the family, which exactly suits me. I feel quite at home and have everything my own way. I don't get lonesome because I have to [do school] work most of the time."[15]

Teachers often visited overnight with various families in their school district, in part as a way to increase communication with the families but mostly as a way to share the boarding responsibility among several families. As an overnight visitor, Rosa Schreurs Jennings found she was eagerly welcomed by the children and their parents.

> I slept . . . under quilts of exquisite needlework, patterns called Twin Sisters, Martha's Choice, West Wind, Wedding Ring, In-

dian Trail, and others. The food was always delicious, possibly
even a blue-ribbon prize winner at the county fair.

Many memories came back to me of those visits I made—
of seeing much "getting along without" with a pride that refused to whine; of lively political arguments with the head of
the house . . . ; of choice, heirloom "receipts" given me by the
mother. Those visits were good for all of us, levelers both ways.
Having once eaten salt and broken bread in these homes, I could
not, had I wanted to, be indifferent to the children's progress
at school; on the other hand, the parents cooperated even to
threatening to "lick the kids" at home if they got a lickin' at
school. [16]

The home visits helped the teachers to know and appreciate the rural
families and their problems and provided the families with the opportunity to be supportive of the teacher.

As a second-year teacher, Bessie Tucker boarded in a home where
she had "a dear little room . . . as charming a little nest as any girl
could wish and is absolutely mine while I am here." [17] Her landlady,
Mrs. Rejman, was Bessie's "mother away from home in my home away
from home." [18] Bessie confided in Mrs. Rejman that she was afraid
the children did not like her. After a long and successful Christmas
program, Bessie's desk was loaded with gifts. "As we drove home,
Mrs. Rejman exclaimed in her broken english, 'You no think they like
you now?' The Christmas spirit truly prevailed." [19]

As wage-earning women, the indigenous teachers were usually of
the same socioeconomic background as their students' families. Their
home visits and their boarding experiences took them to homes much
like their own. In such a setting, it was more appropriate to assume
the role of advocate or proponent than that of civilizer, the stereotypic
role assigned to their mothers. [20] Bessie Tucker explained her "desires"
to improve the community:

It seems a bit presumptuous to hope and pray that one's life might
better a community in any way, but don't think me conceited,
little book [diary], when I say that one of my greatest desires and
constant prayers is that some word or act of mine may brighten
some life, may help someone in a spiritual way and may leave
happy memories of the nine months [school term] I have spent in
their midst. [21]

The Social and Physical Landscape

The schoolwomen were a part of the community where they taught. Their desires to "better a community in any way," impacted on their own lives as well as on the lives of their students through their advocacy of self-betterment through education.

Insects and Other Pests

Regardless of the affluence and the health standards of the homes, insects and other pests were found in every dwelling. The sod houses and schoolhouses were "cool as a cave in the summer while in the coldest weather nothing froze," but they did have their drawbacks.[22] Prairie rodents, insects, and snakes found homes in the sod structures and in the walls and under the floors of the frame schoolhouses. Keith County, Nebraska, Superintendent of Schools Genevieve Giddings Richmond, wrote that no record of pioneer days would be complete if snakes were left out. She recounted stories of occasionally finding bull snakes, garter snakes, and blue racers in the schoolhouse and rattlesnakes in the prairie dog town near the school.[23]

Cassie Wiggins found snakeskins on the beds in the soddy on her claim in Kansas and decided to sleep outdoors while staying overnight the required time to prove her claim. With more than a touch of whimsy or satire, she named her claim, "The Lord Chesterfield," with the buffalo wallow dubbed, "Lake Victoria."[24]

Flies and mosquitoes were ubiquitous. Sarah Jane Price, two younger brothers, and her father lived in a sod house near Phillips, Nebraska, where she campaigned against the pests:

Friday July 18th 1879

The mosquitos were too bad to write [in my diary] last night. I will write this evening before night so I can have time. I have to get supper after night because they are harvesting and the rain has thrown them back so with their work that they are greatly hurried. I am getting along nicely with my study of Nat. Philosophy and like it very much. I hope to complete it this summer. I finished my essay for next sabbath today. The [weather] has been cooler since monday and I hope will have no more very hot weather.

Jane Price. . . .

Tuesday september the 2nd 1879

I washed today and washed my straw ticks [mattresses] and Ed

filled them. I found a great many bugs and I hope have got rid of
them for a little while. I hope we will not live in a sod house
always.

Jane Price[25]

Influence of the Weather and Seasonal Changes

As can been seen in these diaries of short-term and long-term
teachers, the physical aspects of the living and working conditions for
schoolwomen were largely shaped by the weather and the seasonal
effects on daily life and work. The omnipresent prairie winds that blew
in the spring rains, the summer dust, and the blinding blizzards of
January were as much a part of daily life as the uninterrupted rolling
prairie. For the second generation growing up on the prairies and
plains, the wind was part of being home. Beryl Decker, a twentieth-
century western teacher who had taught in several states, described
the heart-felt longing for the land of a displaced prairie woman: "I
have stood on a summer day in other fields, quiet and undisturbed by
the wind, and my heart has cried with loneliness for wide prairies with
grasses bent to the ground, some nearly uprooted by a dust-ridden
tearing blast under a blistering sun. I love Nebraska and its wind."[26]

While rainfall was needed for crops, excess moisture could prove disastrous for the older sod or dugout schoolhouses and homes that could
collapse after repeated heavy rainfalls. A trip to town, to church, or
to visit the neighbors was affected by the weather, as even horses had
difficulty getting through the late winter mud or drifted snow.

While teaching near Wakarusa, Kansas, 1884–1885, Clara Conron
lived with her parents and usually rode her horse, Fanny, to school.
In cold weather, Fanny "wanted to run so much that [Clara] could
hardly hold her."[27] When the mud was too deep to ride Fanny, Clara
Conron had a thirty-minute walk to school. She described a winter
week in February 1885:

Monday, February 9th
    The storm increased all night, and now this morning is a regu-
lar Kansas "Blizzard." I did not venture out to my school, and
have hugged the stove pretty closely. . . .
Tuesday, February 10th
    Twelve degrees below zero. Went to school and had eight

scholars. Got stuck in the drifts and had to get off and crawl through the hedge, in doing which I scratched my hands and tore my dress. . . . I nearly froze my feet. . . .
Wednesday, February 11th
    Very cold. Had to go around by the school house this morning. Bert was sick and did not come to school today. Played blind man's buff with the children. . . .
Thursday, February 12th
    Very cold this morning and all day for that matter. Fanny wanted to run away from me. Had not many scholars but a pleasant time. John sent home this P. M.
O good only 3 more days of school—not that I don't like it, but I am tired and it is so cold. [28]

The pleasant walk or horseback ride through the prairie grasses on a balmy, dewy, autumn morning could leave the teacher's long skirt wet to the knees. That same trip was a feat of daring when the creeks were out of their banks or when the snow drifted over the fence rows. When Agnes Briggs started teaching school in 1867 in Hamilton County, Iowa, she had to wade across seven creeks to get to her school each day. [29] She lived at home and walked five miles to school rather than pay over half her salary to board with a family whose customs she could not accept.

The seasonal changes brought pleasures as well as the discomforts. During her long walks to and from her country schoolhouse in the 1860s and 1870s, Agnes Briggs observed the cyclic changes and kept a calendar for "bud and flower and leaf." [30] In her writing she captured the sense of pleasure and personal freedom she found in the spaciousness of the prairie.

    Not the least of my pleasures was the sense of boundless freedom, of being no longer shut in. Here was elbow room, breathing space. . . . [31]
    . . . above, the vast blue canopy of heaven; beneath, a deep gulf of billow verdu[r]e, and the great glad sun pouring its radiance over all and everything so clean, so pure, so fresh. [32]

Clean, pure, and fresh, except for mud that was an aspect of every rainfall and thaw. At times, schools with dirt floors had to be closed until the muddy floors dried up.[33] In Martha Bayne's ten years of teaching in Kansas, most of her schools were soddies, and only three of her schoolhouses had wooden floors.[34] Mud was a great source of fun for some Nebraska schoolboys taught by Bessie Tucker. After school, one Friday in December, the boys plastered the outside of the schoolhouse with mud balls. When the weather turned sharply colder over the weekend, the mud balls froze, making the boys' Monday morning clean-up job a very difficult one.[35] Jane Jackson recalled her schoolmaster in Arkansas about 1906, who made the children take off their muddy shoes and leave them outside in the rain so they wouldn't track in mud. After the Jackson family moved to Kansas, she didn't have to take off her shoes at school. During her teaching career in and around Chanute, Kansas, beginning at age twenty while still attending high school, and continuing to age sixty-six, Jane Jackson never made her pupils leave their shoes outside.[36]

The diaries of Bessie Tucker reveal her love of the open country of Nebraska. Despite her fondness for the prairies, she was honest about her disappointment over missing a date due to the weather on an early spring day in eastern Nebraska in 1918: "This is a beastly day!! Rain and snow and SCHOOL! It's Saturday and we are making up a day. . . . I had a date tonight, canceled because of the storm. There is just no end to my MISERY."[37]

For their daily trips to school, to town, or to visit neighbors, teachers and children walked or used horses such as Mollie, Fanny, Old Bill, Sir Walter Raleigh, and Lady Jane Grey.[38] Some horses were put on picket ropes near the schoolhouse, or, in bad weather, were stabled in a neighbor's barn. As a Kansas high school student in 1914, Jane Jackson drove her grandmother's buggy six and a half miles to school, then tied the reins to the buggy and the horse went back home.[39] Alta Hull usually walked the mile and a half to the school she taught near Fredonia, Kansas, during 1918–1920. In severe weather, she rode a horse to school, then sent the horse home.[40]

Not only horses were pastured in and near the school yard. Martha Bayne recalled that when she taught in Kansas in the 1880s, "it was nothing uncommon for scholars to bring their herds near the schoolhouse and study their lessons on the range, and come in to recite with their classes. This was not in accordance with school law. But common experience in pioneer toil and suffering begot common sympathy, and the teachers as well as parents and children had learned the old adage: 'Emergency knows no law.'"[41]

Leaving Home

Even with a pleasant place to board, the teachers missed their families and looked forward to letters and visits from home. The proliferation of railroad lines in the 1870s and mail delivery to the towns increased the ease of travel and family communications. These forms of progress did not help Anna Webber in her first teaching position in Mitchell County, Kansas. Webber's diaries of May and June 1881 described her first teaching position, the weather, the countryside, her loneliness, and desire to see her family:

> Monday, May 23.
>
> The children have brought me some pretty flowers, some of the first roses I have seen this spring. I took a walk on the hills yesterday. I saw quite a number of new plants. I gathered my pockets and hands full of curious stones and flowers. Saturday Eve. and Sunday until afternoon I was certain some of My folks would come to see me, So I kept watch of the road over the hills all the time, but I did not see any of them. I think they might have come. I should like *tolerable* well to see them. . . .
> Friday, May 27.
>
> The wind blows again today as if it had the intentions of blowing the [school] house down. . . . We have so many flowers here. There is so many and such pretty ones to. There are some of the prettiest wild roses I ever saw. There are large yellow lilies, and larkspur, Solomon flowers, cactus, and innumerable others. The children bring them to me by the armfuls, I can hardly find room for them all. . . .[42]

The technological progress of the early twentieth century—railroads, rural mail delivery, the telephone, and the automobile—aided seventeen-year-old Bessie Tucker in accomplishing her goals of teaching school. After answering an ad in the newspaper, Bessie Tucker traveled alone by train from Ponca in eastern Nebraska to the Sandhills in the western part of the state, where a few years earlier, she, her mother, and sister had farmed the family's claim. Arriving in Hemingford, Nebraska, at 4:00 A.M., she walked four blocks to the hotel, where she waited for a ride with the Star Route Mail Carrier.

He took her and her one suitcase to within two or three miles of the home of the school director where she was to be boarded. She walked, unafraid, through the blowing sand, feeling at home in this area so near the claim her family had sold to a cattle rancher.[43]

Bessie Tucker found that the school director was not well liked in the area. His wife, badly crippled with arthritis, was the school moderator; their son was the treasurer; and their two daughters were the only pupils in the Bessie Tucker's school. In this, her first teaching position, she was appalled at the director's home:

> Such a dirty place! The mother laid there, bless her heart, completely helpless, crippled with arthritis. Her husband carried her from bed out to couch every morning and back at night. Uncared for!

When asked if she had to stay at that house, Bessie replied:

> That's all there was! . . . [After the long train trip and walk] I was dirty and I asked for a pan of water to wash my hands. Oh, they poured a little water in a pan, you know, in a granite wash basin. That thing! All the way around it, there was a ring of just grease! I asked for some soap and they gave me a bar of homemade soap—old lye, homemade soap. That was their soap. Well, I took the soap and cleaned the wash basin. Then I got some fresh water and I washed my face and hands.[44]

Although Tucker stayed with friendly neighbors every weekend to get away from the director's house, she felt sorry for the wife and helped the young girls clean the house. After three months, she heard about a teaching position at a school three miles away. She applied for the job by telephone, was hired based on the telephone interview, and moved into a satisfactory home for the next school term.

Bessie Tucker obtained a teaching position for her second year when she rode in her friend's car to church after prayer services on a Wednesday night. There on the church steps, she was interviewed for the position by the members of the school board, all of whom had attended the prayer meeting. She was disappointed that the only question they asked was, "Have you had experience?" They didn't ask where or what kind of experience she had had.[45]

In her four years of teaching, Bessie Tucker taught at four different schools; each change brought improvements in her life. Her path to self-improvement was typical of many beginning teachers who were not compelled to stay in one area because of family or other considerations.[46]

Courtship and Marriage

On the prairies and plains there does not appear to have been a widespread prohibition of hiring married women during the period from the 1860s to the early 1900s, but it was expected that women would leave teaching when they married regardless of the local school district policy. While most women quit teaching after marriage, some taught for a term or two until they became pregnant, or they returned to teaching when their children were of school age. Bessie Tucker quit teaching when she married Lee Gilmer, but she recalled having a pregnant teacher when she was a child in the Sandhills of western Nebraska in the early 1900s.[47] The teacher had her baby between fall and spring term, but the school remained closed during the spring term for want of a teacher. Few teachers with young children taught unless they had no other source of income. Societal assumptions about women's place being at home and the limits those assumptions placed on the duration of a teaching career severely restricted most women's advancement in the profession as they were forced out of careers they enjoyed and in which they were successful.

While unmarried women also were expected to shoulder family responsibilities, it was acceptable for them to continue teaching throughout their adult lives unless they were needed at home to care for an invalid parent or a relative's orphaned children. Perhaps some women did not marry because they preferred to continue teaching, but their decisions based on personal choice and family responsibilities were necessarily individually determined. For Sarah Jane Price, an unmarried long-term teacher who had raised her younger brothers and cared for her widowed, aging father, choices in life beyond teaching were hard won and self-generated. At times she regretted that she was without a marital partner, and then she forged ahead, buying another farm, taking in her widowed young brother and his children, giving the Fourth of July oration, and attending yet another teachers' institute.[48] Eliza Morgan, preceptress of Peru State Normal School, considered her young women students to be her family. After her father was permanently injured in a runaway accident and her sister's three children came to live with the family, fourteen-year-old Margaret S.

Barger of Davenport, Iowa, needed to earn money to help her family. "In 1882 teaching was the most honorable for a young woman and also the best paying," so Margaret lived at home and attended the Davenport Teacher Training School for two years. The next fifty years, she taught in the Davenport public schools. Family financial problems encouraged Barger to become a teacher. Her reasons for not marrying remain unknown.[49]

The problem of losing teachers to marriage was persistent, as evidenced by this semiserious commentary in the *Grand Island, Nebraska, Times* in 1883:

> The marriage of Miss Alice Tomilson reminds us that our premium school teachers are being gathered into the matrimonial net by men who place self above the public welfare. Suppose all the marriageable female teachers in the world were to be married tomorrow, the country would go to rack and ruin. It won't do. A law must be enacted limiting the number of female teachers who shall be permitted to marry in each county during a certain period of time.[50]

A county superintendent in 1866 in Kansas complained: "Within a few months, Hymen—relentless Hymen—had enticed to the marriage altar, a number of our best female teachers. These, of course, are lost to our temples of learning."[51]

Judging by these statements, the teachers must have had their share of admirers and suitors. Some young women wrote about their boyfriends in their diaries and gossiped in their letters to their girlfriends. Frania A. Albert sent the latest news from Douglas Grove, Nebraska, to Nancy Higgins, who was attending a boarding academy away from home in 1881:

> I tell you it is a lonesome place here now. There is not a Girl left in the valley. Louis[e] went away last Tuesday to teach school at the same place she taught last summer. And as for Dan, did you see that in the Leader about him, it is splendid isent it. . . . I supose you heard that Smith Waterbury is married, dont it make you feel bad:- it would me if I were in you'r place. . . .
>
> I dont go any place only to the P. Ofice every mail night. I tell you there is a good looking Mail Carrier now. That is what takes me over more then any thing-els. . . . I dont know what to write

about. I don't hear any news and there is nothing going on in this valley. [52]

If a teacher did not share the community's expectations regarding the respectability of her behavior, she moved to another school. Wanting to be seen as respectable was part of the motivation to teach. In Elsie Petsel's hometown in northern Nebraska in the 1920s,

> the only highly respectable jobs for girls after they were graduated from high school were nursing, teaching, or clerking in a store. Since my dad ran a general store, and since I was somewhat familiar with that, clerking wouldn't be any fun, and by the time I'd completed my normal training in high school I'd still be too young to go into nurse's training. I *was* going to be respectable and *was* going to earn a living. So I became a teacher. [53]

Like many schoolwomen, Rosa Schreurs Jennings's social life was virtuous, as there was

> little opportunity to go wrong. Teachers were surrounded with prohibitions, some by contract, others by custom—no drinking, no dancing or card-playing where the community attitude was against it, no "gallivantin' around," no slang. . . . we wore ruffled thing-a-mabobs to conceal our maidenly forms. Neither did we show our legs—high-button shoes and three petticoats, one short and two floor-length, under a dress five yards around the bottom, took care of that. [54]

The schoolwomen of the early 1900s were somewhat open in their writings about their feelings, their boyfriends, and love affairs as seen in the letters and diaries of Nellie Kenmir, Sarah Gillespie Huftalen, and Bessie Tucker Gilmer. Nellie wrote to her girlfriends in an earthy and hilarious manner, describing her activities as a student taking spring term courses to get her teaching certificate. As a beginning teacher in North Dakota in the summer of 1904, Nellie found, "More dances going on than you can attend." Small wonder that she wore out her shoes in a month! She was offered the school for the fall term, but thought she might "accidentally get married." [55]

In Sarah Gillespie Huftalen's diaries, she often included accounts of men she admired or who came to call. She described her brother and her unstable and abusive father in critical and scathing detail, but it was only after her husband's death that she wrote about him and their life together.[56]

In her diary, Bessie Tucker disclosed her Protestant concerns about dating a Catholic boy. When she later met Lee Gilmer, the entries contain joyful accounts of their dates and her love for the man who became her husband.[57]

Religion in the Lives of Schoolwomen

Some schoolwomen used their diaries to help them cope with loneliness, with problems of the day, with love affairs, and for some women, to reaffirm their religious faith. In their diaries, there are expressions of faith in God and the desire to be righteous, but few references to specific denominations. Anna Webber reflected on her quiet surroundings and the presence of God all around her.

Thursday, May 26.
   This is another pleasant morning. I do wish that it wasn't so quiet tho'. It is certainly the most quiet place I ever was in, that is a place having as many inhabitants as this has, yet it is one of the most pleasant. You may go a quarter of a mile from a house, and I don't believe you would see a person, except in the fields at work or hear a sound beside the singing of the birds, and the noise made by the wind. I hardly [know] whether it is the most quiet on the Sabbath or the week days. To me the Sabbath Day seems different from all other days. There is a calm, soothing, peacefulness in the very air, the Sun seems to shine brighter and all Nature seems trying to remind us of the Great God.[58]

Prayer and faith were recorded in Bessie Tucker's diary, sometimes as a personal conversation with God, and often as an expression of gratitude.

February 22, 1918 [Dixon County, Nebraska]: As I sit here this evening watching the little patches of the light the sun is making as it shines through the window and plays on my paper I am glad that God is so good to me and has given me so much to be thankful for, but I do feel so sorrowful and humiliated. With such a friend to help and guide me and with all the many precious assurances of His help He had left for me, still I have fallen so far.

The Social and Physical Landscape

Tonight I am homesick for my dear ones. It seems so long since I
have seen them and planned so much on seeing some of them
tonight but I was disappointed. I can't get to the train because of
the bad roads. Nobody wants to take me and I had to give up.
For a time I let my feelings conquer me. But now there is peace
for I have talked with Him and He has heard me and is holding
my hand in His. I know He will go with me all the way. How
wonderful, He does not ask us to take one step alone.[59]

Etta Parkerson was an exception in many aspects of her life, including the poignant intimacy of her journal, 1874–1875, in which she prayed, "Dear Lord help us to fully, *wholly* trust Thee to bring all right."[60] She was born into a New England antislavery family that was sent West by the New England Emigrant Aid Society as part of the campaign to keep Kansas a free state. Although she was called an "invalid" by her family, her hunchback did not prevent her from attending two years of preparatory school at Kansas State Agriculture College, plus one term as a freshman in 1874. She dropped out of college, probably due to lack of money, and kept house for her uncle for one dollar a week. At this point in her life, she was courted by a neighbor, Alvin Reynolds, who was thirty years older than she. Throughout her journal, Etta Parkerson wrote about her future husband, expressing her doubts about herself and her deformity; about Alvin Reynold's character and their relationship; and finally of her love for Alvin.[61]

> I can't help mixing thoughts of Alvin into *everything*. he seems
> to have become a part of my *life*. . . . Oh! why must friends conspire against us! Why can't people know him as he really is! Oh!
> they don't *know* how *much* we love each other. . . . Dear Lord
> help us to fully, *wholly* trust Thee to bring all right.[62]

Etta Parkerson and Alvin Reynolds were married in February 1876, when Etta was twenty-two and Alvin was fifty-one. She had been unable to find a teaching job as a single, handicapped woman but was hired to teach in the town where she and her husband lived. In her case, being married seemed to substantiate that she was strong enough to teach, although she was only four feet tall. Etta Parkerson Reynolds taught school, had two sons, was active in the antiliquor and antitobacco campaigns, and wrote for the *Manhattan, Kansas, Nationalist.*

Chapter 3

Her health gave out when she was in her mid-thirties, and she died at age thirty-five, but the "invalid" woman had accomplished her dreams.

Religion was for many schoolwomen a part of everyday life. In addition, the religious meetings in homes or schoolhouses, camp meetings, Sunday schools, and church services were significant as both social and religious events where the settlers could enjoy the company of their neighbors, share their hopes, values, and when needed, their earthly goods. The early religious meetings on the prairies and plains "were the focal points of organized social life before the 1890s, and they were open to all."[63] Mary Ward Smith, Linn County, Kansas, described how the schoolhouse was used for religious meetings, 1856–1860, and humorously relates one such event:

> When a preacher came into this part of the Master's vineyards, even though he were a Methodist who believed in slavery, or a Baptist who believed in washing feet, an old or new school Presbyterian, or even a Universalist who did not believe in endless punishment, he was cordially invited to preach there [at the school] on Sunday. . . .
>
> One Sunday, a stranger traveling through the country, named Brother Kezad, signified his desire to preach. . . . Another hymn, and Brother Kezad began, taking for a text, "For it shall be given you in that same hour what ye shall speak." During the long discourse, his eloquence waxed warm, and warmer, reaching a climax when he touchingly related the thrilling story of an honest little boy who cut down his father's cherry tree with his little hatchet and could not tell a lie, tearfully closing with these words, "and that little boy, my brethren and sistern, was your humble servant, Brother Kezad." This was Bro. Kezad's last sermon at Prairie Ridge.[64]

As the population increased, specific denominational churches were formed with women as prominent workers in fund-raising, construction of the buildings, organizing Sunday schools, mission work, and community activities.[65] The progress of development of denominational churches paralleled the organization of the schools: the men were in the leadership and administrative roles of the churches and denominational organizations, but the women organized and directed the church's religious, social, and civic activities.[66] Historian Sandra L.

Myres further likens church work to school work because it "gave women opportunities to participate in community activities and gave them an increased sense of their own worth in the eyes of both man and God."[67] Mabel Carney, author of pedagogical textbooks and director of the country school department in the Illinois State Normal University in the early 1900s, saw this relationship between church work and school work as a responsibility for country teachers and preachers to "understand the daily life of those for whom he works" and to "know agriculture and the social and economic conditions of farm life."[68]

As extensions of women's sphere, the beneficent and social endeavors of the churches put women into leadership and roles of activism that were largely accepted by "other women and society in general."[69] While "creating and reaffirming communities," through the social and organizational structures related to the religious associations that were largely Protestant on the prairies and plains, women, including the long-term teachers and educational leaders, found community leadership, social involvement, and recognition through church-related voluntarism.[70] Church activities were "outlets for [their] talents and interests that the home could not always satisfy."[71]

Expected to be moral members of the community, the schoolwomen pursued church work in addition to their work at home and in the schoolhouses. Throughout her diaries of 1878–1895, Sarah Jane Price, long-term teacher, wrote about the church services, her work in organizing the Sunday school and ladies' aid, her opinions of these religious endeavors, and hopes for her own salvation.

> Sunday No. 1st 1878
> I attended church today. Brother Grundy preached. Did reasonably well. His text was the parable of the grain of mustard seed. His grammar and elocution are very faulty but he seems in earnest and I believe will yet make a preacher whom the multitudes will respect. Our sunday school was well attended and a good degree of interest manifested in the lessons. Our quarterly meeting will be held here two weeks from today and tomorrow. I hope we shall have a good time of refreshing from the presence of the Lord.[72]

The shift from the ecumenicism of the early churches to the sectarianism of denominations brought about changes and conflicts in some communities. No longer did all members of the community gather in one meetinghouse on Sunday to share spiritually and socially. While the public school building continued to be a unifying structure and concern of the community, sectarian conflicts arose concerning Bible reading and prayers in the school and regarding the religious affiliation of the teachers. Sarah Gillespie Huftalen, a Unitarian, left a teaching position in Iowa when the community became embroiled in conflict after she was elected the superintendent of the Union (Protestant) Sunday School.[73] Protestant Ethel Hale felt she was always an outsider when teaching in a predominantly Mormon community in Utah.[74]

Iowa State Superintendent of Schools Henry Sabin addressed the issue of nonsectarian schools by emphasizing the public school's role in moral instruction: "Honesty, reverence, temperance, purity, patriotism, justice, mercy, obedience, whatever tends to add to the usefulness of the citizen or the stability of the government."[75] Sabin expressed his support for the Iowa legislation that provided for separation of the church and the public schools: "The church and the Sunday school teach religion. They touch upon the side of the child's immortality. The common school should teach morals, thus touching upon the side of his humanity. The one regards the future life of the child, the other regards his relations to this world, to himself, and to his neighbors."[76]

The public views of separation of church and school were implemented according to what was acceptable within each community as evidenced by the inclusion of prayers, hymns, and Bible reading in the school programs well into the twentieth century. For the schoolwomen themselves, religious beliefs and affiliations were for the most part based on family indoctrination and the accessibility of specific denominational churches. From the diary entries of those women who included religious thoughts and prayers, their religion and faith constituted a personal relationship with God.

Temperance

The moral character of these accepted and recognized forms of women's endeavors through their churches, "encouraged women who worked in them to slip over into activities with a stronger aura of social reform about them."[77] In the antebellum generation, antislavery was the great moral cause of Northern Protestant women, but following the Civil War, the "epicenter of American prohibitionism seemed to lie on the fundamentalist Great Plains."[78] Temperance was largely supported by the organized churches through focusing on reform in the homes and the local communities, thus it was a proper sphere for women's activism. The Women's Christian Temperance Union, founded in 1874, not only offered the organizational structure to pursue a social cause but also gave women opportunities in leadership roles in this all-female organization.

The WCTU and the overwhelmingly female Anti-Saloon League campaigned vigorously for prohibition at the local, county, and state levels. By 1905, three western states were won to the cause of prohibition—Kansas, Nebraska, and North Dakota.[79] By 1911, the largest women's organization in the United States was the WCTU, with 245,000 members who were part of the "moralistic tide of progressivism," that led to the Eighteenth Amendment in 1919.

Among the women leaders of the WCTU were teachers, for example, short-term teacher Nancy Higgins Gaddis, was president and a life member of the WCTU in Comstock, Nebraska.[80] The Higgins and Gaddis families were members and leaders in the temperance-supporting Methodist and Free Methodist churches. Sarah Jane Price was a prime mover both in the Methodist church and in the organization of the Good Templars, a temperance lodge for men and women.[81] In Iowa, Sarah Gillespie Huftalen, a Universalist, was the Delaware County president of the WCTU for nine years; treasurer for five years; and was active in the Equal Suffrage Association.[82] Huftalen's mother, Emily Hawley Gillespie, was her model in supporting both temperance and suffrage. Emily Gillespie attended lectures on temperance but missed the suffrage lecture by Susan B. Anthony because her husband wouldn't take her to town. "I *did* so want to go and hear Miss Susan B. Anthony lecture last Monday evening, & *might* have gone, only that it seems to be so much trouble to take me any where."[83]

Sarah Gillespie Huftalen brought her interests and values to her scholars in their Arbor Vitae Summit School near Oneida, Iowa, named in recognition of their on-going planting and outdoor learning projects. In 1904–1905, the school yard contained "Ash heaps, dirt mounds from the new building; sticks and stones, not a tree. [Only] grass and weeds."[84] Huftalen and the children planned the improvements, planted the trees, including many arborvitae (white cedar). The first tree they planted was named in honor of Frances Willard, the suffragist president of the WCTU, and the third tree named for

Harriet Beecher Stowe, champion of antislavery. Their first nineteen trees were named as follows:

Nos. 1 to 10 Arbor Vitae	Nos. 11 to 19 Scotch pines
1. Frances Willard	11. S. F. B. Smith
2. Francis S. Key	12. W. C. Bryant
3. H. B. Stowe	13. Foster
4. Longfellow	14. Fulton
5. Whittier	15. Edison
6. Field	16. McKinley([tree] died—set
7. Dickens	another
8. Hawthorne	17. Washington
9. Lowell	18. Lincoln
10. Stevenson	19. "Grow little evergreens, grow."[85]

Suffrage

Perhaps when the suffrage movement in the West is more fully analyzed, there will be more evidence of the continuum of egalitarian democratic values between mother and daughter, teacher and students. Historian Sandra Myres contends: "Part of the problem in trying to analyze the Western suffrage movement is that there has been so little work done in the field. . . . Western suffrage votes are treated as some sort of aberrant political behavior rather than as part of the mainstream of the suffrage movement."[86]

Under the leadership of Frances Willard, the WCTU advocated women's suffrage because, among other considerations, women would vote against liquor. Indeed, women had the vote in ten of the fourteen states that had adopted prohibition before the Eighteenth Amendment was passed, and those states included Kansas and Nebraska.[87] While this was a compelling argument for the supporters of prohibition, large-scale organized backing for suffrage by western women is difficult to identify.[88] Western suffrage leaders apparently believed when suffrage was tied "to temperance and other moral issues, rather than to economic and legal reform, [it] diluted women's power and left them with an empty victory."[89] Western pragmatism and individualism were not the only factors in the lives of western women that shaped their involvement in the suffrage movement. The scattered population made it difficult to organize concerted efforts. Where temperance had the supportive network of the WCTU with the blessings of the Protestant churches, the cause of suffrage in the West was often disassociated with suffrage organizations in the East and nationwide.[90] The western suffrage leaders were more in tune with "the local and regional issues than most of the Eastern and national leadership . . . [because] they emphasized political, economic, and social reform" in addition to suffrage.[91]

This East-West schism in suffrage leadership did not lead to the establishment of a suffrage association dedicated specifically to the movement is the West. However, the women's clubs in western communities were supportive of the suffrage cause.[92] In 1890, when the hundreds of women's clubs across the nation federated to become the General Federation of Women's Clubs, the message of suffrage reached thousands of "middle-aged, middle-class, conservative women."[93] The clubs within the Federation claimed 150,000 members by 1900, with membership soon reaching a million.[94] Through the clubs the women developed a sense of community and belonging as they confirmed their values through conviviality and expanded their viewpoints through the self-betterment tasks of their organization.

In most areas of the heartland, women had been voting in the school elections and running for the elective school district offices, including county superintendent, since the school districts had been organized. Twenty-three states had given women limited voting privileges for tax, municipal, and school elections by 1910. While these limited experiences with voting did not substitute for full suffrage, many western women believed that "local suffrage was of more immediate importance than voting in national, or even state, elections."[95]

At times, individual women pursued political action in pursuit of equal suffrage. For example, "Who would have guessed that the first woman to vote in Iowa would be named Kizzie?"[96] In 1870, ninety-two Iowa citizens residing in Clarinda (county seat of Page County, Iowa) and Taylor County sent their petition for women's suffrage to the Congress. In October 1871, Miss Keziah "Kizzie" Anderson, a twenty-seven-year old teacher who had signed the petition, voted. Her father, William Anderson, and a family friend who supported suffrage, Edwin Henshaw, were the election judges who determined that her vote was legal under the Fourteenth Amendment.[97]

School and Municipal Voting Rights

Aside from this singular event and involvement in the community organizations, how did the question of suffrage affect schoolwomen whose occupation was generally accepted as within the sphere of womanhood? The course of full suffrage in Iowa, Kansas, and Nebraska came in spurts of progress followed by years of stagnation. Property rights for women in Iowa were established in 1851, but efforts to achieve voting rights in addition to school elections failed until the passage of the Twentieth Amendment in 1920.[98] Nebraska women had voted in school elections and run for school offices since 1867, and finally achieved equal suffrage by 1917.[99] Kansas women had the right to vote and run for office in school elections after 1861. Then in 1887, they were given the right to vote in town and city government elections.[100] The first woman mayor in the United States, Susannah Medora Salter, was elected in Argonia, Kansas, April 4, 1887. In 1912, Kansas became the eighth state to give women full voting rights.[101]

The most direct impact of school suffrage came to the schoolwomen through the elected position of county superintendent. Although men continued to hold the majority of the county superintendencies, women did have the right to run for this position with its higher salaries and recognized leadership role.

The County Superintendency

The schoolwomen's local political involvement in the elected post of county superintendent was more than pragmatic expediency to obtain higher salaries. A county superintendent was in the professional position of direct action for the good of the community through the management of the county schools. The county superintendent, while governed by guidelines, laws, and edicts from the state department of public instruction, could influence the quality of education and teaching in the county through hiring practices, in-service education, and supervision of the teachers and schools. The position of county superintendent was not independent of the vagaries of local, near-sighted, and party politics. The experiences of the county superintendents were distinguished by grass-roots participatory democratic involvement, which, as Huftalen, Hedges, and Stevens and other women county superintendents discovered, did not necessarily result in exemplary decisions.

Sarah Gillespie Huftalen was elected county superintendent of Page County, Iowa, in 1913, following her nationally recognized success as a rural teacher and her leadership in organizing the Rural Section of the Iowa State Teachers Association. Following the final illness and death of her husband, she was defeated when she ran for her second term in April 1915: "I was not re-elected to Superintendency of schools of Page Co. last April owing to the fact that Miss [Jessie] Field [superintendent prior to Huftalen] wanted a Y.W.C.A. Co. Supt. and thru strategy and dirty politics succeeded in finding a tool candidate."[102]

While Huftalen was ever the professional, her energies and efforts may have been diminished by her husband's decline and death. Huftalen's career then moved into teacher education, while the "tool candidate," Agnes Samuelson, held the superintendency for eight years. Samuelson was indeed active in support of the YWCA, was an experienced teacher and superintendent who campaigned by visiting every school in the county.[103] After she left Page County, she became extension professor of rural education for Iowa State Teachers College. Samuelson next served as the Iowa State Superintendent of Public Instruction, 1927–1938, and was elected president of the National Education Association in 1935. Both Huftalen and Samuelson were part of a succession of women county superintendents in Page County, Iowa, and of the competition inherent in the politics of elected school positions.

Flora Hedges, county superintendent of Rock County, Nebraska, 1916, became embroiled in the politics of establishing a county high school. The earlier rivalry for county seat and the interests of the Northwestern Railroad entered into the implementation of the state law requiring the establishment of high schools. During a meeting called by Hedges to select representatives from each of the county commissioner districts, a lawyer for the railroad and a man who was opposed to public high schools burst into the meeting and took over the proceedings, effectively stalling plans for the high school. On advice of the state superintendent, Hedges and the county treasurer, C. M. Anderson, appointed three members of the board of regents and began the negotiations for buildings and teachers. The high school opened in fall, but shortly thereafter,

> Court proceedings were instituted to oust the appointed board and the Northwestern sent one of its attorneys up to assist (the local attorney representing the opposition). Our County Attorney had only "God and His good sword," in this case Supreme Court decisions, and our prayer, for his aid and comfort. . . .

So, naturally, the outcome was in our favor. Thus Rock County High School was brought into being. . . .

I thanked God for a judge who was incorruptible; and took my defeat for re-election that next fall with PRIDE knowing that the children would have greater opportunities for learning. . . . I am grateful that God gave me, Flora M. Hedges, the privilege of making a better education possible for the boys and girls of Rock County.[104]

In the election to the county superintendency of Blue Earth County, Minnesota, in 1890, Sarah Christie Stevens was supported by "women's groups, the local Alliance [party], and the Prohibition party."[105] A local newspaper editor summarized her support in the bitter campaign that was fraught with attacks on the gender and character of Stevens:

She ran well in the country towns, especially where she is best known. Our foreign born people, except the Irish, are averse to a woman's holding office, and the Germans and Scandinavians generally voted against her. The Irish supported her heartily, as did most of the Americans. The women in our city [Mankato] mostly voted against her, excepting the most intelligent and progressive, while those in the country supported her.[106]

As the county returned to its usual affiliation with the Republican party, Stevens lost in her bid for a second term, defeated by those people who "disliked precisely the 'goody-goodies,' suffragists, and Populists she stood for."[107] In Stevens's third and last bid for the county superintendency, she again lost to those voters who believed that "personal accomplishments were desirable but not sufficient for the superintendent of schools. Though on the one hand, aggressiveness may antagonize voters, ladyhood may also cripple the aspirant to office."[108]

This dichotomy of aggressiveness versus "ladyhood" epitomizes the clashing values implicit in the socialization of the second generation of women through their new experiences on the prairies and plains. They were "pulled between two sets of influences, their identification with the land about them and their parents' dogged efforts to instill values and traditions from another world."[109] In their political experiences, the schoolwomen were most often active at the local level as observers and, as legislation determined, as participants.

Public Meetings, Clubs, Lodges, and Community Events

Long-term professional teachers and the educational and community leaders were found among the residents of the established towns where organizations that were open to all members of the community thrived.[110] While membership in the women's clubs, the Masons, Odd Fellows, and Eastern Star were gender-specific, there were literary societies, singing classes, temperance lodges, and community events that involved men and women together. Literary societies flourished with meetings in members' homes, where men and women would share music, readings of poetry and prose, political debates, dramatic presentations, and social evenings. The educational value of these organizations is often overlooked, but learning took place through discussions and debates of current problems and concerns such as: a woman is as capable of governing a school as a man; women's suffrage, the unsolved problem; the greenback question; man's ability depends on natural ability vs. education; and women's influence is greater than a man's.[111] At other times the meetings would feature an evening's entertainment with a farcical debate on a topic such as "That a hen and chickens are more destructive in the garden than a pig."[112]

The moral, political, and patriotic causes were popular topics for public meetings at the schoolhouse that brought both traditional and unprecedented outlooks to the settlers and their children. Mary Ward Smith recalled the "Free State Meetings," in Iowa before her family moved to Kansas, about 1860.

> I remember the eloquence of those men when "Crimes against Kansas" were discussed. Owen Lovejoy's oath of "Eternal Hostility to African Slavery" was made their watchword. These men were proud of the fact that in their native state, some of them had been promoters of the Underground Railroad for Slave Refugees. All were rank abolitionists. Fired by the spirit of Charles Sumner and Wendell Phillips, what wonder that they should feel compelled for conscience sake to join the free state migration, espouse the cause of freedom and unforeseen struggles and hardships,

To cross the prairies as of old,
our fathers crossed the sea
to make the West, as they the East,
the homestead of the free. [113]

A generation later, Cassie Wiggins, a girl of about fifteen, found the presidential election of 1888, between Democrat Grover Cleveland and Benjamin Harrison, an "interesting diversion." The torchlight parades and rallies were events that involved the community, including the teenage girls who wore caps "bearing the names of their favorites." Cassie, who had been strongly influenced by her prohibitionist, Populist mother, wore a cap bearing the name of Belva Lockwood. Lockwood ran twice for the presidency, 1884 and 1888, on the ticket of the National Equal Rights party of the Pacific Coast. [114]

Although Cassie Wiggins expressed little interest in her journal about the presidential election of 1892, she found the conflict between the Populists and the Republicans in 1894 fascinating. As a teacher in Hoxie, Kansas, Wiggins had to miss part of the afternoon speeches.

> Sometimes I clipped off a few minutes of school-time and hurried to the hall. A seat at that hour was an impossibility and one was lucky to find standing-room. I never grew tired of the speechmaking, though much to my regret, I never heard John H. Ingalls, the Republican [senator from Kansas, 1873-1891], nor the Populist Jerry Simpson, known as "Sockless Jerry." I heard Mary Elizabeth Lease in her masterful and rather masculine way proclaim the gospel of Populism, urging the farmers to raise less corn and more hell. And then there was little Mrs. Anna Diggs, so refined, smart, aware, convincing with the same gospel, but so differently presented. [115]

During World War I, the patriotic meeting at the schoolhouse, May 18, 1918, in eastern Nebraska, was one long remembered by twenty-year-old Bessie Tucker as she responded patriotically and competitively to the selling of savings bonds:

> After the patriotic speech the speaker began selling Savings Bonds. Names were posted on the blackboard. Most of the young

men were buying $50.00 bonds. I did the same and up went my name on the board. Later some of the men told me how surprised they were to see me from my small salary able to compete with the young men.[116]

Patriotic celebrations involved everyone with picnics, games, and speeches especially on the Fourth of July. Other patriotic gatherings reflected the national concerns, as described by Ora J. Patton, high school teacher in Guthrie, Oklahoma, to her fiancé in the U.S. Army, October 7, 1917:

> The Seniors have made me their class Mother and I'm so proud. They are a dear bunch and I do enjoy my Senior Classes. . . . But being Class Mother gave me stage fright the worst I ever had it last Wednesday when we marched to the train to see 14 more boys go (Oscar Hayman, Don Vickers, Roscoe Miller, etc) The High School led the long procession and as I led the Seniors I had to go first. And you know I could never walk straight or keep step and when we got into town in the crowd I was terribly embarrassed. The old soldiers were having a reunion here and 55 of them marched with the lads who were going. It was a touching sight. . . . Last week was hard.[117]

Conclusion

The prairie schoolwomen were working women from lower-middle and middle-class families who aspired to independence, self-betterment, and the opportunity to be of service to the community. They were at home in the setting of the prairies and plains where they were the second generation of Anglo women to struggle with the conflicts of perceived ideal womanhood in a changing social and political environment. They made new rules of conduct for themselves by traveling alone, working independently in one-room schools, living away from the family, running for political offices, and by achieving more education for themselves and their heartland children. Through their daily lives, the schoolwomen, as both leaders and followers, played their multiple roles as daughters, mothers, and wives; as teachers, principals, and superintendents; as leaders and workers in churches, Sunday schools, women's clubs, WCTU, and the suffrage movement. As members of their communities, they worked to improve themselves, their homes, and their communities by seeking improved education, temperate and healthy living conditions, increased equality, and more salvation. Although they pursued "the Stars Through the Wilderness," their feet were planted firmly on their home ground of the prairies.[118]

Phebe Sudlow began teaching as a teenager in a log schoolhouse. When she became the first women superintendent of a city school system, she demanded and got "a man's pay for a man's job," in the Davenport, Iowa, Public Schools, 1874. (State Historical Society of Iowa—Iowa City)

County Superintendent Jessie Field, Page County, Iowa, 1909. "The automobile shown was won by Page County for its display of school work at the National Corn Exposition in 1909." (Mabel Carney, *Country Life and the Country School* [Chicago: Row, Peterson, 1912], 291) (State Historical Society of Iowa—Iowa City)

Chapter 3

In 1914, when Agnes Samuelson was elected Page County, Iowa, superintendent, children and townspeople met her at the train with this hand-drawn cart. (Agnes Samuelson Collection, State Historical Society of Iowa—Iowa City)

A group of county superintendents at the home of Agnes Samuelson. (Agnes Samuelson Collection, State Historical Society of Iowa—Iowa City)

The Social and Physical Landscape

CHAPTER
FOUR

Teaching and Learning in the Schools of the Prairies and Plains

O little country school! In vain
May critics hold you in disdain.
The greatest lessons that you taught
Were not by chalk and pencil wrought.
As ope'd your door on fields, and sky,
So likewise just as wide and high,
You opened to the eyes of youth
The principles of love and truth.
—Ed. Sabin. From the back of a photo of Pleasant View School,
Page County, Iowa. Agnes Samuelson Collection. State Histori-
cal Society of Iowa.

This sentimental and idealized depiction of the little country school's lessons testifies to the central role of education in the lives of the heartland settlers. They had developed their sense of ownership of public education by building and managing the schoolhouse, directing the educational progress of their children, and utilizing the schoolhouse as a multipurpose community meetinghouse. However, the critics and the leaders in rural education found innumerable problems and shortcomings in the country schools and their teachers. By the turn of the century, the typical teacher was characterized as an "uneducated slip of a girl from city high school or neighboring community," lacking in both teacher education and supervision.[1] The schoolhouse, once the center of the community, was aging and in poor repair and did not have facilities to provide a high school education for the rural youngsters.[2] Teaching materials were scarce and operating revenue for salaries and maintenance of the school buildings was minimal.[3] And yet, the nostalgic and fictional views of the country schools of Iowa, Kansas, and Nebraska, 1860s to the early 1900s, tend to accentuate learning the three Rs, the fun and games, the hardships, the special events, and the long-term friendships. While these memories of the school programs, the spelldowns, and the pot-bellied stove are charming reminiscences, the stabilization of the settlements brought continued educational progress to the schools on the prairie and plains. The institutional accounts of schooling underscore the development of the state courses of study; implementation of compulsory education; increased requirements for the length of the school year and for certification of teachers; and school achievement as measured by the number of students who passed the countywide eighth grade examinations.

What teachers tried to teach and what children probably learned can be explored through several sources: U.S. census reports citing the number of citizens who could read, write, and had attended school; the "Programme" or daily schedule for one-room schools as recommended by the normal courses and state departments of education; the content of the normal courses and the professional education journals of the time period; the content of the available textbooks; and the reminiscences and diaries of schoolwomen, their observers, and the people who attended the country schools.

Nationwide, the census takers asked heads of households whether each person listed, other than infants, could read and write and whether each had attended school within the year.[4] This data determined that the literacy rates in Iowa, Nebraska, and Kansas were among the highest in the nation between 1870 and 1900.[5] While these appraisals are based only on information from the heads of households, the consistency of the responses lead to the conclusion that reading, writing, and attending school were valued by the settler families in these states.

The schoolwomen's personal documents reveal their personal motivation and educational aspirations; their interpersonal relationships with their students; their struggles with the dichotomy between the prevailing faith in education and self-doubts relating to their ability to support adequately that expectation. The hectic schedule of twenty to thirty classes a day explains in part why most teachers did not write much in their diaries and letters about the everyday routine. Writing about the daily events in the schoolhouse would be akin to writing about the mundane occurrences of homemaking. Teachers understandably wrote about the unusual or special events in which they took pride: the school program; individual children who were exceptionally brilliant or who showed significant improvement in learning and behavior; how many of their students passed the county examinations; and lessons that were remarkably successful or unusual in some way. They also wrote about problems related to lack of school supplies, bad roads, unruly children, troublesome parents, personal loneliness, professional isolation, and fears of failure in their work.

Further dimensions of understanding of what was taught and what was learned can be uncovered from the documents of persons who were students in the schoolhouses on the prairies and plains, that is, when their accounts go beyond the remembered long walks to school, the effects of severe weather, and the pot-bellied stove. Regardless of the nostalgic coloration of reminiscences, a sense of community centering in the schoolhouse is depicted in the personal documents while illustrating the changes in the teaching methods, the content, and purpose of the curriculum throughout this transitional period.[6]

The Physical Conditions of the Schoolhouse

In identifying the "lessons that you taught," the physical conditions of the schoolhouse provide the setting for the more important considerations: the teacher's management of the classroom activities; the teacher's instructional skills; and above all, the teacher-student relationships.[7] The physical features of the town or country schoolhouses, the school yards, equipment, and facilities, had many similarities from one district to another, depending on the age of the settlement, its tax base, and the values and stability of the settlers. The school generally went through a series of transitions. The first school in a district may have been in a settler's home; an abandoned soddy or dugout; or the "huts and shanties" described by the superintendent of Leavenworth County, Kansas, in 1869.[8] Once there were enough people and development in a district to generate sufficient taxes to build a schoolhouse, the next step was accomplished. Often the equipment and supplies such as manufactured desks, blackboards, and books, were bought piecemeal as tax funds allowed. Other "conveniences" and improvements, such as two outhouses, a well, and a fence were added later.

The next phase of progress was that of maintaining the school site by painting the outbuildings and the schoolhouse white. (The little *red* schoolhouse seems to be a tradition more often found east of the Mississippi than on the prairies.) The minutes of the meeting, March 14, 1864, of the Electors of LeRoy Township, Benton County, Iowa, cite the costs of upkeep and improvement for the schools: $15 for fuel, $5 for repairs for Sub. Dist. No. 1; $25 for fencing, $15 for painting, $20 for Privy, $15 for fuel and $5 for repairs for Sub-Dist. No.3; and $15 for fuel, "$100 for digging & walling a well and building a curb, about the same for building two 'Out Houses' and repairing S[school]. H[ouse]. in Sub-Dist. No 4."[9]

Cleaning the buildings was usually the teacher's daily job. Even in the 1920s in Iowa, Anna Johnson had her janitor work to do, "such as sweep the floor, empty the waste basket and burn the papers, clean the blackboard and erasers, empty the water cooler, and bank the fire. . . . and set the mouse traps in my desk drawers."[10] The sod schoolhouses had the additional maintenance problems because they were havens for insects, rodents, and snakes.

Reminiscences abound with accounts of school stoves. Those who sat close to the pot-bellied stove got baked; those farther away from the stove froze. Supplying fuel and cleaning stove pipes were the responsibilities of the school board, but coping with the ashes, soot, and heating the school was the job of the teacher. Soot in the stove pipes caused endless dirt and heating problems for the teacher. Students were sometimes given the daily job of carrying in the fuel for the stove and taking out the ashes, each with the accompanying dirt. When the stove pipe fell down spewing soot throughout the schoolhouse, Sarah Gillespie and her scholars "worked extremely hard for three hours when we had to give it up and go home."[11] Bessie Tucker found that a furnace wasn't necessarily the answer when she got the job at the "new modern schoolhouse," where the furnace smoked out the pupils and the teacher. A reliable, old fashioned pot-bellied stove was installed while the school directors worked on repairing the furnace.[12]

The funds to maintain the schoolhouse and yard, provide supplies, and the teacher's salary came from the district's taxes. The weather and daily wear and tear on a schoolhouse demanded on-going funding for upkeep. In 1889, when Iowa had been a state for more than forty years, there were about fourteen thousand schoolhouses. [13] Of this number, about one-tenth were classified as being in poor condition; one-fifth were without adequate outhouses (none, one, or poorly maintained outhouses); more than half of schoolhouses were rated as in only fair condition. Similar conditions prevailed in the other heartland states where the schoolhouses were growing older. It was one phase of progress to build a schoolhouse. For some districts, the more difficult step was to maintain and improve the schoolhouse and its facilities while coping with the economic effects of the grasshopper invasions of the mid 1870s, the great blizzards of '88 and other years, and the ever-decreasing amount of land to be homesteaded and taxed.

The school yards of some rural schools were fenced to keep out the free-roaming stock. Other school yards remained open with no trees or playground equipment. If the weeds in the school yard were mowed, it was done by one of the neighboring farmers who had children in the school. Outdoor play time was what the teacher and children could make it, usually with active games such as poison tag, drop-the-handkerchief, crack-the-whip, sledding in winter, and endless varieties of ante-over and tag. [14] Mabel Townsley, teaching near Hartford, South Dakota in 1900, wrote to her friend, "When four o'clock comes, I have a romping game of tag with the children (which always makes me wonder at myself.)" [15]

The establishment of Arbor Day was observed in the towns and rural areas by planting trees in the school yard. However, with the rapid turnover of teachers, it was difficult to develop continuity in the maintenance of an attractive school site unless the school directors and the children were involved. The county superintendent of Cheyenne County, Nebraska, 1908, reported that in District 36, "The teacher here has created a fine spirit, and the board is going to move the school house, plant trees, and, what is more, take care of those trees during the summer." [16] Under Sarah Gillespie Huftalen's direction, the children of the Arbor Vitae Summit School, Oneida, Iowa, planted trees, gardens, and transformed the school yard into a park. These cooperative learning projects won nationwide recognition through exhibitions at the Iowa State Education Meeting, 1908; National Forestry Convention, 1909; and the World's Fair, Seattle, 1909. Obviously, not all teachers could or would carry out such ambitious projects. Sarah Huftalen wrote many articles for education journals and newspapers describing how outdoor projects could be planned, implemented, and used for learning, but not many teachers had the drive and support to carry out these diligent projects.[17]

Health and sanitation practices at school were similar to those in local homes. Everyone at school drank from the same dipper in the water bucket; everyone washed in the same basin with the same water, in many cases carried from a neighboring farm. Not until ambitious health campaigns were implemented did the water dipper give way to a water jug with a spigot and individual cups for the children. Any contagious disease swept through the scholars. "Suddenly the black diphtheria plague of 1877 struck, claiming eight victims in the community, four from our school including Daisy and her brother. One by one their graves appeared in the cemetery. School was closed and parents guarded their children close for two months."[18]

After Jane Jackson's country school near Chanute was closed during the influenza epidemic of World War I, she took a teaching job in a small town in the area. Shortly after she arrived, the principal died. Because Jane Jackson, in her second year of teaching, had more seniority than the other teachers, she was named the principal of the school building. In addition to teaching full time, she had to keep the school clean, keep the heating stoves burning, and, at times, had to cut and haul the wood herself.[19]

Everyone, including the teacher, carried their lunches, usually in a tin lard bucket or some other covered pail. Lunch might consist of fried mush; a slab of meat; pie; or, most often, just bread, butter or lard, and jam. In winter, if the lunches froze in the cloak room, they could be thawed on the stove.

Most schools had outhouses, one for the girls, one for the boys. A few had one privy for all; and some schools even in the twentieth century had no outhouses, "so the boys went up the hill in the bushes, and the girls went down the hill in a deep ditch."[20] While the outhouse might afford a temporary escape from school work in moderate weather, surely only dire necessity would cause any scholar to linger on a steaming, summer afternoon or on a winter's day when the blasting prairie winds blew straight through the privy's walls. Nebraska State Superintendent J. M. McKenzie reported in 1873 that 517 school districts had no privies; over 400 districts had only one outhouse; and only "200 districts out of the 1,800 . . . have provided suitable out-houses."[21] McKenzie laid the blame for these inadequate facilities on the school boards.

Can it be sheer thoughtlessness, or is it that parsimonious, short-sighted, criminal economy, that will risk the destruction of all those inherent natural instincts of modesty, the ruination of the moral character of their children, for a few paltry dollars? Even in our towns and cities may be found these incipient—shall I say dens of vice? . . . I charge the school boards with complicity in this matter, and call upon them, as men who value the good of the community, to abate all such nuisances at once![22]

While the physical features of the schoolhouse and its facilities certainly added to its comfort or adversity, there were other accoutrements that made teaching more pleasant and effective. The earliest schools used plank benches for the children; had only the books that the children could bring from home; and were supplied with few or no teaching materials such as a dictionary, map, or chalkboard. Sadie Hanna, District 16, Cheyenne County, Nebraska, 1908, reported to the periodical, *The Ranch Teacher*, "We are rejoicing over the arrival of some new desks, which we have needed so long."[23] Much of the burden of supplying or improvising teaching aids and making the school pleasant fell on the ingenuity of the teacher. Rosa Schreurs Jennings described this aspect of the teacher's role in the 1890s.

Teaching helps were scanty—a few old maps, no globe, a reading chart for beginners, also a chart to teach effects of the use of alcohol and tobacco to satisfy the Women's Christian Temperance Union sponsored legislation, a dog-eared dictionary. Because there was so little blackboard, I painted sections of the wall black to help out. We did what we could to pretty things up, with sash curtains at the windows, pictures—blessed be Perry prints—on the wall, painted gourds, strings of bright "calico" corn, colored leaves, abandoned birds' nests, in their season.[24]

The normal school texts indicated that "No curriculum is complete, no matter how scientifically framed, which does not make ample provisions for the aesthetical side of the child's nature."[25] It was up to the individual teacher to provide for the arts and a little beauty in the schoolhouse.

Beginning in the late 1800s and extending into the twentieth century, the school districts moved toward consolidation and the transportation of the children to schools in town where it was hoped they would have more opportunities for a quality education through graded schools and high schools. In the early 1900s, the familiar, one-room, white schoolhouse gradually moved to town where there were rooms for each grade from kindergarten through twelfth grade. The reluctance to close country schools was more than an attack of nostalgia on the part of the farmers and ranchers: it meant the loss of direct control of the school by the residents through the growing bureaucratization of the schools. By 1984, there were only 835 one-teacher schools in operation in the United States, with 360 in Nebraska where the residents apparently do not want to lose their low taxes, control of the schools, traditions, and what they refer to as basic educational values.[26]

Organization of the School Day

The one-room schools were ungraded, that is, children, ages four through twenty and older, attended school together in the same room. Children's attendance fluctuated as they were needed to help at home; however, they were accepted into the school at any time during a school term. There could be as few as two children or as many as forty or more scholars with one teacher. Within this span of ages and learning abilities, the teacher, with few records of the children's academic achievement, placed each child in a class by themselves or with other children who were at approximately the same grade or reading level. In the early days of a school district, the lack of school records of achievement seemed to doom some children to repeat the same books several times, but the brightest children in the ungraded school went at their own pace and were rarely held back by teachers because of the artificial boundaries of grade levels. Children were grouped according to the textbooks they could comprehend, not by chronological age; nor were they kept in any given class, such as the second grade, for the entire school year. As they passed or completed a textbook in any subject, they progressed to the next book. It was common for a teacher to have children of various ages learning from the same textbooks at the same level. This form of school management implemented vertical grouping of children of various ages, with individualized, self-paced instruction and emphasized independent study, which, in current educational jargon appears quite progressive. It was, however, an expedient way to manage a diverse group of scholars.

The school curriculum was largely shaped by the content of the textbooks that were available, even though in the early days of a school district, "The diversity of text-books [was] a great drawback to scholars, and an especial inconvenience to teachers."[27] The textbooks, which "were as various as the flowers on the prairie," provided at least a small source of information for the teachers with little formal education.[28] The reliance on textbooks as the basis of learning was the usual solution for directing the independent study by children of widely varying abilities. Teaching the content of the textbooks was a matter of individualization: children learned the content of the textbooks they owned, shared, or could borrow, as books were generally not provided by the school district. As a result, children from families with little ready cash used the same textbooks for several years, not because of developmental shortcomings, but economic reality.[29] As school districts became well populated and financially solvent, textbooks bought by the children or provided by the school district were used more uniformly, making the teacher's job more easily managed. The content of the textbooks largely determined what was taught, but it was the individual teacher who was the "ultimate curriculum planner," responsible for the learning environment, the content, and methods of instruction.[30]

Within the ungraded country school, where the levels of learning spanned preschool through eighth grade and beyond, children had to learn independently and from each other while the teacher met daily with each class. With school management based on independent learning and small group instruction during recitation periods, children had direct contact with the teacher for several ten-minute recitations during the school day and were on their own the rest of the time. The children listened to the other classes in recitation, daydreamed, worked independently, or entertained themselves. The younger children often listened while the advanced students recited a lesson, sometimes memorizing the advanced lessons. Frances Hiltz spoke Czech but little English when she started school where her teacher was from a Norwegian immigrant family. "How I managed to learn to read, write, and think in English that first year, I do not know. I memorized the *Rose Primer* until I knew each page by heart, and to this day I can close my eyes and see each page, the word or words, and pictures that were above the words."[31]

If the enrollment in the school was small, less than fifteen, the teacher gave individualized instruction throughout most of the day. Children who had no difficulty learning proceeded as rapidly as they could to the next textbook. This reliance on independent learning could be disastrous for the children with little educational background or support from their homes and who were slower at learning, unless the older scholars at school were willing to help out. Children who had difficulties in learning for any reason repeated the same textbooks and lessons and were likely to drop out of school. Anna Johnson felt that she was not prepared to teach the slow learners, the physically handicapped, and mentally retarded children who were among her students. "In my own heart I feel that I helped some a lot, a few just a little bit, but each received some of my time and all the knowledge that I had."[32]

In Dixon County, Nebraska, in 1914, Bessie Tucker's eighth grade teacher, Miss Anna Sheffel, taught "high school courses" to the eighth graders, and read to them every day. Bessie Tucker's mother and grandmother encouraged her interest in reading by borrowing every book available at the schoolhouse to read aloud in the evenings for entertainment for the family. Tucker hated to miss school because Miss Sheffel read every day to the youngsters: *Evangeline*, *The Last of the Mohicans*, and other books. Miss Sheffel also helped Bessie with her mathematics homework and encouraged her to take the county teacher examinations. After Bessie Tucker passed all the teacher examinations, Miss Sheffel tried to keep her in school, but Tucker was eager to find a teaching position and earn a salary.[33]

The organization of twenty to thirty classes daily made up of various combinations of children was an on-going challenge, inasmuch as the enrollment varied with the agricultural seasons, parental demands, student behavior, and with the ebb and flow of settlers. Eleven children dropped out of Sarah Gillespie's school by February 1, 1884.

> Four Tripp children took their books home to night. Guess they will be back again. The reason was because the teachers before me have always sided in with them and Susie Cook and "pounded" the other scholars & I will not be partial.
> That makes 11 that have quit school.
> 1. Mattie Mohr came one wk. age 18. Mother sick.
> 2. Cora Allen-17-Runrounds or blotches cover her body.
> 3. Emma Trip
> 4. Norma ″   Think it is a tough set of scholars and they [the
> 5. Nora   ″   Tripp children] are greatly misused. [Preston
> 6. Alfred ″   boys] Had to mind the teacher.

7. Charlie Preston
8. Alrah Preston
9. Edward Smith-Required at Home.
10. Maggie Schmidt-Too small to go.
11. Cora Anderson-Too small to go.[34]

The "harmonious development of the *whole being,* the *moral,* the *physical,* and the *intellectual,*"[35] was at risk in the ungraded school except where reasonable order was maintained. Independence and cooperation were expected, self-direction was encouraged, and the teacher had to involve the able students as teacher aides and tutors for the other children. To aid the teachers in this task of organizing a school, the county superintendents, the normal courses, and the state departments of education offered various examples. *The Course of Study and Manual for the Ungraded Schools, of the State of Iowa 1877-1879* recommended a "Sample Programme of Recitation and Study."

Instruction, Content, and Methods

It was no accident that in the recommended schedules of a school day, about half of the time was occupied with reading, language, grammar, spelling, and writing. The priority of reading and the language arts, as stressed in the organization of the school day, enabled children to read, write, and learn the common values of their society as portrayed by the content of the reading textbooks.[36] While many different textbooks were available, the widely used *McGuffey's Readers* were typical in content that promoted piety, patriotism, and moral teachings.[37] The early editions of *McGuffey's Readers,* 1836–1837, sold only 7 million copies as they were judged by the public as too sectarian, sectional, and too ecumenical in religious principles.[38] The revised editions of 1879, which sold more than 60 million copies, apparently achieved an acceptable compromise or balance of moral content without raising sectarian conflicts.[39] Among the prevalent themes of the stories in the readers were morality, generally defined Christian tenets, national unity and pride, and self-betterment. The message of self-betterment was often portrayed as in "The Good Reader," in the 1879 edition of *McGuffey's Fifth Eclectic Reader,* which features Ernestine, a poor girl who reads well and thus is rewarded.

In 1874, Nebraska State Superintendent J. M. McKenzie exhorted teachers and parents to read to and with children every day. Generating a love of reading was seen as the "great work" of parents

SAMPLE PROGRAMME OF RECITATION AND STUDY.

FORENOON.

BEGINS.	CLOSES.	TIME.	PRIMARY	1st CLASS	2d CLASS	3d CLASS	4th CLASS	5th CLASS
9:00	9:05	5m			Opening	Exercise.		
9:05	9:15	10	Reading, etc.	Reading	Reading	Reading	Arith'ic	Arith'ic
9:15	9:25	10	Printing	Reading, etc.	Reading	Reading	Arith'ic	Arith'ic
9:25	9:35	10	Printing	Numbers	Reading, etc.	Reading	Arith'ic	Arith'ic
9:35	9:50	15	Numbers	Numbers	Numbers	Reading	Arith'ic	Arith'ic
9:50	10:05	15	Numbers	Printing	Numbers	Arith'ic	Arithmetic	Arith'ic
10:05	10:20	15	Drawing	Drawing	Drawing	Drawing	Drawing	Arithmetic
10:20	10:25	5	Gen. Lesson	Gen. Lesson	Writing	Arith'ic	Geogra'y	Drawing
10:25	10:30	5	Recess	Recess	Gen. Lesson	Arith'ic	Geogra'y	Geogra'y
10:30	10:45	15			Re	cess.		
10:45	11:00	15	Printing	Printing	Writing	Arithmetic	Geogra'y	Geogra'y
11:00	11:15	15	Printing	Writing	Writing	Copying	Geography	Geogra'y
11:15	11:30	15	Printing	Writing	Printing	Copying	Reading	Geog. or His'y
11:30	11:45	15	Numbers	Reading	Printing	Writing	Reading	Reading
11:45	12:00	15	Drawing	Reading	Reading	Reading	Grammar	Reading

AFTERNOON.

BEGINS.	CLOSES.	TIME.	PRIMARY	1st CLASS	2d CLASS	3d CLASS	4th CLASS	5th CLASS
1:00	1:07	7	Reading, etc.	Reading	Reading	Reading	Grammar	Grammar
1:07	1:15	8	Printing	Reading, etc.	Reading	Reading	Grammar	Grammar
1:15	1:25	10	Printing	Printing	Reading, etc.	Reading	Grammar	Grammar
1:25	1:35	10	Printing	Writing	Copying	Reading, etc.	Grammar	Grammar
1:35	1:50	15	Numbers	Drawing	Spelling	Spelling	Grammar	Physiol'y
1:50	2:05	15	Drawing	Reading	Spelling	Spelling	Drawing	Grammar
2:05	2:25	20			Writ	ing.		
2:25	2:40	15	Recess	Recess	Spelling	Spelling	Writing	Physiol'y
2:40	2:55	15			Re	cess.		
2:55	3:10	15	Printing	Reading	Reading	Writing	Spelling	Physiology
3:10	3:18	8	Reading, etc.	Reading	Reading	Writing	Spelling	Spelling
3:18	3:25	7	Drawing	Reading, etc.	Reading	Drawing	Spelling	Spelling
3:25	3:35	10	Printing	Writing	Reading, etc.	Drawing	Spelling	Spelling
3:35	3:50	15	Numbers	Printing	Copying	Copying	Spelling	Spelling
3:50	4:00	10			Gen	eral Exer	cises.	

The condensed type denotes the recitations and the Roman letters denote what the other classes should study. . . .

This programme must be modified to suit the circumstances of each school. Have fewer classes, if possible, and give more time to some of the recitations. If there are other advanced classes, they can recite every other day, alternating with the highest classes given in the above specimen programme. . . .

A copy of your programme should be left in the teacher's register for the use of your successor.

Chapter 4

and teachers because it led to intellectual strength and was a sign of the educated teacher, scholar, or parent. McKenzie emphasized the responsibility of the teacher to

> constantly advance . . . the horizon of his circle of
> knowledge. . . . In order to [do] this, whatever may have been
> his preparation, he must *read*, digest, assimilate. . . .
>
> The teacher must positively find time to read. . . . to gather
> thought, to gain intellectual strength. . . .
>
> The school will readily feel the quickening influence of the
> reading teacher; his manner and conversation will give evidence
> of the work he is pursuing.[40]

This importance of reading, so similar to the curricular priorities of the late twentieth century, was emphasized in the state courses of study along with guidelines and recommendations on how to prevent disorder and directions on how to teach the first- through fifth-grade readers.[41] The Iowa, Nebraska, and Kansas courses of study from the 1870s presented numerous instructions to the teachers as to how to teach various skills and information. Shaping these instructions were the Pestalozzian principles of education which Henry Barnard called "the common property of teachers and educators throughout the world."[42] The principles were also found in the content of the normal school and institute courses and in the teachers' examinations. The examination papers of May 1884, Davenport [Iowa] Training School emphasized understanding child nature, object teaching, development of the mental faculties, and questioning strategies as seen in this excerpt from Alice Harmon's examination paper:

> A Principle derived from the study of Child Nature. Stated and
> Illustrated.
>
> Activity is a law of childhood. Accustom the child to do. Educate the hand. We learn by doing. Strength is the result of
> exercise. . . .
>
> In this way they gain practice in doing for themselves & so
> making them independent of the teacher. Knowledge is fixed in
> the mind more readily.[43]

The Iowa *Course of Study and Manual for the Ungraded Schools* of 1878, summarized the Pestalozzian "principles of the *art of teaching*," which gave a basis for school management and instruction that could be implemented in the ungraded school. These principles, which are also familiar in today's lexicon of pedagogy, encouraged the children's independent learning and short, repetitive lessons that "proceed step by step."

> Begin with the senses, and never tell a child what he can be led to discover readily for himself.
> Reduce every subject to its elements, one difficulty at a time is enough for a child.
> Proceed step by step, be thorough, the measure of information is not what a teacher can give, but what the pupil can receive.
> Let every lesson have a point, either immediate or remote. . . .
> Proceed from the known to the unknown, from the particular to the general, from the concrete to the abstract, from the simple to the difficult. . . .
> Fasten every principle by frequent repetition.[44]

Teachers renewing their certificates and normal school students could repeat these principles in their examinations; however, application in the classroom may have been more hit or miss.

In 1875, the state of Kansas issued a survey in an attempt to ascertain what "Methods of Instruction and Discipline" the teachers were using at that time.[45] While the data from the survey are incomplete because the total number of respondents is not included in the state superintendent's report, the responses do give some clues as to how teachers taught and what they saw as important both in content and methods. Approximately one-third of the survey questions concerned the teaching of reading and the language arts, an indication of the state's emphasis on those subjects. More than half of the respondents required their pupils "to give the substance of the reading lesson in their own language, orally or in writing"; "usually question[ed] the pupils about the reading lesson, either before or after the recitation"; and 64 per cent "usually or sometimes require[d] pupils to write compositions upon a given subject."

The responses related to discipline practices and problems are especially interesting, given the stereotypic view that the three Rs were "taught to the tune of the hickory stick." According to this survey, 58 percent of the respondents were satisfied with their method of dis-

cipline, and only 15 percent of the respondents used corporal punishment. Whispering and idleness were identified as the most cited discipline problems, with bigger students and boys having a slight edge
as being the most difficult students.

John Ise described his school days in Kansas when, after twenty
strokes with the rawhide, the teacher ceased her physical abuse of a
defiant schoolboy.

> Again she raised the whip, but she happened to glance around
> the room, and saw faces that caused her to stop—faces of the
> older girls, some of whom were crying, wide-eyed in horror and
> anger at this exhibition of brutality. She hesitated a moment,
> poised the whip for another stroke, but those eyes were upon
> her. She laid the whip back on her desk, and ordered Danny to
> his seat.
>
> . . . The teacher stood by, but said not a word, defeated, not
> altogether by the stubborn will of this fearless boy, but by the ris-
> ing standards of humanity . . . [which] had rendered her prin-
> ciples of school management obsolete. The frontier was becom-
> ing civilized.[46]

Loulie Ayer Beall recalled her schooling in the 1880s, when the big
boys in the school ganged up on their punitive male teacher and
burned the eighteen-inch black rubber ruler that he used to beat the
children. The boys then carried the teacher outside and "rolled him
over and over in the snow, and admonished him to 'study his lesson'
for the rest of the afternoon. School kept as usual the next day, with
no reference to the incident. My parents refused to listen to the remarkable drama of that day, and little comment was made concerning
it in the neighborhood."[47]

In these two accounts, the sense of community among the children
had effected the change in the teacher's method of discipline. In the
extensive diaries of Sarah Gillespie Huftalen, this shift in discipline
problems and procedures is also seen. In 1883, her first year of teaching, she describes scolding two brothers: "Had a time with the Preston
boys. While I was shaking one for talking loud in school the other
came at me & when I went for him Alrah took up a stick of wood &
came at me. I sat Charlie down so hard that he stayed there & then I
sent Alrah out doors 'hooping' & did not let him in till he begged like
a good fellow. Made them mind though."[48]

Teaching and Learning in the Schools of the Prairies and Plains

Twenty years later, Huftalen's discipline problems consisted of con-
tending with a sassy girl and trying to get the boys to stop soiling the
seats in the water closet.[49] Not only had Huftalen matured in her
teaching methods but also the general view of appropriate behavior
and disciplinary actions in the schools had shifted. Homer Seerley,
president of Iowa State Normal School, reported to the Iowa State
Teachers Association in 1898: "The savage spirit of physical punishment has given way to a more rational treatment of the individual . . .
and an era of love and sympathy for childhood has come."[50]

Seventy-five percent of the responding teachers in the Kansas survey had little difficulty with parents, but the teachers were indeed
evaluated by parents and the general public in terms of the observable
results of what the children were learning. The content, management,
and methods used in the one-room schools mirrored the expectations
of the parents who were concerned that their children knew how to
read, to write, and were competent in arithmetic.[51] For the parents,
proof of adequate learning was their children's performance in the
school programs, passing to the next grade or next textbook, and passing the county eighth grade examinations. Teachers were expected to
keep order in the schoolhouse, teach every child, and handle discipline fairly. The saying, "as is the teacher, so is the school," covered
a multitude of sins and successes.

Schoolwomen received public recognition every time they presented a school program. From the teacher's point of view, the school
program was a source of hard work, pride, and anxiety. Sarah Gillespie described her school program at Little York No. 2, Delaware
County, Iowa:

> Friday, 20 [February 1885] All we did to day was to get ready for
> evening. I did up all the girls hair & we cleaned up some and
> went twice through the programme for evening. Let them go
> home at 3 p.m. & then we got back early. I undone & done up
> all their hair and combed all the smaller boys hair. . . . [The
> programme] lasted two hours & not a blunder was made
> either. . . . I looked for some of our folks up. It was so pleasant,
> but none of them came.[52]

While Sarah was disappointed that her family did not attend the
program, she was pleased that her scholars did well, especially because
there were visitors from another school eager to "have some fun with

the little dutchmen & schoolmam."[53] In her journal, she listed all thirty-six presentations including recitations of poetry, essays, tableaux, songs, and dialogues, such as these:

> The two church spiders by Eddie Morris
> "What I like"—Bertie, Eddie, Glenn, Lori, Maud, Mary, etc.
> "The dying childs request" by Lori Minkler
> "The lips that touch liquor shall never touch mine"—Addie Lear
> Burlesque. "All the great men are passing away—there's Lincoln
> & Washington & Garfield—I don't feel very well myself" by
> Glenn Minkler[54]

On Saturday, the day after the program, Sarah went to the school to take down the "fixings" and leave the building in "quite a respectable shape."[55]

The school programs or picnics culminated each school term by showing off to the parents and other members of the rural community what the children had learned. Essays written by the scholars were often part of the school program. Amelia Phoneta Bruner, an eighteen-year-old student in the school near West Point, Nebraska, welcomed visitors to the school program on behalf of her classmates and teacher, December 18, 1872:

> Kind teacher, dear friends and schoolmates: a kind welcome to each. We are very happy to meet you all here this evening. Today being the last schoolday of this term, and as we are going to have a few weeks vacation, we thought that we would read our compositions, recite our declamations, speak our dialogues &c this evening, and invite some of our friends to spend a pleasant hour or more with us. . . .
>   . . . . We are only beginning to labor in the vast field of education, (figuratively speaking) therefore you can not expect as much of us as though we were some great savans. But, we desire that you excuse and forgive us if we say or do anything this evening that is not exactly correct, which we think you will willingly do, especially those of you who remember the time when you went to school, and used to write compositions and read them, speak pieces &c. [56]

Writing essays was a method of teaching children to use ideas, words, and sentences, as well as giving them an opportunity to master spelling and penmanship. Sarah Jane Price had her students write essays and then read them to the rest of the scholars. She described such an event in her diary.

> Friday Feb. 7th 1879
> This has been a very nice day. I had a full school. This afternoon was the time for essays. Addie had one on old bachelors which was responded to by Will Arnold on old maids. Very humorous. Sherman had one on natural history which was very funny. David Tyler had one about our old brown hen which was so funny he could hardly read it himself.[57]

Student attempts at writing weren't always successful, as Bessie Tucker found out.

> I have one pupil who thinks me a perfect tyrant because I will insist on his studying his lessons and will not allow him to let them go and read story books in school time. After neglecting his grammar for said purpose he came to class with a poorly prepared lesson and a great tale of woe. After having to forfeit his recreation period to complete the neglected work I received this doleful sentence, *"The lesson was long and hard."* He looked so abused when he handed it to me it was only by a strong effort of will power I refrained from laughing.[58]

Music was part of the curriculum, especially if the teacher could sing or play a guitar, piano, or pump organ. Patriotic and folk songs were included daily, and songs were also used to memorize multiplication tables and the alphabet. States and capitals were learned through singing geography:

> Maine, Augusta, on the Kennebeck River; New Hampshire, Concord, on the Merrimac River; Vermont, Montpelier, on the Onion River; Massachusetts, Boston, on the Boston Harbor.[59]

Arithmetic was essential in every schoolhouse. Superintendent Samuel Townsley of Knoxville, Iowa, observed percentages being taught sixth graders in a Des Moines school: "The class had prepared solutions of examples placed on the board at their seats. These were explained. Their teacher collected examples original with [the] pupils and had these solved on being read. . . . Then a pupil gave [a] demonstration. The plan worked admirably."[60]

Not all teachers were able to teach arithmetic "admirably." Catharine Wiggins recalled that it was only after she had been teaching several years and had returned to finish high school, that she found out from "the best instructor of my life" why the divisor was inverted when dividing by fractions.[61] Up to that time, she had memorized the rule without understanding the reason. Arithmetic learned through memorization was to Wiggins and many other children and teachers summed up as follows:

> Multiplication was a vexation,
> Division was as bad,
> The Rule of Three perplexed me,
> And fractions drove me mad.[62]

Cipherdowns and spelldowns were commonly used forms of drill and practice that involved the whole school. E. Mary Lacy Crowder recalled that when the last scholar was spelled down, everyone sang:

> Oh, dear! Oh, dear! I shall never learn to spell;
> I shall always be a dunce, I know very well.
> For the letters get mixed up in such a queer way
> That I never can tell what they mean to say.[63]

At times the school programs took the form of spelling bees or ciphering competitions with other schools. The ciphering competition between Van Huss and Turkey Creek Schools in the early 1890s near Leon, Kansas, was vividly remembered by Roscoe Conaway, one of the "duelers." First the youngest children, the "pin-feathered warriors," competed, then the older scholars matched wits. "This battle between embattled figurers consisted in a series of duels between individuals, one from each school at a time. Accuracy outranked speed. Incorrect answers rated zero."[64] Although eleven-year-old Roscoe Conaway went down on a problem of cancellation, bested by a sixteen-year-old girl, the Van Hussians defeated the scholars from Turkey Creek. In doing so, they vindicated one of their number whom they felt had been unduly collared by "Her Volcanic Majesty," the teacher from Turkey Creek.

The Changes in Educational Practices

The stereotypes of the unchanging country teachers and the good ol' basics taught in the rugged schoolhouses obscure the positive changes that took place in the late nineteenth and early twentieth centuries. For the teachers who were required to attend institutes yearly, changes crept into their repertoire of methods. Diverse and inventive teaching methods, including individualized instruction, were implemented in the one-room schoolhouses. Wayne E. Fuller indicates that "their critics might have considered them progressive had they not been country teachers."[65]

The professional education journals that reached and spoke for the teachers and other schoolwomen were filled with first-hand descriptions of changing and successful teaching practices and some observations by the county superintendents and other educational leaders. The April 1860 issue of *The Iowa Instructor*, published by the Iowa State Teachers' Association, included an article on "Opening School," in which teachers were told how to teach their rules to the children, in much the same manner as supported by twentieth-century research on effective schooling.[66] Announcements and minutes of state, county, and local professional meetings and institutes were included, as well as an assessment of the problems associated with giving prizes at school and an article by a teacher about how she encouraged two German immigrant children to learn.[67]

School Work and Literary Notes, the official journal of the Nebraska State Board of Education, included much of the same range of information: "From a Sod School House, What to do with Small School on Stormy Days"; "Methods, A few Words of Advice to Young Teachers"; a review of *How to Study U. S. History; or, United States by the Brace System;* and resolutions from a teachers' association supporting the development of school museums.[68]

The Ranch Teacher, published in Box Butte and Cheyenne counties, Nebraska, reported the news from the districts schools. For example, District 92 had a box social with receipts of "$22.50, to be used for school library, window shades and lamps for the school house." The county superintendent's descriptions of visits to the district schools cited the name of the teacher and positive comments about the school.

March 4 [1908], p.m.—Miss Hill is teaching in district 69. Here I found some fine new desks, and what is more, those desks are well taken care of. The geography classes were very good, because the pupil and not the teacher did the reciting. It is a bad method to ask questions that can be answered by "yes" or "no," or to waste time by repeating the answers after the pupils.

March 5—A stormy day. Miss Kidd has an interesting school in district 57, and was very good about taking advice. Here there is the second set of good wall maps I have seen on my trips.

March 5, p.m. Miss Ruth Millett, who has a homestead in Cheyenne county, draws $50.00 a month in district 32. There is a good average attendance here.[69]

In addition to these features, *The Nemaha County Teacher*, of Auburn, Nebraska, listed the Missouri Pacific Railway timetable and announced the Boys Corn Growing Contest and the Cooking Contest of the Girls Domestic Science Club. The Perry Picture Company of Malden, Massachusetts, announced their bird study picture sets and asked, "Is there a picture of Washington in every room in your school? Are there beautiful Art Subjects in every grade?"[70] Children's essays in the section, "The Nemahas by the children and for the children," included "Our School-Room," by twelve-year-old Lydia Greer. From the essay by thirteen-year-old Blanche M. Snodgrass of District No. 24, we learn, "There are eighty one school districts in Nemaha county." The essay lists the crops raised in the county, the canning factory, grain elevators, quarries, and the special events such as the annual German-American picnic, the Farmers Institutes, and basketball teams. Young Miss Snodgrass concluded, "the people of Nemaha are prosperous, well educated, highly civilized people."[71]

The prestigious *American Journal of Education* published articles of scholarly interest, research, and leadership, but few classroom teachers had access to this journal. The schoolwomen read their teachers' association journals and county education periodicals, where they received the news of their locale, obtained public recognition for their work, read about new teaching methods and "tried and true" teaching strategies, and maintained their professional contacts.

The National Education Association appointed Henry Sabin, Iowa State Superintendent, 1888–1892 and 1894–1898, as chairman of the prestigious Committee of Twelve on Rural Schools, established to identify the problems in rural education and recommend steps for remediation. In his report to the NEA, Sabin summed up the fifty years of change in education by the early 1900s as a shift from memorization, dependence on textbooks, and the "word of his teacher" to "the skillful presentation of choice material suited to the child's mind." Sabin challenged the teacher education programs and educators: "We demand that they [the teachers] shall know what and how to teach. The next and more important step, is that they shall know *why* they do thus."[72]

Another assessment of educational progress was described by Agnes Samuelson, whose career began in 1905–1906 in the Pleasant View School, Page County, Iowa, and then included the positions of county superintendent, Iowa state superintendent of public instruction, and president and staff member of the National Education Association. Through her forty-seven years as a professional educator, Samuelson was one of many schoolwomen who participated in instituting the many educational changes she described:

> Once the names of all the bones in the body. Now the rules of health and hygiene.
>
> Once only dates in history. Now an understanding of American and world problems.
>
> Once fox and hound problems. Now studies in space exploration.
>
> Once jawbreakers in spelling. Now words most commonly used.
>
> Once the birch rod discipline. Now pupil participation, study of child development and the importance of mental hygiene.
>
> Once the curriculum of reading, writing and ciphering. Now flexible units of study based on the changing needs of modern living.[73]

The changes in curriculum and methods as recommended by the educational leaders and normal schools were beginning to be implemented in the late 1800s and early 1900s. There was a gradual, increased acceptance and recognition that knowledge and the processes of learning extended beyond simple memorization of textbooks. The interests of the growing literate prairie population could be seen in the expanding curriculum shaped by the state courses of study, the classification of the students by grade level of learning, and by the enduring teacher-student relationship. The jobs of the teacher and the county superintendent evolved during this period to become full-time professions with school terms of six to nine months. The requirements for certification continued to increase so that the teachers' institutes and summer sessions for continuing education occupied one to three months per year. Health and safety standards of the school facilities were improved, along with provisions for lunch programs and transportation of pupils. Improvements in teachers' salaries and opportunities for advancement were negligible, but by the mid-twentieth century, gradually and falteringly teachers became organized to negotiate for them. The conditions of the frontier schoolhouse were part of the memories of a generation older than the schoolchildren and their teachers.

Teacher-Student Relationships

What did not change was the motivation of the successful schoolwomen, which was based in the ideal of helping others and acceptance of self, the scholars, and the community. Their income was essential in meeting the economic needs of the schoolwomen and their families; however, substantial monetary rewards have remained notably missing from the professions in education. Through the teachers' concerns about the education, morality, and well-being of their pupils, there developed an affection between teachers and the children similar to the relationships in an extended family. Catharine Wiggins described this atmosphere when teaching in the Goodwill School, near Sterling, Kansas, as "more like a large, well-ordered, and congenial family of some 24 members."[74] With all the school-age members of a family and their cousins in one schoolroom, "family" was a somewhat literal description of some school enrollments. Sarah Huftalen and Mary Jones called their Iowa schoolhouses their "school-homes" in recognition of the kinship, both real and developed, the affection, and the responsibilities of the children and the teacher.[75]

The concept of the school family and its linkage to the children's homes was part of a Nebraska teacher's description of how she taught reading to the beginners:

> When a little child first enters school he comes into a strange
> new world to him. All his ideas are of home and mother. So we
> spend the first few weeks in getting acquainted, and in trying to
> get the little one to talk freely. Hence the family is the first
> thought emphasized. This is done in many ways. In little talks

Teaching and Learning in the Schools of the Prairies and Plains

bringing out what each one has done for his family to help mother. The little songs and games that are taught, the sentences that are read all breathe the spirit of family love. Really our school is a family.[76]

Emma Pospisil, Bohemian immigrant to Nebraska in the 1880s, described how Mrs. Cedalia Collins, her teacher for one year, established the physical and affective environment of the school.

The schoolroom was transformed into a habitable place. Potted plants and crisp curtains were in the windows and pictures were pinned on the ugly grimy walls. . . .

Classes were heard with concern, not indifference such as we had known before. . . .

During the noon hour we used to gather around her like one big family, from the smallest to the biggest boys and girls, and talk of various things, usually of incidents or events that happened in the homes or the neighborhood. We were learning life not only from books but from the teacher's lips as well. I liked to be close to her. Once, after much planning, I edged up to her and kissed her.

"Thank you!" She was surprised but gracious. I have been glad many times that I bestowed upon her this highest expression of affection. . . .

In my early hour of need she had filled an aching void. She showed me the ways of kindness where I had known harshness before. I could have followed her across the world. . . . She is my lode-star still.[77]

Mrs. Collins brought acceptance to this immigrant child through her openly expressed affection and interest in the children's daily lives, their games, and through helping them learn about life. Pospisil's reminiscence glorifies the teacher who had such a positive impact on her; however, the foundation of teaching is this teacher-learner relationship.

In the following excerpts from Bessie Tucker's dairy, the teacher-child relationship is seen from the teacher's point of view. Tucker struggles with discipline and questions her own ability to manage the schoolhouse. She complains about the children's behavior, perseveres at being friendly, then works out her problem with concern for the children's well-being and concludes that teaching is fun—at least most of the time.

> *Sept. 18, 1918:* Little Book, isn't it funny how everything goes wrong some days. This has been one of those days. I am quite discouraged. I tried to win the children by being good to them— that worked so well last year, but it won't this year—NOT AT ALL! Now I am going to keep right on being friendly to the children *but they have to obey me! After all I am the boss and they have to recognize that!* Today wasn't the day to start my new program for as I said before things went wrong from the beginning and neither of us was in any mood for experiments. But I have a problem to solve I know, for with 45 naughty children that all do the same thing at the same time it is rather hard to know just what to do but I must find a way. So long until I find it.
>
> *Sept. 19, 1989:* I've found it. I've just asserted my authority with a will today and I really was amazed with the results. We got along fine and I was as jolly as anyone could wish at recess and did my best to make the children see that I love to play as well as they did, joining in the usual running games, etc. Then during the noon hour we washed the windows and did some other things and some of the big boys hung around and used their strength in the more difficult jobs showing their superiority. . . .
>
> *Sept. 20. 1918:* I am glad I am a school mom. It's fun to teach school, just lots of fun, really. No two days are alike.[78]

On the surface, this is an account of a teacher trying to gain an authoritarian control of the school. However, the elements of concern and interest in the children and the ability of the teacher to change enable Tucker to cope with the conflict of the personal and academic needs of the children. Bessie Tucker felt like a failure because her initial plans did not work out well; nevertheless, she was able to modify her strategy with the children, maintain her ability to enjoy playing with the children, and show her positive consideration for their schoolwork. The teacher-child relationship of this short-term teacher was one of honest warmth and acceptance while expecting the children to learn, cooperate with the other students, and independently complete their school work.

In another excerpt, Bessie Tucker relates more of her views about the teacher-child relationship. In this incident, she isn't eager to like a new boy in her school who tries to flirt with her.

> *Jan. 9, 1919:* . . . . I had two new pupils today, boys far bigger than I am. . . . I think I like school best when there are no big boys coming. . . . One of them winked at me today and I treated him about like a second grader from then on. No more smiling on my students. No-sir-ee! I had enough of that last year. But that was the only offence by said pupil and I think I shall like him fine. I like the other one fine already. It's funny how a teacher learns to love her pupils, every one, isn't it? And one can see beneath the surface and excuse so much in them. It may be because of the home training they had, little defects in manners, etc. It is easy to see how a mother may spoil her children. Now please don't think I'm spoiling mine. I'm not!
>
> The two boys mentioned above have no mother but live with their father. I feel so sorry for them and wish I could make it up to them some way. I am going to make school life just as pleasant as I can for them all. Their mother just died recently and I know they must miss her so much.[79]

In this excerpt, Tucker expresses her concern about behavior of the boys on one hand and then considers their home life and determines that she will make school pleasant. Tucker does not tell how she taught the school subjects: she tells what she worried about, how she related to the children, and how she responded to their personal and academic problems. She defines her role as a teacher in terms of the interpersonal relationships.

Whether by disposition or education, undoubtedly not all teachers were able to relate to children purposefully and affectively. When Sarah Huftalen supervised nine rural schools for a year as a member of the Rural Department, Iowa State Teachers College, she found that three of the nine teachers were poor: "If they could be called a teacher at all, did the best they knew but it is surprising sometimes how some ever passed an examination or 'got a school.' Of course there is at times a director who has a girl who wants to earn some money and stay at home while doing it. Pity the children in such schools."[80]

Ineffective teaching could be found at all levels of education. Evelyn Bolte Hurlbut remembered her seventh grade teacher in Davenport, Iowa, about 1915, who wrote the assignments on the board, then sat at her desk and cried day after day. The children did their assignments but never knew why she was so sad.[81] When Superintendent Samuel Townsley visited the Pleasantville, Iowa, schools he observed a teacher he thought should be fired.

> In the second room I found, *I found*—a regular old style driver, a fighter, a stormer, a woman badly out of her sphere. She uses the rotund voice and that right freely. She requires her pupils to use it, too. She had good behavior on the part of her pupils, secured it by terrorizing them. While present I heard her give sharp, cutting reproofs (perhaps 1/4 of her talk was on that line) saw her shake one innocent looking little girl for laying her left hand on a desk by her while standing in class and heard her promise several times to stay with them until sundown or a little after if necessary in case certain tasks were not performed.
>
> Her frowns are terrible (I saw one of them and it wasn't leveled at me either.) The Board had better pay her her salary to stay away from the building and hire another teacher. . . .
>
> I learned later that she has a rube for a husband and was hired doubtless through sympathy. *Ability as a teacher it seems to me is the true ground* of selection.[82]

Townsley, as an experienced teacher and administrator, saw that the rigid compulsory conformity in this classroom was a destructive relationship. He tried to convey to the teachers he hired and supervised in the Knoxville, Iowa, schools that

> The Live Teacher must be in full sympathy with child nature. . . . If the pranks . . . of children are a vexation to the teacher he needs to cultivate a personal acquaintance with them.
> . . . The sentiment of the children must be for a good working school. The sentiment of a majority of the pupils makes or mars the success of a teacher. At first the teacher can easily win this feeling. He must earn the good will of the people, he can hardly expect more.[83]

This sentiment is seen in Huftalen's description of her interpersonal relationships with her pupils and her methods of school management.

> To this day it is easy to visualize our school close; children scampering about the room, some assigned to one thing and some

to another, dusting erasers, emptying [the] water pail, books and pencils in orderly arrangement in desks, waste basket on top of desk nearest stove, black boards washed; crayon trough cleaned and chalk put in its box etc. and the five going straight to the fuel house to do their apportionment. Then not a child failing to say good night in most friendly manner; many caresses included.[84]

Organization and personalization had its rewards for Huftalen as well as for her students.

Conclusion

The problems of teaching and learning in the heartland schools persisted into the twentieth century: too many recitations each day because of classes consisting of one or two students;[85] lack of uniformity of quality of teacher education and the resultant good, bad, and indifferent teachers; lack of professional supervision and support for beginners and experienced teachers alike; lack of funds for adequate teaching materials, supplies, upkeep for the schoolhouse, and for teachers' salaries. For children, the problems of becoming educated were exacerbated by the lack of textbooks and other teaching materials such as maps, charts, and libraries; the lack of health standards for the water supply and toilets, control of contagious diseases, and adequate lunches; the lack of standard preparation for high schools, and the lack of high schools within appropriate daily commuting distances; the lack of respite from a ineffective or biased teacher. For the schoolwomen, the obstacles remained: poor salaries and inadequately supplied schoolhouses; salaries that had to be supplemented by second jobs or by the teacher's family; little or no way to advance within one school district; preparation for teaching and maintaining a teaching certificate that was often limited to courses offered through the institutes because of lack of personal funds to attend a college; school enrollments that varied with the seasons, making for a lack of continuity of instruction; and continued professional isolation. While the two-tiered level of teacher preparation demanded less of those who taught the rural schools than those who taught the graded schools in towns, the rural teachers were viewed with disdain by other teachers.

With all the challenges to education in the heartland, the paradox remains: the residents of Iowa, Kansas, and Nebraska were among the most literate populations within the United States during the late nineteenth and early twentieth centuries. The schoolwomen, daughters of the homesteaders, who taught the children of the prairies and plains, were the survivors who shaped their visions of the future with the practicality and discipline born of making a living from the land despite drought, grasshoppers, blizzards, epidemics, and economic instability. They found comfort and direction from their religious faith and from the love, support, and guidance of their friends and families. They saw both beauty and caution in the open skies, the vast land, and the changing seasons. They found time to learn, to work and have fun, to be homemakers, leaders, and followers. They were multidimensional working women who discovered that teaching and working in the schools brought them recognition and respect for their personal achievements, albeit small; affection and acknowledgment of their authority from their students; justifiable pride in the accomplishments, independence, and cooperation of their scholars; and satisfaction in knowing that their work was of value to others in their emerging society.

Martha Bayne recorded her reason for teaching as "perhaps victory":

> [Twenty dollars a month] . . . a meager sum for what a teacher had to endure. Often as we rode over the prairies thru winter winds and summer heat, in spite of every effort to look on the bright side, we would find ourselves asking the question: "What is there in all this?" and then came the answer of Garibaldi to his men: "Hunger, cold, suffering, sickness, death—perhaps victory." But victory came. The children that sat on those hard benches on dirt floors are now filling important places.[86]

District No. 1, Merrick County, Nebraska. Decorations and instructional materials included the chalkboard, children's schoolwork, paper windmills, pictures of the presidents, flowers, and people. (Nebraska State Historical Society)

Jackson Township School No. 5, Sac County, Iowa, 1907–1908. Susan Conklin and her scholars lined up in front of the large chalkboard, next to the organ. (State Historical Society of Iowa—Iowa City)

Country school, Emerson, Nebraska, early 1900s. The daily schedule and the lesson outline, "Position and Area of Nebraska," were written on the chalkboard. The schoolhouse had patent desks, globe, books, framed prints, a calendar from the Farmer's State Bank, and the heating stove. (Nebraska State Historical Society)

Teacher and children with their lunch pails, 1909. (State Historical Society of Iowa—Iowa City)

Teaching and Learning in the Schools of the Prairies and Plains

Recess time with teacher, Sadie M. Beach, Page County, Iowa, 1907.
(Agnes Samuelson Collection, State Historical Society of Iowa—
Iowa City)

Bess Owinn taught Chadron, Nebraska's first kindergarten, 1893–1894.
(Nebraska State Historical Society)

Chapter 4

Elizabeth Hewitt's third grade class of about forty pupils, North
School, Fremont, Nebraska, 1904. (Nebraska State Historical
Society)

Eighth grade graduation was an important rite of passage to high school or to work. York County, Nebraska, Eighth Grade, June 6, 1903. (Nebraska State Historical Society)

"O little country school . . ." Agnes Samuelson began her career as a schoolwoman in Pleasant View School, Page County, Iowa, 1905–1906. (Agnes Samuelson Collection, State Historical Society of Iowa—Iowa City)

Part II.

Seeing the Context,

Hearing the Voice

Introduction to Five Lives

The prairie schoolwomen's stories in their own words are frag-
mented, interrupted, and incomplete chapters found among their diaries, letters, photograph albums, scrapbooks, school notes, reminiscences, oral histories, and family stories. To touch the private lives of
schoolwomen without the historical setting is to find their motivations, idealism, hardships, pain, and triumphs merely interesting but
singular stories. When set in the context of their public lives, these
private narratives work together to construct a historical perspective
while they depict real people with actual experiences, not romanticized or cardboard characters.

The narratives of five schoolwomen make up the second section of
this book. They are Nancy Rebecca Higgins Gaddis, Missouri and
Nebraska, 1862–1942; Sarah Jane Price, Ohio, Indiana, Iowa, and
Nebraska, 1841–1920; Sarah Gillespie Huftalen, Iowa, 1865–1955;
Bessie M. Tucker Gilmer, Nebraska, 1898– ; and Ethel Hale Russel,
Nebraska, Idaho, Utah, Iowa, and Michigan, 1895– . The short-term
teachers, Nancy Higgins Gaddis and Bessie Tucker Gilmer, provide
differing views, from the nineteenth and the twentieth centuries, re-

spectively, but there are basic similarities in their perspectives. Both valued education and their experiences as teachers; both continued their community involvement and contributions; the family connections of each represent stability and continuity. The diaries of Sarah Jane Price, long-term professional teacher, reveal this unmarried woman's approach to life as she pursued teaching, homemaking, and farming. Sarah Gillespie Huftalen and Ethel Hale Russel, the educational and community leaders, add further dimensions of schoolwomen's lives through their leadership roles, social activism, and the combination of the public and private aspects of their lives.

Nancy Higgins Gaddis at age thirteen and thirty-five-year-old Sarah Jane Price were emigrants to central Nebraska in the 1870s. Both stayed in Nebraska for the rest of their lives, Gaddis married, had four children, was a pillar of the church and active partner in the Gaddis stock farm; Price never married, was head of her household, entrepreneur in land holdings, active farmer and teacher, self-taught intellectual, and leader in her church. Their lives were lived in similar environments and time spans, but were played out in different ways.

Sarah Gillespie Huftalen, Bessie Tucker Gilmer, and Ethel Hale Russel were all born west of the Mississippi, the second generation on the praires and plains. Huftalen's mother had come from Michigan to Iowa where she met and married her husband. Gilmer's parents had lived in several locations in the West, including South Dakota and Nebraska. Russel's mother had immigrated from Ireland as a young child with her widowed mother, living first in Illinois, then in Nebraska.

Gaddis attended the district school built on her father's land and attended a boarding academy for one semester before beginning teaching. Price also attended an academy, numerous teacher institutes, and pursued her intellectual quest by reading voraciously. Over the years Huftalen and Russel completed their master's degrees, and both attended and taught at the institutes. Gilmer had less than eight years of formal education before she began teaching, but Russel completed high school and attended the state normal school for two years before teaching.

Huftalen, married but childless, taught throughout her adult years until she was compelled by state law to retire at age seventy. Gilmer and Gaddis left teaching for marriage and homemaking, and Russel taught until her second child was born, then directed her energies toward civic improvement. Three of these schoolwomen wrote for publication: Huftalen for professional education journals; Gilmer as a

Introduction to Five Lives

newspaper correspondent and as a participant in senior citizen writing workshops; and Russel was author of a reading textbook and news-letters for the American Association for the United Nations.

Gaddis, Price, Huftalen, and Gilmer taught in one-room school-houses, but Russel attended graded schools as a child and taught in graded schools. As teacher educators, Russel and Huftalen taught pre-service and in-service teachers for both the rural ungraded schools and the graded schools.

Five varied but overlapping lives combine to tell the story of the schoolwomen of the plains and prairies based on their own narratives.[1] While the narratives of these five lives are different in form and con-tent, they represent the criteria for inclusion. First, there are sufficient documents to represent their lives over a substantial period of the women's lives, not each schoolwoman's entire life, but large portions of her existence. The documents are not limited to reminiscences and oral histories, but include diaries, letters, photographs, and memo-rabilia that are not dependent upon the individual's memory or con-scious selection of the story to be told.

The second and more important consideration in choosing these five schoolwomen is that their overlapping lives represent a period of transition in the schooling of children, the education of teachers from the frontier to the established school systems, which is interlaced with the experiential stream of the women's life cycles. The public facets of the lives of each of these schoolwomen extended beyond their schoolhouses to the concerns of the community and the affairs of their contemporaries. The private aspects of their lives show us how they coped with the multiple demands placed upon working women; how they managed their individual pursuits of education, power, and selfhood; and how they sought to accomplish their guiding principles and values. The lives of these schoolwomen are part of the profes-sional heritage of teachers imbedded in the transitions of the history of education.

In general, the short-term teachers' stories are largely incomplete, ending abruptly when the woman moved to another location, was married, or no longer felt the need of confiding in a diary. Often there are portions of stories about teaching included in reminiscences, told years after the event, but identifying teaching as a peak experience in the woman's public life during which she made a recognized contribu-tion to her society. Sherrill Daniels's analysis of more than four thou-sand reminiscences housed at the Nebraska State Historical Society, identifies "the people to leave reminiscences are the ones who see their lives as successful."[2] Through the reminiscences, other narratives, and the preservation of the family stories and memorabilia, the importance of teaching in a women's life for even one school term comes into focus. As schoolwomen, they both comformed to and challenged the expectations of their gender. They achieved, if only briefly and minimally, a position of independence, leadership, and power that received positive public regard. They were, after all, earning a salary and doing good as defined by their society through educating children. The environment of the frontier and early settlement days put these short-term teachers into the situation of isolation in their one-room schoolhouses where they had to be in control or leave and admit failure. Those who failed as teachers, as Daniels has found, usually did not publicly record their reminiscences of failure.

Schoolwomen's accounts of intractable children, problems with parents, complaints about the weather, loneliness, and the hazards of prairie life may seem to the casual reader like pleas for escape from a miserable existence. The context of the writing must be examined to determine the writer's goal. The diary took the place of the intimate friend who would listen and be nonjudgmental. It was a safe place to criticize the landlady's children, the school director, or parents who failed to come to the school program. The diary of the beginning teacher who was isolated from family, friends, and professional support was the place to acknowledge the indecision about school management and teaching; the loneliness; and often the anger at not knowing how to proceed or at failure to accomplish a task. The beginning teachers' diaries were statements of private thoughts. Their tone is often adolescent as these beginning teachers were typically teenaged girls on their own for the first time.[3]

Bessie Tucker Gilmer's diaries are unique in that they cover a wide span of time, 1918–1979, with notes and additions through 1984. Gilmer, a short-term teacher, tells her own story through her diaries, her oral history, a reminiscence written in her eighties, her photographs, and her letters to the author. The diaries of Sarah Jane Price and Sarah Gillespie Huftalen are rich in detail about their work and their families as these schoolwomen used their diaries as their confidantes. Price is terse, with little embellishment. Huftalen rages passionately and with great detail in her dairies. In her reminiscent and public writing, she is didactic, pious, and, at times, pompous.

The diaries give perhaps the closest view of the life of another person's mind that we can reconstruct from their historical documents. In reading the private writings of the prairie schoolwomen, listening to the voice from the past or memories spoken in the oral histories, we question why disparate documents were preserved, why certain stories, fictional or true, were maintained, and we wonder what events have been omitted or rendered emotionless. The schoolwomen recorded their daily lives and the tasks of teaching without much detail or explanation as they did not expect others to read their private writing. It was unnecessary to explain in a letter to a friend or in a diary, the relationships of the people mentioned, or to elaborate on the chores and duties at hand. The writer's own story is found among the descriptions of her daily chores and the events she has chosen to include in her private writing. It is for the modern reader to speculate, to search out the relationships and meanings, and at time to merely wonder how the people and the events fit into the texture of the time and circumstance.

Among the long-term schoolwomen, there seems to be an abundance of reminiscences that relate the schoolwomen's teaching and other life experiences.[4] The memoirs and reminiscences document the events as remembered from the past, sometimes colored by time, enhanced or enlarged, but usually including the accounts of emotional impact and importance to the writer. The content and attitude or style of the schoolwomen's reminiscences are consonant with Daniels's analysis. She identifies the elements of pioneer reminiscences as including, but not limited to, moving West and establishing a home, and

> the blessings and curses of the new world of weather . . . natural
> pests and disasters . . . trials and hardships, family life, church
> life, community life, . . . education. . . . Being first at anything
> counts. . . . one may not complain about the climate. . . . And
> one does not tolerate self-pity in one's self or in others for any
> length of time. . . . In fact one may not complain about much of
> anything.[5]

Numerous biographical sketches about educational and community leaders focus on the schoolwomen's public accomplishments but omit their private lives, as though they lived apart from their families and communities.[6] Long-term teachers and leaders claimed the role of teacher as their identity, and in that capacity, became role models for each other and for their scholars. But that role was only one part of

Introduction to Five Lives

their personas. The blend of idealism, domesticity, and professionalism is found not only among the prairie schoolwomen of the 1860s to the early 1900s but also in Vaughn-Roberson's research on the teachers of the twentieth century in Oklahoma, Texas, and Colorado.[7]

The distance between the professional leaders and the beginners is too far to grasp without the essential humanity of their everyday lives as part of the narrative. Biographical canonization tends to remove the leaders from their potential importance as female role models. In Sarah Gillespie Huftalen's extensive diaries, scrapbooks, and school notes, we find the complexity of the life of a professional schoolwoman coping with her dying mother, a rigid and perhaps unbalanced father, her love for her husband, and the demands of her creative teaching style, self-imposed intellectual curiosity, and social conscience. The narrative of her life, public and private, which she chose to deposit at the Iowa State Historical Society (Iowa City), bursts with emotion, pride, anger, fears, love, and integrity based in her profoundly understood principles of life.

By contrast, the oral history of Ethel Hale Russel is largely concerned with her public accomplishments. However, even in shared memories, there is self-awareness that her life is governed by her self-determined social conscience. Through her strong, vibrant personality, one hears and feels her ardent devotion to global understanding; the liberating force of education in her life; and the empathetic relationships with others as teacher, wife, mother, friend, and as progressive leader in educational and community development. But most aspects of her personal life remain private. Through the historical perspective of this actively thinking woman in her nineties, there is the spirit of integrity with a few regrets.

The exploration of both the public and the private lives of the prairie schoolwomen reveals the individuals within the collective histories of the frontier, of the West, of education, and of community development. This analysis identifies ordinary women as influential in accomplishing a major goal of society: establishing schools and educating children. The prairie schoolwomen were ordinary women whose life stories are generational models, a heritage for the community of women and of teachers, and their contemporaries.

CHAPTER
FIVE

"A Sense of Unity"

Nancy Rebecca Higgins Gaddis, Missouri, 1862–1875; Nebraska, 1875–1942

> our family had a sense of unity which has never left us and I feel
> quite sure the basic values of life are largely unchanged. We find
> happiness as we make our contribution to the world around
> us.—Ruth Gaddis Wilson, *"There is no place like Nebraska."*

Nancy Higgins Gaddis of Comstock, Nebraska, was a short-term schoolteacher of the early 1880s. Her only written record of her life is the small, brown, paper-covered attendance book representing the two years that she taught. This book has been carefully preserved for over a hundred years first by Nancy, then handed on to her daughters, Ruth Gaddis Wilson and Elsie Gaddis McKinney, and granddaughter, Eleanor McKinney.[1] Also cherished were Nancy's life membership certificates for the Women's Christian Temperance Union and the Women's Foreign Missionary Society; a handful of letters from her teenage girlfriends; her wedding certificate; a few undated newspaper clippings; and two handwritten teaching contracts. The first contract promised to pay Nancy Higgins twenty-six dollars a month for the term of two months, beginning May 1, 1882; the second contract, made out to Nancy R. Gaddis, also promised twenty-six dollars a month, beginning May 8, 1883. If there were other contracts, they are missing.[2]

There are a few photographs of Nancy's parents, Adrian and Mary Jane Higgins, and her childhood home near Douglas Grove, Nebraska; Nancy's picture at age seventeen; her wedding picture; and pictures of the timber claim and home that she and her husband, William C. Gaddis, developed into the Golden Rod Stock Farm. Also preserved is a collection of photographs of Nancy and William's children and grandchildren.[3]

Within these few documents and artifacts and the family narratives lie the essence of a short-term schoolwoman and her contributions to the growth of western settlement. Nancy Higgins Gaddis's life story which includes her two years of teaching is important because she was typical of the settlers who stayed with the land and became the foundations of a developing prairie society.[4] William and Nancy Higgins Gaddis's daughters, Ruth and Elsie, retold their mother's stories for the successive generations. From these family stories, and at the insistence of her grandson, Ruth Gaddis Wilson wrote the family history, "*There is no place like Nebraska.*" The small, self-published book contains the family's reminiscences, plus Ruth's childhood memories of growing up on the plains. In *Make Mine Blue*, Elsie Gaddis McKinney, "a true storyteller," wrote a semi-fictionalized account of her mother's emigration experiences from Missouri to Custer County, Nebraska, in 1875.[5]

During the Civil War years, the Higgins family lived near Bethany, Missouri, where their farm was an underground railroad station. In this border area, the abolitionist family was often threatened by Southern sympathizers, even in the years following the war, when the "people were consumed by revenge and anger so that reconciliation became quite difficult."[6] Trees lined the ravines and hollows around Bethany where it was hard to find pure water and well-drained land for crops. Martha, the oldest of the Higgins children, and her husband, Charles A. Hale, a circuit-riding Methodist preacher, had emigrated to the fertile Middle Loup River valley of Nebraska. The antagonism from some of the Higginses' Missouri neighbors, the poor water and land, and the chance for government land near Martha and Charles, led the Higgins family to pack up and head west in 1875. Traveling with three other families, the large Higgins family occupied two of the seven wagons from Bethany that headed for Plattsmouth,

Nebraska, with their livestock and watchdogs. Fording the Missouri River at Plattsmouth was remembered as the most frightening and dangerous part of the trip that eventually brought these settlers to Custer County, Nebraska.

The Custer County land that was "rough and rugged in the extreme" was first claimed in the winter of 1873, by W. D. Douglas and L. R. Dowse.[7] In the spring of 1874, Charles Hale and eight others established their claims near Douglas's claim, which became known as Douglas Grove. In the spring of 1875, the Higgins family "added greatly to the population" with Adrian and his wife, Mary Jane, and their eight children, Amanda Eliza, Sophrona Hanna, Mary Jane, Nancy Rebecca, Lizzie Ellen, William "Billy" Porter, Elcena "Ella" Seaton, and Alfred Anglin.[8]

Leaving the turmoil of postwar Missouri, the Higgins family came into "Custer county, with its numerous, constant streams of pure water, its valleys of hay land and its hills of splendid grazing grass land, [that] became the mecca of the cattlemen."[9] The Higginses, with the help of neighbors, built shelters for the stock, fenced the farmyard, and built a house of "nicely hewn cedar logs . . . the finest home in the Middle Loup Valley."[10] The following summer the grasshoppers "bared the fields of vegetation and corrupted the water in the 'dug wells.'"[11] This was a difficult time for the families until the crops were harvested the following summer. "Many settlers were left entirely destitute and getting through the winter posed a dreadful problem. Barrels of beans and a few other products were shipped from the east. Rev. Hale [Martha's husband] received much of his aid for distribution but even his own children burst into tears almost daily at the sight of 'those old beans' again on their table."[12]

Following Custer's defeat in the Battle of the Little Big Horn in June 1876, there were rumors of an Indian uprising in Nebraska. Nancy's story of this event was recounted by her son, Birney: "Then there's the story of the fort the settler's built at the time of the Custer massacre to which Grandfather would not go. Mother went to bed those nights wondering if she might not hear the warhoop before morning. She was 14."[13] Fortunately, no uprising occurred.

During the autumn of 1876 and the spring of 1877, the Olive brothers of Texas, established a ranch along the South Loup River. They brought several thousand long-horned Texas cattle to the ranch. Nancy's brother, William Porter Higgins, recalled:

A Sense of Unity

This was before the period of Barbed wire pasture and ranchers generally had corrals made of poles and logs sufficient to hold their saddle horses and part of their cattle that they might run them through the branding chute.

These cattle wandered all over that country and became a source of great annoyance to the homesteaders destroying their crops and rendering it next to impossible to stay on their claims.

The Olives asserted that it was not farming country. That they could not obey the herd law of Nebraska and that the homesteader had no right that they would respect, and threatened dire vengence on any one who dared to interfere with their stock.[14]

In the fall of 1878, the conflict between the Olive brothers and the homesteaders came to climax when Ami "Whit" Ketchum and his partner, Luther Mitchell, found their fences cut, the fields full of Olive longhorns, and their corn destroyed. Ketchum retaliated by going after the "slow elk" in the canyons of Custer County and selling the meat in Kearny. When the Olive brothers discovered the cattle rustling, they wangled a sheriff who "was not too fastidious in these matters" to deputize them and their cowboys so they go after Ketchum and Mitchell "legally."[15] The gun battle that followed left one of the Olive brothers dead and another member of their crew badly wounded. Ketchum and Mitchell eventually surrendered to the authorities only to be lynched and their bodies burned by the Olive gang.

The site of the shoot-out was about ten miles from the Higgins farm. Billy Higgins, who was about fourteen years old, went to pick up his gun that Ketchum was to repair and found the following scene: "When I came on the hill a short distance from the Mitchell and Ketchum home I discovered that the hay stacks, outbuildings and the roof of the sod house had been burned and everything of value for the homesteader had been destroyed."[16] The dying Olive brother was at a ranch half a mile away, but young Higgins declined when asked if he wanted to see the wounded man. The "Mitchell and Ketchum Tragedy" was made famous by publication of H. M. Hatch's photographs of the burned bodies and the Solomon Butcher photographs of re-enactments of the events.[17]

In the midst of this anything but peaceful setting, the Higgins family established churches and schools and developed their farm as they carried their culture and values to the new environment. The conflicts between the ranchers and the homesteaders do not appear in the family histories written by Elsie and Ruth but are told by their Uncle Billy some forty years after the event. The family history includes descriptions of the rugged land, the visits of churchmen and other travelers, the daily events of a farm family, and the hardships that were overcome.

Nancy's father, Adrian Higgins, was described as "a patriarch in Jesus, a staunch upholder of the teachings of Wesley, and it was under his roof that Elder Lemin, the pioneer of Methodism in Nebraska, preached and held the first quarterly conference in the county."[18] Mary Jane, Adrian's second wife and Nancy's mother, had been an uneducated hired girl, considerably younger than Adrian. They kept the doors of their home open to travelers and for worship services. However, Mary Jane Higgins was described in her widowed later years as difficult to live with and unable to "adjust to pioneer life and the lives of her grown children and their families." She tried living with various members of the family but always to returned to live with Nancy and her husband.[19]

The middle child of nine children, Nancy Rebecca Higgins was thirteen when the family emigrated to this turbulent plains setting. At home with her mother and sisters, she learned women's traditional skills in quilting, cooking, gardening, and caring for others. Amanda, Sophrona, and Mary were older than Nancy, perhaps old enough to have thoroughly learned their gender roles before emigrating to Nebraska. Nancy, however, was regarded as her father's best livestock herder and a trusted horsewoman even in her early teens. She herded the cattle to the range land in the morning and to the fenced stockyard for the night.

It was not unusual for a teenaged girl such as Nancy Higgins to herd cattle. As a tall thirteen year old, she was probably more physically able to herd than her brothers who were only eleven and five. Especially during the first few years of settlement, the children of the settlers were essential members of the working unit of the family. They did the essential homemaking, ranching, and farming tasks, and herding was one of the most common tasks for children.[20]

Her teen years "were spent quite largely in the saddle," and she continued to handle horses and cattle throughout her life.[21] Nancy was an active partner with her husband William, in the work of their stock farm. Their son, Porter, relayed with apparent pride, the stories about his mother's horsewomanship:

A Sense of Unity

There were rattlesnakes a-plenty, and Mother could kill one with her whip [without getting off her horse]. . . .

My Mother did not lose her ability to handle horses. Father always wanted a team of mules. One day he came in the house and told mother he was about to trade his "Old Charley," a family type of horse for a team of small mules. He said they were broken all right, but it would not be safe for her to drive at least for a time. Mother did not consent to the trade and said that if they got them, she would drive them. He made the deal and a short time afterward Mother told him she must go to town and to hitch up the mules to the spring wagon. She took Birney [Porter's brother] and me with her. They started out for a mile or two in a gallop. Mother just held them to the road and let them go. And as they got tired, Jack got lazy and she had to use the whip on him, and she did that too! She brought us safely home, and I think Father was glad to see her.[22]

Because Nancy had confidence in her ability to handle the team, the mules proved to be no barrier to her determination to go to town.

Nancy was educated at the district school built on her father's land and the coeducational Gibbon Academy, a Baptist boarding school at Gibbon, Nebraska. The first school near Douglas Grove was organized in 1875, with Mrs. E. D. Eubank as teacher of the subscription school.[23] The Eubanks had settled in the area during the spring of 1874, along with Nancy's older sister, Martha Hale, her husband Charles, and their children. By the fall of 1875, District No. 1 was organized, and plans were made to build a log schoolhouse. Before the elected school directors, including Adrian Higgins, could agree on the location of the school, a prairie fire destroyed the logs, so a sod school-house was built on the Higgins farm where Nancy and her brothers and sisters attended school. In 1882, after Nancy had attended the boarding academy for a semester, she taught her younger sisters, brother, nieces and nephews, and her neighbors' children at the District No. 1 schoolhouse.

Supplies for the Higgins family that could not be homegrown were obtained from Grand Island, seventy-five miles away, or Kearney, about sixty miles distant. When Nancy was fourteen, her father brought home a load of supplies, including fabric for new dresses for all the girls. Unfortunately, he brought red fabric for Nancy, who really wanted a blue dress, hence the name for Elsie's book about Nancy,

Make Mine Blue. She refused the red yard goods and was the only Higgins girl without a new dress that fall. "When [Adrian] made his list for the next trip, he made this notation: 'Five yards of serge. Blue it shall be.' He also took with him a letter [Nancy] had written to the storekeeper, suggesting only blue would be acceptable."[24]

The merchant, T. C. Robert, was pleased with her beautiful hand-writing and awarded her a pair of shoes. Nancy kept the letter.

> Kearney March 26, 1876
> My little Friend Nancy
>   I received your very welcome and very well written letter some time ago and I assure you I was glad to hear from you and in deed it does you credit. There are very few little girls of your age that can excel you in your writing. I think you are fully entitled to the Shoes and when you come down again you can select any you wish out of my store. . . .
>   . . . you should make it your duty to do everything in your power to make your Father and Mother happy whilst they are with you for you never know how to appreciate them until they are taken away . . .
>   . . . . Wishing you a happy and continued life and my kindest regards to all I am
>   Very Truly Your Friend
>   T. C. Robert
>   Tell your Father I will look for him as soon as the weather gets good.[25]

The preservation of a small collection of letters Nancy received as a teenager remains one of the puzzles in discovering her story. Were these letters saved because they were addressed only to Nancy? These letters, written by several of Nancy's girlfriends from 1879 to 1882, are delightfully adolescent accounts of the events and people who were important in her life at that time. In Carrie Callen's letter of October 18, 1879, to seventeen-year-old Nancy, there are regrets at having missed company and promises of good times to come.

> Sunday Afternoon Oct. 18th, 1879
> Miss Nancy Higgins
>   Dear Nancy
> As the girls are all gone away but Eliza and I, I will write you a few lines to pass away time. Nancy I am sorry I was not at home

last Friday evening, for I would surely went home with them.
I have wanted to come up and see you but I did not get any
chance to come. Our folks went after plums. They were not very
far from your place. I did not go. I suppose you are having good
times riding your pony. Wait till I come up we will have another
horse back ride. . . . I must go and get (dinner supper). So I will
close hoping to see you soon.

Please excuse all mistakes and poor writing. This paper is all I
have so please excuse.

Give my respects to all.

Carrie Callen

P. O. Balsora

Sherman Co.

Come & see me when you can. Tell Billie [Nancy's brother] I lay
the blame all on him because you have not been down here. Tell
him I will pull his ears good when I come up there.[26]

In the fall of 1881, when Nancy was nineteen, she, her sister
Lizzie, aged fifteen, and seventeen-year-old brother Billy, attended
Gibbon Academy, the Baptist boarding school seventy miles from
home. Her parents must have valued education to have sent the
three children away to school. They may have been sent together
for company and so that they could live together, sharing boarding
expenses. Perhaps Nancy was detained from going to the academy
earlier because she would have traveled and lived alone at Gibbon.
Sending the three teenagers together may also have been an attempt
to educate them so that they could earn their own living and not
go astray like the next oldest sister, Mary Jane. According to the
family stories she may have had a child out of wedlock and disappeared while in her teens. When School District No. 1 was organized
in 1877, school was held in "A dugout belonging to Mary Jane
Higgins on the south side of the creek."[27] The rest of her story
is unknown.

Like many students attending the forerunners of the public high
school, the Higgins children rented rooms and fixed their own meals;
there were no dormitories at Gibbon Academy. In Frania Albert's letter of September 28, 1881, she asked about Nancy's housekeeping,
responded to Nancy's homesickness, and relayed the news about various boyfriends in the rest of her letter.

Chapter 5

Douglas Grove
Custer Co., Nebr.
Sept. 28th 1881
 Miss Nancy Higgins,
 Dear Friend
 I will try and answer your kind and welcome letter. I was very
glad to hear from you, but sorry that you was feeling so lonesome
& homesick. Try and keep up good cheer for you know, *such is
life*. Well Nancy we are all well, but . . . I have had the Tooth-
Ache for the past Week. I haven't seen Will___Wa___ since
you are gone, *Oh* yes I did once and a sick looking fellow he was.
I know he mourns your absence. . . . well how do you like House-
keeping, dont it make you feel old but I supose you are taking a
lesson for the future. I wonder if it would ent be a good Idea for
me to do the same what do you Think about it.
 Nancy I remember the long talk we had the sunday I was at
your place. I would give a small farm to see you today. I could tell
you more than I care to write, and as for me geting married,
There is many a slip—twixt cup and lip, as the old saying is.
I cant tell you yet what I intend to do. There is nothing new
happened out here for me to write so I cant write a long letter
this time, but I would like to see some of those nice fellows down
there. And tell Willie [Nancy's brother] not to let some of those
pretty Girls take his Eye . . . And as for Lizzie [Nancy's sister] I
don't ever expect to see her back agen for she will step off with
some good looking chap, and then she will say
 Good-by, Douglas Grove.
Well I will close for this Time hoping to hear from you soon. . . .
from your friend
 Frania Albert[28]

In Frania's letter to Nancy in November 1881, she again sympa-
thizes with Nancy for being lonely and expresses her longing for her
previous home in Wisconsin.

Douglas Grove
Nov. 6th 1881
Nancy Higgins,
 Dear friend, it is some time ago since I re'd your letter, you no
doubt think I have forgotten you but such is not the case. I often

think of you and feel sorry for you to think you are Homesick and haveing so much Trouble. . . . Raths folks moved over on there clame last Week. Dick Eubanks intend to move soon. There wont be any one left around here after while if they keep on a going as they have lately. I whish you were here. It would do me good to see you and have a talk with you. I get so Homesick sometimes I don't know what to do. I never wanted to go back to Wis. as bad as I do now, since I'v been here. I would go tomorrow if I could get to the Railroad. . . . Please don't wait as long as I did before you answer this, and dont think unkind of you friend,

    Frania Albert
    my love to all and a good share for yourself.
Good By. Write soon.[29]

The letters between homesick girls must have provided welcomed support and understanding. Frania, a relative newcomer to Nebraska, was homesick for Wisconsin and was concerned about the families moving away from Douglas Grove. Although Nancy was with her brother and sister, she longed for the family farm in Custer County, Nebraska.

In March 1882, shortly before Nancy started to teach, she received a letter from her Gibbon Academy schoolmate, Metta Dungan. Metta had dropped out of the academy, was very lonesome at home, and reported on her successful visit at Gibbon Academy.

Newark Neb. March 28, 1882
Miss Nancy Higgins:
Dear Friend, It has been sometime since I received your letter but have been very busy ever since. You will perhaps be supprised to hear that I have quite going to school, I am thinking of teaching dont know how it will be yet. I know how to sympathize with you in my lonelyness. I have been terrible lonley since I come home. I came home two weeks ago. have been back to Gibbon once, went over last wednesday and came back Thursday had a very pleasant time. . . . on friday night I went to the Literary, saturday night—to the Drama, sunday night—church. monday night a party. tuesday night a sencible. wednesday night—prayer meeting. I came home thursday morning on the Denver at 3 o'clock. . . . You aught to have been here valentine day. We had a glorious old time sending valentines. Some of us girls got

to-gether and sent ten. I got two. . . . Do you think you will ever come back to Gibbon to school? I think I will go back next fall. It is getting late I will close. Write soon.

> Your schoolmate and Friend
> Metta Dungan
> Direct: Newark Kearney Co., Nebr. [30]

The academy provided both social and educational experiences for Nancy and her friends, in much the same way as the teachers' institutes did for other young people on the plains.

Nancy received another letter from Metta in May 1882, written during recess at the school where Metta was teaching. She still longed for her friends from Gibbon Academy and was full of comments about her pupils, attendance at an institute, and feeling lonely.

> Newark, May 6, 1882
> Miss Nancy Higgins:
> Dear Friend,
> I received your letter sometime ago, was glad to hear from you. It makes me shudder yet to think of that night you were lost. Weren't you terribly frightened. If you weren't you are a great deal braver than I am. Well I have begun teaching. Have about eighteen pupils and they are all so full of mischief they dont know what to do with themselves. One little girl said one day that she was so full of tickle she could not behave herself. I felt like taking the tickle out. If my letter is not very well connected you will have to excuse it for every few minutes some one of the scholars will come *rushing* in to tell me that such a one pinched them or something.
> O Dear, one little thing has come in squaling like fourty. I had an awful time to get her settled. Some of the girls had slapped her or something. . . . I attended an institute at Minden last week had a real pleasant time.

Metta then gossiped about a boy they both knew and named six girls, their classmates from Gibbon, who were beginning to teach. She concluded with her complaints of being lonesome on a rainy day. [31]

These few letters reveal the substance of lives of the young beginning teachers: minimal education; eager for the company of their peers, both female and male; lonely when away from their families; not sure about teaching school; somewhat resigned to the conditions at hand; speculative about marriage for themselves and others; and full of local gossip.

By the spring of 1882, Nancy had earned her teaching certificate through the courses at Gibbon Academy, and had signed a contract to teach District No. 4, Custer County, a sod schoolhouse with an enrollment of forty-five children ranging in age from four to seventeen. Her handwritten contract was for

> . . . the term of two months commencing on the 1st day of May, A. D. 1882; and the said teacher agrees faithfully to observe and enforce the rules and regulations established by the district board, and agrees to keep herself qualified. The said John Draper [school director] in behalf of said district, agrees to keep the school-house in good repair, and to provide the necessary fuel, and to pay said Nancy Higgins for the said services as a teacher, to be faithfully and truly-rendered and performed the sum of twenty six dollars a month . . . to be paid on or before the 15th day of July 1882. Provided, that in case said teacher shall be dismissed from school by the district board for gross immorality, or violation of this contract, or shall have her certificate annulled by the county superintendent she shall not be entitled to any compensation from and after such dismissal or annulment. In witness whereof we hereunto subscribe our names this day of May 1st A. D. 1882.
>
> Approved by John Draper, Director,
> Thos. S. Woddard, Moderator
> Nancy Higgins teacher[32]

After only one term at District No. 4, Nancy moved for the fall term of 1882 and taught at District No. 1, on her father's land. Nancy recorded the names, ages, and attendance of all her pupils in her attendance book. Although her salary did not increase, she had only sixteen scholars and could live at home. Among her sixteen pupils were her sisters, Lizzie, age sixteen; and Ella (Elcena), fourteen; and her five nieces and nephews, ages six, eight, nine, eleven, and thirteen. Perhaps luckily, four-year-old Charlie Webster only attended once a week. She used the margins of the attendance book to list some of her expenses representing close to a month's salary:

Chapter 5

7.50 shoes	.25 book
3.25 hat	1.30 4th of July expenses
8.00 dress	2.40 dry goods[33]

Nancy's youngest brother, Alfred, aged thirteen, joined his sisters and cousins during the spring term of 1883. Having family members as her scholars was common for any teacher who lived at home and was most likely a trial for many teachers as their brothers and other relatives tested their teacher's control and patience. "[Nancy] often told of the trouble she had with her brother Alfred and [her nephew] Burt Hale who went to school to her. They would reach into the sod wall behind their seats and pinch out clods of sod and flip them at other students when [Nancy] wasn't looking."[34]

While Nancy was living at home and teaching, William C. Gaddis, a homesteader from Iowa, staked a timber claim just three miles from the Higgins farm in the fall of 1882. According to the Timber Culture Act of 1873, legislation enacted in a futile to attempt to forest the plains, 160 acres could be added to the homesteader's land holdings if trees were planted on at least forty acres within four years of settling. While nine out of ten such claims were not forested, William Gaddis planted several hundred trees on about ten acres and made improvements such as digging a well and building a sod house twelve by sixteen feet.[35] While making these improvements, William courted Nancy. In October 1882, Nancy wrote a sentimental love poem, possibly the lyrics to a song, in her attendance book.

Sunday Oct. 29th 1882
I have loved you to fondly
To ever forget
The love you have spoken to me
And the kiss of affection
Still warm on my lips
When you told me how true you would be
. . . But I know that I love
you whereever you roam
I'll remember you love
In my prayers.[36]

On the next page, she listed her expenses for April 11, 1883, the day she and William were married. Among such typical wedding expenses

A Sense of Unity

as $2.00 for photographs and $2.25 for the trip to Grand Island, were the practical necessities of life: salt, $.10; sugar, $1.00, and plough fixed for $3.35. Nancy also listed $1.00 for "certificate." This may have been her teaching certificate for the next term, as she taught at least one term after she was married.

From her teaching salary, Nancy bought "brilliantine" yard goods for her wedding dress that was "a shiny, golden brown with silk threads running through."[37] For the wedding festivities, a table had been set up outside with a white tablecloth. Before the ceremony began, bees swarmed in the tree above the table, and the ceremony was delayed while the men hived the swarm. Sugar was expensive and often hard to obtain, making the unexpected "gift" of a swarm of bees welcomed by the newlyweds. William hired a cabinetmaker to build a pine cupboard as his wedding gift for his "Wifey," his pet name for Nancy. The cupboard is now owned by a granddaughter.

The Gaddis farm was among the last farmland homesteaded in the county, then "Free range land was at an end."[38] They soon had 400 acres, and eventually they bought land adjacent to theirs bringing the Golden Rod Stock Farm to 720 acres. Their daughter Ruth described her mother's garden at the farm:

> There was a large, fenced yard with several fruit trees, a straw-
> berry bed and a row of rhubarb. This area was almost sacred to
> Mother for it was her beloved garden. She did most of the work
> because she was so particular we seldom offered our services lest
> we pull a radish instead of a weed. There was a small never-
> mowed lawn area as lawn mowers had not yet made their appear-
> ance on the rural scene. Large cedar trees lined the path to the
> front door and later Mother planted a row of Lombardi poplars to
> protect the house from winter winds.[39]

Nancy's son, Porter Gaddis remembered:

> Mother was a great provider for the family. She always raised a
> good garden and canned a lot of tomatoes. We picked wild
> fruit,—gooseberries, chokecherries, and plums chiefly. We cured
> meat, her "Smokehouse" being a large barrel. She made all of
> our clothes with the exception of the big drought-year of 1894
> when "aid" was shipped in from the East to local churches. Bir-

ney and I each had an overcoat and a cap, gifts from some boys back East.[40]

Nancy's teaching days ended shortly after she was married. Her contributions, all well within woman's sphere, to the family and leadership in the growing community continued throughout her life. She had a strong soprano voice and "led the singing and superintended the Sunday School in a little Free Methodist Church, with which they united around 1890."[41] Always a staunch supporter of temperance, Nancy was a life member and president of the Comstock Women's Christian Temperance Union. She was also a life member of the Women's Foreign Missionary Society. Nancy sewed without pay for those who needed help, and she was proud of her fine quilting stitches. In fact, she was known to remove quilting done by others if the stitches didn't measure up to her standards. Her favorite patterns were flower garden, log cabin, morning star, the hand of friendship, and trip-around-the-world. She helped others in time of illness, death, and childbirth, delivering about thirty babies.

It was apparently important to Nancy and William to be kept well-informed, as they subscribed to the *Chicago Daily News*, which came by mail a week or two late, and various religious, home, and farm magazines. The children regularly read *Youth's Companion*. During the period 1880–1900, newspapers and magazines became numerous and inexpensive, with 80 percent of the magazines costing only ten cents a copy by 1900.[42] The family kept up with national and local politics, partly the influence of Nancy's brother, Billy, who was a Populist state legislator for one term in 1892, and was re-elected as a Republican in 1894. When the old schoolhouse was torn down, the voting records found there revealed more of the consistency in Nancy's life. She was the one woman in the school district who never failed to vote in the school elections.[43]

The measure of this family's values can best be seen in the ways in which their successive generations were educated and acted upon the family's moral and ethical beliefs. William Gaddis had only a sixth grade education. "Through rigid economy and sacrifice," however, he and Nancy made it possible for their four children to be well educated.[44] The oldest three Gaddis children, Birney, Porter, and Elsie, began their educations in the sod schoolhouse, District No. 143, with Mrs. Alma Howard, wife of the Congregational minister, as their teacher. The family moved to Orleans, Nebraska, a hundred miles from the farm, when the boys, Birney and Porter, were seventeen and fifteen, so that they could attend the Free Methodist Seminary. Elsie was nine and attended school in town, and Ruth Elizabeth was still a baby. The family moved back and forth from town to farm and finally stayed on the farm when Ruth was ready to begin ninth grade.

Birney and Porter next attended Greenville College, the Free Methodist College in Illinois. Porter came home to the farm for the summer and was hired to teach in District No. 143 at forty dollars a month. Birney married Myrtle Graham, his girlfriend from Orleans (Nebraska) Seminary, and together they went to the Free Methodist Seminary at Evansville, Wisconsin, where they taught and boarded students. After being in business for several years, Birney then served the Free Methodist Church as publishing agent and church treasurer, and he established the church's radio ministry. In recognition of his service to the church, Birney was awarded an honorary doctorate from Greenville College.

After his marriage to Merle Wilson, Porter's teaching career included teaching Greek at the college level; and teaching agriculture for about eleven years at the University of Nebraska. He then worked in land insurance and headed a land program for the federal government under Franklin Roosevelt.

Elsie attended Orleans Seminary when the family lived in town and there met Chester McKinney. After Chester graduated from Orleans, he attended Evansville Seminary in Wisconsin. Elsie finished high school in 1911 at the Evansville Seminary while living with Birney and Myrtle. The rules of the seminary and living with her brother and his wife, must have made courting a real challenge for Chester and Elsie. During the summer of 1912, both Elsie and Chester attended the Junior Normal School at Alma, Nebraska. Elsie's father allowed them to use the family buggy for their daily, six-mile commute to summer school classes. Elsie taught country school while Chester finished his bachelor's degree at Evansville. When he graduated, he took the position of principal of the Anoka, Nebraska, High School, and took his bride, Elsie, with him.

The move to Anoka gave Ruth her opportunity to attend high school while living with Elsie and Chester. Later Ruth and her husband, Leonard Wilson, stayed close to the land as county extension agents in agriculture and home economics in Nebraska and Indiana.

This educational heritage and continuity of the settlers in this area of Nebraska was carried on by a number of members of the community.

At least three of Nancy's pupils from 1882–1883 became teachers in District No. 1: Mary Hale, 1886; Alice Dowse, 1894; and Eliza Dowse. At an anniversary of the founding of School District No. 1, it was determined that twelve of the former teachers, from 1875 to the 1930s, lived in or near the district.[45]

The importance to the settlers of family, education, religion, and the land, are brought together through the lives of William and Nancy Higgins Gaddis. They lived to see their children and grandchildren well educated as farmers and business people, church workers and missionaries, librarians and teachers, responsible citizens. While there are gaps in the narrative of Nancy Higgins Gaddis, her life is shared through stories selected for remembrance by her daughters and sons, and preserved by her granddaughter, Eleanor McKinney.

Nancy Higgins, age seventeen, homesteaders' daughter and horsewoman, Douglas Grove, Nebraska, 1879. (Photo by M. Murphy, Grand Island, Nebraska; courtesy of Eleanor McKinney)

The Higgins home was open to visitors, travelers, and church meetings. (Courtesy of Eleanor McKinney)

Among the scholars in Nancy Higgins's school were her sisters, her neighbors' children, and the Hale children, her nieces and nephews. (Courtesy of Eleanor McKinney)

Pages in Nancy Higgins's attendance book were used for recording a love poem, and her expenses for her wedding day, April 11, 1883. (Courtesy Eleanor McKinney)

A Sense of Unity

William C. and Nancy
Higgins Gaddis, married
April 11, 1883,
Douglas Grove, Nebraska.
(Courtesy Eleanor
McKinney)

The rolling land of Wil-
liam and Nancy Gaddis's
timber claim, where
planting several hundred
trees and maintaining a
home were requirements
for proving up. (Courtesy
Eleanor McKinney)

Chapter 5

The rugged terrain of the Grand Cañon, part of the Gaddis's claim. (Courtesy Eleanor McKinney)

The Gaddis children attended the sod schoolhouse, No. 143, with Mrs. Alma Howard as their teacher. Birney and Porter Gaddis also taught at No. 143. (Courtesy Eleanor McKinney)

A Sense of Unity

Nancy Higgins Gaddis was a life member of the Women's Christian Temperance Union, as were many of her contemporaries. (Courtesy Eleanor McKinney)

Picnics were a favorite outing for the Gaddis children and their friends while attending the Seminary. Elsie Gaddis, center, front row, attended the Evansville Seminary, Wisconsin, to complete her high school education, 1911. (Courtesy Eleanor McKinney)

Chapter 5

Elsie Gaddis lived with her brother Birney and his wife, Myrtle, when they taught and boarded students at the Evansville Seminary, Wisconsin. (Courtesy Eleanor McKinney)

Courtship under the strict rules of the Seminary wasn't easy, but childhood sweethearts, Elsie Gaddis and Chester McKinney, persevered. (Courtesy Eleanor McKinney)

A Sense of Unity

Elsie Gaddis and Chester McKinney attended the Junior Normal School, Alma, Nebraska, 1912. (Courtesy Eleanor McKinney)

After completing high school and attending the Junior Normal School, Elsie Gaddis taught near home, District No. 29, Comstock, Nebraska, 1912. (Courtesy Eleanor McKinney)

Anoka Public High School, 1914. When Chester McKinney completed college at Evansville Seminary, he was hired as the principal of the public high school, Anoka, Nebraska. Chester and Elsie went to Anoka as newlyweds in 1914. (Courtesy Eleanor McKinney)

A Sense of Unity

Prairie citizens: William and Nancy Higgins Gaddis, front row, center, with their children (names in italics) and grandchildren at their Golden Rod Stock Farm, 1922. Front row, left to right: Birney and Myrtle's daughters, Kathleen Gaddis Hicks (homemaker), Bernardine Gaddis Biddulph (missionary, Columbia); *Elsie Gaddis McKinney* (teacher, homemaker, book reviewer), Elsie and Chester's daughter, Eleanor McKinney (professor of librarianship, Western Michigan University), Nancy Higgins Gaddis, William Gaddis; Porter and Merle's daughter, Mildred Gaddis (professor and musician, University of Delaware). Back row, left to right: *Birney Gaddis* (manager, Free Methodist Publishing House); Porter's daughter, Marian Gaddis Deuser (homemaker); Myrtle Graham Gaddis (Birney's wife, homemaker); Chester A. McKinney, (professor of business education, Rider College, New Jersey); Elsie's daughter, Doris McKinney MacLaclan (teacher, homemaker); Merle Wilson Gaddis (Porter's wife, homemaker); *Porter Gaddis* (professor of agriculture, University of Nebraska, land grant supervisor for the U. S. Government, and for Equitable Insurance); Leonard Wilson (Ruth's husband, county extension agent in Nebraska, then executive secretary, of Indiana Implement Dealers Association); *Ruth Gaddis Wilson* (teacher, homemaker, county extension agent in Nebraska, then with Indiana Implement Dealers Association). (Courtesy Eleanor McKinney)

Chapter 5

"Greater Usefulness in My Calling"

Sarah Jane Price, Ohio, 1841–1843; Indiana, 1843–1874; Iowa, 1874–76; Nebraska, 1876–1920

July 20th, [1880]

. . . My Algebra, Physiology, and housework occupied most of the time [today]. I hope I am gaining little by little and preparing myself for greater usefulness in my calling and hope to make a more successful teacher in the future. Today has been remarkably cool and pleasant for the time of year and tonight is too cool for mosquitoes, even on the cow. When I went to milk, she did not have to fight them as she always does. The moon is shining very clear and bright and it is light as day out of doors.—Jane Price

As a teacher, homemaker, independent thinker, community leader, farmer, and landowner, Sarah Jane Price represents the pioneer as defined by Jesse Bernard: those women who "had the dynamism associated with maleness harnessed to the people-oriented, humanitarian achievement values associated with femaleness."[1] Sarah Jane Price was a pioneer of the prairies, an independent, unmarried woman whose daily activities and thoughts were recorded in her extant diaries, beginning in November of 1878 and extending into 1895. Jane Price, as she signed her diary entries, wrote sparsely, to the point, and without many details, emotions, or elaborations.[2]

In her recorded thoughts she sought "greater usefulness in [her] call-ing" through knowledge and self-improvement, generally in keeping with her Christian values and with the "moral imperative . . . to care, a responsibility to discern and alleviate the 'real and recognizable trouble' of this world."[3] Jane Price often used the "language of respon-sibility" and caring as she wrote about her relationships, observations, and opinions of events and people.[4] And as for those who "unreason-ably" didn't agree with her, Jane could get along "without their good opinion." The intrepid spirit of Jane Price and her life are documented throughout her almost daily journal entries, a description of her trip to an international Sunday school conference in Europe in 1907, and a few school notes, all housed at the Nebraska State Historical Soci-ety, and the family memorabilia and recollections of her nieces and grandnephew.

The events of her first thirty-seven years, and the years from the early 1900s to her death in 1920, are the puzzle pieces drawn in part from U. S. Census Records of Indiana and Nebraska, Nebraska prop-erty records, and histories of Rush County, Indiana, and Hamilton and Hall Counties, Nebraska. Additional clues are found throughout Jane Price's diaries and miscellaneous papers, and in the letters and documents preserved by family members.

The Price family had lived in Ohio where five of the children, in-cluding Sarah Jane, were born. In 1843, they moved to a farm near Rushville, Indiana. The Census of 1850 for Rush County, Indiana, lists Daniel and Sarah A. Price and their six children. Abigail, thir-teen, William C. (Christy), eleven, and Sarah J. (Jane), eight, at-tended school that year, but John, aged four, and two-year-old Charles were too young to go to school. Fourteen-year old Elizabeth (Lib), the oldest child, is not listed as attending school. Although there were three academies in the Rushville area in the 1840s, she may have completed as much schooling as the growing Price family could afford, and she was most certainly needed to help at home. In Indiana, four more sons were born to Daniel and Sarah A. Price: Jeremiah, 1843–1846; Francis Marion (Frank), 1851; Alonzo W. (Lon), 1856; and Daniel Edgar (Ed), 1858.

By the mid-1850s, free schools in Rush County were apparently mistrusted by "those who desire for their children something more in the way of educational facilities than they believed possible under the new system and the 'seminary' idea persisted."[5] In 1855, the Rushville area had five academies, including the Richland Academy. "The academy inspired a taste for intellectual things . . . and the presence of so many interesting young people brightened social life and gave it a marked literary tone."[6]

Jane's brother, Christy (William C.) is listed as an arithmetic teacher at the Richland Academy in 1861.[7] At the outbreak of the Civil War, John McKee, principal of Richland Academy, "recruited a company (K Company, Thirty-seventh Regiment, Indiana Volunteer Infantry), half of the members of which had been students at the academy, and went to the front. . ."[8] Christy's lame foot may have prevented him from joining the Union Army along with others from the academy. Despite his lameness, however, Christy joined Company C, 134th Regiment on May 6, 1864, and was mustered out when his 100-day term expired.

The events of Jane Price's life during the 1850s to mid-1870s are sparsely documented by a few references in her diaries and her Iowa teaching certificates of 1874–76. Jane occasionally notes in her diaries the anniversary of her mother's death and her deceased siblings' birthdays and states how old they would have been on that date. Jane's mother, Sarah A. Price, died at age forty-six in 1858, leaving at home five boys under the age of twelve, including the baby, Ed. The three older children may no longer have been living at home as Jane, at age seventeen was remembered by the family as the "mother of them all" after Sarah died.[9]

A few years later, in 1866 and 1867, both Christy, aged twenty-seven, and Abigail, aged thirty, died of consumption.[10] Jane remembered Christy as "dear Christy, our brother, / Our love, our pride, his equal, no other, / He was diligently perusing divinities books." Abigail was characterized as "our gentle sister, Abbie with hands so fair, / Was making a garment which I was to wear." Gentle Abbie, like Jane, had her own opinions, as she debated with brother Charles "the matter of strife, / Which is the greatest slave, the negro or wife."[11]

The 1870 Census of Rush County, Indiana lists the family as consisting of Daniel, 57, farmer, Sarah J., 28, housekeeper, Francis M., 19, Lonzo W., 16 and Daniel E., 14. John was attending Illinois Wesleyan University, and then taught in Illinois before moving to Nebraska in 1873. Elizabeth was married and living in Indiana, and Charles had moved to Iowa.

About 1874, when Jane was in her early thirties, she moved west to Polk County, Iowa accompanied by her father, Daniel, and younger brothers, Lon and Ed. Jane taught school for three years in Iowa while the family lived near Charles. They then moved to Hamilton County, Nebraska to live near John who was teaching children during the day, and adults in the evenings at College Corners School.[12]

As her diaries open in 1878, Jane was thirty-seven years old. Her father, aged sixty-five, and brothers Ed, twenty-two, and Lon, twenty-four, lived with her in a sod house near Phillips, Nebraska. "The boys," Lon and Ed, worked on the Price farm, hired out as threshers, and, according to Jane, spent too much time going to dances. Her father, Daniel A. Price, occupied his time visiting various neighbors, his married children in Nebraska and Indiana, and doing some of the less demanding farm chores such as churning. The 1880 Census for Hamilton County, Nebraska, lists Daniel as crippled with rheumatism, but Jane never mentions this affliction.

The Price family along with other settlers from Illinois, Missouri, Iowa, Ohio, Indiana, Wisconsin, Germany, and Sweden, found the soil of Hamilton County, south of the great Platte River, was well-suited to general farming but dependent on sufficient rainfall. Even though the available homesteads in the county had been claimed by 1873, an 1876 booklet advertising the benefits of Hamilton County to prospective settlers lauded the land as ideal for sheep and swine raising, stock breeding, general gardening, and listed its major products as "wheat, oats, rye, barley, flax, hemp, corn, broom corn, buckwheat, millet, . . . , sorghum, peas, beans, Irish and sweet potatoes, peanuts, onions, turnips and all vegetables of the field."[13]

Jane Price's farming and gardening supports this impressive list of products. Her garden produced potatoes, corn, asparagus, rutabagas, tomatoes, horseradish, strawberries, peas, cucumbers, squash, pumpkins, sweet corn, cabbage, beets, peppers, melons, huckleberries, currants, raspberries, and flowers. She harvested the garden produce for her family's use, traded some among her neighbors, and peddled onions, garden crops, eggs, baby chicks, and old roosters in town. In addition to her typically female chores such as gardening, homemaking, milking, and feeding the stock, Jane produced, bought, and sold wheat, corn, and livestock. She planted, cultivated, and harvested acres of wheat, corn, and onions, shoveled manure, trimmed the orchards, built the privy, smokehouse, and the hen house, and lathed the bedrooms in preparation for the plasterer. Jane planted a large number of trees on the farm and on her lots in town: silver maples, cottonwoods, walnuts, black locust, and, anticipating an orchard, peach pits. Brothers Lon and Ed were also actively involved in all the farm labors, hired out as threshers, and played in a band, but it is evident from Jane's diaries, that she was in charge of the farm's management.

Hamilton County was a different agricultural region than the range-land of Custer County where the Higgins family settled amid the range wars of the early 1870s. The major conflict of Hamilton County was the "county seat war," which pitted the political forces of the young communities of Orville, Aurora, and Hamilton against each other. After five elections extending from 1870 to 1877, Aurora finally had a majority of eighty votes and the court house was built at Aurora. By the 1880s, Orville became the site of the county poor farm, "while Hamilton has almost become a deserted village."[14] Out of the county seat controversy, the Greenback Party emerged, bringing defeat to the Republican ticket.[15]

The Greenback following did not help Jane when she ran for county superintendent on the Greenback ticket in 1879. Her brother, John T. Price, who had been one of the first teachers in the county and the third county superintendent of schools, 1874–75, may have encouraged Jane to run. She was hesitant, but wrote, "I don't suppose I can, but I should like to have it, if I could fill the place successfully." While the records indicate that she ran on the Greenback ticket, Jane indicated that she was an independent candidate. Viewing herself as independent may have been the only way that Jane, who believed that everyone should be "Republican and Methodist," could run against the incumbent.[16] She made no mention in her journal that she had campaigned for the elected office against the well-established Republican E. B. Barton. She was defeated by Barton who held the post 1877–1883 and 1885–1889.[17] When Jane got the election results, it does not appear from her diary that she was particularly surprised or disappointed in the results. Or, perhaps, she thoroughly understood her personal feelings, so there was little need to write about them. She noted on November 7, 1879, "learned what I had felt certain was so before: that I am elected to stay at home and let Mr. Barton attend to the Supt. office which is satisfactory to me." Although Jane and E. B. Barton were political rivals in 1879, he continued to be her superintendent and signed her teaching certificates.

Apparently a gregarious woman, there were few days, except during the most severe weather, when Jane did not visit with the men, women, and children who were relatives and neighbors. Jane repeatedly determined that it had been a pleasant day, "barrin' the wind," and wrote descriptions of the weather, such as on October 8, 1879: "This has been a very warm day and windy enough to astonish anybody but a Nebraskan." The Nebraska wind and weather did little to keep Jane from becoming well known. Indeed, "'Aunt Jane' was considered an 'Institution' in Hamilton County, with her outstanding personality and leadership. She was an authority on many subjects and throughout her lifetime was revered by a wide circle of friends and admirers."[18] She enjoyed visiting with her friends, and attended reunions, Fourth of July celebrations, Christmas and New Year's parties. Important aspects of Jane's femininity were her ongoing attachments, "social interaction and personal relationships" with her friends.[19] After a basket meeting (pot luck dinner) at St. Joe, Sunday July 16, 1883, Jane wrote: "Altogether I enjoyed the day very well . . . We ate our dinners at Mrs. Lutz's. Bro. Millers, Purdys, Doc Arnolds and us united our supplies and set a large table. Had a good social time. Doc and some of us had a 'set to' on baptism which I enjoyed very much. I believe I beat the doctor at last. The day was very fine and pleasant."

Often friends stopped at the Price home to visit, have supper, and stay overnight. Jane and Sister Dunn visited together often just to have a "good old talk." There were many pleasant contacts among Jane and her neighbors, the Ball family, Isaiah, Sarah, and their children, Lottie, Kattie, and the twins, Charly and Lora, and the Lutz family. Mrs. Lutz, Susie, and Lon were related to Jane by the marriage of John Price to Nancy Kinsey, Mrs. Lutz's daughter by her first marriage. Jane quilted at the Sampsons and enjoyed calling on Mrs. Adams where she "had a pleasant time, was much pleased with her [Mrs. Adams'] evident intelligence, and common sense" (April 25, 1882).

Jane wrote essays for the literary societies, church meetings, and special occasions such as the Fourth of July. A few essays preserved by the family indicate the religious and moralistic tenor of her writing.[20] For her own pleasure and as a means to express her feelings, she tried her hand at religious and inspirational poetry. In one of her poems that appeared in her journal in the spring of 1880, she speaks of true friendship as the "flowers of the mind."[21]

I seek a bouquet of flowers rare,
Picked from the gardens of friends I love . . .
The flowers I seek are not all of earth . . .
Flowers of the mind, of matchless worth
Of the heart and soul that nought can blight.
Then dear friends, will you give me the flowers I love?
Pure friendship and truth without alloy . . .

Her social activities included church activities, literary societies in St. Joe and College Corners, and the Good Templars Lodge, a temperance organization, which she helped to organize and in which she served as an officer. "Aunt Jane," along with her brothers, John and Alonzo, organized the Union Sunday School which later evolved into the Methodist and Baptist churches. [22] In the Methodist Church of College Corners, and later at Phillips she was a teacher of various Sunday school classes, superintendent of the Sunday school, a member of the Ladies' Aid Society, and was involved in the organization and maintenance of the church. When the Methodist Church was organized in Phillips in 1884, Jane Price, and two men each gave $100 for the building fund. One hundred dollars was equivalent to about three months salary from teaching school. The official board of the Phillips Methodist Church of 1893–1894, included Jane Price and six men. Her place in the church was always in the first pew. [23]

In her diaries, Jane frequently wrote about what she was reading and at times, what she was thinking, but she gave very few clues about her physical appearance and strength. Once, when she met a woman for the first time, she wrote: "Jan. 2, 1883. Mr. Reiter's mother is a very large woman. I think almost as heavy as I and fully as pursy." On another occasion, she was visiting a sick neighbor, when Indians who were camped nearby came to the door. "Mrs. Arnold was afraid of them but they did no harm. One tried to come in the house but I pushed the door in his face. 'Are you a man?' said he. 'No, but I am as stout as a man,' I replied. There are about fifty of them camped down on the river" (February 6, 1882).

Webster's Common School Dictionary of 1867 defines pursy as fat and short-breathed; stout, as strong, brave; large and fleshy. Jane saw herself as a large, heavy set woman, who was diligent and undaunted. In her farming and extensive gardening, her physical endurance is apparent as the work on many occasions seems overwhelming. The strength of her opinions and values, and her independence of thought show up throughout her diaries as she enjoyed debating at the literary society with both men and women on the teams; gave Fourth of July orations, led the Sunday school, spoke for suffrage, and determined that one of her suitors, Brother Auten, was entirely unsuitable and "hopeless."

In a poem, Jane described herself as "leaving her hoe, / Out in the garden where the flowers grow. / She smiled and said 'The garden was good.' / . . . She quite often laughed, her face wore a smile, / Good nature was written there all the while."[24] This ebullient disposition was characteristic of Aunt Jane. Her grandnephew, DeRoss Andrews, recalled her laughing as she sang, "I'm an old maid, sitting in the shade, drinking lemonade . . ."[25] Her niece, Betty Merrill, remembered Aunt Jane's full skirts with large pockets containing peppermints for the children.[26] The children enjoyed the opportunity to drive Jane's horse, Charley Lazybones.

Jane's responsibilities at home included cooking for her father and brothers, for threshers and harvesters, and for occasional overnight guests and boarders. She wrote about baking bread on Saturdays and trying out or rendering the lard when a hog was butchered. Occasionally, Jane noted baking or fixing some special dishes such as nut cakes; pie plant (rhubarb), squash, and custard pies; gallons of plum butter and plum jelly; sweet tomato pickles; souse (pickled pigs' feet and ears), and sausage. She also made vinegar and yeast for her own use. Her diary from the fall of 1884 gives some insights into how she managed to teach and fulfill her homemaking tasks. "I had a nice school today and a pleasant time generally. Have been very busy since I came home, ironing, baking bread, getting supper and dressing a chicken. Am tired tonight. It has been warm but windy today." In another entry, September 15, 1884, Jane Price wrote that she had "churned this morning before school and in addition to my other work, it made hurrying to get round in time for school." She did the washing after school along with the other daily chores.

Jane Price sewed for herself making and remaking dresses, basques, sunbonnets, aprons, and underdrawers. She made shirts, socks, and overalls for her father, shirts for the boys, and sheets and towels for the family's use. Aunt Jane made clothes and toys for brother Ed's children after his wife died and they lived with her for a while. Many winter hours were spent in the company of other women, making quilts with pattern names such as rising sun, double star, hit-and-miss, hexagon, humming bird, and medley.

Chapter 6

In addition to teaching almost every term, she was "another of our first lady land owners in Town 11, as Phillips precinct was then called."[27] She was involved in buying, selling, and renting various parcels of farm land, and city lots in Phillips and Grand Island, beginning in the fall of 1879, when she bought her first farm. Her rural entrepreneurship included loaning money to neighbors and members of the family, from a few dollars up to holding notes and mortgages. Gradually throughout the 1880s, her farming and other business affairs took on more importance. Jane carried out her teaching responsibilities with thoughtful vigor, but it did not seem to be critical to her, financially or personally, to teach every term as her farming and land ownership became more successful. By the spring of 1894, she paid taxes of $118.10 on her land. At the time of her death in 1920, her estate included five lots in Phillips; two lots in Grand Island; a quarter section and eighty acres in Hamilton County. She was not a large land owner, but through her own management of her financial affairs she was independent.

Her business ventures became a very satisfying part of her life, but being a woman added frustrations to ordinary transactions. In this diary entry, she could not cash a bank draft without help from a male bank officer.

Saturday, Dec. 31st 1881

I went to Grand Island with Cliff today, had a cold ride. The wind began to blow soon after we started and blew very hard all the way over and was quite high till I came back, but we had it to our backs as we came home. I got my draft cashed but would have had trouble if I had not known Mr. Thummel. My draft was in favor of S. J. Price Esq. and the cashier would not let me have the money without it was corrected, but when I told him Thummel could identify me, he said that would do. So I went up to Thummel's office and he told me if I would endorse, he would cash it, which he did and saved me farther trouble. I got thirty five yds. of sheeting, eleven yds. of domestic, three of toweling and a pr. of overalls for father. I took over two doz. and nine eggs, and got 56 c. worth of beans for them. I ate dinner at Bro. Smith's and called at Isaiahs. All seemed well. I saw Father Dempster at Bro. Smith's. I sent for Harpers magazine and the InterOcean by money order $4.60. We got home about seven o'clock.

A Greater Usefulness in My Calling

In the course of one day's diary entry, Jane combines the important elements in her life: her friends and neighbors, home responsibilities, marketing the products of her farm, her land ownership, and self-improvement through reading. This balance of substance in her life is consistent in many of the diary entries.

Jane was a complex woman who delighted in the company of others, relished her intellectual pursuits of reading and debating, and also usually enjoyed her solitude. "I am thankful for the education which enables me to enjoy myself though alone and without agreeable society. My mind may be filled with happy thoughts when my surroundings are not all that I could desire them to be" (October 28, 1883). At this point of her life, Jane was living comfortably in her own home, but her surroundings often lacked intellectual stimulation other than what she generated for herself through reading.

Jane Price was an avid reader with broad intellectual interests. She had attended one of the academies in Rushville, Indiana, and perhaps the educational attainments of her brothers, Christy, John, Charles, and Frank, also had influenced her devotion to a wide variety of books. Christy had attended college and taught in an academy in Rushville, Indiana. John T. Price had attended Illinois Wesleyan University and taught school in Illinois before moving to Hamilton County in 1873. He was one of Hamilton County's first "schoolma'ams," and was the third county superintendent of schools, 1874–1875.[28] Brother Frank, with his family, studied at Oberlin College, then went to China, Japan, and Micronesia as pioneer missionaries, returning to the United States in the 1920s. Frank was fluent in eight languages, translated prayers and portions of the Bible into Chinese, and wrote *Christ's Life* in Chinese.[29] Charles and his wife Eva also attended Oberlin. After Charles graduated at age forty-one, they went to China as missionaries, 1889–1900, where they and their daughter were killed during the Boxer Rebellion.[30] The Memorial Arch on the campus of Oberlin commemorates the Prices and other missionaries who lost their lives during the Boxer Rebellion.[31]

The family's devotion to religious interests can be seen in Jane's reading list which included *Compendium of Methodism* by Porter; *The Lives of Popes* by the brilliant German historian, von Ranke; a five-volume *History of the Reformation* by d'Aubigné; *The Works of Josephus*; and *The Life of St. Paul*. She also read *Notes by the Wayside*, a travelogue of England and France; and an occasional novel. She doesn't indicate her source of the books, however, Grand Island had estab-

lished a free public library in 1882.[32] In 1894, her subscription to
InterOcean included several books, *Pilgrims' Progress*, *Dickens' Child*,
History of England, *Emerson's Essays*, and *The Vicar of Wakefield*. Jane
was part of "a small portion of people (less than 5 percent) [who] had
attended high school [or an academy in Jane's case] and the book-
reading public was probably drawn primarily from this more highly
educated group."[33] If Jane didn't go visiting or have company, she usually read after church and Sunday school, as on December 23, 1883:
"I have read quite considerable and passed the day very pleasantly. . . .
I feel thankful and happy tonight. My lot is a pleasant one and I am
blessed above many. My home is comfortable. I have many friends and
enjoy the delights of literature and converse with the ancients."

Although the ten-cent, pulp magazines accounted for 80 percent of
the magazines purchased nationwide from the 1880s to 1920, Jane's
subscriptions reflected another balance in her life. Among her subscriptions were the periodicals for "thinking people," religious writing,
women's concerns and homemaking, the events of the nation and
world.[34] Jane subscribed to *Harper's*, *InterOcean*, *The Christian Advocate*, and *Ladies Repository*. She eagerly read the *Cincinnati Enquirer*,
the *Register* from Iowa, and other newspapers.

Her enthusiasm for reading, her staunch faith, and values may have
been influenced in part by her mother, Sarah A. Price. Other than a
few pages of recollections about her mother in her journal of 1885,
Jane never mentioned her mother; however, that description reveals
some of the foundations of Jane's character and values:

> Her educational advantages were limited, coming to that new
> country when it was just beginning to be settled. Schools were
> scarce and a large family of little ones made her presence at home
> necessary. She only went to school about three months to Uncle
> Frank Keith, but learned to read and by diligent use of the
> knowledge, she became an intelligent reader. I have heard her
> tell how when she had an interesting book she would sit up till
> after midnight to read it. She delighted in Pilgrims Progress and
> kindred works. Was quite a reader of biography. She was very
> anxious to have her children enjoy the benefits of education.
> I remember how glad she was to have me go to the academy and
> how proud she seemed of Christie's success. She could talk intel-
> ligently on most subjects especially on moral and religious ques-
> tions. Was a woman of radical views. I remember her denuncia-

tion of slavery as portrayed in the pages of Uncle Tom's Cabin. She was also an earnest advocate of temperance, could hardly bear to have drunken men come about our place lest we children should hear the rude language. [35]

In Jane's diary entries, the totality of each day is pulled together, balancing the demands she felt on her time, considering others' opinions but following her own self-determined directions. Her diaries detail the working woman's conflict of time and energies diffused among her work as a teacher, the demands of her home, her business ventures, and her intellectual pursuits. At the time of this entry, Jane, her brothers, and father had been living in a sod house in Nebraska for about two years. She expresses her desire to improve her school, and refers to her unnamed cares. Among the trials Jane Price had experienced in Nebraska were the harsh winters, the threat of grasshoppers in the summer, and the lack of intellectual stimulation.

Monday Nov. 2nd, 1878
I have spent today in the schoolroom. I am trying to carry out some of the suggestions of the institute. The pupils seem to be very much interested in their studies and I hope to be able to accomplish some good this sessions. Lon is away threshing and father and myself are alone at home tonight.
This has been a lovely day and I am in hopes bad weather will not set in for some days yet. We have had a pleasant fall and winter so far and such good roads and dry healthy air. I feel almost as I used to in the days of "old Lang syne" when my heart had not known so much of care as at present and I had the vigor and buoyancy of youth. I feel a slight reaction since the institute closed and a longing for the companionship of those with whom I became acquainted there. I think of Marion Lounsbury, and remember the pleasant communion we had together. I hope I may have done her good. I must close . . . . [36]

Her longing for the companionship of other teachers was a typical response to the welcomed professional association and socializing found at the institutes. Jane usually enjoyed the good company, the opportunity to learn, and to upgrade her certificate, but occasionally the institute was not a success.

Chapter 6

Fri. 24th [August 1883] . . . got there about ten o'clock, staid till
five. Had a pleasant time . . . Prof. Drummon gave a good recitation in grammar but Prof. Seaman did not do much in Arithmetic, and Prof. Halleck was a failure . . . . I got home about
dark somewhat tired but feeling very well.

One of the few times that Jane discloses her feelings of loneliness
comes upon leaving the fellowship and stimulation of the institute.
A month after the institute, Jane was continuing to improve her
teaching, doing her homemaking tasks after a full day of work at her
schoolhouse, and making plans for further professional studying.

Monday-eve Dec. 9th, 1878
I come to my journal late tonight. I am trying out lard. When I
returned from school this evening, I found they had been butcher-
ing and I had to go into the lard business, but it is nearly cooked
now and I shall be glad when it is finished. I am working my best
at my school. I had a new scholar today . . . . My pupils are most
of them trying and I believe they are learning very well . . . .
This evening I did not get out until sundown. I find it necessary
to use a good deal of firmness in managing the school and I think
I shall get along very well. I hope to give satisfaction to the most
of the district and if there are a few unreasonable ones I hope to
get along without their good opinion . . . .
Wednesday Dec. 11th, 1878
We had a good day at school. One episode a little unpleasant,
Geo. King was throwing something from his seat into the coal-
pail. I told him if he wished to put anything into the pail to ask
permission to do so. Almost immediately he threw something
else in and I called him out on the floor. I guess he will learn by
and by not to attempt to run the school . . . . I feel an earnest
determination to pursue some systematic course of study [to improve myself]. I must make of myself a workman who need not be
ashamed in any department connected with my profession . . . .

The winter of 1879 brought surprisingly mild weather with continuing illnesses among the neighbors and the schoolchildren. The pioneer saying that a green winter will fill the graveyard was well-founded
as the *Centennial History of Hamilton County* cites the numerous graves
of children who died in the winter of 1879 and during an unnamed

epidemic in October 1882.[37] The school children died of typhoid, diphtheria, and scarlet fever. Measles and mumps kept children out of school and cut back attendance at church and Sunday school. Whooping cough killed the babies, and childbed fever took the new mothers. In one week in September 1882, Jane recorded the deaths of three babies and one woman all from "some throats and lung difficulty originating in the whooping cough."

Jane's descriptions of illnesses and deaths seem understated, yet the sparseness of her comments brings a haunting poignancy to the following accounts as they are interfaced with the humorous essays read at school:

Sabbath eve, Jan. 19th, 1879
This has been rather a profitless sabbath to me as we had no sabbath-school and no meeting . . . . Ida is better but not quite well yet. I hope she will entirely recover.
    Susie Lutz is better and Lon also.[38] Nels Miller is very bad. I hope they will all get well and we will see the people in their accustomed health. I have school tomorrow and will then decide whether to continue all week or not . . . .
Monday, Jan. 20th, 1879
Today has been a beautiful day. The sunshine was warm and the air was so balmy, it seemed almost like spring. I had three scholars at school . . . . I will try lying over a little while giving myself a little rest and perhaps the health will be better next week.
    Susie is not yet out of danger but I hope will get well. Lon is still somewhat bad also. Addie is sick today so that none of them [are] at school. I hope they will not have scarletina as there are so many there to have it, they would hardly get over it this winter.
Thursday Feb. 6th, 1879
. . . . I had fifteen scholars today. Those who have essays to write were busy as tomorrow is the day to read them . . . . Susie is no better, indeed she is somewhat worse. I fear she will never be any better . . . .
Friday Feb. 7th, 1879
This has been a very nice day. I had a full school. This afternoon was the time for essays. Addie had one on old bachelors which was responded to by Will Arnold on old maids, very humorous. Sherman had one on natural history which was very funny.

David Tyler had one about our old brown hen which was so
funny he could hardly read it himself.
Tuesday, Feb. 11th, 1879
I have not written any in my journal since last Friday because I
have had no time, so I will snatch a few moments tonight, although I must sleep a little less. Susie died on last Saturday. Lon
came home about three and said they thought she was dying and
wanted me to come and so I got ready without delay and went,
but got there just as she died. She knew everything until the last
and talked very good to them. All said she died *so* happy and
hoped they would all die as she was dying. Her funeral was
preached by Bro. Smith, a very good sermon and I hope much
good was done. I helped to dress her and washed her myself. She
had a sweet smile on her face. It is better so, as her name was
stained in a way she was in no way to blame for, but must have
felt she is taken from the evil to come . . . .

Jane's journals gave no clues as to how teenager Susie's name had
been stained, nor the nature of the "evil to come." The closeness
among neighbors and between teacher and scholar are seen in Susie's
deathbed wish to see Jane. With Jane's brother, John, married to
Nancy, Mrs. Lutz's eldest daughter, there were additional ties between
the Lutz family and Jane. Jane's concern for her family, her neighbors,
her friends, and for her scholars is consistent throughout the diaries.

In the midst of death, Jane planned ahead for the next institute and
hoped that her scholars, Addie and Eva, could attend the institute.
For Jane and other survivors, life indeed went on. The rest of the
winter was occupied with school, with the highlight being the teachers' institute in Aurora, Nebraska in early March.

Sat., March 8th, 1879
I have just returned from Aurora where I have been attending
Institute all week since Wednesday. We had a good institute.
I enjoyed it very much, made many new acquaintances and became better acquainted with many others. I hope we shall have
pleasant times together hereafter. I passed examination, did not
need to do so but thought best to as I hoped to get a better grade
in some of my studies. I think I passed very well and look for a
good grade . . . . I hope the girls [Addie and Eva] will get a good

A Greater Usefulness in My Calling

certificate and be able to teach a good school. I am too sleepy to write more . . . .

The institute accommodated the experienced teachers like Jane, and the beginners, Addie and Eva. Here was the place they could get together as teachers and as friends, learning and socializing together. In mid-spring, contagious diseases again claimed children.

> Thursday, May 8th, 1879
> I had no school today. I went to the schoolhouse where I learned that Jennie Tompkins was dead. She was one of the most pleasant and kind-hearted girls I ever knew. I dismissed school and attended the funeral . . . . She died of scarlet fever and Diphtheria. Her mother took it very hard. She was only sick two days. Our little graveyard is filling up very rapidly.

The understated response to the loss and sadness carry into the next day at school which was lonely for the Jane and her school children.

> Friday, May 9th, 1879
> I have spent today rather unpleasantly. It seemed so gloomy all the forenoon and there were only seven scholars at school which made it seem lonely, but I hope to feel better tomorrow. This evening has been pleasant, the warmest for a week. I have finished Redpath's History of the U. S. and pronounce it good.

Deaths and illnesses were frequently recorded in Jane's journals as she sat up with the sick, the dying, and the bereaved. In response to a suicide and an accidental drowning, Jane drew her own moralistic conclusions.

> July 12, 1883
> . . . . I have learned that Kittie Bacon committed suicide last night by poison, how terrible it seemed, but she lacked a good honest heart and purpose in life. Poor rash silly girl. She has hurried herself unprepared into the presence of her Maker, a warning to many others . . . .
> Sunday July 22nd 1883
> Just at the close of the Sabbath school Jeff Thompson came by with word that Lew Ham drowned in the Platte. Everyone rushed

Chapter 6

off to the river except the women. I came home pretty soon. All day the men were searching the river for the body but up to a late hour this evening had not found it. It seems sad to think of the child of Christian parents being drowned in the river on Sunday but boys will run these risks and perhaps these were no more guilty than many others who were not drowned. May we all heed the lesson these things teach us and be always ready.

If her frailties or those of others discouraged her, she used her journal as a written prayer for guidance and increased faith. In her journal entry on her fortieth birthday, Jane seeks her ideal as finding and following the will of God: "Well, I must wait the will of providence and try to follow the guidance of him who holds my destiny in his hand, taking up life's duties as they come to me and finding my big best joy in the service of my heavenly master." Jane frequently expressed the desire to achieve a "greater usefulness in her calling"; and to have better attendance and dedication at church affairs.

A few times, Jane mentions being alone and unmarried, perhaps regretfully, or as a simple observation of her reality: "I am alone tonight as I was last night. I suppose I must get used to being alone as I am expecting to live an 'old maid.'" (January 28, 1881). In her early twenties, Jane had other expectations as she wrote to two Union soldiers from Indiana. Her six letters from Benjamin E. Bear, 1864–65, are accounts of his efforts to maintain his Christian beliefs and his hopes that temperance would become widespread. Her correspondence with William Ell begins in August 1862:

> Memphis, Tennessee
> Miss Price, It is with pleasure that I have taken my pen in hand to address a few lines to you to inform you that I am well and harty and hope these few lines may find you and the rest of them enjoying good health. You may think it strange of my writing to you as we are almost strangers to each other. We have had but little acquaintence with each other yet, but we may have after this war is over if we should live to see the end of the rebellion. Even if we should not see each other I consider it no harm to pass a few lines to each other in the way of friendship. [39]

William Ell described the hot, dusty camp and hoped to hear from Jane. The remaining letters through January 3, 1864, are written from

A Greater Usefulness in My Calling

Fort Pillow, Tennessee, where the 52d Regiment, Indiana Volunteers, was engaged in making raids on the Confederate forces. In William's letter of November 2, 1862, he confides in Jane, his "respected friend," that he missed his friends in Rush County, Indiana, and feels quite alone. His family is scattered "to the four winds of the Earth," in Missouri, Kansas, Pennsylvania, and North Carolina. He concludes his letter hoping to hear from Jane soon, and remained her friend "till death."

The dreary Christmas at Fort Pillow was spent expecting to be attacked by the Confederates. William wishes Jane "a happy new year. A long and happy life and plenty of friends, that you may never want for anything. As for a Christmas gift, I have nothing but a ring which [I] will send you in this letter. It was captured in Covington, Tipton County, Tennessee. It is but a small gift but you are welcome to it, if you will receive it."

William's letter March 29, 1863, contains a cheerful description of the lovely spring weather and a graphic account of the capture of seven drunken deserters. "All that I have to say about souch men that they augh to suffer for their disobedience." William responded to Jane's question of whether he was a democrat.

> I am no politician my self . . . I am no one sided party man. The man that I think is the best calculated for place that he is candidate for, that is the man for me whether he bee democrat [or] republican. I see by your letter that you are a Lincoln woman. If you will allow me expression, the women are not allowed any hand in the election of our officers. But still I like to here their minds spoken in the choice of their candidates. If they were allowed the write to vote, their centiments have a great affect on the mind of men. At least some have on mine any how.

In July of 1863, for the second time William criticizes the men who were marrying women in Tennessee.

> I think that they only married during our stay here at Fort Pillow [because] they have about eighteen hundred dollars a piece in gold and I think that is what they think the most of . . . You said that you did not want all of them to get married down here. The ladys look verry attempting. But I hope there will be one left for you as you said probably you might want a husband your self. It

may be that you have your mind fixed on one now. If you have and he is in the army, I hope that he may be sp[a]red to return home a gain where you can enjoy the pleasure of his society. I have no more time to write this time . . . for the horn is blowing for to saddle up our horses and be off . . . Write soon.

In December 1863, William was discouraged:

. . . our Sunday school has plaid out here and turned to a debating school. Preaching is also scarce here. The chaplin has hung his religion on a bush and forgot where the bush is. It is hard to find a Christian in the army.. . . I don't kno of one in the regiment . . . I belong to old nick yet and he may close the mortgage on me yet before I can get shet of him, but I hope not.

In William's letter of January 3, 1864, perhaps his last, he sadly writes about several men who had frozen to death. "People may talk about the Sunny South but give me the wintery north. I have felt cold weather but never was I pinched with cold like I have been for the last two days." He also responded to Jane's request for his picture.

If you had it, you would say that it was not mine. I am so much flesheyer than when I left home and have so much beard on my face that you wouldent kno me at all. I am verry fleshey and weigh 212 pounds. That is about 30 pounds more than I weighed when you last saw me. I am so ugly that I am a shamed to get it taken.

Probably I may send it in my next letter. If I do, I must ask yours in return. . . . I will close hoping to here from you soon.

It is unknown if Jane received a picture of William Ell, or whether she had her mind "fixed on" a man in the army. Other than the wartime correspondence, there is no further evidence of the friendship between Jane and William.[40]

Being unmarried certainly did not prevent Jane Price from fulfilling her ambitions of leadership in church, school, and community affairs and of financial and intellectual independence. In addition, she seemed to accept her role as a woman including the care-giving responsibilities as evidenced by her satisfying relationships with her family members and neighbors. Her ideal of perfection was that of successfully fulfilling her self-determined moral obligations as a teacher, a leader in the Methodist Church, head of her family, and as a friend. Imbedded within the feminine structure of her life, were her actions outside the social norms for an unmarried woman. Jane Price was a land-owner, an active and successful farmer, and managed her own financial affairs. She fulfilled leadership roles in organizations made up of both men and women, as found in her church, the literary societies, and in the temperance lodge. She supported suffrage, but even without the vote, she saw herself as equal to men in the importance of her contributions to the developing prairie society. Indeed, Jane Price's life included the "strategies and activities that challenge those norms [of womanhood]," as she was both the "changer and the changed."[41]

September 1879, brought changes into Jane's life. On September 2, after washing the straw ticks and getting rid of many bugs, Jane hoped "we will not live in a sod house always." A few days later, after three years of living in a Nebraska soddie, Jane looked at a farm, a quarter section of "good, wet soil," that she hoped to buy.

Saturday, September 6th, 1879
I have bought a farm at last. Mr. Force was here tonight and we agreed on the terms. I pay four hundred down and the remainder in a year, assuming the mortgage of four hundred due in two years. I hope I have made a good trade and got a piece of land that will make me a good home sometime. I never did much trading before and I felt rather awkward, but I got through rather better than I anticipated. Now if I can only make the payments without trouble, I shall be satisfied with myself and everybody else . . . .
Saturday, Nov. 29th, 1879
I went to Grand Island today and paid off my Force note at the office of Thummel & Platt. I bought a blank book for my journal at Mullins. I was very cold riding but I was well wrapped and did not suffer. I hope my cold will be no worse . . . .
Saturday, June 25th, 1880
I went to Grand Island today. John was going over and I went with him. I paid Thummel $200 on the Force note, and loaned Mr. Morgan $40 to pay interest on the mortgage when due . . . .

I bought me a new hat, the first in four years. I don't know how I shall like it. Cost me two dollars . . . .

This property which she bought for $1250, she sold in September 1882 for $1750, with the buyer assuming the mortgage of $450 and paying the taxes for the year. As she became more adept at buying and selling land and farm products, she gained in confidence and seemed to enjoy bargaining, but she did not move into her own house until March 1883.

Her Saturdays continued to be the time to be fully involved in homemaking tasks, unless there was business to attend to in Grand Island. Sundays were dedicated to Sunday school, church meetings, and visiting with friends and family.

> Saturday, November 1st, 1879
> I washed, scrubbed, baked, and ironed today. My rising did not come so I did not get to bake bread. I fear I shall have to bake biscuits all of this week of which I shall get tired. Lon shot a goose today, so we will have a roast tomorrow. Isaiahs [neighbors] are coming to dinner . . . .
> Sabbath, Nov. 30th, 1879
> . . . I went to Sabbath school this morning and pleased with the attendance and interest . . . I had company to dinner . . . . We spent the time very pleasantly . . . . I have filled a volume in my journal and shall lay it away for future reference. Its record covers a year and I feel that there is much to regret but also much to be thankful for. And while I see many errors, there is much I have learned and temptations overcome and trials past. I hope the rec-ord for next year will be better and nobler and whatever trial may await me, that I may be so happy as to pass through them with-out harm and gain a home at last where the wicked cease to trouble and the weary are at rest . . . .

The winter months were spent in teaching, reading, church activi-ties, and the temperance discussions at the Good Templars Lodge meetings. The extremely cold weather made school attendance low, and Jane closed the term in January 1880, feeling less than successful. "I believe it is about as near a failure as I ever made in teaching, not from any fault of my own, but because there were so few scholars in the district and they mostly [are] so small that they could not attend regularly in cold weather. But I am through and glad of it and hope I have done some good."

In February, Jane looked unsuccessfully for another school for spring term. Her time, however, was well-filled with lectures on temperance and suffrage, prayer meetings, more reading, and an attempt by Brother Parker to discuss evolution.

> Sabbath, Feb. 1st, 1880
> I have just returned from prayer meeting at College Corners. Bro. Parker was there and took the lead. He is not a good leader. He told the story of the tadpole from which man is supposed to have sprung by a certain school of philosophers, and that set the baser sort to laughing, and they could not be quiet afterward. I was sorry I let him lead but hope no harm was done . . . .
> Thursday, Feb. 5th, 1880
> I have just returned from St. Joe where we have been having a course of two lectures on temperance by Mr. Vinton. They were the best lectures I ever listened to and did much good in arousing the temperance people to a more earnest interest in the work . . .
> Monday, Feb. 9, 1880
> It was cold this morning but is warmer now. I washed this morning and scrubbed the floor. I have begun "Put Yourself in His Place," but wish I had not because I shall want to finish it and it will take too long. But I hope to learn something from it, if nothing more, at least how little there is in the novel . . . .
> Tuesday, Feb. 10th, 1880
> I have just returned from St. Joe where I heard a lecture by Mrs. Robinson. It was entitled "The Unsolved Problem," mainly devoted to the question of Women's Suffrage. She handled her subject well but her voice was not in good condition, she having a cold. I believe the lecture was well-received . . . .

Four years later, Jane Price gave her first suffrage speech.

> January 10th 1884
> I have just returned from literary, we had a pleasant time. I made my first speech in favor of woman's rights. I also read the Cottars Saturday night. Today was cold and windy but tonight was still . . . There was a good crowd at literary.

During the spring of 1880, Jane studied algebra and read d'Aubigne's five-volume *History of the Reformation.* and Prescott's *Ferdinand and Isabella.* Lodge attendance, singing school, church activities, "choring around," the garden, and farming filled her days, along with occasional business in town. Spring also brought numerous illnesses and deaths of mothers and babies.

Tuesday, May 4th, 1880
I attended the funeral of Mrs. Beymer today. Went down yesterday supposing it would be yesterday evening, but Mr. Beymer thought they had better put if off till this morning. The corpse was very offensive. She died about daylight Monday morning. Had childbed fever, her babe was about one week old. She expressed a hope in Christ toward the last and sang a verse of a hymn, "Beautiful Land of Rest." Bro. Smith preached her funeral at the house and attended to the grave. I was there all night and came home after the funeral . . . .
Wednesday, May 12th, 1880
I went to singing [school] at St. Joe last night and consequently did not have time to write. I finished reading D'Aubigne, History of the Reformation, today. Have been much pleased with it and have been benefitted by it in many ways. I shall begin Prescott's Ferdinand and Isabella immediately. I hope to make a success of this summer's study . . . .
Sabbath, May 23rd, 1880
We had a small attendance at sabbathschool and church this morning owing to the fact that the measles are so bad. Brother Auten preached. He lives over on Hamilton circuit. Does tolerably well for a local preacher. Our quarterly meeting will be held at College Corners, Tuesday and Wednesday of this week . . . .

The summer months brought more studying, reading, and the Fourth of July celebration.

Friday, July 2, 1880
I visited Lizzie's school today, afternoon. She had twenty scholars. All seemed interested and I believe are doing well. Today has been very hot and it is still warm this evening. The mosquitos are very bad. I am digging into Geometrical Progression in Alge-

A Greater Usefulness in My Calling

bra and like it very well. I am almost through Vol. I of [von]
Ranke, Lives of Popes . . . .
Monday, July 5th, 1880
They had a tolerably good time at St. Joe today The parade was
real good and seemed to be very much enjoyed by all. The Ragga-
muffins came in and made quite a display. Some of the masks
were very comic. We had some good music by the band and some
excellent singing, footracing, horse racing, croquet, and a few
other exercises. Tonight they are to have a "hop" to finish things
off nicely which . . . I think could be safely dispensed with . . . .
Tuesday, July 6th, 1880
I have not felt right well today. I guess I ate too much yesterday
so this morning I woke with my head feeling a little heavy and
very unpleasant feeling all over. I did not wash as I intended but
put it off till tomorrow . . . .

In September 1880, Jane returned to another term of schoolteaching and coped with the unwelcomed attention from Mr. Beymer,
whose wife had died in the spring. Her father and Ed brought home
three bushels of plums, and Jane spent a couple of days making two
gallons of plum butter, a gallon of plum jelly, and two gallons of mar-
malade. At the temperance lodge meeting, Jane and the men debated
the question, "that a man's success in life depends more on natural
ability than on education."

Tues., Sept. 21, 1880
I had twenty-six at school today and spent a good day taking all
in. All this afternoon it rained, commencing at one o-clock. I
got to ride home as J. B[eymer] was there with his buggy. I would
almost as soon have walked through the mud as to have rode
with him but hated to refuse, so I came flying home . . . .
Wednesday, Sept. 29th, 1880
I had a good school today. Think I am getting along nicely. Have
introduced a written spelling exercise which I think is a good exercise. Mr. Beymer came and wanted me to go to the fair at
Grand Island with him, but I did not wish to do so. He brought
me home. I think he wants something he won't get, but he may
think differently . . . .
Friday, Oct. 1st, 1880
I am alone tonight. It is now nine o'clock and the boys have not

returned from work yet. I suppose they have gone to the "Caucus." I had good attendance at school today. Mrs. Skelton and Mr. Beymer came about half past three . . . . he wanted to come home with me but I did not wish to do so. I spoke rather plainly to him. I think he will come to the conclusion to let me alone hereafter . . . .

Sabbath, Oct. 3rd, 1880

I went with Mr. Beymer and Ava to St. Joe to Sunday school this afternoon. I had quite a number picking at me and could not help having my face a little bit red, but I don't care. I hope I shall have independence enough to let him know he is not wanted.

Mr. Beymer then disappeared from her journal. As a recognized land owner, Jane's financial independence was well-known. Because she was almost thirty-nine years old, she may have felt that Mr. Beymer was mainly interested in her land and needed a housekeeper. At any rate, she definitely was not interested in his company. As her success in teaching and land ownership became increasingly more secure, Jane was more confident in her ability to be independent.

The changing point in her life seems to come in 1882, when in her early forties, she became progressively more successful in her land deals, continued to manage the business of the farm, and bought her own home in October 1882. In March 1882, Jane learned that Lizzie has applied for the teaching position that Jane wanted.[42] "I leave it all with a good providence. Shall try to believe whatever is, is for the best." The next day, Jane discovered "that fire has been on my place and destroyed some of my trees. I hope I may learn who set it out." In this entry, after spending the day alone, but busy studying arithmetic, reading, sewing, and caring for a sick cow, Jane despaired "for a better life, more in keeping with the character I profess."

Sat., March 18th, 1882

. . . . Another week with its busy cares is gone and I am thankful the record is no worse. I feel a desire for a better life, more in keeping with the character I profess, but my way seems hedged up. Lord, undertake for me! I desire to feel resigned to the will of God in all things, to trust my all in His hands Spiritually and Temporally . . . .

A Greater Usefulness in My Calling

The character of Jane Price seems torn among several roles: that of the conventional homemaker and farm woman; that of the self-taught intellectual who teaches the young and "converses with the ancients;" that of the religious woman who could lead others toward faith and salvation; and that of the business entrepreneur, buying and selling land and farm produce. This constellation of conflicting roles and responsibilities, the domain of working women across time, left Jane Price seeking guidance in finding her true character.

In the following month, Jane finds that Lizzie did indeed get the school for the spring term. "I hope she will be successful. I suppose I shall be idle this summer again but hope to make a successful summer's study." The month of April seems to be a month of marking time doing the "little every day duties that take so much of my life."[43] In late April, after a rainy, lonely Saturday, Jane wrote one of her first poems in her diary.

> And we toil and strive in vain,
> When the labor seems too great
> And we long for rest from pain . . .
> While we strive, success still wooing,
> Wearied with our hope deferred,
> With our faith "faint yet pursuing,"
> Soon will come the brighter day . . .
> When our darkness shall be o'er . . . .

Again, a poem in her diary expressed Jane's frustrations with herself and those around her.

> Tuesday May 2nd '82
> . . . . Though foes assail us every hour.
> And e'en our dearest friends forsake, . . .
> We labor hard but find no fruit
> Of all our toil beneath the sun.
> We court success but find our suit
> Ever denied while life rolls on . . . .
> Our toil shall have a rich reward
> Though long deferred, our victory's sure
> And He who is the sparrow's guard
> Our safe deliverance does assure.

Chapter 6

Jane's poetry, more than her prose diary entries, conveys her feelings of frustration that her work at home, in the church, and in land ownership, had not yet produced visible success. In each poem, she concludes with a strong statement, or perhaps a wish, that her faith in God will bring rewards in Heaven, if not sooner.

By May, Jane had made several decisions about her properties and, perhaps unconsciously, about the direction of her life. Within a few days, Jane put her lots up for sale.

Friday May 5th 1882
Today is Abby's birthday, she would have been forty-five if she were alive now, almost fifteen years ago she died. I went to G. I. today. Lon went up with a couple of hogs and had a chance to go. I put my lots on the market, hope to be able to sell them in a few days. Isaiah is the agent who acts for me. I was at Mr. Ball's for dinner. I took over some eggs to West's and got some garden seeds which I must plant in a short time. Lon got 6 1/2 c. for his hogs today.
May 8th 1882
I went to Aurora today. Lon and Father went down to prove up on his claim. I went to attend to a loan which I was trying to secure from Major Miller. I sent in my application and hope I have it all right this time. I am to have $450 at 9% for five years. Rec'd eight dollars of the balance due me and am to receive the remainder when my release comes.

I took dinner at Tuttles which seemed like home. I bought me a hat at Mrs. Cassell. It cost me two dollars and five cents. I also bought Father a pair of shoes at Sawyers, 1.79. It was cold going down but pleasant coming home.

During this month, Jane wrote several poems, read many books, planted her garden, visited with her neighbors, the Kizers, and sat up many nights with a neighbor who was suffering from chronic rheumatism. By June, the garden was growing well, and she had an offer on some of her land for "two thousand if I get the crop but $2,200 if I let them have immediate possession. I am in no hurry to sell at those figures, but think best to sell which I am." Jane set aside any decisions on buying and selling land for the summer. However, her involvement in buying, selling, and renting property continue to be included throughout the remainder of her diaries.

A Greater Usefulness in My Calling

The end of June brought the happily anticipated visit from Jane's sister, Lib, and her husband, Brother Wheeler.

Friday, June 30th, 1882
I have baked, ironed and done a great deal of work today, was expecting Lib [to arrive from Indiana by train] this evening, but she has not come yet (10.30) and I am going to bed. I suppose the boys have not got here and staid at St. Joe.

Sat., July 1st, 1882
Lib is here, came today. She and her husband , they seem very much pleased with the country. It seems natural to see Lib but she is older. It is warm tonight and I am afraid the mosquitos will be troublesome. I must get to bed and be ready to get up and to work tomorrow morning. I read my essay to Sister Dunn this evening, she pronounced it fine.

Sabbath, July 2nd, 1882
We have spent the day very pleasantly and I trust somewhat profitably. Bro. Wells preached at College Corners this morning and we all attended but Lon and Father. Bro. Wheeler [Lib's second husband] was much pleased with the meeting and the preacher. I enjoyed the meeting very much. We spent the afternoon pleasantly visiting with our relatives. I think I shall like our new brother very much. Lib seems to be enjoying her visit very much. I never enjoyed anything more and only fear I shall have to give her up too soon. It is quite warm tonight, the mosquitos are bad.

July 3rd, 1882
We drove down to my place this morning going through St. Joe. We found things all right and Bro. Wheeler seemed much pleased with my place. Lib seemed pleased too. We got home about half past twelve. I have been busy ever since, have most of my baking for the fourth done and my chicken cleaned. I am enjoying Lib's visit very much. I fear I shall be too busy to prepare fully with my essay, but it must go through this time certainly, as I have promised to give [it] and will keep my word. I fear I shall not be satisfied with all that goes on there.

Tuesday, July 4th 1882
We attended the celebration at St. Joe today. I read my essay and was complimented highly on it. Bro. Wheeler seemed highly pleased. Bro Wells and Uncle John Foster were very much pleased with it. Lew Shuman complimented me and Mrs.

Skelton said I did better than all the rest together. We had a pleasant time till about four o'clock when they began to dance and we came home . . . . The crowd was not large but all passed off pleasantly.

Jane's well-received essay must have brought great satisfaction to her. It was not unusual for women to be included in the Fourth of July orations. In neighboring Clay County, a woman usually read the Declaration of Independence, except during the 1876 festivities when, in recognition of the large numbers of immigrants in the area, the Declaration was read in English, German, and Swedish.[44]

Brother John and his wife, Nancy, left the next day, and Lib and her husband left a few days later, leaving Jane where she felt at home.

Wed., July 5th, 1882
We all went to Grand Island today with Johns to see them [John and family] off to the Loup once more. I got my picture taken, gave one to Lib and the other to Nannie . . . .
Saturday, July 8th, 1882
I went with Lib to the train last evening so had no opportunity to write. We staid until they started at one-twenty [A.M.] when Lon and I came home. They forgot their lunch basket and Mr. Wheeler's Sunday pants. We got home and to bed about three, but I have felt very tired and sleepy today. I have not done much but read. The weather was very fine, looks some like rain tonight.

After Lib left, Jane "rambled around awhile hunting seeds" of various prairie plants to send to Lib, perhaps to share some of the beauty of the prairie with her sister and as a remembrance of their good visit. Jane and Lib had shared the plants and seeds of their gardens and environs for many years.[45]

In October 1882, Jane paid taxes on her lots in town, bargained for land a couple of weeks with the Kizers, and finally made her decision to buy her own home.

Monday, Oct. 23rd 1882
I have bought the old Kizer homestead today, am to pay twenty-six hundred for it. I think it is little high but am not sure it is too

much. I think I shall like my home very much. I have quite a
start of small fruit and garden herbs in abundance. I hope it will
prove a good investment. I don't like very much to get in debt
again but perhaps it is as well . . . .
Tuesday, Oct. 24th 1882
I had a small school today but got along nicely. The day was
pleasant and everything went along smoothly. I think of my trade
with a good deal of satisfaction. The more I think of it, the better satisfied I am. I hope to enjoy my new home very much. "If
God wills" and I shall hope to make it pleasant for myself and all
who may come to it . . . .
Saturday, Oct. 28th 1882
. . . went to G[rand] I[sland] to get the deed for my land. Sister
Kizer did not wish to sign it and seemed very much out of humor
some way, but we got the matter arranged satisfactorily, got the
deed all right. I paid Bruce $1,130.85 in cash. Traded him the
boys' note for $435.15 and a school order for thirty-four dollars.
I am well satisfied with my trade and better satisfied the more I
think of it.

A month after Jane bought the Kizer farm, she felt happy and
confident that her goals were being implemented according to her
plans. An unexpected and unwelcomed letter from a local preacher
rated scant comment in her diary. This was the second time that
Jane encountered an unanticipated suitor shortly after she acquired
property.

Sat., Nov. 25th 1882
. . . received a letter . . . from Bro. Auten offering me his hand,
heart and fortune. I hope he is not much smitten as the case is
utterly hopeless. I rented my place to [brother] Ed today so that is
off my mind now.
Sabbath, Nov. 26th 1882
. . . . The day has been lovely and tonight is superb. I feel thankful and happy tonight. All my plans have worked out so far so
much better than I had reason to hope and my path seems so
pleasant and good. My spiritual sky seems clear and I feel so confident and happy and a tranquil sense of peace and joy, a bright
hope of everlasting life . . . .

Chapter 6

Finally, on December 4, 1882, Jane wrote a letter to Bro. Auten,

> . . . respectfully declining to correspond with him on the subject
> of matrimony. I hope this will be the last of this as I have no
> time to trible away in that way.

There seems to be no question about Jane's having "independence enough" to pursue her own way of life. She was not governed by the traditional viewpoint that a woman needed to be married in order to function financially or socially. Her rich social life put her in contact with many friends, both women and men, who were neighbors, members of the church, Lodge, and literary societies. Moving into her own house the following spring brought her more confidence, pleasure, and more farm work.

> Tuesday, March 13th, 1883
> Yesterday we moved into my house on the Kizer place. Kizers left
> a little after noon and I began cleaning right away. The boys
> could not fill the straw ticks till today so we slept on the floor last
> night . . . . I have a good deal of my fixing up to housekeeping
> done and am well pleased with my house. I trust I may be per-
> mitted to enjoy many happy days here and that this house may
> ever be devoted to good and noble purposes.
> March 15, 1883
> . . . I have most of my goods arranged for the present. The house
> begins to seem homelike.

During the next ten years, Jane planted a wide variety of trees, bushes, vegetables, and flowers. Her work for the church was an ongoing responsibility and comfort. She occasionally taught school; continued to learn through her reading; and "chored around" her home. In September 1893, Lizzie, brother Ed's wife, died after the birth of their third child. Ed and his daughters, Frankie and Earle, moved in with Jane, while Lizzie's mother cared for the baby, Mary Elizabeth. Jane sewed for the children, made rag dolls for their Christmas presents, and sat up with them when they were sick. Ed's children went with Jane to Sunday school and to visit with the neighbors. Jane's quiet times for reading and contemplation were filled with the care of the young children.

Even with her increased family responsibilities, a typical day for

Jane in the spring of 1894 combined farmwork and visiting with friends: "I put in the forenoon cleaning out my stable. Wheeled out twenty-eight barrow loads. Clara Cramer and Mrs. Boyce with Frank's baby were here in the afternoon. Also, Bro. Sutton and wife were here and got a setting of eggs. It was pleasant."

There does not seem to be a specific time when Jane ceased to teach. Teaching school is mentioned less and less during the late 1880s as she becomes more successful in her business ventures. Although her father lived with her much of the time, she also rarely wrote about her father until the summer of 1894, when he was so gravely ill that Lib and brother John came to Jane's home. He recovered, but by fall Jane was "feel[ing] so much like I was hedged in all the time. I scarcely know what to do but hope to sometime be free once more." Ed and the children were still living with her and undoubtedly, as the unmarried daughter, Jane had the major care of her father while he was ill and in his declining years. He died at eight-five in 1898. Her family responsibilities had all but overwhelmed her own pleasures and activities.

By January 1895, Jane had achieved a more balanced life, but longed for a quiet home: "Another lovely day, seems hardly like January. Spent as most of the days are at home. I am glad to have a comfortable home and tho there are some things unpleasant yet I have many blessings. I hope to see the time when I shall have my own quiet home again."

Jane's journals abruptly end in June 1895, or were somehow lost. She apparently regained her independence in the ensuing years as she became increasingly involved in church and Sunday school leadership and her farming. In May 1907, Jane achieved the culmination of her lifetime of reading and religious thought when she went on a seven week tour of Europe. She attended an international Sunday school convention in Rome and toured the major sites of Italy and London with other delegates. Judging from the depth of her reading, and her enthusiasm for history, her understanding of the historical significance of Rome and other European sites must have been more than generally expected of a nineteenth-century prairie schoolteacher.

She sailed on the steamer *Nord American*, May 3, 1907: "The convention began when we started from N. Y. on all the steamers carrying delegates. On the Nord American we had prayer meetings every morning at Nine, and every afternoon at 'five.' These meetings increased in Spirituality and power till the last few days when they were

'Pentecosts' . . . . The moral tone of the cabin was very good, very little trifling and nothing immoral."[46]

There is no question of Jane's Protestant viewpoint as she described the religious relics of Rome: "There is a picture of the virgin here [Church of St. John Lateran] said to be miraculous, also said to have been painted by Luke, both statements are not true."[47]

The historical significance of the Appian Way, "the oldest road in western Europe, paved . . . more that two thousand years ago," did not escape her attention. Jane called Michelangelo's Moses "The greatest work of the greatest sculptor that ever lived. Words fail when we attempt to describe such a work. Think of a statue twice as tall as an ordinary man of pure white marble every muscle showing great strength. Then think of every noble quality pertaining to humanity and them all portrayed in the face."[48]

Among the speakers at the convention, were the granddaughter of Garibaldi, who welcomed the delegates to Rome; Lloyd Griscom, the American Ambassador to Italy; and Madame Reiler, the daughter of D'Aubigne, historian of the Reformation. To have read D'Aubigne in her prairie home, and then hear his daughter in the historical setting of the Reformation was a remarkable experience for a country schoolteacher.

In London, Jane was delighted to find that in Westminster Abbey, "England has done herself honor by placing the name of our Longfellow among her own. I ran upon a tablet of white marble to John and Charles Wesley . . . and the famous sayings of John Wesley recorded on the tablet."[49]

Three years later, Jane traveled to another Sunday school convention in Washington, D. C., where twenty-six to thirty thousand delegates met "working sweetly and harmoniously together for the upbuilding of the great cause of sabbath schools."[50] She toured many historical sites in the eastern United States, then stopped in Indiana, "my old home in Indiana, they let me teach my old class and gave me a chance to talk at the S. S. convention in the afternoon, also . . . in the evening."[51]

After hearing a speaker at this convention who was confined to lie in a wheelchair, Jane wondered "sometimes if there are any obstacles which cannot be overcome." With good books, magazines, and newspapers to read; friends and family to visit; the Sabbath for its time of contemplation; and her mind and her land to call her own, Jane Price was a survivor who generally had a pleasant day, "barrin' the wind."

A Greater Usefulness in My Calling

Sarah Jane Price, teacher, homemaker, independent thinker, community leader, farmer, landowner, ca. 1890. (Courtesy DeRoss Andrews)

Chapter 6

CHAPTER
SEVEN

"To Be a Teacher"

Sarah Gillespie Huftalen, Iowa, 1865–1955

I have been weaning myself from my beloved "Arbor Vitae
Summit" [School] all the year. In the early mornings before the
children came I have gone from window to window & looked out
long and silently on my little yard and trees. I have planted my
love in their rootlets. I felt sad but brave not to show it.—Sarah
Gillespie Huftalen, Oneida, Iowa, May 28, 1909.

On her last day as the teacher of Arbor Vitae Summit School,
Oneida, Iowa, Sarah Gillespie Huftalen heard her pupils give their
recitations at the school program and, surrounded by "lilacs & flowers
& flags," she promoted them.[1] When Sarah, a Universalist, was
elected the superintendent of the proposed Union Sunday school, the
community became embroiled in the controversy, questioning her
theological commitment to the Protestant tenets. In addition, the
new leadership of the public school directors was uncertain about
Sarah's unorthodox teaching methods. The factions of the Union
Sunday school rancor and among the old and new school directors
"used the school to thresh each other."[2] The result was that their
nationally acclaimed rural teacher, Sarah Gillespie Huftalen, reluctantly moved on to another school.

Throughout Sarah's life there were circumstances, often not of her own making, that forced her to move on, to take "the next step to . . . leadership."[3] The transitions of her life presented a mosaic of obstacles and opportunities. Her route, most often, was toward the fulfillment of her personal sense of duty and moral imperative, which included family responsibilities, educating herself and others, promoting social progress, expanding and enriching the quality of rural education, and bringing professional recognition to the rural teachers. Sarah's moral ideal appears to be based on "the fulfillment of an obligation, the repayment of a debt, by giving to others without taking anything for oneself."[4] She was cognizant of how the power of morality tied her to others through her dependence on them and her commitment to them.[5]

At the core of Sarah Huftalen's commitment to others was, as she put it, "love for my chosen field of work for I believe I am fitted and well prepared by experience, training and above all by native choice: it being all but a passion within me."[6] In Sarah's research of her family heritage, she found the motto of the Scotch-Irish Gillespies was "I Serve." Her mother's family, the English Hawleys, had moved from England to Holland, seeking religious freedom under the motto, "Follow me."

> As we are the Summum Bonum of our forbears I suppose some of their traits have come my way, viz.: The domesticity and love of home of the Hollander; the tenacity of the English; the humor of the Irish; and the integrity of the Scotch. A combination of these remote ancestral characteristics, modified by the more immediate, evolved in the gift of teaching which has dominated my life.[7]

This love of teaching was to be the center of Sarah's life for fifty-two years.

Sarah began writing diaries in childhood, and throughout her life she wrote essays, journals about her teaching, and articles for newspapers and educational journals. When she married William (Billie) Huftalen, Sarah's diaries ceased for twenty-two years, then resumed six months after the his death. These extensive diaries, journals, scrapbooks, photographs, and school notebooks document the life of Sarah Gillespie Huftalen.

Sarah's mother, Emily Hawley Gillespie, referred to her own diaries as "My Only Confidant."[8] Sarah's diaries take on this quality also, as she emotionally and, at times, melodramatically expresses her opinions and comments on her hopes and fears. In Sarah's school notebooks and in her public writing about teaching, she used the plural forms *we* and *us*, indicating the cooperative planning that was an essential part of her teaching strategy. In some contexts, however, her use of *we* and *us* became more pontifical in tone. In this account, Sarah indicates that she and her students did not believe in keeping children after school for punishment, but refers to herself in the plural form. "We thought six hours of happy, busy work enough. (However there was seldom a night that pupils did not keep us to visit and plan and ask questions of importance to them. Many times we would saunter back to the porch and sit until moonlight and talk and talk.)"[9]

In Sarah's public writing, she is both the cheerleader urging progress and the moralist, promoting righteous behavior for teachers, school directors, parents, and children. In her article, "The Use of the Hand Book in Rural Schools," published in *Midland Schools*, 1910–1911, Sarah calls for "every school home [to be] a beacon light of temperate living, sober thinking, chaste being, every boy growing more noble and manly, every girl becoming more graceful and womanly." But intermingled with such pious statements are the following incisive pronouncements related to the content of the handbook:

> She [the rural teacher] is handicapped in all too many instances by meager salary and by unsanitary and poorly equipped buildings and grounds. . . .
>
> Why the rural teacher should be compelled to get up socials for school benefits is past explaining. Her contract calls for all needful apparatus and supplies . . . and all other necessaries. Perhaps it is partly the teacher's fault as well as the directors. She does not ask, or becomes fearful it once refused, and he does not volunteer. . . .
>
> The teacher who does not give daily instructions in reading and writing in the very best manner and method possible is a stumbling block to the pupil's progress and advancement in all the other branches. . . .
>
> Let us urge directors and township boards to live up to their side of the contract, and let us not neglect our own side of the same document.[10]

To Be a Teacher

Sarah's blend of traditional piety and spirited drive for better school conditions emerged from a childhood that was relatively conventional for the time and the place. Sarah was born in 1865, near Manchester, Iowa, the second child of her pioneer parents. Her education began with her mother's lessons at home. When Sarah, age four, and her brother, Henry, started school at Coffin's Grove, Iowa, her young aunt was the teacher. Henry was twenty-two months older than Sarah, "but we entered school together and were kept together until the academy we attended later was absorbed into the public high school. We were not only in the same classes; we were dressed in suits of the same color and if one had red mittens the other had the same."[11]

Her mother, Emily Hawley Gillespie, had taught school before she married James Gillespie, a farmer. Emily supplemented schooling for Sarah and Henry with lessons at home. She wrote diaries for thirty years, from age twenty to shortly before her death in 1888, and encouraged Sarah and Henry to do the same by giving them journals as gifts.[12] Emily's diaries reveal her interest in the temperance movement, the Universalist church, her daily house and farm work, the family financial records, and, as her "only confidant," her diary became a record of the increasingly antagonistic, devastating behavior of her husband.

Emily Huftalen raised turkeys to help pay the school expenses for Henry and Sarah. She was so apprehensive and critical of their teachers that she organized a petition drive to oust one teacher and kept the children at home where she taught them. Emily believed that "[people's] happiness lies in their children with fond hopes that *they* may rise higher."[13] When her husband, James Gillespie, would not take Emily to town to hear Susan B. Anthony speak about woman suffrage, she complained in her diary "that it seems to be so much trouble to take me anywhere," but she determined, "I *must* not give up *no no*, my children are too noble, I must use every effort to help them to be what I might have been. tis my only pleasure to see them happy."[14]

Emily enjoyed socializing and the arts, and from time to time, saw herself as an aspiring but frustrated artist and writer. But as James preferred to stay home alone, Emily invested her efforts of domestic efficacy into her children who then became her universe, her hope for the future.

Sarah characterized her mother "as a martyr to her children" in a letter to Henry in 1948, as she prepared to send her mother's diaries to the Michigan Historical Commission: "It grieves my heart to review my dear mother's sorrows. She gave her life a martyr to her children. Naturally cheerful, prayerful, hopeful, the burdens became too heavy to bear and the light of her candle of life went out. I wonder what she would say could she know her prayers for her children were fully answered; I trust as an honor to her."[15]

In the verbal and physical battles with James, the children sided with their mother as she sought to make amends with James, to protect Sarah and Henry, and to make their lives better than hers had been. Emily was critical of divorce but found herself trapped by convention and economics in an increasingly unhappy marriage.[16]

For Sarah and Henry, their mother was their champion, seeking the best education for them and dealing day by day with their moody, repressive father. James Gillespie was unpredictable in his angry outbursts as he accused Emily of trying to kill him and tried to choke Henry and force him off the farm.[17] As Emily's health declined in the mid-1880s, James continued his verbal abuse of her, causing Sarah and Henry to fear for her safety. With the help of a lawyer, Emily forced James to leave the family for a year. At the end of the year, Emily moved to a house in town, where she died in 1888.

Throughout these trying years, Sarah and Henry pursued all the educational advantages that Manchester, Iowa, had to offer. In 1879, when Sarah was fourteen and Henry sixteen, the Normal College and Commercial Institute, commonly called the Academy, was established in Manchester. This school provided the opportunity for further education for the Gillespie children. In writing about her "Transition from the Country School to the Academy," fourteen-year-old Sarah was eager to attend the Academy in Manchester, Iowa, but found it somewhat different from the country school.

> Mon. Nov. 19th 1879, Commence to go to the Academy; study Appleton's Fifth Reader, Robinson's Progressive Higher Arithmetic, Reed and Kellogg English and Swinton's Spelling; that's all. Like it very well but it seems a little different from our school up here. . . .
>
> Fri. 7th Oct. [1881] . . . I don't like Trig very well and then again I do. Same with Latin. . . . I will sketch a few of the dresses etc. that Ma made for me for school and of each . . . I wrote, "I think it is real nice, or real pretty." Same of the cloaks.[18]

To Be a Teacher

Sarah's interest in new clothes for the academy was supported by her mother's skills as a milliner, dressmaker, tailor, and shoemaker. "She made even our heavily lined overcoats and cloaks; and my father, brother, and I never wore clothing purchased in the stores until after my mother died in 1888." [19]

Sarah's education prior to teaching consisted of attending

> . . . [the Academy] for two years taking a double course and from which we would have received diplomas of graduation had it not been we were prevented from attendance that last semester by illness . . . [I] served in assisting in the teaching of a large class in Double Entry Book Keeping and I was also supply teacher in a class in Elocution numbering 54. . . . There were Normal Training summer schools in Manchester each year of six to eight weeks and these I attended thus being in readiness to teach should opportunity come to the longing desire of my heart. [20]

The Academy plus the summer normal school sessions and institutes constituted Sarah's formal education until she was fifty-two, when she completed a bachelor's degree at Upper Iowa University in two years, while teaching there full time. At fifty-eight, she completed her master's degree at the State University of Iowa, and began taking courses toward a doctorate.

Sarah's beginning years of teaching near home in Delaware County, Iowa, were filled with learning how to cope with the rusty stove pipe that fell down; spit balls on the ceiling; the sixteen-year-old who chewed tobacco in school; and going home overnight with the scholars. "I went home with Charlie Anderson last night. Oh! Cats! the smell! ugh! Although Charlie is a nice swede boy." [21]

On another occasion, Sarah "Went up to Mr. Giffords home with the children. Mr. Giffords nephew Ed Moss, from Greene, Butler Co. Iowa, & Amy Gifford were very nice to come and visit the school last evening so I could ride home with them. . . . ta-ta-, young clerk—Had a good visit, they are Universalists & believe in Phrenology [as did Sarah's family]." [22]

When Sarah needed the buggy to go to the school director's home to find out about a teaching job in the fall of 1884, her father did not want her or her mother to drive. James's control over the horse and buggy also stifled Emily's ability to socialize. But Sarah would not wait for her father to relent and harness the horse.

I expected Pa would be mad for we have not taken the team in over a year. And he thought he had them so we could not drive them & we'd have to stay at home only [go] when he said we could go. Of course the buggy is old but there's always some excuse. Well he was mad—so mad he wouldn't harness. Thank the Lord I knew how. I harnessed & hitched up & we [Emily and Sarah] went. Pa said if we got killed or run away with we needn't blame him & that he'd "like the team once in a while." . . . [The school director] said he'd let me know as soon as possible . . . We got home about seven . . . We had a good ride and a good visit and Pa & Grandpa I hope will feel better. They had a good? talk I guess. Pa never said a word but G—pa told Ma when we first came in that he knew no one could drive "that horse" without her jumping & getting nervous, etc. They can if they treat her half decent. I can do any-thing with her.[23]

Sarah often thought that her father had strange thoughts and "mad fits."[24] Sarah overheard her parents' discussion over Emily's property, which she would not sign over to him. Pa was sure he would not live another year and was "A humming—'O Dear,' 'Well, well,' all the time. I can hear him. Ma is writing. The rest have retired, 9 o'clock. I must also for I am to go to the Normal to-morrow. I pray that all will be well—Good night. Beautiful moonlight."[25]

Throughout Sarah and Emily's diaries there are accounts of James's emotionally cruel behavior that appears to be unbalanced and erratic. Their diaries passionately describe his behavior and their feelings of anger and fear. This candor, which is somewhat unusual for diaries that have been placed in archival collections, is part of Sarah's private writing throughout her life. Her entries describe the events in her life and what she thought, said, and felt in the situation.

As a twenty-year-old teacher, Sarah had to cope with the weather, a sore throat, and with the amorous attentions of a married man.

Tues. 6 [January 1885] Have a very sore throat and bad cold. Taught school. Snowed and blowed a perfect blizzard all night. When I got to school at 8:30 a.m. the Pogue boys were there and had built a fire. My underclothes were ringing wet—and I had no chance to dry them. It was knee deep & the stickiest, wettest snow I remember of seeing. . . .

Wed. 7. Taught school—am about sick—no one seems to

To Be a Teacher

know it though. When we were eating supper who should come but Mr. Seger. I was glad to see him. In the evening he wet a towel in cold water & bound it on my neck. He had me put my stocking around over the towel. Well, I don't suppose it looked very nice but he kissed me good night. I was very near given out—so near I did not much care about any-thing . . . Mr. Alcorn & Mr. Seger sat up till after 12 & then the 1st thing I knew the cats were on the seed corn knocking it down on the dishes and raising an uproar in general. . . . Mr. Seger took me to school & was loth to leave me so sick with my bad cold. . . . As we were going he said—"O Sadie if I only had a wife like you I'd be happy—" said he "knew it was wrong but he couldn't help it—He did love me with his whole heart," and that "if he were a young man I should never teach another term of school"—I told him it was wrong for him to feel so, that Mrs. Seger is a great deal better than I & that he must not allow himself to think different—I will try to not give him the least bit of a chance to even speak to me. Taught school—I think a great deal of my school. Pleasant.[26]

Sarah's admirer erroneously thought he was offering her the best by saying that if he were a young man, she'd never teach school again. Not to teach would have been prevented Sarah from fulfilling the treasured goals of her life.

At Little York School No. 2, Delaware County, Iowa, Sarah signed a one-year contract, probably one of the first rural teaching contracts for more than one term. The school directors wanted to give her a contract for five years, but her mother's declining health prevented her from accepting it. Sarah had taught school for several years and was reluctant to leave teaching to stay home to care for her paralytic mother, but she had no choice. Henry was attending college and her father was unwilling or unable to care for Emily. Sarah recalled this stress-filled and physically exhausting period preceding her mother's death in 1888.

> . . . I was bloodless from loss of blood caused by the years
> of heavy lifting until I would fall and my voice and sight were
> nearly gone from the continued strain of years of ceaseless care
> and toil. Dr. Sherman said he was afraid I could not last to hold
> out before ma would go. Thank God I did. But from ten years to

twenty-two were given entirely to the duties and cares and anxiety of her whom had given me life and the awful care and stress of those years in her behalf all but took mine.[27]

Sarah saw herself from age ten on, as being the major care giver of her mother, but both children were supportive of their mother in the on-going arguments with James.

During the last two years of Emily's life, William "Billie" Huftalen, a sixty-year-old pawnbroker who boarded with the Gillespies, brought comfort, love, and support to Sarah. Billie was forty years older than Sarah when he asked Emily

> . . . on bended knees by her bedside at the farm for me and told her in his way that I must have care and that he would care for me as I needed so much and she told him he could have me, but I would not [admit] outwardly yet [what] I had inwardly known since the first time I met him at the age of sixteen in his store that I was his. Then finally when I talked it over with ma that winter before she died in March and I was to tell him when he came to noon day meal for he boarded with us in town then . . . how overjoyed I was in the thought and eager for his coming . . . he took my hand and said if I so wished it, so should it be. I was in bliss in mind and heart yet no emotion on either part—most silently were we. Then when Henry came . . . I was sad and glad to tell him but he said it must not be . . . I broke it to Billie and broke our hearts, and suffered it for 4 years.[28]

Henry's reaction to Sarah's engagement does not seem unusual coming from a protective older brother. In considering Billie as Sarah's future husband, his somewhat questionable occupation and the forty-year difference in their ages certainly raised legitimate concerns. Henry may well have felt that his intelligent and attractive sister could do better than marry a man who was older than their father. He may also have wondered if Sarah would be as unhappy and repressed as his mother had been with a man of that generation. At the time of Emily's death, Henry was attending college with the goal of becoming an Universalist minister. For Sarah to obey her brother reflects her admiration of Henry and his aspirations, as well as her expected conformity to the masculine domination in her family.

Emily expressed her concerns and hopes that Sarah would not have the unhappiness that she, Emily, had lived with. "Ah, *marriage is a lottery.* how full of deceit do they come with their false tongues and *'there is no one as dear as thee'* until one is married *then 'you are mine now we have something else to do besides silly kissing'*" (April 26, 1887).[29]

In the period after Emily's death, Sarah traveled to New York, Ohio, and Michigan, visiting friends and family while recovering her health. The physical and emotional exhaustion of caring for her mother was gone, but legacy of Emily's empathetic, loving support contributed to Sarah's strength. She asserted her adult independence and was no longer governed by her father or her brother as she left home and took a secretarial job in Des Moines. She did not leave a clue about the events that led this dedicated small-town teacher to take an office job in Des Moines and meet Billie there. Surely, there had been plans that led to Sarah and Billie's marriage. Marrying Billie at a hotel in Des Moines in September 1892 was Sarah's most defiant act against the domination by her father and Henry's so-called protection. Emily's death and Sarah's marriage to Billie four years later mark significant transitions in Sarah's private life. "It happened to be in Des Moines where I was writing for Jesse B. Herriman. . . . [Billie] had come from the Hot Springs in Ark. on his way to anywhere. We were married [September 14, 1892] at the Savery annex and remained there a month and then to the East side . . . where we remained until spring and then went to Manchester to live." [30]

Sarah's father and brother continued to disapprove of her marriage, and returning to Manchester did not mend this schism in the family. Sarah returned to teaching in the fall of 1893, and, having left the traditional role of dutiful daughter, she entered into a time of stability and growth in her teaching and social activism in her community service. Sarah was a frequent speaker on behalf of the temperance movement and was the president of the county WCTU for nine years. The Manchester Equal Suffrage Association was also led by Sarah. On the occasion of the fiftieth anniversary of the equal rights convention at Seneca Falls, New York, July 20, 1848, Sarah delivered the address, "Woman's Sphere," at the City Hall in Manchester, Iowa. After recounting some of the accomplishments of women and the importance of public coeducation, Sarah concluded:

> Thus we see that with the advancement of the history of our nation, woman too, as time and place demanded, has met these changed surroundings until we find her to-day capable of filling

innumerable positions. With keen intuitive perceptions and with intelligence equal to brothers and fathers, she feels that she is a necessary factor in the upbuilding of a nation, knowing too that the home is the bulwark upon which the rise or fall of a nation rests, does it not seem right that her voice should be counted in all questions of morality that constantly arise among a people and which environ her home with the results of a polluted or un-polluted ballot box? . . .

It is difficult for us to imagine a time when it would be consid-ered a disgrace for women to preside at public meetings, let alone their occupying pulpits, (it is said there are 18 denominations that ordain women and there are 1,800 women now occupying pulpits,) mounting the rostrum as orators, inscribing M. D. and other like initials after their names and the hundred and one other things which call forth praise, instead of censure, at the present time.

Surely, a wonderful advancement has been made during these fifty years which the younger people scarce can realize—an advanced condition that has placed woman in a new world of thought and action, and she accepts it with all its privileges and blessings and gives thanks to those pioneers who opened the way. Every advantage gained, every privilege granted to woman is the result of her own efforts.[31]

The Cosmos Class, a group that Sarah helped to organize, stud-ied the social, intellectual, and religious nature of "mankind," and worked toward community improvements such as a public rest room for women and children. Despite their well-developed plans and solici-tations, the rest room project failed for lack of funds "from the busi-ness portion of the town."[32]

These years of 1892–1903, in Manchester, Iowa, were calm and happy for Sarah and Billie, until Billie "failed in debt while keeping [a] second-hand goods store in Manchester. He insisted on my signing the note and not letting the public know our circumstances which was right enough, but at the time it was a very hard thing for me to do. . . . In a way it was a good thing for it put me in my realm of public school work."[33]

This unfortunate circumstance was the catalyst in Sarah's public life. Financially they could not maintain the status quo, so Sarah sought the best-paying teaching job where she was in her "realm of public school work." The next five years in Oneida, Iowa, living eighty rods east of the schoolhouse, were happy but stressful, frugal years. While Sarah taught school, Billie "got the meals and tended the large lawn and garden." One year, they "grew $70.00 worth of onions and did all we could while teaching." With Sarah's salary, and the meager profits from the garden, "It took eight years of the most frugal living and saving to clear the debt."[34]

In addition to the debt was the community controversy stemming from the election of Sarah, a Universalist, as the superintendent of the proposed Union Sunday school. The forced move to another school brought Sarah into the next stage of her teaching career, with a higher salary and additional freedom to develop her teaching style and leadership in public education. Billie, now in his late seventies, had many regrets and sad memories, but he persevered in his devotion to Sarah and as the househusband.

> Billie never overcame his heart griefs . . . Charity's death [his second wife], the loss of his hotel by fire, and his having me sign the note for debt to Simmons for store and house rent.. . .
>
> We were at Norwich (Page Co.) nearly four years and Billie kept up the chores, got the breakfast (always had since we were married) and the meals and did the dishes. . . .
>
> . . . And he was so lonesome while I was away during the day. We would talk it over and try to think of some way different to do so I could be at home, but as [I] could never come to the point of undertaking any thing else, he would say, he would get along and for me to come as soon as I could, and was anxious for me to be on time. I was not away a great deal at night. Had to be some time. . . .
>
> I do know he idolized me and was precious of my life. I am sorry to have suffered so much pain and caused him so much worry therefore. How tenderly he nursed and cared for me as but few men would have done.[35]

Sarah's parents' relationship had been the antithesis of the partnership in homemaking that she and Billie had developed. Billie was the understanding father figure she never had and the loving supportive husband her mother was denied. While Sarah had been the devoted care giver for her mother, she never understood her father's peculiarities and mean-spirited actions.

Chapter 7

Throughout her twenty-two-year marriage, Sarah continued writing dated notes about her pupils, her teaching methods, and the school events, but her daily diary entries ceased. With Billie as her confidant and companion, Sarah had little need of writing about her hopes and fears. Billie's love of Sarah and his role as househusband freed her to identify and create her leadership role as the professional rural educator.

One of the major sources of change in education in the early 1900s stemmed from the state courses of study. When Sarah began teaching in 1883,

> . . . [she] taught Reading arith. gram. spel. writing, geog. and history. New subjects were added from year to year until we now had a curriculum of many subjects besides the fundamentals. Phonics, Music, Nature Study, General Lessons, Palmer Method of penmanship, agriculture, Domestic science, etc. Supervision of the play periods, was a must. Hygiene and the effects of narcotics. So many pages in so many months. Boys and girls club work, Forestry, corn corn corn.[36]

Beginning in 1883, while teaching the Little York School No. 2 in northeastern Iowa, Sarah developed her own teaching style, which came into full blossom in the Arbor Vitae Summit School in Oneida, Iowa, 1905–1909, and continued to develop at Norwich, Page County, Iowa, 1909–1913. The rural school setting gave her the freedom to experiment with different and original instructional methods employing both creativity and practicality.

> We thought that every farm should have a wood lot so we collected hundreds of specimens, learned much about trees and their care and uses. We committed [to memory] tree poems and made beautiful booklets 22 by 28 inches containing poems, drawings, and maps. We drew our homes and the school yard showing the trees and shrubs on each. The sentiment spread through the community, many planting trees and shrubs and beautifying their yards and lawns.[37]

Throughout Sarah's school notebooks, scrapbooks, and articles, her teaching style and philosophy indicate a departure from the stereotypes of the "worn out red school house."[38] She found that her philosophy and methods of instruction were applicable to a variety of rural and town schools. Regardless of the number of children or their age span, Sarah's students worked together on the school projects, each at his or her own level of learning. Sarah's concern with developing a sense of community among the students and a strong teacher-child relationship is found in this excerpt from one of her scrapbooks:

> When children are happily busy and interested in a united effort in their studies, projects and games one need not worry about the so-called problem of discipline. There is none to worry about. With a beautified yard that all hands help make possible establishes interest akin to ownership. And what child does not but enjoy the sensation of ownership; his very own. Complete trusting and confidence between teacher and a child served as a strong tie.[39]

The local patrons and parents were always welcomed at Arbor Vitae Summit and Norwich Schools. The schools were also visited by fellow teachers, superintendents, and teacher educators from around the nation. Sarah's teaching excellence became recognized through her leadership in state and local teachers' associations, institutes, and through the displays of her scholars' work at these meetings. She became known as the best and highest paid rural teacher in Iowa, and perhaps in the nation.[40]

Through her teaching experience, Sarah found that "if engaging in any occupation three things were essential if the goal was worth while . . . time, money and labor." [41] The first projects undertaken in each of Sarah's schools were those that improved the school yard and the schoolroom, because "Environs have a subtle way of influencing the moral atmosphere in a school, home or community."[42] Her concern for morality and healthy conditions extended to the outhouses. "The 'big, bad boy' took up the old desks and seats (caused sore blisters on the inside of both hands). He built two large outbuildings having sanitary seats later. We papered these and woe to a new scholar who dared to mark one or anything else on the grounds. We had one lesson on the law in regard to such effacements."[43]

In terms of time and labor, Sarah Huftalen was a visionary who could facilitate learning mathematics, science, grammar, history, and literature in the context of working together to build a park out of the clay hill and ash heaps that constituted the school yard. Teamwork and cooperation were the basis of labor in her classroom, "two to wash a board; two to dust the erasers; two to do this and to do that."[44] Her students were totally involved in planning, developing, and maintaining their "school home."[45] As Sarah remembered her one-room school at Oneida, she wrote: "Really we were a happy school family in a school home every inch of which we all loved both inside and outside. We were a team in every project and endeavor. Harmony reigned over the hill."[46]

In order to obtain funds for the projects and goals of the school, Sarah organized money-making programs at her schools in which the children displayed their talents and projects. Everyone was invited with an admission of ten cents. Sarah wrote this letter to parents accompanying the schedule of events for the school year, 1908–1909:

Dear Friends:
We want to have the best school in the state, nothing short of it will satisfy us, we are determined to reach the summit of excellence that is founded on true merit and worth. We are willing workers. We want and need supplies and apparatus. We seek your co-operation and helpfulness, such only as parents, patrons and friends can give. We solicit your visitations, interest and suggestions. . . .

The parent, the pupil and the teacher form the trinity of the schoolroom—of education. Let us work together to raise the standard of excellence. . . .
Sincerely and faithfully,
MRS. HUFTALEN[47]

The "trinity of the school," children, teacher, and parents, was the foundation on which the learning projects were implemented. Sarah thought that it was "miraculous for a teacher to lead a pupil beyond home influence which is fairly breathed into the very life and existence of a child."[48] This belief, however, did not prevent her from expecting each child to do her or his very best work. She asked the children to write on their papers, "This is my level best."[49] She hung pictures at the children's eye level to encourage "happy thoughts" about the scenes, animals, birds, children, patriots, and reformers "like some of the Presidents and Frances Willard," the temperance leader.[50]

She also expanded the children's knowledge of the world through reading, but at the Arbor Vitae Summit School she was frustrated with the practice of the township secretary coming to pick up reference and library books before she and the children had completed them. She especially recommended Booker T. Washington's *Up From Slavery* as a "wonderful source, in the way of removing prejudices and of educating the coming generation to the facts relative to the true conditions of the negro race."[51]

In Sarah's classrooms, textbooks were not the only source of information. She used a wide variety of supplementary materials such as the forestry and agriculture bulletins from Iowa State College; exhibits from manufacturers of thread, fabric, kerosene, steel; children's magazines; collections of rocks, shells, wood specimens; scrapbooks and boxes of clippings on "corn, cotton, wheat, weeds, potatoes, coal, gold, etc."; and maps, books, and displays that the children had constructed. In using these materials, children "could help themselves during study periods so each member of the class would have something of interest outside the text."[52] When the children brought "many kinds of texts" to school, Sarah and the children "devised the method of assigning lessons from the different texts on the same topic. This, with the supplemental material we furnished, added interest to the recitation periods."[53]

Sarah's students wrote original dialogues and books that they illustrated and bound. The children's work received honors at various educational meetings in Iowa and around the nation. Children who moved to a graded, city school system had no problem of "fitting in" academically because of the independence, responsibility, and interdependence among children fostered by Sarah's teaching. Her scholars' learning went far beyond memorization through the correlation and integration of school subjects as illustrated in this example from her Arbor Vitae School notebook:

> The 5th [grade] will read DeSoto in reading. Draw map of DeSoto's march in Geog. and recite about DeSoto, Coronado, Vaca and Navarez [Narváez] in history—reciting from the maps.
> In Geog. we started at the school-house & expect to travel all over the world from Oneida as a center.[54]

Each child's work was displayed; each child had a job to do; each child deserved recognition, acceptance, and encouragement. Sarah believed that the "common school graduates from the Rural school deserve recognition in a public manner and I want to do my part in behalf of the educational interest and moral benefits that our boys and girls merit."[55]

As Sarah encouraged children to do their "level best," she expected the same of herself and other educators. She gave children recognition for their achievements within the schoolroom and in the various public programs. Sarah and her scholars wrote numerous newspaper articles about the school activities. In general, however, the rural teachers of the early 1900s had little or no professional recognition beyond their school district, the local institutes and associations. Although the state education associations talked about "the rural school problem," usually implying inferior education, Sarah and others found there was no recognition of rural teachers as professional educators.

During this period of the early 1900s, Sarah came to the fore as the organizer of the Rural Section of the Iowa State Teachers Association, perhaps her most consequential contribution to public education. In 1908, Sarah decided to not only send charts and displays from Arbor Vitae Summit School with her county superintendent but to attend the Iowa State Teachers Association meeting herself. The only person she knew there was her superintendent, and she found not one discussion or lecture for rural educators. She described her leadership and the origins of the Rural Section of ISTA:

> In regard to the organizing of a Rural Section of the Iowa State Teacher's Association the years 1908-1910 were the most momentous to me as the duty of accomplishing it had fallen across my path. I was teaching in a one-room village school at Oneida, Delaware County, Iowa, and had kept abreast of all educational requirements as well as having initiated some of my own. The Normal Training Summer Schools, Institutes and special meetings called by the superintendent had been faithfully attended. Yet there comes a time for re-freshing, for advancing. An inner urge, an intuitive feeling prompted me to desire to attend an educational meeting higher up.
>
> County Superintendent of Schools, Frank D. Joseph, who said it was like a benediction to visit my school, called to select some material as an exhibit for him to take to the State Convention at Des Moines a week hence. I said that I should like to attend to which he replied there was no need for the country teachers to attend. . . . I was to take the material to the station to hand to

him as he would be on the early train on his way to the convention. . . . The train stopped, Joseph alighted, shook hands, accepted the material and re-entered the coach. I followed and passed him without his seeing me and took a seat in the rear. . . . .

. . . above and over all was the blissful anticipation of attending a great, and my first, state meeting.[56]

. . . I walked alone around the Mezzanine floor to find many doors . . . each bearing a placard that served as an invitation and welcome home room or booth of rest and meeting. There were placards for the Romance Language, the Mathematics, Music, College, University, Latin, etc. and on and on but none for the Country teacher. Where was I to feel at Home and at ease! I felt orphaned and lonesome. . . . A truth came forcibly to mind and heart; an Association that is broad enough to cover the state whose specific duty is to father and mother the educational interest of the state and no Rural Teacher's Section, Round Table or department, no nothing for that portion from which springs nearly, if not all of the rest, that portion which serves as foundation and corner stone for much that represents our best and noblest citizenship and statesmanship. How could such a thing be, I argued with myself.[57]

In determination to remedy this omission of the rural teachers, Sarah sought out the state superintendent of schools and asked why there "was no place for such [rural] teachers at the State Convention." He told her that no one had ever thought of it before, but if she could get ten teachers together, they could have a rural teachers' round table. During the following year, Sarah sent out letters, such as the following examples, through the Iowa State Teacher's Association to rural teachers and superintendents urging them to attend the next state meeting, encouraging them to save their best specimens of their scholars' work for exhibits, and generally cheering on the "ruralists."

Come and receive that inspiration that the privilege and opportunity of such a meeting [the Rural Section] affords which will help place the rural schools where they rightfully belong in buildings, equipment and salary. . . .

Under separate cover . . .you will receive a bunch of circular letters which I am going to take the liberty of asking you to hand to the teachers of your county at Institute. . . . Will you urge a large attendance and the importance of it? . . .

Sincerely yours to boost the little old worn out red school house with its weed patch, out; and the large new sanitary and more convenient building with its art and skill inside, and the beautiful setting outside, in.

Mrs. Huftalen [58]

NORWICH, Ia., Sept. 8, 1910

Dear Fellow Teacher:

The Rural school teachers,—the one room faraway country school teachers, who wade through mud and slush, build their own fires, get up box socials to secure apparatus that their contracts say the board shall provide, teach or hear thirty classes and eight grades—these country self-sacrificers are organized for the first time in the history of Iowa into a state assembly that meets at Des Moines November 3-5, 1910.

As you and I are part of this great body of ten thousand, upon whom rests the responsibility of the meeting and of much of the betterment of the conditions of our schools, in equipment, tutelage, salary, etc. May I urge your attendance, your interest, your helpfulness?

Have you an ideal, a question, a topic, that you would like to bring or have brought before the meeting? Come and present it or have it presented. Get your director to come. If he is progressive and a booster he ought to be heard; if he is of the "old-time cradle and hoe" sort he ought to be whaled into line or out of office.

Let us be boosters and progressive ourselves. Let us marshall our forces for the improvement of our Rural Schools, that they may better meet present day conditions and demands.

Our vacations are about ended, we are planning for the coming year's work. Let us include going to Des Moines in November. We have a right to go without loss of salary. We will never regret it. The story of a trip to the capital city will inspire the dummest kind of pupil to loyalty, and a desire to see and to know.

I would like to see you and explain the moment of this meeting of ours, but as I cannot, this meager message of invitation will have to do for now. . . .

Sincerely and faithfully your friend and co-worker,

Mrs. Huftalen.

Leader Rural Teacher's Round Table

I.S.T.A., 1910.

P.S. Save this, my teacher friend, printing 10,000 costs some, and you may not hear from me direct again before we meet in November when I shall expect to see you face to face and we can talk all things over together.[59]

While the state superintendent suggested she gather ten teachers together, Sarah contacted 10,000! In her contacts with the rural teachers, she emphasized her understanding of their problems and praised their work, while urging reform on the part of the teachers and their directors.

When she attended the state meeting in 1909, she asked the chair of the general session to read her announcement inviting rural teachers to meet in room 65 for the purpose of organizing a rural section of Iowa State Teachers Association. "Result that No. 65 was crowded to standing room and in the hall," and Sarah was elected president to plan the program and establish the rural section of ISTA.[60] Although she didn't know the word *networking*, her approach to organizing and recognizing the rural teachers of Iowa was a brilliant example.

Starting with sixty members in 1910, Sarah was re-elected president of the Rural Department of the Iowa State Teachers Association every year until she resigned in 1927. At that point the membership had grown to six hundred members. This on-going professional network of rural teachers and superintendents brought encouragement and enlightenment to many school directors, as they too were invited to attend the rural education meetings. The titles of papers presented at the 1914 state meeting by rural teachers give some insight into their professional concerns: "Entertainments Given by Country Schools, Their Purpose, Their Influence"; "Exhibits and Their Values"; "More Efficient Teacher Service"; "Discussion of Consolidation"; "The Prestige of the Rural School Teacher and Her School"; "What the Country Teacher Thinks of the Average Director"; "The Most Important and the Most Neglected Branches"; "Prize Giving, to What Extent"; "Cooperation of Patrons and School Officers, How Obtained"; and "The Evolution of the Country School."[61]

In the early organizational years of the Rural Department of ISTA, Sarah received support from many county superintendents but got no response from Miss Jessie Fields, who was then her superintendent in Page County. Because of her successful leadership in establishing the Rural Section and her continuing achievements as a rural teacher, Sarah was encouraged to run for the position of county superintendent. Running on the Democratic ticket in a largely Republican county, she won and took office in January 1913.

> Upon our return from the ISTA in Des Moines we noticed some fires about the village. The train stopped and a number of citizens swarmed in the coach, took our valise and umbrella and carried us off the train. The Essex Band was playing a Royal Welcome Home and a large crowd had gathered. We had been elected to the county superintendency of schools and a speech was demanded. We reluctantly resigned our beloved school position. We selected Faith Bailey to come and teach with us a week and folded our tent and quietly stole away to take residence in Clarinda.[62]

In this position, which she held until September 1, 1915, she visited each of 110 schools two or three times during the school year. She traveled by buggy, automobile, and train, staying overnight when necessary in order to reach, guide, and help the teachers throughout the county.

As part of her position as Page County superintendent, and in addition to her school duties, Sarah worked with the Farm Boys' and Girls' Clubs during their summer camp sessions at the Chautauqua meetings each August. She arranged for instructors in domestic science, agriculture, stock raising and judging. Closely associated with the summer programs was her work in organizing the 4-H Clubs in the county with 350 members. Sarah was the secretary and organizer of the annual Farmers' Institute and Exhibition. These additional duties were appropriate for the woman who had worked with children in planting and improving school yards and had won medals for her championship corn in 1908 at the Omaha Exposition.

Billie and Sarah's debts were paid at last, and Sarah was indeed in her "realm of public school work." But the forty-year difference in their ages began to take its toll as Billie, now in his eighties, was in declining health. Occasionally, Sarah would be called to come home as Billie was lost, confused, and looking for his wife. He gradually became weaker and bed-ridden, and with Sarah at his side, Billie died January 7, 1914, at age eighty-six. Just six days later, January 13, 1914, a teacher in Page County was fired by the local school board for being unfit. Sarah referred to the situation as "a 10-day trial for me to serve as judge" and give "my decision of an unfit man teacher."[63]

Six months after Billie's death, Sarah returned to writing a diary in which she recorded her grief in losing Billie, and recollections of their happiness.[64]

> June 28, 1914. Sunday. Clarinda, Iowa. 341- 16th Street.
> It is a bright and beautiful morning. I slept well and woke rested and refreshed after a week's arduous work.
> It is my privilege to be the County Superintendent of Schools of Page County, Iowa since Jan. 1, 1913. I like my work always and am happy in the doing.
> When I awoke I thought I would tidy the house, cook my own breakfast, bathe and go to church.
> But when I began building the fire in our little kitchen stove and handling the things it brought the memories of loved days so thick and fast that I've cried until my eyes are too reddened and my head too painful to see anyone.
> Someway I do not lift from the grief of Billie's going. . . . I know of no reason why I should write in a diary at all as I so seldom have since Ma died in 1888 but in the hopes of finding relief I will attempt it. There are some new friends but none but the Lord to tell one's suffering to. . . .
> [While teaching for five years at Oneida] Billie and I were very happy in the home . . . and as he gradually failed, I would think and say to him, "Billie, I cannot, I cannot have you grow old." It did not seem as though I could.
> Then he would say, "we must all pass by," so quietly, so sweetly, with hands clasped and a dreamy faraway look in his eyes. Those dear eyes.—How they have watched for my coming.

Sarah regretted that she had to be away from home and could not stay with Billie during the day. With the debts paid off, their lives in Page County should have been easier, but Billie had to give up the gardening and the housework. Sarah then recounted his last hours and her own feelings of "a most terrible loneliness." At this point, she began to understand her father's grief.

> I can understand how it doth hurt when the affections be-
> tween those who are one are severed. One feels so lost, so lonely
> and longing to wander away, away. I can see what Pa meant
> when he said he had cried days and days and nights and nights.
> Poor dear Pa. I never fully understood him. I do not see how
> Henry ever stays alone on the old farm and batches it as he has
> during the past two or three years and more. He and Pa were
> never reconciled to my marriage to Billie, so I never feel like say-
> ing any griefs to Henry.
> It has now reached noon and I've wept the forenoon through.
> This has been a hard ordeal, and yet there is a degree of satis-
> faction in it. It is evening and this has been the hardest of days
> for me.

During their last few weeks together, Billie told Sarah about his early pioneering days in the Denver area and in Nebraska. Sarah went to visit his sister-in-law, Carolyne, in Fremont, Nebraska, June 13–16, 1914. Carolyne gave Sarah pictures of Billie's first wife, who died on their journey west, and of Charity, his second wife. While in Fremont, Sarah placed flowers on Charity's grave and "on the graves of those I've loved and known only in spirit this score of years and more."

When Sarah returned home, she once again recalled the details of Billie's death and funeral and visited his grave.

> Sunday, July 12, 1914. . . .
> Can I refrain from tears and loneliness. Can I help longing to
> see him once more . . .
> I've been so very busy with office duties and it's a blessing so to
> be. But it comes again and again on Sundays and crushes my
> bleeding heart. . . .
> Billie died when I was 48. We had been married 22 yrs. He
> was 67 & I 27 when we were married. Sept. 14, 1892. Does not
> that seem strange. If I were to wait 20 yrs. from now and then
> marry some one 20 yrs. younger than I now am? That is what
> Billie did.[65]

In the next diary entry dated January 10, 1915, Sarah again recalled Billie's funeral and remembered how Billie was ever brave and gallant, even in his declining years. She mourned for Billie and for the son they never had.

> . . . Sometimes I feel his presence and once he has spoken distinctly. I only wish that we had had a son like him. I cannot understand why childless I had to roam but I expect it is all for the best someway. . . .
> . . . But why all this—I could go on and on for twenty more years and think and live it all over but no use. This writing is a comforter in a way like speaking to an unseen friend.

Her grief spent, the next diary entries concern her first and enduring love, her work as a teacher and superintendent. Sarah wrote in detail about the teachers' institute she had organized and its successful implementation. The superintendency was a position that Sarah relished inasmuch as it gave her the opportunity to attempt to implement her teaching style countywide. When Sarah was not re-elected to the superintendency in April 1915, it appeared to her that she had lost because "Miss Field [superintendent prior to Sarah] wanted a Y. W. C. A. Co. Supt. and thru strategy and dirty politics succeeded in finding a tool candidate."[66]

In September, rather than accept another teaching position, Sarah joined her brother, Henry, at the home farm near Manchester. Henry had returned to college after their mother's death and graduated as valedictorian of his class from Ryder Divinity College, Galesburg, Illinois, in 1894. He worked in Chicago as the assistant pastor of Saint Paul's Church, and as a carpenter, according to one source, and as an architect, according to his obituary.[67] After their father's death in 1909, Henry returned to the farm.

For Sarah, the return to the home farm was another disappointment following close upon her defeat in her bid for re-election. Although she had been offered various teaching positions, she declined, perhaps feeling that being a classroom teacher was a demotion. The sense of homecoming and "rest and change" that she sought at the family farm eluded her as she and Henry became adversaries. And once again her diary became her "unseen friend."

> At Manchester, Iowa. 10–13–1915.
> I needed a rest and change and so refused several teaching positions that were offered and above all I felt it a duty to come &

keep house for Henry who has been living on the farm alone and batching. I was in high hope and joyed at the thought of coming but I fear the change is too radical. . . .

Strange as it might seem I'm not at home here either in mind or heart. The duties difficult and beyond strength such as have not done since lived here in girlhood thirty years ago. . . . I feel like giving it all up and going away. I must try to get well and God will yet show the way. I'm sure He will. . . .

I guess we do not understand each other. Henry has lived here so long alone and in such a way that thus far I've felt the least at home of any place I've ever been. . . . [I] scarcely dare suggest anything for fear I'll be told I don't know what I want. It has been the hardest initiation I've ever experienced. My back suffers much pain and I have nervous headaches, something I've never had, nervous chills, menstrual periods irregular caused by these nerve shocks and the most tears I ever knew. And he's criticized everything I've brought in one way or another until I wish I'd never come or brought them. I cannot help it. I fear it is the mistake of my life. Sometimes the darknesses have proved disguised blessings. Maybe this will.[68]

At age fifty, Sarah's unrecognized menopausal symptoms were aggravated by her brother's criticisms, perhaps a return to the pattern of their childhood relationship. The shift from a position of leadership to that of the belittled and demeaned housekeeper took its toll on Sarah's fragile physical and mental health. In the months that followed, Sarah tried to clean up the old farm home and find a place for rest and happiness but found her efforts blocked by Henry. Henry was "unnerved" at her bringing furniture, books, and buggy to the farm, and, characteristic of their parents' relationship, he never ceased berating her. During this time, Sarah found out that she too owned part of the farm, although she had never received anything for her share. By the summer of 1917, Sarah had "four very serious days in June and went to Hinsdale Sanitarium on June 12th, was there five weeks."[69] She returned to the farm in late July, and within a few days was again "suffering much."

In August 1917, a phone call brought an end to the "darknesses," as she was invited to attend a methods conference conducted by Iowa State Teachers College "for their critic teachers and associate professors of which I am now to be one." Sarah was now launched into her next period of professional and creative productivity. She returned to the farm after the conference, sold some of her belongings, and packed for the move to Cedar Falls.

> I am to have the Supervisorship of the 9 Rural schools in Bennington Township in Blackhawk County and $105 per mo. which included the $160 voted by the township for the care & feed of the horse. $20 a mo. for 8 mo. The College pays me 85 per mo. to start on.
>
> This is the next step to what I was trying to work out in Page Co., i.e. Township leadership. A "circuit teacher" I thought. . . . Miss Cortz has Lincoln township. We are the only ones in the State or U. S. to try out the new plan.[70]

As Sarah packed for her move back to her professional world, she was apprehensive of leaving some of her belongings at the farm. Although Henry had not included Sarah in any profits from the farm, he had apparently been asking her for money for some time and made one more attempt as she was packing. Sarah dreaded Henry's opinions, just as her mother had feared her father's outbursts. "My heart hurt all night. I was so fearful of what Henry might say when he learned I was looking for a horse. He is so hasty, excitable and wrathy. I cannot understand him. I am sorry so sorry for him. Now I will put this [her diary] in Billie's trunk. Am leaving my pictures, furniture, library and other things in the old parlor. And hope they will not be destroyed."[71]

When Sarah met with Professor of Rural Education Macy Campbell, formerly the superintendent of schools, West Liberty, Iowa, he gave her a choice of positions and asked her to name her salary. Her characteristic response was, "I could not [name a salary] and that whatever they wished would be all right." After Sarah and Billie Huftalen paid their debts, she prided herself on not actively looking for a position nor questioning the salary offered. She obviously believed that it was a form of positive recognition when other school systems sought her out. As evidenced by her scrapbooks of newspaper clippings, she actively sought publicity for the activities in her schools and for her own community involvement. While she stretched the bonds of gender through her leadership roles, and wholeheartedly sought publicity for her accomplishments, her desire for personal recognition did not appropriately include negotiating for positions nor for salaries.

Huftalen's position at Iowa State Teachers College was part of the on-going effort to upgrade rural schools under the leadership of College President Homer Seerley and Dr. Chauncey P. Colgrove, chair of the Department of Education.[72] During the one-year project of 1917–1918, Huftalen supervised

> . . . the most backward township and Miss Anna Cortz [was] in the most progressive township. We were to furnish our own conveyance which was a horse and buggy. . . . It required constant driving and helping at each school all the year. No one wanted the new feature in these townships. . . .
>
> I drove to each school keeping in close touch with their teachers, methods, and curricula for eight months.
>
> Of the nine teachers, three could be called good, one outstanding, three were average and the others poor. All cooperated pleasantly and I sometimes wondered how they could when, at times, at least three of the Rural staff would be at their school on an early morning with suggestions and advice and questions. They would be putting work on the blackboard or preparing a lesson or building fires or other duty. The three poor teachers, if they could be called a teacher at all did the best they knew but it is surprising sometimes how some ever passed an examination or "got a school." Of course there is at times a director who has a girl who wants to earn some money and stay at home while doing it. Pity the children in such schools.
>
> On the whole it proved a happy and successful year's work [and] placing some of the schools on the standardized list was a happy event for the schools and the supervisor for it took hard and persistent work. And this was in 1917-1918 when all schools were required to purchase War Stamps and do various kinds of hand work for our boys in France. Rally Day Programs were held in each district and plans made for complying with all requirements.[73]

This year of leadership through on-site teacher education rescued Sarah from the unhappiness of trying to live with Henry and propelled her into full-time teacher education for the rest of her professional years.

To Be a Teacher

When Dr. Chauncey P. Colgrove left Iowa State Teachers College to become the president of Upper Iowa University, Fayette, Iowa, he contacted Sarah to teach a methods class of eighty "teachers and would-be teachers" and supervise a demonstration school representing a one-room country school during the summer of 1918. Colgrove asked Sarah to remain for the regular school year and was shocked to find out that she did not possess a college degree. With Colgrove's encouragement, she contacted the rural staff at Iowa State Teachers College who released her from her commitment.

> I remained at U.I.U. and took a four-year course in two years and taught during the time. How savagely and furiously I worked day and night with never a holiday or respite. It seems almost incredible but I have the note books to show for it that I wrote over 300,000 words in preparation, class notes, examinations, and reviews during the time. . . .
>
> I taught there including summers from 1918 to 1923, receiving an A. B. in 1920.[74]

While at Upper Iowa, Sarah taught courses in four departments: social science, natural science, physical science, mental science and education. Her students ranged in age from seventeen to seventy-three, with up to eighty students per class. As it had been in every school, Sarah's first steps were to get to know the students as individuals and involve them in cleaning and decorating their classroom.

> My room was on the north side of the hall on the lower floor and I should think at least forty by fifty feet. Old rags were hanging on the glass doors that entered the hall; black soot had run down on the walls where the stove had been used. The wall had been red but was faded and dingy. This was the way it looked when we entered. We proposed to renew it and the students and a teacher . . . helped paint the wall, and I did the whole job of painting the wood work and deep window casing and sills. We hung the class pictures and some others I furnished, and made all glass to shine. I brought my library and book cases and a parlor table for my desk. We then had a cheery and inviting and pleasant room to work in with its chairs, long tables and a reading table in the rear, etc. . . .
>
> The class in Geology was composed of young men; some of

whom were returned War Soldiers. We never discussed that hor-
rible experience. They were thinking of having homes of their
own and same way with the members of the Sociology Class. . . .
I never shall forget how interested we were. The boys would
saunter almost unconsciously up to my desk that stood on a low
platform; sit down on the platform around my feet and ask questions vital to them. These were real heart to heart talks.[75]

Under the presidency of Chauncey Colgrove, Sarah was promised a
life position at Upper Iowa University. With a change in leadership,
Sarah was anxious to resign and be "free from such demands" as were
made by the head of the Department of Education and Psychology.
The new department head demanded detailed planning, analysis, and
evaluation of every lesson in every subject, to be completed "both
before and after classes" and "laid on his desk." She complained, "It
took me two hours and work as fast as possible to fill in the blank
sheets [of questions] in each of the subjects I was teaching: Applied
Psychology, General Psychology, Methods, Sources, and History of
Education."[76] The forms to be completed before and after every lesson
analyzed the assignment and the methods of instruction in minute
detail.[77] While this analysis if applied occasionally could be helpful in
developing teaching skills, the detail and daily repetition were of little
value and insulting to an accomplished, successful teacher. Sarah believed that the department head "was very anxious to dispense with
my services," and had imposed this "most absurd demand ever made a
teacher" because she might have been considered as the head of the
department. "This did not happen and I someway felt an inner glad-
ness in looking forward to be free from such demands." She would
have welcomed the promotion to department head but could see that
her style of leadership would not have been appreciated after Colgrove
had left the college.

Her sense of injustice at being forced out of a "life position" stayed
with her for years to come. After 1935, when Sarah had retired from
teaching, she gathered together 106 pages of these lesson analysis
sheets and sent them to her former professor at the State University
of Iowa, Forest Ensign, hoping "that some student might find them of
interest." In her letter to Ensign, she speculated if the department
head had ever read the plans, he being the kind of leader who would
"get others to do all the work and he get all the credit." She went on,
"I suspect he did the best he knew. . . . He said this, that a leader was

To Be a Teacher

a manager of others and I think he tried hard to be a leader of this kind. My principle is entirely different. Leaders are pioneers who laid the way noting obstacles and showing how to remove them like the man who built the bridge that other generations who followed might cross."[78]

After Sarah left the University of Upper Iowa, she attended Saturday classes at the State University of Iowa from 1921 to 1923, "enjoying it immensely." She completed her M.A. in January 1924, and was then contacted to teach at the Normal Department, Muscatine High School, Muscatine, Iowa. She accepted the position of

> Methods and Critic teacher of the Normal Department in the fall of 1924, and that it was understood that should a Junior College be established I was to be Dean thereof. The board raised my salary twice of its own volition they saying would like to raise it more but owing to other teachers' wage, etc., did not. It was [for] "my willingness to serve, my experience, my influence, and my high standing scholarship and education." Supt. Hayes and I were the only members of the entire faculty holding Master's Degrees.[79]

As she had in every school and classroom, Sarah began her work by involving the normal training students in cleaning, furnishing, and decorating their classrooms. "We sponsored films, sold candy, and held bake sales in order to furnish our department with supplies: globe, clock, hectographs, magazines, besides pictures suitable for each grade, one to eight, gold fish and bowl, vines, and decorations for special days, etc."[80]

In this position, Sarah could disseminate the teaching strategies she had developed during her years of classroom experience.

> We had all the Trainers [normal training students] make sufficient seat work [for children] for a year; also we made lessons for the year (36) in each of the Primary subjects, Grades I, II, & III in Plants, Animals, insects, birds, land, sea, and sky with poems, quotations, and Talks, etc. These really should have been published.
>
> I also taught in Night School and coached private pupils on vacation.

Chapter 7

Once again Sarah lost a promotion to a leadership position due to the resignation of her administrator and the lack of written contracts. The new superintendent, who knew nothing about prior agreements to appoint Sarah Huftalen as the dean of a potential junior college, named her the chair of a committee to investigate the feasibility of establishing a junior college. "We obtained a sufficient number [of students] to warrant the establishing of the college. Miss Wiletta Stran was made Dean."[81]

Despite her disappointment, Sarah found "these dozen years were like a halo of happiness before retiring." Her real sorrow was that she had to retire.

> The Boards of the state made a ruling to retire teachers at seventy. Age is not a criterion of abilities. Neither are degrees.[82]
> . . . . Why cause one to feel as though he should be laid on the shelf and become a recluse when he could not and will not if he could.[83]

The normal school closed "because of the depression," and Sarah reluctantly went home to Manchester once again. Perhaps by 1935, brother Henry had mellowed, and Sarah's strength and confidence was such that she could tolerate him. She kept house for him until 1950. Henry had been

> . . . at various times in his long life a minister, carpenter, architect, author and farmer. . . .
> In 1909 he returned to Manchester to care for his father who passed away that year, and in 1912, he took over management of the farm, where he had lived alone since.
> He was president of the county Farm Bureau for a number of years, and is credited with having introduced Guernsey cows to Delaware county. He took great interest in weed control, and is known for having a farm which was virtually weedless.
> During his lifetime he wrote numerous articles for magazines and he published a booklet on Universalism and Free Masonry . . . [and] a paraphrase on the Book of Job.[84]

The Book of Job seems to be a fitting metaphor for portions of the lives of Sarah and her brother, Henry.

In her retirement years, Sarah continued to write and spent many months organizing the vast collection of her diaries, class notes, histories of various institutions and organizations with which she was associated. She compiled "seven Historical Records including Genealogical lines and branches."

Sarah Gillespie Huftalen's professional work spanned fifty-two years during which substantial changes took place in American public education. Sarah's teaching, writing, and leadership emphasized the significance of the interpersonal relationships between the teacher and the students. Her love of her students and of learning were implemented in classrooms where she respected and encouraged her students to be independent, cooperative, and responsible citizens and learners. Among Sarah's volumes of papers is an undated essay, "Why a Teacher." Her words sum up her personal philosophy of education.

> People are asking what is the criterion of a teacher. The first requisite and last criterion of a teacher is to be a true follower of the Great Teacher, not so much in professing as in living. . . . It means a right attitude toward the profession, toward each subject taught, toward the home, the school, the community and the child. It means to possess knowledge and the ability to interpret it to right uses so that it becomes a power for good in the life of the child. . . .
>
> To be a teacher, many methods of approach are necessary in reaching the minds and hearts of growing boys and girls: these at the levels of the child's abilities to pursue and achieve. And when such happy team work is obtained the teacher continues to walk beside the developing mind and soul; pressing a little here, guiding, directing thoughtfully, prayerfully, ever keeping the goal of a perfected character as the objective sought. . . .
>
> Some one had said that to be educated meant to bring forth and train up all the faculties and powers of the mind and body to their highest possible use. To accomplish this makes it mandatory to live in such manner of thought and activity as will make the whole world better for our having lived in it .[85]

"Sarah L. Gillespie with dinner pail, Elocution book & Analysis note book. Lessons prepared & on the way to school. Teacher, author, lecturer, PROHIBITIONIST." (Huftalen Collection, State Historical Society of Iowa—Iowa City)

"I will sketch a few of the dresses, etc., that Ma made for me for school. . . . " Sarah is wearing this coat in her portrait. (Huftalen Collection, State Historical Society of Iowa—Iowa City)

"All hands busy. A happy family at the school grounds, of course."
Sarah Huftalen and her scholars, Norwich School, Page County,
Iowa, 1910. (Huftalen Collection, State Historical Society of Iowa—
Iowa City)

Scholars and teacher "mending the rickety & rotten old fence" at
Norwich School. (Huftalen Collection, State Historical Society of
Iowa—Iowa City)

The Good of Your Party,
Or The Good of Your Child,
WHICH?

Who will be best for
your child?

OUR CANDIDATE.
MRS. SARAH HUFTALEN

CANDIDATE FOR COUNTY SUPER-
INTENDENT ON THE DEMOCRATIC
TICKET.

Sarah Huftalen, county superintendent,
Page County, Iowa, January 1, 1913–September 1, 1915. (Huftalen Collection, State Historical Society of Iowa—Iowa City)

"The teachers' tent, close to the dining tent," Clarinda, Iowa, Chautauqua, 1912. The Farm Boys' and Girls' Clubs had their summer camp sessions during the Chautauqua. Sarah Huftalen at right. (Huftalen Collection, State Historical Society of Iowa—Iowa City)State Historical Society)

"Country teachers, 1914, at Institute. Lesson Judging by C. F. Garrett." Sarah Huftalen, county superintendent, at right. The man at the far left may be Billie Huftalen, as Sarah's notes indicated a "visitor" at the institute. (Huftalen Collection, State Historical Society of Iowa—Iowa City)

Sarah Huftalen and her students painted the dingy walls and the woodwork, then hung the class pictures. "We then had a cheery and inviting and pleasant room to work in with its chairs, long tables and a reading table in the rear, etc." Upper Iowa University, Fayette, Iowa, 1918. (Huftalen Collection, State Historical Society of Iowa—Iowa City)

Chapter 7

CHAPTER
EIGHT

"Attaining My Lifelong Ambition"

Bessie M. Tucker Gilmer, Nebraska, 1898–

> I am nineteen and will soon be twenty. It's quite nice to be 19
> but I don't know how it will be to be twenty. . . . I'm short and
> weigh 130 pounds which is too much. I have brown hair and
> blue eyes and a dimple when I grin, my one redeeming feature. I
> grin a lot!
>
> I am a school teacher by profession, attaining my lifelong am-
> bition when I was eighteen. . . .
>
> I've got to quit now and sweep this [schoolroom] floor. . . . Good
> night, little book of my dreams, more news tomorrow.—"Jour-
> ney Through Life," the diary of Bessie Tucker, 1918, Nebraska.

Bessie Tucker Gilmer wrote diaries fairly consistently from 1918
through 1920, then sporadically into the early 1930s. Her "Journey
Through Life" then becomes a mixture of occasional diary entries and
reminiscences through the early 1980s.[1] Her early diary entries are
conversational in tone, like a chat with a good friend. The entries in
the 1970s and 1980s, are more reminiscent in tone. She used her diary
entries to express her thankfulness to God and to seek guidance when
she was in doubt or lonely. Her diaries and other writing are touched
with humor as Bessie often laughs at herself and the events of her life.

Her deep religious faith is a constant element throughout her diaries, reminiscent writing, and oral history.

Through these personal narratives of her life and times, her participation in the writing and storytelling festivals for older Nebraskans, and her oral history and correspondence with this author, Bessie tells her story of meeting her lifelong ambitions of teaching school, being married, and raising a family. She relates her "joy that comes from work well done" and her pride and sorrows that emanated from her students, her family, friends, and neighbors.[2] Her life experiences were based in "traditional moral values" and "down-to-earth veneration of family and hard work."[3] Her traditional goals and life-style bridged her near-frontier experiences in the Sandhills to an established farm in eastern Nebraska and her farm family's survival strategies of the Depression years. Bessie Tucker Gilmer was one of the "clear-eyed pragmatic folk," one of the thousands of short-term teachers of the heartland.[4] As a twenty-year-old teacher, she called herself "just an ordinary girl, living an ordinary life."[5] Her story is uniquely hers, and in the broader sense, also the story of her contemporaries who also were steeped in the conventional definition of womanhood.

By the time Bessie was born in Jefferson, South Dakota, 1898, her parents had lived at a gold mining camp in Montana; a silver mining camp in Nevada; and a lumber camp in South Dakota. They had lost one baby boy to whooping cough, and another to being "born frail." They had adopted Mary, the year-old daughter of a friend who died of tuberculosis, and then seven years later, Bessie was born. When the Tucker family moved to Dixon County, Nebraska, Bessie's father farmed various rental properties because land for homesteading was no longer available. Bessie recalled, "We were constantly on the move as the grass was always greener on the other side of the fence."[6]

Bessie's father, who had less than a fourth-grade education, encouraged Mary and Bessie in their education and loved to have them read to him. Bessie's mother had completed fourth grade and was an avid reader as was Bessie's grandmother. Family evenings were spent popping corn and cracking a crockfull of black walnuts, while the mother, grandmother, and Mary read aloud. Bessie recalled: "We read everything! We read every book in the school library. We brought it home regardless of what it was."[7]

As the family moved from farm to farm, Bessie's early education lacked continuity and quality, and Bessie started every day with a stomach ache.

Chapter 8

Our breakfast consisted of pancakes, morning after morning
after morning. My father didn't think there was anything else to
have for breakfast. . . . I liked my mother's pancakes. The
trouble was they didn't like me. And so until the first recess of
each day I suffered with a stomach ache. I could not concentrate
on my studies, only on my stomach. So I received poor grades on
those subjects.[8]

From her own experience as a school girl and as a teacher, Bessie
found that all "'qualified' teachers were not necessarily devoted to the
art of teaching." Teaching, as an alternative to domestic work, was
one of the few occupations open to women, so "those who could afford
the training taught school." The teacher Bessie had in second, third,
and fourth grades punished children for any mistakes by having them
stand in the corner to "ponder" their errors. Bessie vowed to never
have a child stand in the corner.

As a young school child, Bessie's best friend was the daughter of
the director of the school board. The children of the director threatened to tell their papa whenever they felt they weren't being favored.

The teachers must have believed them for things certainly
went in their favor, even when there was solid proof they were
in the wrong. Many of their sins went unpunished for which we
who did not have a "papa" on the school board suffered. Result:
When I taught school all of the children were going to be treated
the same, regardless of "Papa's" position on or off the schoolboard.
I was going to clean up the system. And you know what? I did!
Every child stood or fell on his or her own merits. Sometimes the
members of the schoolboard having children in the school raised
their eyebrows at me a bit but not one of them ever took me to
task. The greatest compliment ever paid me was the statement
that Miss Tucker had no favorites.[9]

Bessie's motivation to teach included the desire to right the wrongs of
ineffectual teachers but was more deeply rooted in the compelling as-
piration to help others.

Finally, in fifth grade, Bessie's teacher was a sympathetic young man
who helped her get caught up in arithmetic, then her grades "soared."
But the following spring, the family moved into another school district where the male teacher's only talent was being able to play ball

Attaining My Lifelong Ambition

with the children. He put Bessie back in fourth grade so he wouldn't have to have only one child in fifth grade. In fall Bessie again had the teacher who had taught her in second through fourth grade, and who, unfortunately, had not improved in her methods of teaching nor of punishment.

The bright spots of Bessie's early education came through the school and church programs.

> My mother and sister began training me in the art of Public Speaking at a very early age. In school and church programs I always gave the longest recitation and was active in small plays and dialogues. At the age of eight years I took part in a speech contest requiring five contestants. This was a Temperance Program. The other four contestants were all adult men and women. But without a fifth contestant the contest could not be held. So my sister volunteered my services and I committed a lengthy speech to memory. Dressed all in white we drove through the rain to the church where the driver picked me up, covered me with a blanket head and foot to protect my finery, and carried me into the church. I didn't receive the gold medal but did cover myself with glory, prolonged applause, and some were even kind enough to assure me I should have received the medal.

This family training for public speaking provided valuable skills for Bessie when she taught school and for her participation in church activities. "All through the years I have been active in public speaking and dialogues and plays. My school programs are always well attended and have become quite noted." [10]

In early spring of 1910, Mrs. Tucker and Mary read an ad in the newspaper for the relinquishment of a quarter section of land filed under the Kincaid Act in the Sandhills of Nebraska. Proposed by Congressman Moses P. Kincaid of Nebraska as an effort to promote settlement and farm production in the dry rangeland of thirty-seven counties of northwest Nebraska, the Kincaid Act of 1904 allowed homesteaders to file for up to 640 acres. After five years of residence and proof that the land had been improved, the homesteader received the patent for the land. Attempting to farm the land often ended in failure with the use of conventional farming practices in this region of little rainfall. The Kincaiders lived a frontierlike existence in their soddies and shacks, and more than a few gave up and sold out before they had completed the required five years of residency. These relinquishments were most often sold to ranchers and others with large landholdings.[11]

For farmers with little capital like the Tuckers, the Kincaid Act and the relinquishments of claims offered the opportunity to obtain land. By answering the newspaper ad, the Tuckers found their opportunity to own land, "and no more drifting from one run down farm to another."[12] Sight unseen, the sale was completed and Mr. Tucker and Bessie's Uncle Ed fixed up a covered wagon complete with a crate of twelve hens; "King Bob," the Rhode Island red rooster; and a string of horses. Mrs. Tucker, Bessie, and Mary planned to go west by train after the men got settled.

Home at the ranch in the Sandhills was at first a corrugated metal shed with the livestock on one side and the men living on the other side. When Mrs. Tucker, Bessie, and Mary arrived, the men then built a three-room house with lumber hauled thirty miles from Lone Pine. Making a living in 1910 by farming in the Sandhills was precariously dependent on the rainfall. After Mr. Tucker was offered only twenty-five cents a load for hauling hay for the neighboring cattleman, he went back to Dixon County where he worked as a farmhand in order to have enough money for the family to get through the winters. So Mrs. Tucker, Mary, and twelve-year-old Bessie had to take over the farm and complete the four remaining years of residency required for ownership of the land.

One of the first and hardest lessons learned in the Sandhills was how to cope with the scarcity of fuel. The wood chips left over from building the house didn't last long. Bessie's mother tried burning twists of hay for cooking but soon had to admit that cow chips were the only practical source of fuel.

> She put on a sunbonnet, grabbed a pail and left for the pasture
> from which she soon returned, tears streaming down her face,
> with a pail full of cow chips. She had conceded. Our fuel prob-
> lem was settled. . . . [We] broke enough sod each spring to make
> a garden where we raised the best vegetables, melons and peanuts
> in the state and enough corn to feed our stock. We mowed, raked
> and stacked the prairie hay. In early fall we went out to the sur-
> rounding pastures with a single box wagon and gathered the de-

spised cow chips which we stacked for fuel. About every ten days
we made a trip with the spring wagon to the nearest grocery
store, ten miles from our home for groceries.[13]

After spending a cold first winter in the small, drafty frame house,
the family built a warm and comfortable soddy. Mrs. Tucker, who had
lived in mining camps and a series of run-down farms, did what she
could to make life pleasant and the home attractive. She used white
tablecloths and bedspreads, and the neighbors thought the Tuckers
were "nice stylish people." Life for Mrs. Tucker, Mary, and Bessie was
enriched through the bimonthly programs at the schoolhouse in which
everyone took part. On Sundays, they attended Sunday school at the
schoolhouse during good weather. Sunday school never met during
the winter months, so Mrs. Tucker sent for the instructional materials
and held the meetings in her home for a year. The traveling missionaries rejected the meetings led by Mrs. Tucker and determined that
Sunday school should be held only at the schoolhouse, and again
the Sunday school closed during the winter.

Bessie's education during the four years in the Sandhills continued
to be erratic in quality. "Because the weather was so severe and the
schools were so far apart with walking or horseback riding the only
means of transportation, the school term consisted of six months,
three months in the fall and three months in the spring. I walked four
miles to school through huge cattle pastures."[14]

The first year in the Sandhills, Bessie had a pregnant teacher who
taught the three-month term in fall. In spring, the teacher stayed
home with her baby, and the school remained closed for lack of
a teacher. In the fourth year, when Bessie was sixteen, "we had our
first nine month school with a wonderful teacher, Tom Dillon by
name. . . . He took an interest in me and advanced me to the seventh
grade. I worked hard and my report card showed it."[15]

In 1914, after four years on the relinquishment land, the Tuckers
sold their "quarter section of sand" to the cattleman and moved
back to Ponca in northeastern Nebraska, where they bought a home
in town.

We sold our stock and moved back to Ponca the first of
March. Mr. Dillon sent my grades and a letter of recommenda-
tion to the Superintendent of the Ponca High School. But he
would not accept me in the seventh grade. So I did not go to

school the rest of that year and started eighth grade the next fall. Again, I had a wonderful, dedicated teacher [Anna Sheffel], and while taking the eighth grade under her I also took the teacher's examinations as they were given under the County Superintendent at the Court House, and passed them all.[16]

With the help of a few effective teachers and her parents' interest in reading and in her education, Bessie received a sufficient educational foundation to prepare her for the normal school at Wayne, Nebraska. At seventeen she attended the normal school for a summer term, earning her room and board by setting and clearing tables. "The next step was to find a school which was in need of a teacher. There were so many teachers starting their first year in our County Seat town there were no vacancies in Dixon County. So I resorted to Newspaper advertisements as did many others and in early December answered one such ad and was accepted."[17]

Bessie Tucker's teaching position was in a school near Hemingford, in the Sandhills, close to the area where the Tuckers had proved up the relinquished claim. Her mother was in full support of this transition from teenage daughter to independent schoolteacher, but her father was reluctant to see his daughter leave home. Bessie went to the bank to borrow fifty dollars " for transportation [by train] and necessities until I received my first pay check, and much against Daddy's wishes was ready to leave on the noon train. When I looked in my purse my money was gone. We searched and searched while daddy calmly ate his dinner. Just when I was ready to give up in despair he told me my money was in a bowl in the cupboard. He had hidden it but couldn't go through with it. And so I was on my way."[18]

Bessie traveled alone by train to Hemingford, arriving at four in the morning. She got a ride with the rural mail carrier who took her and her one suitcase to within two miles of her destination, the school director's home. Bessie boarded with the school director, his bedridden wife, and their two daughters, who were Bessie's only pupils. She was appalled at the dirty home and felt sorry for the invalid mother, so she helped the girls clean the house. Her boldness in seeking and obtaining the teaching position had led her into this disagreeable situation: the director was not well liked, the living conditions were grim, and the schoolhouse was run-down. The only other family in the district, the Bartletts, became Bessie's "family" on weekends. The train trip to eastern Nebraska was too expensive and too long for a visit home until the end of the year. Charlie Bartlett, her good friend, regularly went five miles by horseback after the mail so that Bessie could get the news from home.

After three months in this school, with help of the Bartletts, Bessie was hired through a phone conversation with the woman director of another school. Once again, Bessie had children of the school director, plus a four-year-old "visitor." The school offered better pay, a pleasant schoolhouse, and her boarding conditions were vastly improved. Bessie paid twenty dollars for room and board, but she absolutely refused to slop the pigs. When the director's daughters failed the county eighth grade examination at the end of the school term, she closed the school and refused to come to the picnic on the last day. Bessie planned the picnic anyway, and everyone except the director attended. With a total of six students in two different schools, this first year of teaching provided the necessary "experience" for Bessie to get a school in the more populous and prosperous eastern section of Nebraska.

While visiting a cousin, Bessie happened to go by the church at Elk Valley just as the weekly prayer meeting was letting out. There on the church steps were all the members of the school board who asked Bessie if she had teaching experience and hired her on the spot. This homogeneity of the residents of a school district was a positive factor when they were supportive of the school and educational progress.

The school had thirty scholars in all eight grades and a bell like a church bell. The farmers nearby requested that Bessie ring the bell for five minutes each morning because of its lovely tone. The fall box social raised ninety dollars for supplies for the schoolhouse, including plays and dialogues for school programs and a swivel chair for the teacher. The children pushed Miss Tucker up one aisle and down the next when the new chair arrived.

The eighteen-year-old experienced teacher made it a point to join the children during recess. "While playing with the children today I got in the way of the baseball bat and it collided with my ankle leaving me rather inactive for the rest of the day. I hate to think of tomorrow. . . . theory is no good without practice, is it?" [19]

In her moments of introspection, Bessie found that she was

> realizing more and more, little book, the non-importance of the things that seem to take up so much of our time. Only as they may be a help to others are they important and I am learning to

Chapter 8

make that one of the guiding rules of my life. My little school is teaching me patience but it has a hard pupil and I often feel disappointed at how little has been accomplished, but then such thoughts are unworthy of a dedicated teacher and I must put them forever out of my mind.[20]

Bessie found good friends in Elk Valley, including the people with whom she boarded.

April 1, 1918: . . . . Quite a few of my pupils have left me and quite a few new ones have taken their place. I am learning not to miss the old ones so much and am becoming acquainted with the new. That seems to be the way with life. We just meet and make new friends only to have them pass from our lives in a short time, leaving a sad longing in the heart in the place they have filled. . . . Rev. Ralph Clem and wife Ruby, with whom I have made my home since coming to Elk Valley, left today to take up their new work in western Nebraska. Dear friends! God bless them! I have moved into the home of Loren and Maggie Tilton, for the rest of the school year. Mr. Tilton is moderator of the school board. The walls of my lovely upstairs bedroom are papered with a bright appleblossom pattern in pink and white and a low wide window looks out over the fields and pastures from this window. . . . Guess I've proved myself an early riser as I got up and dressed and came down stairs this morning at 1:10 A. M. I was greeted with shouts of laughter and "April Fool" by the four adults assembled there who had been visiting the night away before Ralph and Ruby's departure for the new charge. What better to do than to call a poor unsuspecting teacher from her rest in the early morning hours? This is one April Fool's day I will long remember. But the children, bless their hearts, were perfect darlings all day.[21]

For several weeks in February and March of 1918, entertainment was in the form of a singing school:

I celebrated last night. A certain well-meaning individual has established a singing school, holding singing lessons in the church once a week. . . . a number of we public minded individuals signed up for a 10 week course for a price, collected in advance.

Attaining My Lifelong Ambition

The first week he showed up complete in swallow tails and a cel-
luloid collar. His music was as antiquated as his attire. . . . Goodness knows he is doing his best, which leaves much to be desired,
however. But I am endowed with a giggle that always displays itself at the wrong time and in this instance it has plenty of company including our honorable pastor. Well, we have to get something for our money and goodness knows we are not getting what
we paid for.[22]

Although the school year had gone well, Bessie was uncertain and
wondered if she were "a success or a failure or a mixture." She decided
not to accept the offer to come back, believing she would do better
with an enrollment of less than thirty children in all eight grades. On
a hot windy day in mid-May, when the children were rambunctious,
Bessie questioned her ability to make a positive difference in the
school:

May 15, 1918: Well little Book, if you haven't got the most disgust-
ing author I don't know who has. This has been such a hot windy
day and the children were restless. Now I am not excusing myself
at all but simply stating conditions. Everything I told them to do
I had to tell them three or four times and in the end I got rather
excited. What in the world is the matter with me? Why can't I
be patient and gentle at all times like I would like to be? . . .
Well, Little Book, I am getting ready to leave and I don't think I
will come back. I believe I can do better, perhaps, in a new surroundings and a smaller school. There are too many pupils here
to do them justice and I would like a smaller school. I am so tired
now though I am glad I don't have to start in right away. There
are many things here that I hate to leave. I hate to leave the
kiddies whom I've grown to love, and all of my friends, and the
school itself has grown very dear to me. . . . Are they going to
care or won't it make any difference that I am not coming back?
There are some who I know will miss me, a few who I know will
care and it is nice to be missed by some anyway. But it is wrong
of me perhaps, to think of these things. God will look after everything and I have prayed to him to guide me aright.

She left good friends behind, including her Catholic boyfriend, Phil
Sorenson. As a Methodist, Bessie was unsure of the propriety of dating

Phil, and rationalized the situation by predicting that she'd be "an old maid."

> May 10, 1918: . . . I like Phil . . . He has been very good to
> me since I came here and so have all of the family. I wonder if he
> likes me. Not that I really care, of course but then it is nice to be
> liked even if one is going to be an old maid and will never be
> anything else. . . .
> . . . [Phil's family] are so nice to me but I sometimes wonder if
> it is right for me to go there as they are Catholics and although
> they seem to respect my religion and never say anything in any
> way about the difference in our beliefs I feel a bit of disapproval
> from my church friends.

In May 1918, there were patriotic meetings in the schoolhouse for the purpose of selling savings bonds. "After the patriotic speech the speaker began selling Savings Bonds. Names were posted on the blackboard. Most of the young men were buying $50.00 bonds. I did the same and up went my name on the board. Later some of the men told me how surprised they were to see me from my small salary able to compete with the young men."[23] It seems to be out of character for Bessie to buy the bond in order to compete with the men; however, she seemed pleased that they took notice of her patriotic actions.

Bessie closed her school year at Elk Valley with a "nearly perfect" school program and with her mother, her sister, her sister's husband, and friends from Ponca in the audience. A week later, pleased to be at home, she wrote in her diary,

> June 5, 1918: . . . I am home and so happy to be here. Fur-
> thermore, I have the whole summer before me as a spring flood
> stopped the trains long enough to make me a week late for the
> opening of the summer Normal School at Wayne so I decided
> not to go. . . .
> June 19, 1918: . . . what a happy week it has been. I've done
> everything from cooking breakfast to painting the floors and then
> all the way back again. . . .

By the end of June 1918, Bessie knew that Phil would be leaving soon for the army.

Attaining My Lifelong Ambition

June 29, 1918: Little book, you must know this is war times, a time when all the nations of the world are engaged in a great struggle and we must all be true and loyal citizens in order that our country and our own Sammies may win. Uncle Sam can be proud of his nephews. Brave, noble boys! How much they are all doing for us. . . .

Little Book, my Sammie is going before long and I want to send him away with a smile. He has been down just once to see me but he is my Sammie all the same. . . . and I am proud of him. . . .

July 29, 1918: Little Book . . . I've got so much to tell you I doubt if I ever get it all told. Some of it I want to just tell and then forget all about it. Phil came again, the next Monday night, came with a box of chocolates to tell me goodbye. He is gone now to Camp Dodge. I gave the candy to Mother and went to visit a dear cousin who could always be relied on to lend a sympathetic ear.

Bessie's patriotism did not diminish, even though she received only a few "short, friendly letters" from Phil and knew that was the "beginning of the end" of her romance with him.

In September 1918, Bessie taught in a public school on an Indian reservation near Wakefield and Pender. On some reservations, the land was allotted, allowing white people to lease and rent the land. With the influx of white people, there was a demand for the establishment of public schools, which theoretically "encouraged assimilation" of the Indian children into the white culture.[24]

Sept. 6, 1918: . . . . I have 43 pupils now and more coming. Quite a joke for the gal who thought 30 was too many. . . . The children are all very nice children and I like them all immensely. . . . This is an Indian Reservation school but among the 40 plus there are only six Indian youngsters. They are a challenge to me. Their father is very progressive, speaks excellent English and had taught the children to do the same, dresses well as do the children; is active in Indian affairs and preaches on Sunday in an Indian church near Winnebago. Their mother is the exact opposite. Wears long skirts and shawl, refuses to speak English and clings to the Indian customs. There are three boys in the second, fifth and seventh grades, and three girls in the third, fifth and seventh grades. They are bright children and do well in their studies. . . . The girl in the 7th grade is very shy. She speaks very low and often when I ask her a question will just sit and look at me. I was a bit puzzled how to handle this problem until I gave the first written tests and she was at the head of the class. So I don't worry about her anymore.

Bessie's lack of understanding of the clash of cultures for the Indian children is somewhat balanced by her acceptance of their abilities as she tried to accept each child on his or her own merit.

At first, Bessie felt like an outsider boarding with a Bohemian family that spoke only Bohemian at home. Bessie offered to teach English to Mrs. Rejman if Mrs. Rejman would teach Bohemian to her. By the end of the school year, Mrs. Rejman was speaking English very well, but Bessie had learned only a few phrases. The Rejman home was filled with good Bohemian cooking, four daughters, five dogs, a dozen cats, and one young schoolteacher who was trying to get her large school organized.

Sept. 11, 1918:. . . . Yester[day] I was dismayed to see a team and buggy drive up and a man and lady get out. It was apparent that they had come to visit the school and I had awful visions as to how it would look to the eyes of strangers. The gentleman turned out to be the Indian Agent of this reservation and he gave a talk to the children. I had heard him talk before and had a low opinion of him. But I really enjoyed his talk yesterday. Then his wife sang for us. I don't think she is a very good singer but I enjoyed her singing yesterday and made a good impression on her by asking for an encore. The children were on their good behavior and that made a good impression. So I came to the conclusion that in spite of the large enrollment I did not have such a bad school after all. Everything looks different to me today. Then a lady was overheard talking over the telephone and made the statement that her little boy liked the new teacher better than the old one. That was a marvelous help . . . I was glad to know they didn't think they had such a bad teacher after all.

In the following week, Bessie went from despair that she had forty-five naughty children to the knowledge that teaching was indeed her special mission in life at that time.

Attaining My Lifelong Ambition

Sept. 13, 1918: . . . Have taught this school for two whole weeks now it is so different from the one I had last year. But I like the children so well. However, they do the funniest things for such big children. Such as sticking pins through the rubbers of their pencils and then sticking each other with them or tapping them on their tablets in unison which sounds about like a flock of wood-peckers. They gaze at me in wide-eyed surprise when I reprove them. I guess I will have to assert my authority a little more.

During the next few days, Bessie "asserted [her] authority with a will" but continued being friendly and playing with the children during recess. They responded by willingly cleaning the schoolhouse and being more attentive to their lessons.

Sept. 20, 1918: I am glad I am a school mom. It's fun to teach school just lots of fun, really . . .

I was trying to encourage one ungrateful little wretch by making him think that he was improving. So I said in my most winning tone, "Oh my, Floyd, I don't like the way you are studying now. That doesn't look nearly as well as the way you worked this morning." A little later I caught him giggling away to himself and asked, "What is so funny, Floyd?" In between giggles he managed to answer, "I didn't study this morning either."

That is just an example of a small part of one day and as every day is different, I don't see how anyone could find teaching monotonous. I taught the pupils a new song at school last night. It is one of the new war songs, "Keep the home fires burning."

The full schoolhouse and the busy Rejman home left little time for reflection until Bessie found a place where she could be alone.

Oct. 5, 1918: . . . I have found a secluded little nook where no one ever follows me where I can sit and watch the stars come out every evening. Where I can dream my own dreams and think my own thoughts and worship my Savior in my own way. I wonder at the beauty of the Heavens on a clear night and it seems I can almost see my Master there. . . . I know he wants me to be bright and cheerful and happy and I mean to be. I know too, there are many lessons He would have me learn and I want to learn them cheerfully and quietly. I want to be more gentle and patient and loving and all that He would have me be. . . .

Little book, I believe that the school is mine at last. I honestly feared for a time that they were going to get the best of me. But I didn't intend to give up without a struggle, you may be sure of that. And not at all if I could help it. I've got them under control now though and the best order prevaileth. Now wish me well that I may have success in keeping it.

Within a week, Bessie's school was closed and she was at home working with her mother in caring for friends, family, and neighbors suffering from the influenza epidemic. It was an experience that Bessie never forgot.

Oct. 10, 1918: At Home, little book, but I hope not for long. I enjoy the vacation but not the reason for it. Because of a terrible disease similar to the grippe which we have experienced for many years during the fall and winter months but which is call the flu, short for influenza, a highly contagious disease . . . the school board decided to close the school. . . . We [Mother and Bessie] work together going from place to place where we are needed. This deadly disease strikes like a rattlesnake, attacking entire families at once leaving no one to care for the sick. Sometimes one or more members of the family are dead within a matter of hours. . . . As many as seven funerals were held in one day in this small town of less than 1,000 citizens. The clergymen were so worn out and the funerals so numerous that only graveside services were held. A few singers would gather around the open grave singing a gospel song or two, a few verses of scripture were read and a few consoling remarks made to the members of the family who were able to attend and the group would move on to the next gravesite. I was privileged to be a part of many of these services. . . . But more important than burying the dead was caring for the living. I had my fair share of this as all of our loved ones were very ill. Molly and Clarence and Little Bobby [Bessie's sister, Mary, her husband and son] were taken care of, mother returned to the farm to care for daddy, and then back to my Uncle-John and his family . . . Eleanor, Floyd, Everett, Raymond and Tommy. . . . Somewhere Tommy read or heard that onions would keep the flu away so he went about eating onions until no one could get near him but it might have paid the rest of us to do the same instead of laughing at him. Know what? HE DIDN'T GET THE FLU, so he had the last laugh. . . . At last the epidemic passed and the people adjusted to their losses. All of my dear ones were spared and I was so thankful that God had seen fit to so bless us.

While Bessie was waiting for her school to reopen, she went to visit her cousins.

When I arrived I found Tom far behind in picking his corn as there was no help to be had. So I said I would be glad to help him . . . . They supplied me with suitable clothes and I sallied forth one cold frosty morning. By noon I was sore and stiff but still game but when we reached the house the long awaited call from the school had come.[25]

Aching and tired, Bessie went to her home, where she was put to bed and diagnosed as having flu. She told the doctor she had to get back to school because it had been closed for five weeks. "I will never forget his disgusted snort, these school moms and their schools, worse than a mother hen with two dozen chicks."[26]

The school remained closed two more weeks, with no deaths among the children.

There was only one casualty. The day the school was closed I was just getting ready to leave when a car drove into the schoolyard. It was the County Supt. coming to visit the school. I invited her in and we went over the records etc. She complimented me on the good work we were doing and the attractive schoolroom etc. She was a large boned, heavyset woman with no physical attractions but an inner beauty just beamed from her face. I only met her that one time. When I returned to school she had been a victim of the flu and gone to her reward. Our loss and her gain.[27]

In order to make up the six weeks that school had been closed, Bessie offered to teach on Saturdays for the rest of the year so that school would be out by the end of May, rather than in July. With forty-five children, every school day was crammed with recitations.

Chapter 8

. . .there was no time for opening exercises, no time for singing
of school songs together or reading of children's books which they
could enjoy. As soon as the school came to order I called my
primer student to class, listened to her read, assigned the next
lesson for her to study and there was only time to answer the
questions of those who were wildly waving their hands in the air
before calling the next class for recitation. I conducted recitation
the entire day and it was often five after four before the last spelling class was over. [28]

While living with the Rejmans, Bessie could not get to church on
Sundays but took time away from the busy household to read her
Bible. Throughout her diary, Bessie recorded her close personal relationship with God, her source of strength and guidance. During the
years that Bessie taught school, religious exercises during school hours
were no longer acceptable, but she often privately asked God for
guidance.

Dec. 20, 1918: . . . . Isn't it queer how something we say will
affect the lives of others. When I was just learning to drive the
Ford and had trouble holding a straight course, Phil used to say,
"Whoop, hold her, hold her." . . . Now just this morning I was
having a struggle with my temper, and I knew that my thoughts
could not be acceptable in God's sight, when those words came
to me, "Whoop, hold her, hold her," and I did. And then I
knew I did not have to do it alone, that God would put His hand
on the wheel and steady it and all would be well. Oh, I am so
happy in Him, and I am happy tonight even though this has been
a hard day for I know He is there and His hand is on the wheel.

Bessie moved again for her fourth and final year of teaching.

From the doorway of the schoolhouse where I had spent the last
year I had looked enviously toward the new modern schoolhouse
on top of a hill in plain view about two miles distant. It was a
beautiful structure with modern facilities, a furnace for heating,
and all new modern desks and equipment. There were 12 pupils
in six grades. They were looking for a teacher. [29]

Attaining My Lifelong Ambition

Bessie met a young man who lived near the home where she was boarding and who occasionally took her to church on Sundays, but all was not well.

> September 15, 1919: I am so tired tonight little book, but I feel the urge to write my troubles all down on paper and perhaps they will become more clear. This is the third week of my new school year and I like it as much as I thought I would. I have such a beautiful little school room and twelve pupils. I am glad there are no more because I am so tired most of the time [as an after effect of the flu] I just couldn't teach anymore. I like this dozen very much and as we get better acquainted we have very good times together. . . .
>
> . . . The problem is Clarence. . . . I have been going with him since last March and in that time he has done everything for me he possibly could. I like his parents and family and they like me. He has been especially nice to me this fall. . . .
>
> . . . But the trouble is Clarence doesn't trust me. . . . I don't like to accept his invitations when I feel this way and I just can't help it. He feels so hurt and shows it so much. . . . He doesn't realize he has hurt my feelings . . . with his jealousy.

Clarence gradually faded out of Bessie's life as a suitor but was her friend for most of her last year of teaching.

By October 1919, Bessie had decided that her parents needed her at home, so she resolved to make this last year of teaching one to be remembered.

> October 2, 1919: Oh it is a grand morning this morning, little book, a morning for holy thoughts and thanksgiving to the Savior who has made such a beautiful world. My heart was singing all the way to school as I fairly skipped along. I am truly sorry this is my last year out here in the country among God's hills. But since this is the last year I am going to make it a year to be remembered with His help. You see I am needed at home. . . . I am not qualified to teach in the town school so the only alternative is to find some other line of work in the town where my parents live.

Bessie wasn't qualified to teach in town because of her limited education. She apparently did not have the funds to attend the normal school for more than a summer session, and the town schools probably demanded a high school education plus normal school.

Bessie gave special attention to her twelve scholars so that all the children were promoted to their appropriate grade. For Frank, the thirteen-year-old "bad boy" of the school, this meant promotion by mid-year from fifth grade to seventh grade.

> I tried him out in the seventh grade and he completed everything except arithmetic which he did make up the next year and passed the county examinations. This was supposed to be the bad boy of the school. Well I always made friends with the bad boys if possible. This one was no problem. He lived alone with his grandmother. I called on her and we became good friends. (Years later I found Frank working at a filling station in South Sioux City. Making conversation while he serviced my car we recognized each other. . . . The last I heard of Frank he was on the Police Force in South Sioux City. We did a pretty good job on him, his grandmother and I. . . . Life long friends were made here and lives intertwined for many years. At the age of 80 I am still in touch with two of them, Helen Polzer Elfrink and Minnie Cobb Cline.)[30]

Bessie's last year of teaching in the "new modern schoolhouse" brought friendship and success in her work. Having a small enrollment, a well-equipped school, and supportive school patrons made this a memorable year. One part of the school equipment, the furnace, left much to be desired, as it smoked out the teacher and the children. A small heating stove was installed while the school director waited for the new parts for the furnace to arrive. Bessie wrote about the cold and her plans for Christmas.

> Dec. 9, 1919: Och, The trials of a poor school marm! Verily I say, they are without number. The weather, the American Express Co., and the size of our stove are my greatest [trials] at present. The weather is stormy and cold, many degrees below zero, the express which is carrying the grates for our furnace is slower than Christmas when it is 364 days away and our stove isn't large enough to heat a 6 x 6 coal bin. So you can imagine how doleful I feel after freezing beside that fire for 6 hours and 20 minutes. . . .

Attaining My Lifelong Ambition

No school yesterday because it was too cold and the furnace wouldn't work. Going home to warm up. . . .

December 15, 1919: We are planning the most charming time for our Christmas program Friday afternoon. Miss Peterson, who teaches the school I taught last [year] is bringing her group and we are going to combine our program. We are going to furnish candy and nuts for all the children and I am going down to Jepsons tomorrow night to help make popcorn balls for the 54 of them. Frank loaned me his saddle horse this afternoon and I rode down to Jepsons to finish making arrangements. The first time I have been on a horse's back for three years. Was it fun? It was a lovely day, lots of snow but not cold. I felt so happy and free in God's fresh air and sunshine. I could just sing for pure joy. Oh, I do love the country and love to be in it but hope I may love the city life just as much next year when I spend a year with my father and mother which I am doing at my mother's request. . . . [I'll] just work part time where work is available. . . .

December 26, 1919: . . . . Christmas was a beautiful day, a white Christmas but the temperature was as warm as spring. One of those rare winter days filled with beauty and sunshine. All we lacked was the Meadow Larks.

After four years of teaching, Bessie believed she had "achieved my first goal in life."[31] Her year at home with her parents was a pleasant time of renewing friendships through the church organizations, clerking in the general store during Christmas rush, visiting with her sister and her family, and dating Lee Gilmer.

Perhaps I should try to describe him to you. I will try to do it in moderate terms for I know Sweethearts are apt to exaggerate. He is just a little bit taller than I, with curly black hair and twinkling blue eyes. . . . he has a smile so big and wide that it fairly envelops you. He is the most wonderful person in the whole world and likes to go hiking and picnicking. He likes the birds, and the wind and the river and the trees and all of the things I like. We both love music. We sing in the church choir and take an active part in the many activities provided for us by the church. . . .

Can you imagine calling me Mrs. Gilmer, in the spring?

We have been so many places together, my Laddie and I. . . .

Chapter 8

always the nicest part was the ride home with the moon shining overhead and everything so still and quiet. . . .

One Sunday afternoon we slipped away all by ourselves and after reaching the river we found a path leading to the very top of one of the large bluffs. . . . I knew that God was with me and my lover's arm was about me and his kisses were on my lips. . . . how many times would I recall that little scene. . . .

Well Little Book, ever since the night he asked me to come with him and together we could build a little nest, . . . my heart has been his and I could not give it to a truer better man. My Laddie says, "I want to spend the rest of my life with you now, Girlie, and I want to live a good Christian life so that after death we may meet again over there and be together again." Oh, I love him so much, Little Book. Wish us happiness now and forever. Good night! [32]

When Bessie married Lee December 30, 1920, she wore the midnight blue taffeta wedding dress he had helped select. The wedding cake was a large fruit cake with white frosting served at the Tucker home after the ceremony at the church. "It was a cold December day, and the sun shone brilliantly on the depths of snow that covered the ground. Only a bobsled drawn by a team of skittish horses could navigate the country roads." [33]

Although Bessie's family arrived at the church after the ceremony was over, another goal had been achieved and her marriage was "the beginning of an era" with Lee.

Laddie loves the out-of-doors, the horses, the cows, the chickens, likes to hear the birds sing and likes the farm because of the beauty of nature, its sunrise and sunsets, and the joy of life that a farm can give a true farmer. This was not always his wish, at one time he hoped to be a doctor and he would have been a wonderful doctor with his gentle hands that can rub away the aches and pains but after finishing high school there was no money available for medical education so he compromised and put everything he had into being the best possible farmer. He worked his way through one year of Ag-College, bought the first tractor in Dixon County and put his education to work. [34]

Bessie and Lee established their home and family and weathered the vicissitudes of their years together.

Attaining My Lifelong Ambition

April 28, 1922: . . . So our dreams have come true and we are very happy. And to increase our happiness I am to be a mother very soon. The time is growing short and I can hardly wait. Lee has been everything a husband could be to me and I know he will make a good and kind father to the little one who is coming. . . .

I have my garden in, and eight hens setting on their nests of eggs which will turn into baby chicks in a couple of weeks. One of the farm's little miracles. Looks like I'm not doing so bad myself. I may make a pretty good farmer's wife yet. . . .

October 19, 1922: . . . Well our family arrived on schedule, a fine bouncing baby boy [Donald] of 8 pounds with blue eyes and light brown hair and a husky voice. . . . He is a bundle of joy. And do you know what? He arrived on my 24th birthday! (May 27, 1922)

Two years later, with no prior indication of pregnancy in her diary, Bessie joyfully announced the birth of twin daughters.

September 1924: This is to announce the arrival of Bonnie Marie and Beth Lorene Gilmer at the home of Mr. and Mrs. R. Lee Gilmer, September 16, 1924 at 7 & 7:20 A.M. Twins! Twin girls! The first Gilmer twins, ever! Just think that we should be so blessed! I just can't realize even yet that anything so nice could happen to us. Of course we put in an order for a girl—but TWINS! Donald goes around saying to each one who calls on us, Little Sissers, *two* of em! No jealousy there. We will be a busy household. But we thank God for his goodness.

January 20, 1925: "Suffer little children to come unto me and forbid them not for of such is the Kingdom of Heaven and unless you become as a little child, Ye can in no wise enter in." This was the text the pastor took as we laid little Beth to rest.

Little Beth was a blue baby and it was very hard to see her suffer during the time she was with us. . . . After the graveside service my only wish was to get back to the baby girl [Bonnie] and the little boy [Donald] waiting at home for us.

Bessie could write about the loss of her baby girl a few months after her death, but the memories of Beth must have been sharply rekindled when many years later, Donald and his wife had twin daughters.[35]

In time, Bessie and Lee fell heir to the old home place of Lee's parents. Lee and Bessie and their children lived on this farm for more than twenty years, however:

> This was not all that simple. There were years of drouth and depression when we barely survived and that was all. When Grandpa passed away . . . we learned there was a three thousand dollar mortgage against the farm at the bank. We were barely making ends meet. By now our family had increased by one son [Donald], twin daughters, Bonnie and Beth, who was just loaned to us for a while, Gayle and Betty. Then Franklin Roosevelt came along with his farm program and saved our farm for us. It took us twenty years to pay off the loan. But pay it off we did and we will always be grateful to him for making it possible. And so a second generation grew up on the old home place in the house that Grandpa built for his family.[36]

Bessie recalled their struggles, faith, and courage during the Depression, drought, and dust storms of the "dirty thirties":

> Febr. 5, 1983: With our family of six, Lee and I and four dependent children. We faced life on the farm in the dirty thirties. With cribs filled with corn which he could have sold for $1.75 a bushel, he finally sold for 40¢ a bushel. At that time 40¢ would buy a ball of yarn. . . . I remember when we could only get 10¢ a bushel so we burned it as it was the cheapest fuel we could get. . . .
>
> I also remember when we had no corn and sold half of our baby chicks to buy feed for the rest. As I went into the chicken yard with my bit of rationed corn the bony chicks flew at me picking at my feet, flying on my shoulders and pecking at my ears, sometimes drawing blood before I could get the corn in the feeders. . . .
>
> Hard as it might have been to sell our corn for 10¢ a bushel, our eggs for 10¢ a dozen and a can of cream for less than $2.00 we saw a day we would have been glad just to have had them to sell. There followed years of depression and drouth. . . . Hopefully we watched from the hill back of the barn, day after day while the crops dried up in the fields. . . .
>
> I made a vow that never again would I complain about prices, mud, or inconvenience if only we had food for ourselves, and the farm animals and chickens.

Attaining My Lifelong Ambition

Dust storms raged filling the air with dust and debris. It sifted in at every crack, and around the windows and doors making it difficult to breathe. Sheets were hung over the openings to catch the dust and clear the air. When the storm was over we could open the house to the hot sun but it was a misty gray.

Families were leaving the farms in Nebraska and Kansas loading what they could in their cars and setting out for California. They just shut the doors of their houses, left the machinery setting in the fields or farm yards and drove away. Of those who stayed many went on county relief. This was the easy way out. They were provided with food, good warm clothing for the winter months, and other things to keep them comfortable. Lee was approached by a good friend and neighbor who was on the County Board, offering help. He said he could manage it so no one would know. Lee thanked him courteously for his concern and kind intentions but told him we could make it on our own. And make it, WE DID! Expenses were cut to the bone. We ate what the farm provided and sold our eggs and cream for the necessities we had to buy. We discontinued the daily News Paper and on Sunday mornings, Lee would walk a mile and one half to his brother's house to pick up the week's Sioux City Tribune which they saved for us. In the afternoon we would catch up on the news. To save gasoline we had taken the wheels off the Essex and put it up on blocks.[37]

Bessie conveys the pride of the pioneer as she recounts their survival through the Depression and droughts of the thirties. The good times of the thirties were brought about because their "neighborhood was just one big happy family." When it was time for work or to celebrate anniversaries and holidays, "Everybody helped everybody else."

Bessie Tucker Gilmer had successfully realized her traditional ambitions: she was a successful teacher, wife, mother, and homemaker. The family was active in the church organizations and community events. Bessie planted the gardens, put by fruit and vegetables for the winter, and sewed for the family. She helped her children with their school work and encouraged them to succeed. For several years, Bessie wrote a weekly children's story for the family page of the *Dixon County Journal* and was the local news correspondent for the newspaper. In later years, Bessie gathered her children's stories into photocopied volumes to share with her children and grandchildren. After twenty-seven years on the farm, the Gilmers moved to Lincoln in 1947, where their daughters, Bonnie, Gayle, and Betty, could continue their educations at Wesleyan University. After the children left home, Lee managed the four-plex where they lived. He continued to work until age eighty-five, when after twenty years with the Good Will Agency in Lincoln, he was forced to retire.

The church continued to be the center of the Gilmer family as their children accomplished their own goals. Betty's husband and Donald were ministers for a few years. Bonnie trained to become a missionary nurse, then answered the call to become a minister in the United Methodist Church as her life's work. After teaching three years, Gayle married a farmer who earned his doctorate. They then settled on a sheep farm in Oregon.

With much of their family living nearby, Bessie and Lee spent fifty-seven years together before poor health confined Lee to a nursing home his last few years. "But this is the end of an era which started with a ride through the snow in a Bobsled. . . . but I am still here. The days come and the days go and he is much in my thoughts. But I must go on alone."[38]

Bessie's life spanned homesteading and breaking the sod, to farming with the first tractor in Dixon County and having a farmer son-in-law with a doctorate. Bessie attended the Sunday school initiated and taught by her mother, and she saw her children become well-educated ministers and teachers. Bessie had about eight years of schooling, but all of her children and many grandchildren are college educated as a matter of course. While her own teaching certification was based on one summer session at the normal school and passing the teachers' examinations, she expected and got well-qualified teachers for her own children. Bessie often walked or rode a horse during her first year of teaching, and she became equally at home driving a Ford. Throughout the technological and educational changes of her life, there is a consistency in the life of this twentieth-century woman. Bessie Tucker Gilmer was a short-term teacher whose life was founded upon the values, virtues, and actions related to and based upon the traditional definition of womanhood: the well-being of the family, the neighbors, and the community.

On her eighty-seventh birthday, May 27, 1985, Bessie Tucker Gilmer wrote the following:

Attaining My Lifelong Ambition

Mother Nature is catching up with me and I feel as old as I am. I am not complaining. I say with Browning, "Grow old along with me, The best is yet to be, The last of life for which the first was made." The love of our children and our grandchildren, and our great-grandchildren is very precious to us. A strong arm to lean on is always there when needed. And so we travel unafraid down the last miles to eternity trusting God and unafraid.[39]

Two of Bessie Tucker's scholars, Dawes County, Nebraska, 1917. (Courtesy of Bessie M. Gilmer)

Eighth graders studied for the county examinations, Dawes County, Nebraska, 1917. (Courtesy of Bessie M. Gilmer)

Attaining My Lifelong Ambition

End of the school term, May 18, 1917, Dawes County, Nebraska. Bessie Tucker at right. (Courtesy of Bessie M. Gilmer)

Bessie Tucker attended the Teachers Institute, Pender, Nebraska, 1918. (Courtesy of Bessie M. Gilmer)

"I love the country." Bessie Tucker. (Courtesy of Bessie M. Gilmer)

"The new modern schoolhouse," near Wakefield, Nebraska, 1919, Bessie's last year of teaching. (Courtesy of Bessie M. Gilmer)

Attaining My Lifelong Ambition

Lee and Bessie M. Tucker Gilmer, married December 30, 1920. (Courtesy of Bessie M. Gilmer)

". . . baby chicks. . . . One of the farm's little miracles. . . . I may make a pretty good farmer's wife yet." (Courtesy of Bessie M. Gilmer)

Chapter 8

CHAPTER
NINE

"Teachers are Leaders"

Ethel Hale Russel, Nebraska, 1895–1916; Idaho, 1916–1917; Utah, 1917–1919; Iowa, 1919–1922; and Michigan, 1922–

Teachers *are* leaders when they know their self worth *and* accept community responsibility.

The life of Ethel Hale Russel illustrates transitions in the education of children and teachers from the one-room schoolhouses with minimally educated teachers to the graded schools in town with professionally educated teachers. She has personally experienced the expansion of the roles of women, shifting from the private concerns of home and family to public and political pursuits. Her narrative, based largely on her oral history, spans more than ninety years and includes her participation and leadership in educational, community, and social change at the local, state, national levels, and efforts to encourage international understanding.[1] She purposefully sought out the transitions in her life, fully realizing that each would bring change and challenge into her existence.

Ethel was born on a farm near Hardy, Nebraska, near the Kansas-Nebraska border. She, her brothers, and sister attended the graded school in Hardy. Ethel's oldest brother refused to attend school beyond the local high school, but the three younger Hale children, Cleo, Russell, and Ethel, attended the state normal school: it was expected of them, and they didn't question their parents' decision to educate them beyond high school. For Mrs. Hale, the children were fulfilling her desire to be educated.

> School was very, very important in our lives. I think it largely
> due to the fact that my mother was the great influence. Now my
> mother had been born in Belfast, Ireland, and her father. . . .
> died when my mother was about a year and a half old. . . . they,
> [Ethel's grandmother and mother, Anna Semple-Hill McKinstry
> and baby, Mary] came to Illinois and my grandmother [may have]
> taught in the school in . . . Peoria.

The young widow, Anna Semple-Hill McKinstry, remarried in Illinois, and then moved west to Avoca, Nebraska, where several children, Mary's half-brothers and sisters, were born. Growing up in Avoca, Ethel's mother, Mary McKinstry, longed for more schooling.

> There was a little college, [I think] it would be called a
> college . . . my mother said . . . how she wanted to go to this
> college and there wasn't any money. Here she was in this particu-
> lar little town where she could have gone if there had been
> money, but there was none. . . . It was in Avoca then that my
> grandmother died, leaving six or seven children, and the oldest
> of that family [the half-brothers and sisters] was about fourteen
> years old.

Anna's death left Mary in charge of the children and the house-keeping.

At Sunday school, Mary met James Matthew Hale from Kentucky who was working on building the railroad. When she was eighteen, she went alone to meet him in a town between Avoca and Seward, Nebraska, where they were married. They first settled on a farm near Nora, then moved to Nuckolls County.

> Apparently, the one thing that was foremost in my father's
> mind was to get land . . . be a farmer. . . . before I was born, he
> had gotten this quarter section in Nuckolls County. . . . It wasn't
> the very best land, but they started there together to work on
> this and to build a house. . . . [They] had laid out the fields and
> had plans for planting trees. Mother was a devoted tree planter.

Chapter 9

On this place then they had planted a fruit orchard and had surrounded it with three lanes of trees: a row of maples, a row of ash, and a row of elm. These were planted pretty close together to be a wind break . . . for the orchard. . . . and for the house. The house was a teeny, tiny house in which we were pretty crowded, but it wasn't too long before my father contracted . . . to build on a dining room, a kitchen and two bedrooms. . . . The old part of the house which was well built and attractive . . . was to be the parlor and then two bedrooms.

Farming must have been going on fairly well, but I know nothing about the financing, where the money came from. Dad [had] . . . about a carload of livestock to fatten as I remember in those early years. Then we had hogs and then we had some fruit from this orchard . . . mostly cherries, fruit trees didn't grow very well.

By the time red-haired, blue-eyed Ethel, the youngest of the four Hale children, started school in 1901, the farm children living near town attended the graded school in Hardy, Nebraska.

. . . my father thought I couldn't walk the mile and a half to school. So every morning, we hitched up the horse, a single buggy, and the four of us drove to school. Dad built a barn on Mr. Beatty's place so that when we got to Mr. Beatty's, we unhitched the horse. The boys put him in the barn and we walked another half mile straight north to the school. In winter time, going straight north wasn't an easy job. . . . We drove Old Bill at first, and Old Bill was a slow-going traveler. . . . and had to be urged on, so it was always, "Get up, Bill! Get up Bill!" Yet when we got to the railroad tracks, we always pulled up. That was one thing we were trained to do . . . . this was a mainline of the Burlington to Denver, and those trains came down that grade just awfully fast.

Ethel's first teacher made sure that the children learned their lessons.

[I] started in the chart class, that is the beginning. I probably had an awfully good time. I'm not sure that I learned very fast, but anyway, one learns from listening to the older children in the

Teachers Are Leaders

next class [grades one through three were in one room] . . . . we began at 9 o'clock and we went through the morning up until 12 and then an hour at noon and back at one in the classroom.

We carried our lunches for years and years . . . . it was mostly bread sandwiches and an apple . . . . We were brought together in a certain place under teacher supervision for our lunch and we gobbled that in order to get out on the playground to play. So we played for just as long as we could . . . .

[Miss Groves was] well-known as a good teacher. Apparently she was an experienced teacher and she was devoted. . . . [She] saw to it that we didn't fail to learn the things that were expected of us . . . . I don't know whether she [had] teacher training or anything of the sort, or maybe she just had taken the examinations. But she had an aptitude for it.

It is apparent that the Hale family valued education. Providing transportation to school for the children assured consistent attendance. Mrs. Hale visited the school to see how the children were progressing, and to see

if we were having trouble. I was always having trouble, especially with arithmetic. She always helped us with our school work. Now my father didn't [help us with schoolwork] . . . but he never objected to her spending time working with us on our school work. . . . all this time, I think this influence of her regard for books and learning and reading touched each of us. . . .

. . . the whole attitude in our family was that schooling, a chance to go to school, read books: this was a real opportunity! . . . we knew that schooling . . . was a *paramount* thing. . . .

Although Ethel remembers having difficulties in school, she skipped a grade in high school and graduated at age fifteen with her older brother. The value her mother placed on education and especially on reading permeated Ethel's life. Gifts at Christmas time always included books, so that the Hale children had

a raft of ten cent books that Mother provided, such as *The Five Little Peppers*. . . . it's in there on the shelf now. And Mother

Chapter 9

read to us, not only did she read to us, she expected us to remember the stories.

. . . I shall never forget her attitude there. Her emphasis upon
books, upon reading, her emphasis upon our doing well in school.

The Hale children went to Sunday school at first in the schoolhouse
in Warwick, Kansas, a quarter of a mile from home, where Mrs. Hale
taught the weekly lessons.

> Then she was teaching a Sunday School class in Hardy. There
> were two churches in Hardy. One was Methodist and one was a
> Lutheran. [After teaching Sunday School at the Methodist
> Church for several years], the superintendent of the Sunday
> School, who was a close neighbor and good friend said to her,
> well, you can't go on teaching a Sunday School class unless you
> join the Methodist Church. . . . So the next Sunday all of us
> were over at the Lutheran Church . . . . it was a good many years
> before we did join this Lutheran church. . . .
>
> She kept emphasizing that one of the things she did was to
> read. She didn't just read the Bible, she read books that com-
> mented on passages of the Bible and she read articles that she
> kept and there were packages of a magazine or two that she kept
> reading that I think probably stimulated her a great deal. Any-
> way, all the children my age and Russell's age were in her Sunday
> School class until [because it was too large] it was split into a
> boys class and a girls class.

Mrs. Hale used her benevolent and religious volunteer work to ex-
pand her influence beyond her home. For her, the denominational
constraints were simply artificial barriers that could be dealt with by
changing churches. This spirited approach to self-determination can
be seen in Ethel's life also.

By the time Ethel was in high school, her older sister, Cleo, was
teaching school ten miles from home. Cleo had a tenth grade education, all that Hardy public schools offered her, and had passed the
teacher's examinations. "Of course, my mother and father were very
pleased that Cleo . . . was out earning some money and successful and
she was being recommended for another school which was a step up
and this pleased the family. . . . I don't know what she was paid, I
think $20 a month there at first."

Teachers Are Leaders

As Ethel and her brother, Russell, completed the newly added eleventh and twelfth grades of Hardy High School, her parents "knew what we were doing even in high school!" During Ethel's senior year in high school, she was allowed to attend a school event with a classmate named Bill.

> . . . I was to get home at ten o'clock, and my father told Bill this when he came. . . . And as we came across this bridge and were coming right along, we were within a half a mile of home, we met up with a man on horseback. And it flashed across my mind, "Why that is one of our horses." And it was a little after ten o'clock. But nobody ever told me about it afterwards, I'd always just guessed this is my father coming out to see that we were on our way home. . . . it was the gait of the horse that made me think it was he.

The consistency of the Hale family permeates Ethel's memories. The family farm home was the center of their work, their social activities, and the foundation of the children's education. Ethel's parents determined that Ethel and Russell would attend Peru State Normal School along with Cleo. When the three Hale children left home to attend the normal school, this supportive family network continued. Cleo paid her own expenses from the $450.00 she had saved while teaching. Mrs. Hale wrote to the children every month "in a flowing hand," and Mr. Hale sent a check for fifty dollars to cover room and board, and to provide spending money of one dollar each for Ethel and Russell. The check was always made out to Russell.

> You see, in those days . . . it would be done that way. So when Russell cashed the check, he was supposed to divide it with me. Well, he had gotten involved, before the end of the first year he'd become interested in one of the girls. . . . So he explained to me, now, I have to take so-and-so to different things and I'm going to have to keep this extra dollar, and he kept it! . . .
> He said, now you just get somebody to take you about. But I was fairly young and . . . I was probably a little slow at developing, but I hadn't been interested in boys and men or anything of that sort. So only, I guess, once during that time did any one of the men, and he was a good deal older than I . . . ask me to do something that cost money. We usually just picnicked, you know,

a group of us would go on a little picnic party. That was mostly our entertainment. It was right on the Missouri River . . . very beautiful country side and right down by Nebraska City.

Ethel recalled with humor the situation of having Russell take care of the money, including Ethel's spending money but was still peeved at the injustice of her imposed inferior position because she was the younger sister.

At Peru State Normal School, Ethel had both men and women in-structors who taught "excellent classes on how to approach children."

> We had good instructors at this Peru State Normal and I remem-ber certain ones of them with real pleasure. I think they put us [through excellent classes on] how to approach children. I think there was some good psychology. . . . I think the training we got in Peru was superior training, was *very good* training. . . . And we had to do practice teaching. And we didn't get just fifteen minutes of practice teaching, you had to go in the room and sit and watch. . . . So we watched really good people at work. That, I think, was one of the things that helped me readily. . . . And that training, I expect, was probably what accounted for my be-ing as enthusiastic as I was when I went to teach.

Ethel graduated from the two-year program at age seventeen.

> Anyway, after two years of this, without question I was going to teach. . . . I didn't have a very serious outlook. The fact of the matter is I think I was having an awfully good time!

Beginning a few days after her eighteenth birthday, Ethel taught second grade in the public school in Fairbury, Nebraska, a position she held for three years. One of her friends left Fairbury and took a teach-ing job in Spokane, Washington. The girl friend's accounts of teach-ing on the West Coast encouraged Ethel in her resolve to "see the world" and to test her independence. Her mother supported Ethel's desire to travel because she "thought that seeking the world was ter-ribly important," but "Father thought I was a little off."

Her first adventuresome step into the larger world beyond Nebraska was to teach for a year in Twin Falls, Idaho. She possibly answered a newspaper ad, and then traveled alone by train to Idaho. The rough atmosphere of Twin Falls was far removed from the calm and settled small towns of Nebraska that Ethel had known. After one school year, she left and accepted a position in Ogden, Utah, where she taught for two years.

She recalled when two of her students in Ogden, Tommy and Walter, who

> asked her if they could come to her place on Saturday mornings to play ball with her. Those lads came from poor homes with older brothers wards of the Juvenile Courts so the mother of the two boys whose home it was [where Ethel boarded] would not allow her sons to play ball. Many of those beautiful Saturday mornings were spent on the mountain side playing "One Old Cat."[2]

The community and the school system of Ogden were well established, but Ethel found herself to be one of the few Gentiles among the Mormon majority. In her teaching, she was enthusiastically supported by her principal but was evaluated in varying ways by four different supervisors. These conflicting evaluations went to the superintendent's office and prompted him to visit her classroom. Apparently, the superintendent agreed with the principal's assessment, that Ethel was a teacher with remarkable qualities.

> It was through the Superintendent that the opportunity of a life time came! In the early spring, I was called to come to his office. He, the Superintendent, told me he was leaving his post in Ogden at the end of the school year. . . . He said that he did not like to go leaving me in the situation [with divided support], and [asked if I] would I be interested in furthering my education.
>
> He was a graduate of the University of Iowa, knew Dr. Ernest Horn, director of the Experimental School and would recommend me, if I cared to apply. I did apply and the almost unbelievable happened. I received the appointment, taught the second grade, did demonstration teaching, had a part in some experimental studies directed by Dr. Horn. [I also] carried courses and received my Bachelor of Science in Education and Masters Degree.[3]

Ethel had dared to leave the comfort and security of teaching near to her home and had the self-confidence to believe those administra-

tors and supervisors who valued her creative teaching style. She found
that the three years at the State University of Iowa, Iowa City, beginning in 1919, "made all the difference in my life." Her conviction
that she was a successful teacher and her inclination to see the world
took her beyond the ordinary expectations of most young teachers.
Ethel had only two years of normal school prior to being employed
at the university elementary school, commonly called the Experimental School, where she felt especially fortunate to be a part of the
courses and research in learning at the University of Iowa. She taught
second grade in the Experimental School, did demonstration teaching
for preservice and in-service teachers, took part in research and experimental projects, and enrolled in college courses. In the cultural
setting of Iowa City, Ethel Hale became a well-educated professional
teacher.

The University Elementary School, founded in 1915, with Dr.
Ernest Horn as director, was housed in an "old, old building, nothing
fancy." The only special room was for the orchestra. The superior
academic education available in the Experimental School was so appealing that enrollment of the children of the faculty had to be limited
to half of the total number.[4] Parents were also eager to have their
children accepted in the preschool at the Iowa Child Welfare Research Station. While the Experimental School and the research station were separate entities, both added to the stimulating atmosphere
of research and scholarship in education. The station functioned "in
a sense, [like] a second psychology department [at the University of
Iowa], not a laboratory school" and was the first scientific research
center in the United States to investigate the growth and learning of
normal children.[5]

Ernest Horn was the coauthor of the widely used *Horn-Ashbaugh
Speller* and author of numerous spelling textbooks for elementary
grades through high school and other texts.[6] Ethel found that Dr.
Horn believed that

. . . teachers *must be well-informed,* had to understand children, and plan for individuality. He wasn't impressed with the
easy-going approach when people do what they want to do, select what they to teach. Children *had to have the three Rs.*

Dr. Horn thought that reading material shouldn't be made up
of simply fairy tales, but should consist of a good deal of factual
stuff. In order to do this, teachers used a wide variety of stories. I

Teachers Are Leaders

read dozens of different kinds of stories to the second graders. He [Horn] was a most remarkable man![7]

Ethel worked with Ernest Horn and other colleagues in studying eye movements in reading and then trained children through the use of "masses of specially prepared flash cards" to read "in swoops across the page." Their goal was that children would "read in order to learn about the world." The emphasis on reading in the Experimental School carried over into Ethel Hale's master's degree thesis, titled "Selection of Reading Texts for Grades I–II–III."

As products of this professionally stimulating atmosphere, Ethel and her colleagues at the Experimental School were in the position to become teacher educators in colleges and universities across the nation. Dr. Horn aided Ethel and others in obtaining positions in higher education and educational leadership. "Helen Davis went to teach in a college in Colorado; Wilma Garnet went to teach in Ohio; and the principal of the Experimental School, Bess Goodykoontz, went to Washington, D.C., as Assistant Commissioner of Education."[8]

In 1922, President D. B. Waldo, Western State Normal School, Kalamazoo, Michigan, went to Iowa City to interview Ethel. His goal was to bring together faculty from Columbia University's Teacher College, the State University of Iowa, and George Peabody College for Teachers in order to obtain the "best of all educational worlds." Ethel joined colleagues from all of these institutions in teaching at the Training School of Western State Normal School, working with children and student teachers, doing demonstration teaching, and teaching in-service teachers. Her starting salary of $2,500 in 1922, which increased to $2,950 by 1929, was comparable to her colleagues in the Training School and in the academic departments. Among the highest paid faculty members were Frank Ellsworth, director of the Training School, with a salary of $4,750, and Roxanna Steele, the associate director, with the salary of $4,000. A relatively new normal school, having been established in 1903, the faculty of Western State Normal School in 1925 consisted of fifty-nine men and fifty-eight women, including thirteen women in the Training School.[9]

She brought with her a well-developed educational philosophy that grew out of her nine years of successful teaching, and her professional education that began at Peru State Normal School and flourished at the University of Iowa. At the core of her teaching was the recognition of the need to plan for the individuality of students. Ethel believed that the successful teacher relates to children as "a good close friend so you can talk to children seriously about what's fine and what's wrong. I was a good friend to my school children." [10]

Among the faculty at Western State Normal School, Ethel met a transplanted Kansas farm boy, Dr. Robert R. Russel, professor of history. Ethel's landlady thought that the young man Ethel dated who had a car was a more fitting suitor for her than Robert who did not own an automobile. However, Ethel and Robert were married on Christmas Day, 1924. Ethel and Robert agreed that she should continue her professional affiliations and employment after marriage.

In this period of the late 1920s and early 1930s, Ethel was at her peak in her teaching career with her work in the Training School. In the evenings and during summer sessions, she taught extension classes to teachers in a sixty-mile radius of Kalamazoo. Ethel was approached by a group of professors from the University of Michigan to join them in writing elementary reading textbooks, but she thought she could do it on her own. The influence of Ernest Horn and her work at the University of Iowa Experimental School carried over into her factual third-grade reader published by Lippincott. She intended to write additional reading books, but "I never got it done as there were just other things to be done." [11]

In 1925, Western State Normal School issued a bulletin, "Speakers Available," but neglected to include any of the women faculty members as potential speakers. The women responded by compiling and distributing a parody, "Western State Abnormal School Bullet, Shriekers Prevailable," which listed women faculty speakers whose topics lampooned those offered by the men. The Shriekers noted, "No men are prevailable this year. Previous years the demand has been so low that it has been thought best to entirely eliminate them. . . . All Shriekers listed are prevailable only for Uplift Clubs, Widowers Clubs and Ace of Clubs." [12]

Ethel Hale-Russel is listed as prevailable on the topics, "Onwards and Upwards," "Canned Goods," "This Is the Life," and "Beauty Parlors and Tea Grounds." Her colleague, Anna Evans of the Department of Rural Education, would speak on "Losing a Vacation," and "Flappers of Today." The seventh-grade supervisor, Louise Steinway, was cited as being "Especially versatile. Has 64 lectures. Renders without notes." Elizabeth Zimmerman, Department of Languages, would speak on "The Wisest Man—Never Born" and "Women—Balanced Creations." The women made their point; six women were among the speakers listed in the next bulletin.[13]

During the late 1920s, the normal school extended the two-year curriculum for teacher certification to three years, and became Western State Teachers College. As a member of the Training School faculty, Ethel was involved in planning these changes in the curriculum. The requirements for teacher certification were continuing to change nationwide through the leadership of the professional teacher educators.

When she and Robert announced to President Waldo the impending birth of their first child, he promised there would be a place for her on the faculty whenever she wished to return to teaching. Ethel took only a brief break from teaching when their first son, Robert, was born in 1932. With the help of a succession of college girls who worked for their room and board by doing housework and child care, Ethel returned to teaching until their second son, James, was born in 1934.

Ethel believed, "Households don't succeed too well unless there is someone who is the grounding point." Her professional career took second place to her taking responsibility for being that "grounding point" and to her husband's career. She was able to be adventuresome as a single woman teacher and was eager to develop her professional role as a married woman without children. But she could not entrust the care of her children to the college girls who worked for their room and board. This went against her beliefs about the role of mothers. Had Robert and Ethel's incomes been sufficient to support a professional nanny and housekeeper, Ethel might have continued teaching. However, she eased into a slightly more relaxed time of exploring the world close to home with her young sons. "When the boys were in school, I got into community affairs. I needed to have some additional interests. I missed teaching, but there wasn't any chance to go back to school [to study] or to teach. As they grew, I was pretty sure that my job was here [at home]. I could have gone back when they were in high school, but I would have to go back to school first."

Going back to school would have meant residing in Ann Arbor, approximately 100 miles from Kalamazoo, in order to pursue a doctoral program at the University of Michigan. Robert's work, their sons, and their home were in Kalamazoo. The physical and emotional distance to graduate school was greater than Ethel could tolerate while maintaining her desire and personal need to be the "grounding point" of the family.

This transition from being a highly involved professional teacher educator to a stay-at-home mother pushed Ethel into her most creative and productive years as an innovative community activist and leader. It is at this point in her life that she expands the boundaries of her definition of womanhood largely through benevolent work, especially related to education. Through her participation in the Parent Teachers Association, she established parent education groups for mothers *and* fathers, the first in this area that weren't exclusively for mothers. After she moved on to other interests, she was appalled that the parent education groups again became known as mothers' study and met only during the day, effectively excluding the participation of fathers. With the welfare of children as her main concern, Ethel was a prime mover in the establishment of well-baby clinics in Kalamazoo, again combining the well-being of children and the educational process. Following these municipal housekeeping interests on the local level, she was appointed to the state Child Welfare Board and was the League of Women Voters' representative to the State Safety Council of Michigan. In these state level positions, she could exert political and educational influence on behalf of children. While she was not employed for a salary, her sons thought of her as a working mother during this period of community and state involvement.

Ethel was happily and productively involved in community affairs, but the Depression years were times of uncertainty because Robert's continued employed was dependent on the variable state appropriations and declining enrollment at Western State Teachers College. Robert recalled the financial hardships and dismissals of faculty as enrollments declined, especially in 1934:

> It was nerve-racking to wait to see where the axe would fall. The relief of finding oneself retained was offset by the sadness of seeing friends and colleagues dismissed for no particular fault, only that the appropriation was too small or the times too bad. It was hard to face those people. . . .
>
> At some time during the Depression, Dr. Paul Sangren, then dean of administration, called several of us in individually and slipped each a little extra money from a small fund he found that was not otherwise committed. I got $50.00. My impulse was to say "Why don't you use the fund to bring back one of the in-

structors dismissed?" But I didn't say it. Instead, I took the fifty, thanked Dr. Sangren ungracefully for it, turned on my heel and walked out.

In general, the Depression years were not Western's finest hour.[14]

For Ethel, the World War II era was a most trying time, when Robert, in his late forties, but true to his convictions of patriotism and duty, enlisted without her prior knowledge and approval. He served as an historian in the U.S. Army for the duration of the war, while Ethel and the boys coped with rationing and the shortages at home. During the school year 1943–1944, Ethel taught for $200 a month at Richland, a small town about fifteen miles from Western's campus, where many prospective teachers did their student teaching. At the close of the war the Russel family was relieved to have Robert return home and resume teaching at Western.

Shortly after World War II, Ethel and several of her friends established the Women's Action Committee for Peace, motivated by the belief that the "search for peace is every thinking woman's cause."[15] Out of this small group of thinking women came the groundwork for establishing the first organization of lay people who worked in support of the United Nations. Ethel identifies her work in founding the American Association for the United Nations as her most important accomplishment. For the next twenty years, Ethel's desire to "search for peace" took form as she worked throughout Michigan as state president of the AAUN, head of the speakers' bureau, and as the catalyst in establishing sixteen chapters of the AAUN. Her definition of the boundaries and responsibilities of womanhood now put her in a public leadership role that extended beyond the state for the cause of international understanding.

For the Nebraska farm girl who wanted to see the world, the American Association for the United Nations was the opportunity to work on behalf of world understanding. Ethel's leadership of the AAUN brought her into contact with Eleanor Roosevelt, also a dedicated supporter of the United Nations. In 1950, Mrs. Roosevelt, at Ethel's invitation, spoke to a standing room only crowd in Kalamazoo Central High School Auditorium, then visited the campus of Western State Teachers College. A framed letter from Mrs. Roosevelt to Ethel hangs in her home, a prized possession. "In her letter she called me an invaluable part of the organization, and said that she hoped I would never leave. I prize and cherish what she said and wrote to me."[16]

In her nineties, Ethel continues to be a "thinking woman," with widespread interests having to do with the welfare of children, the environment, and world understanding. She occasionally writes to her representatives, senators, and others expressing her considered and well-informed views. Robert writes every day, sometimes working on the Russel family history, and often writing in his special field of scholarship, the economic history of the United States. The ties with their children and grandchildren have been the core of family continuity for the Russels. As their lives together continue passed their mid-nineties, they remain relatively independent. However, they

> . . . regret that, as they lose contact with their life's pursuits, they cannot have as much influence upon events that they have seen deteriorating in recent years.
>
> "Robert talks at the TV a lot whenever people are discussing things he doesn't agree with," she [Ethel] confides. "I hear a lot of good lectures [from Robert] while we're watching the news."[17]

Ethel and Robert also have "lively discussions" when they find themselves on opposite sides of a question. This intellectual vitality, while slowed by the inevitability of physical decline in old age, shines on in this partnership. On her ninetieth birthday, Ethel and Robert, her husband of sixty-two years, had enjoyed the bright, clear day at their home. In describing her birthday to this author in the late afternoon, Ethel declared, "The day is bordered with bright colors!"[18] The bright colors of Ethel Hale Russel's life have emanated from her vivacious and expansive spirit in "seeking the world," coupled with the strong influence of domesticity and the Protestant ethic of her family. In March 1989, Ethel was an honored guest at the Women's History Month luncheon at Western Michigan University, formerly Western State Teachers College. She was pleased to see "women coming into their own," while Robert's pleasure was seeing his wife honored for her contributions to education and to the world community.

Ethel Hale Russel continues to believe that "Teachers *are* leaders when they know their self worth *and* accept community responsibility." For this educator and leader, the global community is "every thinking woman's cause" and responsibility.

Ethel Hale, eighth grade graduate, ca. 1908. Completing eighth grade became an educational goal for rural and town children in the early 1900s. (Courtesy of Ethel Hale Russel)

High school graduation, Hardy, Ne-braska, Public High School, May 1911. (Courtesy of Ethel Hale Russel)

Chapter 9

After Ethel Hale completed the two-year program at Peru State Normal School, she taught second grade, Fairbury, Nebraska, 1913. (Courtesy of Ethel Hale Russel)

After teaching six years, Ethel Hale became a teacher at the Experimental School, State University of Iowa, and completed her B.S. and M.A. there. (Courtesy of Ethel Hale Russel)

Teachers Are Leaders

At Ethel Hale Russel's request, Eleanor Roosevelt spoke to the American Association for the United Nations, and visited Henry Hall, Western Michigan University, Kalamazoo, Michigan, 1950. (Courtesy of Ethel Hale Russel)

Robert and Ethel Hale Russel, January 1986, bringing in wood for the fireplace in preparation for a "lively discussion." (Photograph by Carl Bennett, *Kalamazoo Gazette*)

Chapter 9

Epilogue

"They Left Their Mark"

[The women teachers] were physically and mentally strong, fear-
less and defiant of obstacles, determined that they would establish a reputation for all things good and be an example to direct
the young people the higher life, they left their mark on . . .
citizenship that can never be effaced.

The profound changes in American public education during the
period of the late 1860s to the 1920s are illuminated in this regional
assessment of the schoolwomen of the plains and prairies. The educational progress and reforms of the heartland describe those rural
areas of the United States where there was a stable population of
people who rejected a tradition of power belonging to the landed gen-
try or the social elite. These middle- and lower-middle-class farmers
and ranchers believed that it was their democratic right to have access
to public education for all of their children and to have their say in
how education was implemented. They were willing, albeit grudg-
ingly, to support the reforms of public education, elementary through
higher education, through increasing taxes as the amount of new lands
to be taxed diminished.

Both coeducation and the feminization of teaching were begun east of the Mississippi and carried to the West by the emigrants. The feminization of teaching reflects the need for employment of women outside of their homes and the significant lack of other employment opportunities for them, especially in sparsely populated areas. As men rejected teaching for better-paying occupations, women were expected to accept the low salaries because it was their duty to help others, especially children. Thus the feminization of teaching emphasizes the persistent influence of domesticity by specifically identifying women as the care givers and the carriers of the culture. These roles of women extended from the family to the one-room schoolhouses scattered across the rolling western land, to the emerging communities and the institutions of their democratic society.

As the frontier became settled and tamed, homes, schools, and communities became viable institutions undergirded by the stability of the people who made their homes on the plains and prairies. The tax-paying residents of the heartland gradually lengthened the school year from a few months to eight or nine months in order to give children more time to be educated. Through the leadership of the educational professionals, the curriculum expanded from a simplistic approach to the three Rs, based on a hodgepodge of student-owned textbooks, to state-designated courses, content, and texts that were supported by ever-increasing taxes.

The requirements of teacher education and certification became codified and professionalized, no longer based on the whims of local superintendents and school boards but shaped by standards determined by state departments of education and fostered by the state teacher education colleges and the professional associations. Mere literacy as the criterion for employment as a teacher was short-lived as local school boards and county and state departments of education designed and implemented the requirements for certification, which included examinations, normal courses and institutes, and increasingly, college education for teachers.

None of these momentous transitions and reforms transpired without conflict, nor were they implemented uniformly. However, the overall sweep of educational progress placed the populations of Iowa, Kansas, and Nebraska among the most literate in the nation as the environment of the plains and prairies changed politically and socially from the frontier to established communities. Thus the residents of the region, including the schoolwomen, were both the changers and the changed, the reformers and the reformed, the advocates and the recipients of the benefits of advancement and growth of public coeducation.

The constant factor throughout this period of change remains the pervading motivation of teachers based on the satisfaction, recognition, and inspiration drawn from the teacher-child dyad. The role of teaching in the lives of the schoolwomen whose narratives are found in the preceding chapters varied in length and intensity, from a few school terms to a life-time profession. Those who saw themselves as successful, confidently identified themselves as teachers. They found the daily contact with students challenging, reinforcing, and enjoyable. The drawbacks of teaching, such as low salaries, poorly equipped schools, lack of professional contact, and lack of respect from other professionals, were overbalanced by the prospects of guiding learners toward fulfilling their potentials, of seeing children becoming successful, and by the lack of other challenging, respected employment. Some persons who failed at teaching found the responsibilities of being in the leadership role with large groups of children all day, every day, compounded by the stress and the low salaries. Others who failed, faltered under the multiple burdens of the interpersonal relationships between the teacher and the scholars, and the obligation to not only know and guide each student, but also to know the appropriate content and skills and how to teach them. Still other failures resulted simply from the lack of knowledge of the basic content of the school curriculum.

Among these distinctive lives of the schoolwomen of the prairies and plains, 1860s to 1920s, are the commonalities that identify them in human qualities and characteristics. That these schoolwomen were from rural families and spent their childhoods on the prairies and plains does not make them exceptional, but rather emphasizes the prevalence of the rural way of life in this time frame. The schoolwomen of the heartland were among the people who were at home with the land where they were nurtured, educated, taught school, cared for their families, and related to the larger community around them.

The schoolwomen cited in this volume took pride in being teachers whether they taught two years or more than fifty. Being a teacher was the part of their public identity and self image that involved them in "greater opportunities for doing *good*, . . . preventing crime, increasing wealth, protecting property, elevating morals, and promoting general happiness."[1] The schoolwomen believed that they had ideas, skills, and information worth sharing with others and they made the effort in their lifetimes to achieve public recognition for their competencies through teaching, writing, and speaking in a variety of settings.

The schoolwomen whose personal documents have contributed to this research wanted their narratives known by members of their families and by others. They preserved teaching contracts, attendance books, school notebooks, photographs, and diaries and handed them on to daughters, granddaughters, and archival collections as evidence of success in the teaching profession. To share their thoughts publicly and to educate others, they wrote essays, poems, stories, and books, some of which were published or presented in public meetings. In the emerging communities, these rural schoolwomen had ample opportunities to be heard as teachers and as citizens of the community. Through teaching, women had an appropriate, accessible occupation through which they could obtain public approval and self-esteem for their expressions of idealism, while coping with their own economic and family needs.

Their association with students brought them the challenge and opportunity to plan, to implement, and to observe the positive effects of learning on the next generation. These attributes are associated with capable and effective teachers across time and regions. In their diaries, the schoolwomen comment on the human relationships in their schools, indicating that warmth and affection were welcomed by both students and the teachers. While the content of the curriculum was shaped by state courses of study, it was implemented by individual teachers with varying degrees of success, but with the overall result of a high level of literacy.

Schoolwomen often cited their parents, especially their mothers, as significant in developing their love of learning, of books, and of schooling. The foundations of learning, responsibility, and independence were begun in homes where the families expected their children to be educated, to be accountable, and to be contributing members of the family and community. For the rural families, these expectations were essential for survival in the frontier days. Successive generations also regarded children as contributing members of the family, although as they became educated at high schools, colleges, and universities their ties to the land became diffused. The generational influence can be seen through the succession of teachers from mothers to daughters and granddaughters, and from teachers to students. Among the heirs of Nancy Gaddis, Jane Price, Bessie Gilmer, Sarah Huftalen, and Ethel Hale Russel are generations of teachers. The heritage of influence from teacher to student is an expectation of successful teaching.

The schoolwomen's lives propelled them into public roles that stretched the limitations of gender. In addition to their work in schools, the schoolwomen's idealism was applied through public leadership for social and moral causes: public education, suffrage, temperance, and community development in general. The antecedents of current social concerns can be seen in their actions: Gaddis voted in the school elections; Huftalen and Price spoke publicly for suffrage; and Russel was an active leader in the League of Women Voters. Gaddis delivered babies; Price cared for neighbors and family during childbirth, illness, and death; Gilmer helped friends and neighbors when ill and aided others during the flu epidemics; and Russel established well-baby clinics and worked for improved public safety. Price, Gaddis, and members of their families supported the foreign mission work of their churches, while Russel sought to inform people about global concerns through establishing the American Association for the United Nations.

In their private writings and oral histories, each woman emerges as a forceful personality—intelligent, compassionate, strong willed, and devoted to their families and to their students. They were ambitious for themselves, for their students and the members of their families. The well-being of their families was of primary importance so that maintaining a schedule of employment outside of the home was often difficult. The scheduling of school terms not only aided women in balancing home and teaching demands but also imposed unemployment during portions of the year.

The schoolwomen endured personal setbacks, traumatic and tragic events, but they persevered and saw their lives as worthwhile and productive. In the open land of the plains and prairies, they found their own "adaptive strategies" appropriate to the environment, and were part of the continuity of purpose that produced high levels of literacy.[2] From the 1860s to the 1920s, the schoolwomen of the prairies and plains, carried out their profession in a time and place in which traditions were both respected and changed during the transitions from frontier to established communities, from pioneer teacher to professional educator, from crude one-room schoolhouse to multigraded, consolidated schools. They were pragmatic idealists whose lives were shaped by their dual roles as the creators and preservers of their transplanted and transformed cultures of the heartland.

> . . . they left their mark on . . . citizenship that can never be effaced.[3]

Abbreviations

ISHD-HS, Iowa State Historical Department, Division of the Historical Society, Iowa City
KSHS, Kansas State Historical Society, Topeka
NSHS, Nebraska State Historical Society, Lincoln
RHC-WMU, Regional History Collections, Western Michigan University, Kalamazoo, Michigan

Notes

Introduction

1. Earlier generations of teachers mostly east of the Mississippi are found in Nancy Hoffman, *Woman's "True" Profession: Voices from the History of Education* (Old Westbury, N.Y.: The Feminist Press; New York: McGraw-Hill Book Company, 1981), and Polly Welts Kaufman, *Women Teachers on the Frontier* (New Haven: Yale University Press, 1984).

2. "Story of Routt County's Early Schools is Story of Emma Peck," *The Steamboat Pilot* 75th Anniversary, 8B (Steamboat Springs, Colo.: 1959); Emma H. Peck, "Routt County Days of Yore," *Routt County Republican*, Hayden, Colorado, 1916, unpaged pamphlet; Bill May, local historian, S Bar S Ranch, Steamboat Springs, Colorado, to Mary H. Cordier, July 1, 1983.

3. Rebecca Bullard, Diary, RHC-WMU.

4. *Report of the Commissioner of Education for 1902*, 2 vols. (Washington, D.C.: 1903), 2: 2314–15.

5. Herbert Quick, *One Man's Life: An Autobiography* (Indianapolis: Bobbs, 1925), 154–55.

6. Wayne Fuller, *The Old Country School: The Story of Rural Education in the Middle West* (Chicago: University of Chicago Press, 1982), 191.

7. Carolyn G. Heilbrun challenges women "to turn to one another for stories of their lives and their hopes and their unacceptable fears," in *Writing a Woman's Life* (New York: W. W. Norton, 1988), 44.

8. Donald Warren, ed., *American Teachers: Histories of a Profession at Work* (New York: Macmillan, 1989), 3.

9. The "saints' lives" term used by Hoffman, *Woman's "True" Profession*, xv.

Part I. The Educational and Historical Setting

Chapter 1 The Schoolwomen of the Prairies and Plains, 1860s–1920s

1. *Report of the Commissioner of Education for 1902*, 2 vols. (Washington, D.C.: 1903), 2: 2314–15. Measures of literacy were based on the census

questions to the heads of household as to whether each member of the household could read, and whether they had attended school during the past year.

2. Carol Fairbanks, *Prairie Women: Images in American and Canadian Fiction* (New Haven and London: Yale University Press, 1986), Chapter 1: "Introduction," especially 24–25.

3. Frank S. Townsley described Matthews as a "western wonder" in his "Journal, 1883," May 23–24, 1883, ISHD-HS. Teaching was rated "second to none" in "Resolutions of the Teachers' Class of Osceola, Clark Co.," *The Iowa Instructor* 1:6 (May 1860): 238.

4. Elliott West emphasizes that the settlers of the west were families. Elliott West, *Growing Up with the Country: Childhood on the Far Western Frontier* (Albuquerque: University of New Mexico Press, 1989), 1–2. See also, Elizabeth Hampsten, *Settlers' Children: Growing Up on the Great Plains* (Norman: University of Oklahoma Press, 1991).

5. For the nativities of the populations of Iowa, Kansas, and Nebraska, see each state as listed in these Census Reports, published by the U. S. Government Printing Office: *8th Census 1860, Population of the United States in 1860; 11th Census, 1890, Report on the Population of the United States; and Abstract of the 12th Census of the United States, 1900.* A detailed analysis of the population of Nebraska appears in Wayne Wheeler, *An Almanac of Nebraska: Nationality, Ethnic, and Racial Groups* (Omaha: Park Bronwell Press, 1975).

6. John M. Blum, et al., *The National Experience: A History of the United States*, 6th ed. (San Diego; New York: Harcourt Brace Jovanovich, 1985), 446.

7. West, *Growing Up with the Country*, xi.

8. Mary Ward Smith, "Autobiographical Reminiscences, 1856–1860," 1–2, KSHS.

9. Eliza Adaline Mercer (non-teacher), Reminiscences of childhood in Highland, Kansas Territory, 2–3, KSHS.

10. See Chapter 5, this volume, on Nancy Rebecca Higgins Gaddis.

11. West, *Growing Up with the Country*, especially see Chapter 1, "The Frontier," and Chapter 3, "At Home," in which West contrasts the generational differences of experiences.

12. The schoolwomen's documents used in this study have been gathered from the State Historical Societies of Iowa (Iowa City), Nebraska, and Kansas; the Regional History Collections, Western Michigan University; numerous libraries and museums; private collections; published sources; and oral histories and interviews in Michigan, Iowa, Nebraska, and Kansas.

13. Isabelle Simmons Stewart Manuscript Collection, Dorchester, Nebraska, May 8, 1925, 2, NSHS.

14. Alice Money Lawrence, "A Pioneer School Teacher in Central Iowa," *Iowa Journal of History and Politics* 33:4 (October 1935): 376–78.

15. West, *Growing Up With the Country*, 250. See also Andrew Gulliford, *America's Country Schools* (Washington, D.C.: The Preservation Press, 1984), Country Schools as Community Centers, 78–89.

16. Michael P. Malone and Richard W. Etulain, *The American West: A Twentieth-Century History* (Lincoln: University of Nebraska Press, 1989), 205.

17. Excerpt from Robert E. Riegel, *Current Ideas of the Significance of the United States Frontier* (1952), quoted in Blum, et al., *The National Experience*, 448.

18. Frederick Jackson Turner, "The Problem of the West," in his *Frontier and Section: Selected Essays of Frederick Jackson Turner*, with introduction and notes by Ray Allen Billington (Englewood Cliffs: Prentice-Hall, 1961), 127.

19. Malone and Etulain, *The American West*, 6.

20. James H. Madison, *Heartland: Comparative Histories of the Midwestern States* (Bloomington: Indiana University Press, 1988), 4. See also, Dorothy Schwieder, "Iowa: The Middle Land," 286; Frederick C. Luebke, "Nebraska: Time, Place, and Culture," 241; and Leo E. Oliva, "Kansas: A Hard Land in the Heartland," 256; all in Madison, *Heartland*.

21. West, *Growing Up with the Country*, 262.

22. Turner, *Frontier and Section*, 61.

23. James R. Shortridge, "The Heart of the Prairie: Culture Areas in the Central and Northern Great Plains," *Great Plains Quarterly*, 8:4 (Fall 1988): 216–17.

24. Earl Pomeroy, "Toward a Reorientation of Western History: Continuity and Environment," *Mississippi Valley Historical Review* 41:4 (March 1955): 579–600, especially 582–83, 593.

25. Clarence Ray Aurner, *History of Education in Iowa*, vol. 2 (Iowa City: State Historical Society of Iowa, 1914), "Appendix A—A Comparison of the Michigan Law of 1838 and the Iowa Law of 1840," 359–82; "Appendix B.—A Comparison of the Union School Law of Ohio of 1854 and the Iowa Law of 1857," 383–95. Wayne E. Fuller, *The Old Country School: The Story of Rural Education in the Middle West* (Chicago: University of Chicago Press, 1982), chapter 2, "Free Schools for Farm Children," especially 27–30.

26. Fuller, *The Old Country School*, 30.

27. W. Elliot Brownlee and Mary M. Brownlee, *Women in the American Economy: A Documentary History, 1675 to 1929* (New Haven: Yale University Press, 1976), 269.

28. John L. Rury, "Who Became Teachers? The Social Characteristics of Teachers in American History," in Donald Warren, ed., *American Teachers: Histories of a Profession at Work*, 10, 23 (New York: Macmillan Publishing Company, and London: Collier Macmillan, 1989).

29. Ibid., 10.

30. Turner, "The Problem of the West," in Turner, *Frontier and Section*,

63. Recent interpretations of Turner may be found in David Lowenthal, "The Pioneer Landscape: An American Dream," *Great Plains Quarterly* 2:1 (Winter 1982): 5–19; and John Opie, "Learning to Read the Pioneer Landscape: Braudel, Eliade, Turner, and Benton," *Great Plains Quarterly* 2:1 (Winter 1982): 20–30.

31. *First Annual Report of the Superintendent of Public Instruction of the State of Nebraska for the Year Ending December 31, 1869* (Lincoln: 1869), 52.

32. Ibid.

33. *Biennial Report of the Superintendent of Public Instruction to the General Assembly at its Thirteenth Regular Session, Des Moines, January 10, 1870* (Des Moines: 1870), 76.

34. On the development of the schoolhouses in particular, see Gulliford, *America's Country Schools.* On the development and the politics of the school systems, see Fuller, *The Old Country School.*

35. Amelia Phoneta Bruner, "Recollections of Childhood in the 1860s and Early 1970s," Bruner Family Collection, NSHS.

36. Stewart Manuscript Collection.

37. E. Mary Lacy Crowder, "Pioneer Life in Palo Alto County," *Iowa Journal of History and Politics* 46 (1948): 184.

38. *Third Annual Report of the State Superintendent of Public Instruction for the Year Ending December 31, 1871* (Lincoln: 1872), 160.

39. *Biennial Report of the Superintendent of Public Instruction to the 16th General Assembly of the State of Iowa, 1874–1875* (Des Moines: 1876), 31.

40. Ethel Hale Russel, interview with author, Kalamazoo, Michigan, June 10, 1982, oral history tape recording, RHC-WMU; NSHS.

41. Kenneth Wiggins Porter, ed., "Catharine Emma Wiggins, Pupil and Teacher in Northwest Kansas, 1888–1895," *Kansas History* 1 (Spring 1978): 18.

42. Ibid., 19–20.

43. *Third Annual Report, Nebraska, 1871,* 141.

44. Clarence Ray Aurner, "Some Early Educational Leaders in Iowa," *Iowa Journal of History and Politics* 22 (October 1924): 555; *Ninth Annual Report of the Superintendent of Public Instruction of the State of Kansas for the Year Ending December 31, 1869* (Topeka: 1870), 23.

45. [C. C. Nestlerode], "Editor's Table," *Iowa Instructor—An Educational Journal* 1 (April 1860): 222–23.

46. Schwieder, "Iowa: The Middle Land," in Madison, *Heartland,* 286.

47. Blum, et al., *The National Experience,* 487.

48. David Tyack and Elisabeth Hansot, "Silence and Policy Talk: Historical Puzzles About Gender and Education," *Educational Researcher* 17:3 (April 1988): 34–36; and David Tyack and Elisabeth Hansot, *Learning Together: A History of Coeducation in American Public Schools* (New Haven and London: Yale University Press, 1990), 46–49.

49. Tyack and Hansot contend that there is little evidence that instruction and discipline were gender-specific in the one-room schools. David Tyack and Elisabeth Hansot, *Learning Together*, 69–72.

50. Rury, "Who Became Teachers?" 20.

51. See Chapter 2, this volume.

52. Nancy Hoffman, *Woman's "True" Profession: Voices from the History of Teaching*, (Old Westbury, N.Y.: The Feminist Press; New York: McGraw-Hill, 1981), xviii.

53. Rury, "Who Became Teachers?" 16.

54. Geraldine Jonçinch Clifford, "Man/Woman/Teacher: Gender, Family, and Career in American Educational History," in Warren, *American Teachers*, 299, 293–343.

55. Sandra Acker, "Women and Teaching: A Semi-Detached Sociology of a Semi-Profession," in Stephen Walker and Len Barton, eds., *Gender, Class and Education*, 123–40 (Falmer House, Barcombe, Lewes, Sussex, England: The Falmer Press, 1983).

56. "Resolutions of the Teachers' Class," *Iowa Instructor*, 238.

57. Support for equal pay came from the teachers associations. For an overview of this support, see Edgar B. Wesley, *National Education Association: The First Hundred Years, The Building of the Teaching Profession* (New York: Harper and Brothers, 1957). In 1863, the Iowa State Teachers Association, in its eighth session, determined that women who "had not been required to pay any fees" to the Association, should pay on an equal basis with men because they had been "counted worthy to take the place of the brave boys who have gone to teach rebels the consequences of secession." In Clarence R. Aurner, *History of Education in Iowa*, vol. 2, part 6, "Teachers Associations," 189–254.

58. Alison Oram, "A Master Should Not Serve under a Mistress: Women and Men Teachers 1900–1970," in Sandra Acker, ed., *Teachers, Gender and Careers*, 29 (New York: The Falmer Press, 1989).

59. Susan B. Carter, "Incentive and Rewards to Teaching," in Warren, *American Teachers*, 49.

60. *Fifteenth Biennial Report of the State Superintendent for the Years Ending July 31, 1905 and 1906, Kansas* (Topeka: 1906), 9.

61. Marianne A Ferber, Professor of Economics, University of Illinois at Urbana-Champaign, "The History of Women in the Labor Market—How Present Day Conditions Evolved," paper presented March 22, 1990, Western Michigan University, Kalamazoo, Michigan, sponsored by the Women's History and Research Network and the Commission on the Status of Women.

62. *Thirteenth Biennial Report of the State Superintendent of Public Instruction to the General Assembly of Iowa, January 13, 1868* (Des Moines: 1868), 87–88.

63. *Fifteenth Biennial Report, Kansas, 1905–1906*, 8.

64. See Chapter 5, this volume, on Nancy Higgins Gaddis.

65. Mary Frances (Frankie) Patton Clark to Ora Jim Patton Mann, January 14, 1928, Mann Family Collection, RHC-WMU.

66. Rosalie Trail Fuller, ed., "A Nebraska High School Teacher in the 1890s: The Letters of Sadie B. Smith," *Nebraska History* 58:4 (Fall 1977): 450.

67. See Chapter 8, this volume, on Bessie Tucker Gilmer.

68. See Chapter 7, this volume, on Sarah Gillespie Huftalen.

69. Lawrence, "A Pioneer School Teacher in Central Iowa," 385, 390.

70. Alta Hull, interview by Betty Rowan, 2 April 1983, Fredonia, Kansas.

71. See Chapter 8, this volume, on Bessie Tucker Gilmer.

72. Fuller, *The Old Country School*, 187–89.

73. Ibid., 69–71.

74. Employment data adapted by Carl N. Degler from David Stern, Sandra Smith, and Fred Doolittle, "How Children Used to Work," *Law and Contemporary Problems* 39 (Summer 1975): 99, quoted in Carl N. Degler, *At Odds: Women and the Family in American from the Revolution to the Present* (New York: Oxford University Press, 1980), 70.

75. Degler, *At Odds*, 69–71.

76. Ibid., 309.

77. Gulliford, *American's Country Schools*, 35.

78. Rury, "Who Became Teachers?" 15.

79. Thomas Morain, "The Departure of Males from the Teaching Profession in Nineteenth Century Iowa," *Civil War History* 26:2 (1980): 161–70. See Table 1, "Growth of Number of Public Schools and Number of Teachers," this volume. A wider discussion of "women's jobs" appears in Julie A. Matthaei, *An Economic History of Women in America, Women's Work, the Sexual Division of Labor, and the Development of Capitalism* (New York: Schocken Books, 1982), part 2, "Women's Work and the /Sexual Division of Labor Under the Cult of Domesticity," chapter 9, "The Development of Sex-Typed Jobs," 187–234.

80. Rury, "Who Became Teachers?" 23.

81. Ibid, 23.

82. For growth statistics, see Table 1, "Growth in Number of Public Schools and Number of Teachers," and Table 3, "Growth in Number of School Age Children, School Enrollment, and Average Daily Attendance."

83. Fuller, *The Old Country School*, 191.

84. Blum, et al., *The National Experience*, 487–88.

85. *Fifteenth Biennial Report of the State Superintendent for the Years Ending July 31, 1905 and 1906, Kansas* (Topeka: 1906), 9.

86. To obtain the estimated numbers of prairie women who were school-women during some part of their lives, I used the total number of women teachers cited for each state in Table 1, "Growth of Number of Public Schools and Number of Teachers." From these totals listed roughly by decades, I estimated the number of teaching positions held by women for each year. Based on Dayoff's 1905 estimate of the length of teaching career as less than four years, I used 3.5 years as an estimate for 1870 to 1890s. From this data I estimated the number of women who had taught or who were teaching in the 1890s.

87. Rury, "Who Became Teachers?" 28. Clarence Aurner reports that by 1877, in Iowa, the minimum age for women teachers was seventeen; for men, nineteen. In 1889, eighteen became the minimum age in Iowa for both women and men teachers. Aurner, *History of Education in Iowa*, vol. 1, 324. In 1901–1902, in nine Nebraska counties, only 45 teachers out of 654 were under the age of eighteen; 79 were eighteen; 88 were nineteen; 200 were twenty; 245 over the age of twenty. *Seventeenth Biennial Report of the State Superintendent of Public Instruction for the years 1901–02*, vol. 1 (Lincoln: 1903), 117.

88. Elliott West defines the demands on pioneer men as the providers for the family security who must "raise himself up in the world." West also describes the special attention afforded children by men who were lonesome for their own families. West, *Growing Up with the Country*, 162–67.

89. Robert L. Griswold, "Anglo Women and Domestic Ideology in the American West in the Nineteenth and Early Twentieth Centuries," in Lillian Schlissel, Vicki L. Ruiz, and Janice Monk, eds., *Western Women: Their Land, Their Lives*, 29 (Albuquerque: University of New Mexico Press, 1988).

90. Catherine Beecher, "Address on the Evils Suffered by American Women and American Children," 1846, in Hoffman, *Woman's "True" Profession*, 51.

91. For more information on Catherine Beecher and the teachers sent west under Beecher's leadership by the National Board of Popular Education in the mid 1800s, see Polly Welts Kaufman, *Women Teachers on the Frontier* (New Haven: Yale University Press, 1984). See also, Kathryn Kish Sklar's definitive biography, *Catherine Beecher: A Study in American Domesticity* (New York: Norton, 1973).

92. Kaestle cites opposition in the West to the National Board of Popular Education, in Carl F. Kaestle, *Pillars of the Republic: Common Schools and American Society* (New York: Hill and Wang, 1983), 189–90.

93. Madeleine R. Grumet, *Bitter Milk: Women and Teaching* (Amherst: University of Massachusetts Press, 1988), 43.

94. "Resolutions of the Teachers' Class," *The Iowa Instructor*, 238.

95. Sarah Gillespie Huftalen, "Normal Training Department, Muscatine High School, Muscatine, Iowa," in "Personal No. 2, Sarah L. Gillepsie Huftalen, Manchester, Iowa, I Remember This & That," 102, box 8, vol. 11, Huftalen Collection, ISHD-HS.

96. Bessie Tucker Gilmer, "Journey Through Life," March 18, 1918, 2, NSHS.

97. See Chapter 4, this volume, for additional information on the sense of community within the schoolhouses and on what was taught.

98. Anna Johnson, "Recollections of a Country School Teacher," *Annals of Iowa* 42 (Winter 1975): 491–92.

99. Clara S. Conron, Diary, October 29, 1884, KSHS.

100. Ibid., December 1, 3, 4.

101. Genevieve Giddings Richmond, Reminiscence, Delta Kappa Gamma file, 1, NSHS.

102. Rosa Schreurs Jennings, "The Country Teacher," *Annals of Iowa* 31 (July 1951): 44, 48.

103. Ibid., 62.

104. "Resolutions of the Teachers' Class," *Iowa Instructor*, 238–40.

105. Ibid.

106. Wayne E. Fuller, "School District 37: Prairie Community," *The Western Historical Quarterly* 12:4 (October 1981): 424; Gulliford, *America's Country Schools*, 78–89.

107. *Fourteenth Biennial Report of the Superintendent of Public Instruction to the General Assembly at its 13th Regular Session, Des Moines, Iowa, January 10, 1870,* (Des Moines: 1870), 45.

108. *Sixteenth Biennial Report of the Superintendent of Public Instruction to the 15th General Assembly of the State of Iowa* (Des Moines: 1874), 130–31.

109. *Nineteenth Biennial Report of the Superintendent of Public Instruction to the 18th General Assembly of the State of Iowa* (Des Moines: 1879), 77, 99.

110. *Fifteenth Annual Report of the Superintendent of Public Instruction of the State of Kansas, 1875* (Topeka: 1876), 71.

111. David Sands Wright, *Fifty Years at the Teachers College: Historical and Personal Reminiscences* (Cedar Falls: Iowa State Teachers College, 1926), 53–56.

112. Gulliford, *America's Country Schools*, 89; Fuller, *The Old Country School*, 245.

113. Brownlee and Brownlee, *Women in the American Economy*, 269.

114. Grumet, *Bitter Milk*, 86.

115. See Chapters 5–9 of this volume.

116. Richard W. Rathge points out that the interdependence of tasks of

the farm family has not been appropriately recognized, and thus women's farm work traditionally has been identified as that of the helpmate "whose labor is only indirectly related to agriculture." Richard W. Rathge, "Women's Contribution to the Family Farm," *Great Plains Quarterly* 9 : 1 (Winter 1989): 36. See also, Joan M. Jensen, *With These Hands* (Old Westbury, N. Y.: Feminist Press, 1981).

117. Rathge, "Women's Contribution to the Family Farm," 41–47.

118. Ibid.

119. Rury, "Who Became Teachers?" 28–29.

120. Addington is cited in *Twenty-eighth Biennial Report of the Superintendent of Public Instruction of the State of Iowa, November 1, 1897* (Des Moines: 1897), 112. Numbers of women county superintendents are cited in David Tyack and Elisabeth Hansot, *Managers of Virtue: Public School Leadership in America, 1820–1980* (New York: Basic Books, 1982), 187.

121. *The 1915–16 Educational Directory*, Bureau of Education, issued by the Interior Department indicates that of the 12,000 "conspicuous positions, largely of an adminstrative character," 2,500, or 20 percent, were held by women, in "Women as Leaders in Education," originally published in, *Instructor Magazine*, January 1916, and reprinted in *Instructor Magazine* 100 : 3 (October 1990): 24.

122. Department of the Interior, U.S. Bureau of Education, *Educational Directory, 1915–1916*, Bulletin, 1915, No. 43 (Washington, D. C.: Government Printing Office, 1915), 36–37, 42–43.

123. Ibid., 16–17, 20–21.

124. Tyack and Hansot, *Managers of Virtue*, 187–89.

125. *Seventeenth Biennial Report of the State Superintendent of Public Instruction of the State of Nebraska for the Years 1901–1902*, vol. 1 (Lincoln: 1903), 134.

126. Tyack and Hansot, *Managers of Virtue*, 190.

127. Grumet, *Bitter Milk*, 56.

128. Sophia N. Hapke, "Pioneer Women in Education: Margaret Barrette, Taught in Davenport Schools 1884 to 1934" (Davenport, Iowa, Delta Kappa Gamma, Alpha Chapter, 1949). Typescript in author's possession.

129. Bessie Tucker Gilmer, "Journey Through Life," September 19, 1918.

130. Ibid., May 31, 1918.

131. Sarah Jane Price, Diaries, October 30, 1881, NSHS.

132. Huftalen, "Arbor Vitae Summit, Taught by Sarah Gillespie Huftalen, 1904–1909, Oneida, Iowa," Notebook, June 22, 1907, 22. Huftalen Collection.

133. Huftalen, "Personal—No. 2, Sarah Gillespie Huftalen, Manchester, Iowa, I Remember this & that," 75, Huftalen Collection.

134. The National Education Association attempted to identify the

310

problems of rural education and solutions to the problems in the *Report of the Committee of Twelve on Rural Schools, July 9, 1895* (Chicago: University of Chicago Press, 1897). Wayne Fuller contends that rural teachers were unfavorably compared with urban teachers because of the "anti-rural bias." The professional educators were convinced that the small school district system provided poor education; and that the teachers could be "cured" of their poor teaching through the teacher education programs in which the professionals had vested interests. Fuller, *The Old Country School,* 163–64.

135. Examples of community and educational leaders are documented in these sources: Sherrill F. Daniels, "The Community Builders, Architects of Nebraska [Ruth Calkins Oldam]," in *Perspectives: Women in Nebraska History, June 1984 Special Issue* (Lincoln: Nebraska Department of Education and the Nebraska State Council for the Social Studies, 1984), 62–73; Cornelia Mallett Barnhart, "Phoebe Sudlow," *Palimpsest* 38:4 (April 1957): 169–76; Delta Kappa Gamma file, typescript articles on Susan Frazier, Eliza Morgan, and Genevieve Giddings Richmond, NSHS; Sarah Gillespie Huftalen, Huftalen Collection, Ellen Payne Paullin, "Etta's Journal, January 2, 1874 to July 25, 1875," *Kansas History, A Journal of the Central Plains* 3:3 (Autumn 1980): 201–19; and 3:4 (Winter 1980): 255–78; Dorothy Ashby Pownall, "Agnes Samuelson, A Dedicated Educator," *Palimpsest* 43:11 (November 1962): 497–544; Ethel Hale Russel, retired teacher and community leader in Nebraska, Montana, Utah, Iowa, and Michigan, interview with author, Kalamazoo, Michigan, 10 June 1982, oral history tape recording, NSHS, and RHC-WMU. See also, Chapters 5–9 in this volume.

136. Schwieder, "Iowa: The Middle Land," in Madison, *Heartland,* 278.

Chapter 2 Educating the Schoolwomen of the Heartland

1. *Third Annual Report of the State Superintendent of Public Instruction of the State of Nebraska for the Year Ending December 31, 1871* (Lincoln: 1871), 36.

2. Jurgen Herbst, "Teacher Preparation in the Nineteenth Century"; and William R. Johnson, "Teachers and Teacher Training in the Twentieth Century," in Donald Warren, ed., *American Teachers: Histories of a Profession at Work,* 213–36, 237–56 (New York: Macmillan Publishing Company, and London: Collier Macmillan, 1989).

3. Mary Ward Smith, Autobiographical Reminiscences, 1856–1860, 7–8, KSHS.

4. E. Mary Lacy Crowder, "Pioneer Life in Palo Alto County," *Iowa Journal of History and Politics* 46 (1948): 197.

5. The current terms for teachers' institutes are in-service education, continuing education or teachers' workshops.

Notes to pp. 38–46

6. Rosa Schreurs Jennings, "The Country Teacher," *Annals of Iowa* (July 1951): 61.

7. Geraldine Jonçich Clifford, "Man/Woman/Teacher: Gender, Family, and Career in American Educational History," in Warren, ed., *American Teachers,* 310. See also, Chapter 1, this volume, on the feminization of teaching.

8. In "Man/Woman/Teacher" Clifford reports that by 1910, two-thirds of the teachers had a high school education, and 5 percent had additional education, in Warren, ed., *American Teachers,* 309–10. Sandra L. Myres acknowledges the minimal education of teachers on the frontier, and the increasing demands for additional education and passing examinations for the certification of teachers, in Sandra L. Myres, *Westering Women and the Frontier Experience, 1800–1915* (Albuquerque: University of New Mexico Press, 1982), 184–85, 250–51.

9. Exemplary research can be found in Kathleen Underwood, "The Pace of Their Own Lives: Teacher Training and the Life Course of Western Women," *Pacific Historical Review* 55:4 (November 1986): 513–30. Underwood reports on 315 women graduates of Colorado State Normal School, during the period 1890–1900.

10. Overviews of teacher education centering on the normal schools appear in Herbst, "Teacher Preparation in the Nineteenth Century"; and Johnson, "Teachers and Teacher Training in the Twentieth Century," in Warren, ed., *American Teachers,* 213–36, 237–56.

11. Wayne E. Fuller, "The Teacher in the Country School," in Warren, ed., *American Teachers,* 110. Fuller also discusses the education of the rural teachers in Wayne E. Fuller, *The Old Country School: The Story of Rural Education in the Middle West* (Chicago: University of Chicago, 1982), Chapter 9, "Teachers Are Born," 157–84.

12. See Chapter 5, this volume, on Nancy Higgins Gaddis.

13. Ibid.

14. Enid Bern, "Memoirs of a Prairie School Teacher," *North Dakota History* 42 (Summer 1975): 6.

15. See Chapter 6, this volume, on Sarah Jane Price.

16. See the following works edited by Kenneth Wiggins Porter: "Catharine Emma Wiggins, Pupil and Teacher in Northwest Kansas, 1888–1895," *Kansas History* 1:1 (Spring 1978): 16–38; "College Days at Cooper Memorial, 1895–1898," *Kansas Historical Quarterly* 26:4 (Winter 1960): 383–409; "Country Schoolteacher, 1898–1902, Rice County, Kansas," *Kansas Magazine* (1961): 38–44.

17. Rosalie Trail Fuller, ed., "A Nebraska High School Teacher in the 1890s: The Letters of Sadie B. Smith" *Nebraska History* 58:4 (Fall 1977): 447–73.

18. Examples of community and educational leaders are documented in these sources: Sherrill F. Daniels, "The Community Builders, Architects of Nebraska [Ruth Calkins Oldam]," in *Perspectives: Women in Nebraska History, June 1984 Special Issue* (Lincoln: Nebraska Department of Education and the Nebraska State Council for the Social Studies, 1984), 62–73; Cornelia Mallett Barnhart, "Phoebe Sudlow," *Palimpsest* 38:4 (April 1957): 169–76; Delta Kappa Gamma, typescript articles on Susan Frazier, Eliza Morgan, and Genevieve Giddings Richmond, NSHS; Sarah Gillespie Huftalen, Diaries, Huftalen Collection, ISHD-HS; Ellen Payne Paullin, ed., "Etta's Journal, January 2, 1874 to July 25, 1875," *Kansas History, A Journal of the Central Plains* 3:3 (Autumn 1980): 201–19; and 3:4 (Winter 1980): 255–78; Dorothy Ashby Pownall, "Agnes Samuelson, A Dedicated Educator," *Palimpsest* 43:11 (November 1962): 497–544; Ethel Hale Russel, retired teacher and community leader, Nebraska, Montana, Utah, Iowa, and Michigan, interview with author, Kalamazoo, Michigan, 10 June 1982, oral history tape recording, NSHS, and RHC-WMU. See also, Part II, Chapters 5–9, in this volume.

19. See Chapter 7, this volume, on Sarah Gillespie Huftalen.

20. See Chapter 9, this volume, on Ethel Hale Russel.

21. Report of the Board of Visitors for 1866, State Normal School, Emporia, Kansas, in *Sixth Annual Report of the Department of Public Instruction, of the State of Kansas, 1866* (Leavenworth: 1867), 45.

22. Chauncey C. Colgrove, *The Teacher and the School* (New York: Charles Scribner's Sons, 1912), vii–viii.

23. Ibid., viii.

24. *First Annual Report of the State Superintendent of Public Instruction for the Year Ending December 31, 1869* (Lincoln: 1869), 82.

25. *Biennial Report of the Superintendent of Public Instruction to the Eighteenth General Assembly of the State of Iowa* (Des Moines: 1879), 80.

26. Ibid., 65–66, succeeding quotes in this paragraph are from this source.

27. Gladys McArdle, "An 1878 Model Kansas School, Lebanon, Smith County, Sixth District," 1–2, KSHS.

28. *Sixteenth Biennial Report of the Superintendent of Public Instruction of the State of Iowa, 1871–73* (Des Moines: 1874), 46–58.

29. Mari Sandoz, *Old Jules* (Boston: Little, Brown, 1935), 366.

30. Mari Sandoz left teaching and worked at a variety of different jobs while a part time student in English and writing at the University of Nebraska. Sandoz was recognized as an author of books set in the pioneering days on the plains, especially after the publication of her biography of her father, *Old Jules*. She returned to teaching in the 1940s as a successful author and taught college courses in creative writing. Barbara Sicherman and Carol Hurd Green, eds. *Notable American Women: The Modern Period, A*

Biographical Dictionary (Cambridge, Mass.: Belknap Press of Harvard University Press, 1980), 621–22.

31. Huftalen, "Aug 7 1881–Aug 28 1882, Didactics by Prof. Rose, of Davenport, Iowa," in "Note-book in Analysis," 16, Huftalen Collection.

32. See Chapter 6, this volume, on Price.

33. B. A. Hinsdale, *Horace Mann and the Common School Revival in the United States* (New York: Charles Scribner's Sons, 1900), 145.

34. *Fourth Annual Report of the Superintendent of Public Instruction of the State of Nebraska for the Year Ending December 31, 1872* (Lincoln: 1872), 225. For a more detailed, serious discussion see: J. A. Smith, "The Superintendent's Relation to the Normal Institutes and Hints for the Management of the Same," presented at the Convention of County Superintendents, Lincoln, Nebraska, January 27, 1880, in *Twelfth Annual Report of the State Superintendent of Public Instruction for the State of Nebraska for the Years 1879–1880* (Lincoln: 1880), 28–31.

35. *Biennial Report of the Superintendent of Public Instruction to the General Assembly of Iowa at its 12th Regular Session, January 13, 1868* (Des Moines: 1868), 39.

36. Hinsdale, *Horace Mann*, 136–37.

37. Clarence Ray Aurner, *History of Education in Iowa*, vol. 2 (Iowa City: State Historical Society of Iowa, 1914), 151–52.

38. *Thirteenth Annual Report of the Department of Public Instruction, of the State of Kansas, 1873* (Topeka: 1873), 23.

39. Fuller reports that, although some townspeople charged unfair prices, most charges for room and board at the institutes were appropriate. Fuller, *The Old Country School*, 174–75.

40. Barbara Miller Solomon, *In the Company of Educated Women: A History of Women and Higher Education in America* (New Haven: Yale University Press, 1985), 64–66. Solomon reports tuition costs of $20 at the University of Illinois in 1868; in 1905, they were $30 at the University of Michigan, $350 at Wellesley, and $100 at Smith.

41. Crowder, "Pioneer Life in Palo Alto County," 196–97.

42. [C. C. Nestlerode], "Editor's Table—Teachers' Institutes," *Iowa Instructor, an Education Journal* 1 (May 1860): 253.

43. A. E. Parsons, "Penmanship and Drawing Dept.," *Johnson County Teacher* 8:1 (January 1896): 23.

44. Ibid.

45. Fuller, *The Old Country School*, 170.

46. Ibid., 170–72.

47. *Sixth Annual Report of the Superintendent of Public Instruction of the State of Nebraska for the Year Ending December 31, 1874* (Lincoln: 1874), 53.

48. For examples, see the following: Faculty of the State Normal School, Peru, Nebraska, in *Fourth Annual Report, Nebraska, 1872*, 96; presenters,

leaders, and presidents of sections of the Iowa State Teachers Association, conference program for 1893, in *Biennial Report of the Superintendent of Public Instruction of the State of Iowa, November 1, 1893* (Des Moines: 1893), 77–83; faculty of Iowa State Normal School, 1891–1893, Ibid., 87.

49. For a detailed description of the development of the institutes from their inception to a sequential three-year program, see the Kansas Course of Study, in *First Biennial Report of the Department of Public Instruction for the School Years Ending July 31, 1877 and 1878* (Topeka: 1879), 12–40, 47–49, 401–24; *Fifteenth Annual Report of the Superintendent of Public Instruction of the State of Kansas, 1875* (Topeka: 1876), 120–24.

50. Fuller, *The Old Country School*, 172.

51. Charles H. McGrew, *Institute Manual; or, Graded Courses of Study, and Note Book, for Normal Institutes*, 2d ed. (Ottumwa, Iowa: Press of J. J. Bowles, 1884), unpaged, ISHD-HS.

52. Ibid.

53. Sarah Jane Price, Diary, March 8, 1879, NSHS.

54. Ibid., November 2, 1878.

55. Ibid., March 3, 1879, March 8, 1879.

56. Huftalen, Diaries, August 1884, Huftalen Collection.

57. Lewis Atherton, *Main Street on the Middle Border* (Bloomington: Indiana University Press, 1954), 116–18.

58. Ibid., 116.

59. "Nebraska Teachers' Reading Circle, 1904–1905," NSHS. Additional informal may be found in "Reading Circle Work and Teachers' Certificates," Bulletin No. 3 (1907), NSHS.

60. Ibid.

61. "Nebraska Teachers' Reading Circle, 1902–1903," NSHS.

62. Clara S. Conron, Diary October 3, 1884–July 1, 1885, October 22 and 24, 1884, KSHS.

63. Ibid., January 23 and 31, March 5, 1885.

64. Ibid., February 10, 1885.

65. Ibid., March 17–20, 1885.

66. Lila Gravatt Scrimsher, editor, "The Diary of Anna Webber: Early Day Teacher of Mitchell County," *Kansas Historical Quarterly* 38 (October 1972): 323.

67. Ibid., 324.

68. Ibid., 326.

69. Ibid., 336.

70. Ibid., 337. The "school" was the summer institute at Beloit, Kansas.

71. For detailed descriptions of courses at the normal school from the student's and the instructor's viewpoint, see Huftalen's "Note-book in Analysis" and the "Personal Scrapbooks," Huftalen Collection. Huftalen kept her class notes as a student and her notes when she taught in normal

schools. The Huftalen Collection is unusual in the depth and quantity of documents; class notes of any detail do not seem to appear in other schoool-women's documents.

72. Herbst, "Teacher Preparation in the Nineteenth Century," in War-ren, *American Teachers*, 224–25.

73. "Eastern-Iowa Normal School, General Statements," Supplement, ca. late 1883, unpaged. Two pages of five-column folio sheet, possibly *The Normal Index*, published in Columbus Junction, Iowa. Eastern-Iowa Normal School file, ISHD-HS. About 1880, E.I.N.S. moved to Columbus Junc-tion, Iowa, when presented with land and a building.

74. Ibid.

75. David Sands Wright, *Fifty Years at the Teachers College: Historical and Per sonal Reminiscences* (Cedar Falls, Iowa: Iowa State Teachers College, 1926), 57.

76. Kenneth Wiggins Porter, ed., "College Days at Cooper Memorial," 396.

77. Wright, *Fifty Years at the Teachers College*, 75–78, 84–88.

78. The community societies, church organizations, and literaries are de-scribed in Atherton, *Main Street on the Middle Border*, 186–90.

79. Porter, "College Days," 396.

80. Ibid., 408–9.

81. Ethel Hale Russel, interview with author, 10 June 1982.

82. See Chapter 9, this volume, on Ethel Hale Russel.

83. Ethel Hale Russel, interview with author, Kalamazoo, Michigan, 25 July 1985.

84. See Chapter 9, this volume, on Russel.

85. Geraldine Jonçinch Clifford, *Lone Voyagers: Academic Women in Co-educational Universities, 1870–1937* (New York: The Feminist Press at the City University of New York, 1989), 18–20.

86. Ibid., 19–20.

87. Fuller, *The Old Country School*, 166–67.

88. Clifford, *Lone Voyagers*, 37.

89. Louise W. Mears, "Miss Eliza Morgan—A Short Biography," *Ne-braska History* 17 (April–June 1936): 133–35; and Delta Kappa Gamma file, "Miss Eliza C. Morgan."

90. Delta Kappa Gamma file, "She Loved Her Work [Susan Frazier]," undated; Huftalen, "Personal Scrapbook No. 1, I Remember this and that," page 1, chronology of Huftalen's education and career, Huftalen Collection. See also, Chapter 7, this volume, on Huftalen.

91. Huftalen, "Upper Iowa University, Fayette, Iowa," in "Personal No. 2, Sarah L. Gillespie Huftalen, Manchester, Iowa, I Remember This & That," 94, Huftalen Collection.

92. Huftalen, "Normal Training Department, Muscatine High School, Muscatine, Iowa," in "Personal No. 2," 102–3, Huftalen Collection.

93. Herbst, "Teacher Preparation in the Nineteenth Century," in Warren, *American Teachers,* 224.

94. *Sixth Annual Report of the Department of Public Instruction of the State of Kansas, 1866* (Leavenworth:1867), 43.

95. *Tenth Annual Report of the Department of Public Instruction of the State of Kansas, 1879* (Topeka: 1870), 184.

96. *Fourteenth Annual Report of the Department of Public Instruction, of the State of Kansas, 1874* (Topeka: 1874), 172.

97. *First Biennial Report Kansas, 1877 and 1878,* 327.

98. *Third Annual Report of the State Superintendent of Public Instruction of the State of Nebraska for the Year Ending December 31, 1871* (Lincoln: 1871), 45.

99. *Fourth Annual Report, Nebraska, 1872,* 101.

100. R. McLaran Sawyer, "No Teacher for the School: The Nebraska Junior Normal School Movement," *Nebraska History* 52:2 (Summer 1971): 191.

101. *Seventeenth Biennial Report of the Superintendent of Public Instruction, of the State of Iowa, 1875–1877* (Des Moines: 1878), 104–5.

102. Wright, *Fifty Years at the Teachers College,* 22.

103. Ibid., 28.

104. William C. Lang, *A Century of Leadership and Service: A Centennial History of the University of Northern Iowa,* vol. 1, *1876–1928* (Cedar Falls, Iowa: University of Northern Iowa, UNI Alumni Association, UNI Foundation, 1990), 177.

105. William C. Lang, "Higher Education at Cedar Falls: Town and Gown in the First Hundred Years," *Palimpsest* 64 (May–June 1983): 71.

106. Lang, *A Century of Leadership and Service,* see chapters 1–4.

107. *Twenty-seventh Biennial Report of the Superintendent of Public Instruction, of the State of Iowa, 1895* (Des Moines: 1895), 14.

108. *Twenty-eighth Biennial Report of the Superintendent of Public Instruction, of the State of Iowa, 1897* (Des Moines: 1897), 38.

109. Sawyer, "No Teacher for the School," 191.

110. *Sixth Annual Report of the Department of Public Instruction of the State of Kansas, 1866* (Leavenworth: 1867), 22.

111. *Eleventh Annual Report of the Department of Public Instruction of the State of Kansas, 1871* (Topeka: 1871), 53.

112. Lawrence B. de Graff, "Race, Sex, and Region: Black Women in the American West, 1850–1920," *Pacific Historical Review* 49:2 (May 1980): 295–96.

113. Clifford W. Griffin, *The University of Kansas: A History* (Lawrence: The University Press of Kansas, 1974), 209–10.

114. *Seventh Annual Report of the Department of Public Instruction, of the State of Kansas, 1871* (Leavenworth: 1867), 97.

115. *Twelfth Annual Report of the Department of Public Instruction, of the State of Kansas, 1872* (Topeka: 1872), 223.

116. *Thirteenth Annual Report, Kansas, 1873*, 241.

117. John D. Reynolds, Assistant State Archeologist, Kansas State Historical Society, telephone interview with Mary H. Cordier, 22 February 1991.

118. *Fifteenth Biennial Report of the State Superintendent for the School Years Ending July 31, 1905 and 1906, Kansas* (Topeka: 1906), 74.

119. *Twelfth Biennial Report of the State Superintendent for the School Years Ending July 31, 1899 and 1900, Kansas* (Topeka: 1900), 79.

120. As of February 1991, the fate of the Quindaro site is still in limbo. Quindaro is a rich archeological site with hundreds of artifacts. John D. Reynolds, interview with Cordier, 22 February 1991.

121. Richard L. Guenther, "The Santee Normal Training School" *Nebraska History* 5:3 (Fall 1970): 360, 365.

122. Ibid., 375.

123. Ibid., 367.

124. *Thirteenth Biennial Report of the State Superintendent for the School Years Ending July 31, 1901 and 1902, Kansas* (Topeka: 1902), 140.

125. Margaret Connell Szasz, *Education and the American Indian: The Road to Self-Determination Since 1928*, 2d ed. (Albuquerque: University of New Mexico Press, 1977), 9–12.

126. Thomas Thompson, ed., *The Schooling of Native America* (Washington, D.C.: American Association of Colleges for Teacher Education, in collaboration with the Teacher Corps, U.S. Office of Education, 1978), 142, 171.

127. National Education Association, *Report of the Committee of Twelve on Rural Schools, July 9, 1895* (Chicago: University of Chicago Press, 1897), 84.

128. Ibid., 79–86.

129. W. T. Harris, quoted in Colgrove, *The Teacher and the School*, 32–33.

Chapter 3 The Social and Physical Landscape of the Schoolwomen's Living Conditions

1. Bessie Tucker Gilmer, "Journey Through Life," Diaries 1918–1979, with notes and additions through December 1984, February 20, 1918, NSHS.

2. Wayne E. Fuller, *The Old Country School: The Story of Rural Education in the Middle West*, (Chicago: University of Chicago Press, 1982), 44–45.

3. Ibid., 120, 215–17.

4. Carl F. Kaestle cites research about teachers: Martha E. Coons, "The Feminization of the Wisconsin Teaching Force, 1850–1880" (seminar paper, University of Wisconsin, 1976), and Ann Weingarten, "Women Common School Teachers in Michigan, 1836–1860" (senior honors thesis, University of Michigan, 1976), which indicate that the majority of the teachers, 82 percent and 67 percent respectively, were single and living at home

with their parents; 7 percent and 1 percent were married; and 11 percent and 32 percent were boarding or living independently. The Michigan study cites an earlier generation of teachers than the Wisconsin study, or than would be found in Iowa, Nebraska, and Kansas. Carl F. Kaestle, *Pillars of the Republic: Common Schools and American Society, 1780–1860* (New York: Hill and Wang, 1983), 126, 241.

5. Mabel Carney, *Country Life and the Country School* (Chicago: Row, Peterson and Co., 1912), 136–37.

6. Agnes Briggs Olmstead, "Recollections of Pioneer Teacher of Hamilton County," *Annals of Iowa* 18 (October 1946): 104.

7. Rosa Schreurs Jennings, "The Country Teacher," *Annals of Iowa* 31 (July 1951): 41.

8. Mollie Dorsey Sanford, *Mollie—The Journal of Mollie Dorsey Sanford in Nebraska and Colorado Territories, 1857–1866* (Lincoln: University of Nebraska Press, 1959), 87.

9. Ibid., 97.

10. Ibid., 93.

11. Phoebe Athey Nater, "Telling Tales," in Ainsworth Area Retired Teachers, *The Sway of the School Bell: Schools and Histories of Brown, Keya Paha, and Rock Counties, Nebraska* (Ainsworth, Nebr.: Ainsworth Area Retired Teachers: 1976), 9.

12. Ibid., 9–10.

13. Jennings, "The Country Teacher," 55.

14. Ibid., 57.

15. Rosalie Trail Fuller, ed., "A Nebraska High School Teacher in the 1890s: The Letters of Sadie B. Smith," *Nebraska History* 58:4 (Fall 1977): 457.

16. Jennings, "The Country Teacher," 52.

17. Gilmer, "Journey Through Life," February 20, 1918.

18. Ibid., 18.

19. Ibid.

20. Armitage sees the role of civilizer as a stereotype because of the implied passivity of women. They were actively involved in developing the communities, but did not see themselves as heroic. Susan Armitage, "Through Women's Eyes: A New View of the West," in Susan Armitage and Elizabeth Jameson, eds., *The Women's West* (Norman, Oklahoma: University of Oklahoma Press, 1987), 13–15.

21. Gilmer, "Journey Through Life," April 18, 1918.

22. Kenneth Wiggins Porter, editor, "Building a Kansas 'Soddy'—1885," *Kansas Magazine* 7 (1942): 18.

23. Delta Kappa Gamma file, Genevieve Giddings Richmond, Reminiscence, NSHS.

24. Kenneth Wiggins Porter, editor, "Catharine Emma Wiggins, Pupil

and Teacher in Northwest Kansas, 1888–1895," *Kansas History* 1:1 (Spring 1978): 37.

25. Sarah Jane Price, Diaries, 1878–1895, and miscellaneous papers, NSHS.

26. Beryl Decker, "The Wind in Nebraska," in Ainsworth Area Retired Teachers, *The Sway of the School Bell*, 8.

27. Clara L. Conron, Diary, October 3, 1884–July 1, 1885, KSHS.

28. Ibid., February 9–12, 1885.

29. Olmstead, "Recollections of a Country Teacher," 94–95.

30. Ibid.

31. Ibid., 96.

32. Ibid.

33. *Eleventh Annual Report of the Department of Public Instruction, of the State of Kansas, 1871* (Topeka: 1871), 100–101.

34. Martha Bayne, "Reminiscences of Mrs. Martha Bayne, a Teacher in the Country Schools of Russel, Lincoln and Osborn Counties in the '80s," 1–2, KSHS.

35. Gilmer, "Journey Through Life," December 10, 1918.

36. Jane Jackson, retired teacher, interview by Betty Rowan, Chanute, Kansas, 3 April 1983,

37. Gilmer, "Journey Through Life," 38.

38. Mollie belonged to Genevieve Giddings Richmond, Delta Kappa Gamma file; Fanny took Clara Conron to school, Conron, Diary; Old Bill was remembered by Ethel Hale Russel, interview with author, Kalamazoo, Michigan, 10 June 1982, oral history tape recording, NSHS and RHC-WMU; Sir Walter Raleigh, was owned by Susan Frazier, Delta Kappa Gamma file; Lady Jane Grey was Catharine Wiggins's horse described in Kenneth Wiggins Porter, ed., "Country Schoolteacher, 1898–1902, Rice County, Kansas," *Kansas Magazine* (1961), 44.

39. Jackson, interview.

40. Alta Hull, interview by Betty Rowan, Fredonia, Kansas, 2 April 1983.

41. Bayne, "Reminiscences," 2.

42. Lila Gravatt Scrimsher, ed., "The Diary of Anna Webber: Early Day Teacher of Mitchell County," *Kansas Historical Quarterly* 38 (October 1972): 323–25.

43. Bessie Tucker Gilmer, retired teacher, interviews with author, Lincoln, Nebraska, 12 and 13 July 1983, oral history tape recording, NSHS.

44. Ibid.

45. Ibid.

46. Ibid.

47. Ibid.

48. See Chapter 6, this volume, on Sarah Jane Price.

49. Delta Kappa Gamma, Alpha Chapter, "Pioneer Women in Education," article by Elsie Sindt, "Margaret S. Barger, Taught in Davenport Schools 1884 to 1935," Typescript in author's possession.

50. *Grand Island Times* quoted in [*School Work and*] *Literary Notes* 10:15 (September 15, 1883): 174.

51. *Sixth Annual Report of the Superintendent of Public Instruction, of the State of Kansas, December 16, 1866* (Leavenworth: 1867), 14.

52. Frania A. Albert to Nancy Higgins, November 6, 1881, Douglas Grove, Nebraska, private collection of E. McKinney.

53. Elsie Petsel Hallock, "Sweet Sixteen," in Ainsworth Area Retired Teachers, *Sway of the School Bell*, 63.

54. Jennings, "The Country Teacher," 55.

55. Nellie Kenmir to Mamie Goodwater, July 11, 1904, Dunseith, North Dakota, in Elizabeth Hampsten, comp., *To All Inquiring Friends: Letters, Diaries and Essays in North Dakota* (Fargo: Department of English, University of North Dakota, 1979), 50, 54.

56. Sarah Gillespie Huftalen, Diaries, 1877–1889 and 1914–1917, Huftalen Collection. See also, Chapter 6, this volume, on Huftalen.

57. Bessie Tucker's Catholic boyfriend was the subject of many entries during May, June, and July 1918. Lee Gilmer appeared in the entries in November 1918 and throughout the rest of the Diaries. See also, Chapter 8, this volume, on Bessie Tucker Gilmer.

58. Scrimsher, ed., "The Diary of Anna Webber," 323–25.

59. Gilmer, "Journey Through Life," February 22, 1918.

60. Ellen Payne Paullin, ed., "Etta's Journal: January 2, 1874 to July 25, 1875," *Kansas History—A Journal of the Central Plains* 3:4 (Winter 1980): 258.

61. Paullin, ed., "Etta's Journal," *Kansas History—A Journal of the Central Plains* 3:3 (Autumn 1980): 201–19; and 3:4 (Winter 1980): 255–78.

62. Ibid., 3:4 (Winter 1980): 258.

63. Lewis Atherton, *Main Street on the Middle Border* (Bloomington: Indiana University Press, 1984), 186.

64. Mary Ward Smith "Autobiographical Reminiscences, 1856–1860," 5–6, KSHS.

65. Sandra L. Myres, *Westering Women and the Frontier Experience, 1800–1915* (Albuquerque: University of New Mexico Press, 1982), 205.

66. Ibid., 203.

67. Ibid., 204–5.

68. Carney, *Country Life and the Country School*, 51–52.

69. Carl Degler, *At Odds: Women and the Family in America from the Revolution to the Present* (Oxford: Oxford University Press, 1980), 306.

70. Elliott West, *Growing Up with the Country: Childhood in the Far Western Frontier* (Albuquerque: University of New Mexico Press, 1989), 171.

71. Degler, *At Odds*, 301.

72. Price, Diaries, 1878–1895.

73. Huftalen, Arbor Vitae Summit School Record Book, 1904–1909, box 10, vol. 3, unpaged. Huftalen Collection.

74. Ethel Hale Russel, interview by author, Kalamazoo, Michigan, 23 August 1985.

75. *Biennial Report of the Superintendent of Public Instruction, November 1, 1889* (Des Moines, 1889), 119.

76. *Biennial Report of the Superintendent of Public Instruction, November 1, 1891* (Des Moines, 1891), 155.

77. Degler, *At Odds*, 302.

78. Michael P. Malone and Richard W. Etulain, *The West: A Twentieth-Century History* (Lincoln: University of Nebraska Press, 1989), 61.

79. Ibid., 61–63.

80. Ruth Gaddis Wilson, *"There is no place like Nebraska,"* (by the author, 1984), unpaged.

81. Price, Diaries, November 21, 1878, January 29, 1879. The Good Templars are mentioned on varying dates, once a month into 1880.

82. Huftalen, "Personal Scrapbook No. 1, I Remember This & That," 1. Huftalen Collection.

83. Judy Nolte Lensink, Christine M. Kirkham, and Karen Pauba Witze, " 'My Only Confidant': The Life and Diary of Emily Hawley Gillespie," *Annals of Iowa* 45:4 (Spring 1980): 304.

84. Huftalen, "Arbor Vitae Summit School," a notebook of school events, 7, Huftalen Collection.

85. Ibid., 6.

86. Myres, *Westering Women*, 234–35.

87. Seven western states were among the ten states that had passed both suffrage and prohibition prior to passage of the Eighteenth Amendment in 1919: Utah, Montana, Kansas, Oklahoma, Nebraska, South Dakota, North Dakota. Reference Department, Kalamazoo (Michigan) Public Library.

88. Myres, *Westering Women*, 235.

89. Ibid., 237.

90. Ibid.

91. Ibid.

92. Ibid., 207.

93. John M. Blum, et al., *The National Experience: A History of the United States*, 6th ed. (San Diego and New York: Harcourt Brace Jovanovich, Publishers, 1985), 485.

94. Ibid.

95. Ibid.

96. Louise R. Noun, *Strong-Minded Women: The Emergence of the*

Woman-Suffrage Movement in Iowa (Ames, Iowa: The Iowa State University Press, 1969), 174–75.

97. Ibid.

98. Glenda Riley, *Frontierswomen: The Iowa Experience* (Ames: The Iowa State University Press, 1981), 154–55.

99. Myres, *Westering Women,* 219.

100. Leo E. Oliva, "Kansas: A Hard Land in the Heartland," in James H. Madison, ed., *Heartland: Comparative Histories of the Midwestern States,* (Bloomington, Indiana: Indiana University Press, 1988), 260.

101. Joanna L. Stratton, *Pioneer Woman: Voices from the Kansas Frontier* (New York: Simon and Schuster, 1981), 265–67.

102. Huftalen, Diary, October 13, 1915. box 7, vol. 5, Huftalen Collection.

103. Dorothy Ashby Pownall, "Agnes Samuelson—A Dedicated Educator," *Palimpsest* 43:11 (November 1962): 518.

104. Ainsworth Area Retired Teachers, *The Sway of the School Bell,* 84–85.

105. Jean Christie, "'An earnest enthusiasm for education': Sarah Christie Stevens, Schoolwoman," *Minnesota History* 48:6 (Summer 1983): 249.

106. Ibid., 250.

107. Ibid., 253.

108. Ibid., 254.

109. West, *Growing Up with the Country,* 260.

110. Atherton, *Main Street on the Middle Border,* 185–86.

111. These topics are drawn from Sarah Jane Price's diaries as examples of literary society topics. Price, January 1, 1880; February 10, 1880; August 27, 1880; September 1, 1880; October 7, 1880.

112. Porter, "Country Schoolteacher," 24.

113. Mary Ward Smith, "Reminiscences," 6–7.

114. Porter, "Country Schoolteacher," 18–19.

115. Ibid., 34.

116. Gilmer, "Journey Through Life," May 18, 1918.

117. Ora J. Patton, Letters to Delbert Mann, October 7, 1917, Mann Family Collection, RHC-WMU.

118. State motto of Kansas, "To the Stars Through the Wilderness," Ad Astra per Aspera.

Chapter 4 Teaching and Learning in the Schools of the Prairies and Plains

1. Mabel Carney, *Country Life and the Country School* (Chicago: Row, Peterson and Company, 1912), 139, 142.

2. Ibid., 139, 142–43.

3. Ibid.

4. Information from National Archives and Records Service Catalogs:

"Federal Population Censuses, 1790–1890"; "1900 Federal Population Census;" "The 1910 Population Census"; and from specific information sought by United States Census Schedules for 1870, 1900, 1910.

5. *Report of the Commissioner of Education for 1902*, vol. 2, (Washington, D.C.: 1903), 2:2314–15.

6. The time period and regional focus of this research find substantive change in schooling, while Larry Cuban contends that teaching methods have not changed substantially from 1890 to 1980. Larry Cuban, *How Teachers Taught: Constancy and Change in American Classrooms, 1890–1980* (New York: Longman, 1984).

7. For an assessment and application of recent research in the areas of interpersonal relations in the classroom, see Vernon F. Jones and Louise S. Jones, *Comprehensive Classroom Management: Motivating and Managing Students*, 3d ed. (Boston: Allyn and Bacon, 1990), part 2, "Creating Positive Interpersonal Relationships in the Classroom," 61–130.

8. *Ninth Annual Report of the Department of Public Instruction, of the State of Kansas, 1869* (Topeka: 1870), 141.

9. Minutes of LeRoy Township, Benton County, Iowa, ISHD-HS.

10. Anna Johnson, "Recollections of a Country School Teacher," *Annals of Iowa* 42 (Winter 1975): 493–94.

11. Sarah Gillespie Huftalen, Diary, December 20, 1883. Huftalen Collection, ISHD-HS.

12. Bessie Tucker Gilmer, "Journey Through Life," Diaries, December 9, 1919, and December 26, 1919 (written December 31, 1919), NSHS.

13. *Twenty-fourth Biennial Report of the Superintendent of Public Instruction of the State of Iowa, November 1, 1889* (Des Moines: 1889), 109.

14. Kenneth Wiggins Porter, editor, "A Little Girl on an Iowa Forty, 1873–1880—Catharine Wiggins Porter," *Iowa Journal of History and Politics* 51:2 (April 1953): 149.

15. Mabel Townsley to Helen Myers, February 17, 1900, in Andrew Gulliford, Project Director, *Country School Legacy: Humanities on the Frontier* (Silt, Colorado: Country School Legacy, 1981), 26–27.

16. "Superintendent's Visits, Cheyenne County," *Ranch Teacher* 1:2 (May 1908): 30 NSHS.

17. Huftalen, "Arbor Vitae Summit School," a notebook of school events, unpaged section in notebook, Huftalen Collecion.

18. W. H. Hotze [non-teacher], "Pioneer School Days in Southwest Nebraska: A Reminiscence," *Nebraska History* 33 (March 1952): 45.

19. Jane Jackson, interview by Betty Rowan, Fredonia, Kansas, 3 April 1983.

20. Ibid.

21. *Fifth Annual Report of the State Superintendent of Public Instruction*

of the State of Nebraska for the Year Ending December 31, 1873 (Lincoln: 1873), 90.

22. Ibid., 90–91.

23. "News Notes," *The Ranch Teacher* [Box Butte and Cheyenne Counties, Nebraska] 1:2 (May 1908): 31.

24. Rosa Schreurs Jennings, "The Country Teacher," *Annals of Iowa* 31 (July 1951): 45.

25. Henry Sabin, *Common Sense Didatics: for Common School Teachers* (Chicago: Rand, McNally, 1903) 216. Henry Sabin was Iowa State Superintendent of Public Instruction, 1888–1892 and 1894–1898, chairman NEA Committee of Twelve on Rural Schools, 1895, and an experienced institute leader and superintendent.

26. Andrew Gulliford, *America's Country Schools* (Washington, D. C.: The Preservation Press, 1984), 113. See also, Mark M. Kindley, "Little schools on the prairie still teach a big lesson, *Smithsonian* 16:7 (October 1985): 118–28. For an in-depth discussion of school consolidation, see chapter 11, "Consolidation," in Wayne E. Fuller, *The Old Country School: The Story of Rural Education in the Middle West* (Chicago: University of Chicago Press, 1982).

27. *Sixth Annual Report of the State Superintendent of Public Instruction for the Year Ending December 31, 1875* (Lincoln: 1874), 173.

28. Martha Bayne, "Reminiscences of Mrs. Martha Bayne, a Teacher in the Country Schools of Russell, Lincoln and Osborn Counties in the '80s," 1, KSHS.

29. The names and dates written in *Cornell's Intermediate Geography*, a textbook published in 1855, span the time from 1864 to 1914. Whether all the children from the Brenner family of DeGraff, Ohio, who signed their names used the book at school isn't known. Book in author's possession.

30. J. Galen Saylor, *Who Planned the Curriculum? A Curriculum Plans Reservoir Model with Historical Examples* (West Lafayette, Indiana: Kappa Delta Pi, 1982), 171.

31. Gulliford, *Country School Legacy*, 34.

32. Anna Johnson, "Recollections," 500.

33. Bessie Tucker Gilmer, interviews with author, Lincoln, Nebraska, 12 and 13 July 1983, oral history tape recording, NSHS.

34. Huftalen, Diary, February 1, 1884, Huftalen Collection.

35. Edward A. Sheldon, "Object Teaching," *American Journal of Education* 14 (March 1864): 93.

36. Carl F. Kaestle explores how diverse published reading material, newspapers, magazines, and books presented "a common culture to a diverse people." Carl F. Kaestle, "Literacy and Diversity: Themes from a Social History of the American Reading Public," *History of Education Quarterly*, 28:4 (Winter 1988): 523–49.

37. Anna Marie Murphy and Cullen Murphy, "Onward, upward with McGuffey and those Readers," *Smithsonian* 15:8 (November 1984): 184.

38. John H. Westerhoff, *McGuffey and His Readers: Piety, Morality, and Education in Nineteenth Century America* (Nashville: Abington Press, 1978), 23.

39. Ibid., 23–24.

40. *Sixth Annual Report, Nebraska, 1875,* 20–23.

41. *Nineteenth Biennial Report, Iowa 1877–79,* 41–56.

42. Barnard is quoted in Report of the Committee on the Primary Schools, Oswego, New York, "XI. Primary Instruction by Object Lessons," *American Journal of Education* 12 (December 1862): 605.

43. "An Examination—Subject: Methods of Instruction. All the Class represented," in *Davenport Schools, 1884, Training Department,* unpaged; one of a collection of handwritten, bound volumes of school papers from first grade through high school and the Teacher Training Department. Davenport School Museum, J. B. Young Junior High School, Davenport, Iowa.

44. *Nineteenth Biennial Report, Iowa, 1877–79,* 47.

45. *Fifteenth Annual Report of the Superintendent of Public Instruction of the State of Kansas, 1875* (Topeka: 1876), 8, 101–15.

46. John Ise, *Sod and Stubble: The Story of a Kansas Homestead* (Lincoln: University of Nebraska Press, 1936), 239.

47. Loulie Ayer Beall, "Early School Experiences in Nebraska, A Webster County School," *Nebraska History* 23 (July–September 1942): 200–201.

48. Huftalen, Diary, December 28, 1883. Huftalen Collection.

49. Huftalen cites the on-going campaign to keep the boys' toilets clean during 1905–1906, in "Arbor Vitae Summit, Taught by Sarah Gillespie-Huftalen, 1904–1909, Oneida, Iowa, Delaware County," Huftalen Collection.

50. President Homer H. Seerley, Iowa State Normal School, quoted in Keach Johnson, "Elementary and Secondary Education in Iowa, 1890–1900: A Time of Awakening," part 2, *Annals of Iowa* 45:3 (Winter 1980): 194.

51. Wayne E. Fuller, "The Teacher in the Country School," in Donald Warren, ed., *American Teachers: Histories of a Profession at Work* (New York: Macmillan Publishing Company, 1989), 107.

52. Huftalen, Diary, February 20, 1885, 105, Huftalen Collection.

53. Ibid.

54. Ibid., 106–7. Among the thirty-six recitations in this program were the "Lord's Prayer," "Mary's Lamb," "Kittie and Mousie," "Little Star," "Little Boy's Pocket," "My Home, My Mother," "The old & new," "Sculptor boy," "American Forest Girl," "Tableaux in 4 Scenes—The Rose Bush," accompanied by "*splendid* music produced by Mr. Ferdinand Shoultz on his

elegant accordian," the "Old Schoolhouse," "Nobody's Child," and concluded with "Parting Piece," presented by Sarah Gillespie.

55. Ibid., 108.

56. Amelia Phoneta Bruner, composition welcoming parents and friends
to the school program, December 18, 1872, Bruner Family Collection, NSHS.

57. Sarah Jane Price, Diaries, 1878–1895, and miscellaneous papers,
NSHS.

58. Gilmer, "Journey through Life," September 18–20, 1918

59. Kenneth Wiggins Porter, ed., "School Days in Coin, Iowa,
1880–1885—Catharine Wiggins Porter," *Iowa Journal of History and Politics*
51:4 (October 1953): 306.

60. Frank S. Townsley, Journal, May 23 and 24, 1883, 15HD-HS.

61. Kenneth Wiggins Porter, "Catharine Emma Wiggins, Pupil and
Teacher in Northwest Kansas, 1888–1895," *Kansas History* 1:1 (Spring
1978): 30.

62. Porter, "School Days in Coin, Iowa, 1880–1885," 307.

63. E. Mary Lacy Crowder, "Pioneer Life in Palo Alto County," *Iowa
Journal of History and Politics* 46 (April 1948): 186.

64. Roscoe Conaway, Reminiscence, KSHS.

65. Fuller, 106.

66. C. C. Nestlerode, "Theory and Practice of Teaching, No. 6, Opening School," *The Iowa Instructor, An Educational Journal,* 1 (April 1860):
207–10. Applications of current effective schooling research may be found
in Carolyn Evertson, et al., *Classroom Management for Elementary Teachers*
(Englewood Cliffs, N.J., 1989).

67. M. Ingalls, "Prizes in Schools," and, by a teacher, "A School Incident," *The Iowa Instructor: an Education Journal* 1 (September 1860):
353–58, 366–68.

68. [*School Work*] *and Literary Notes* 10:15 (September 15, 1883), NSHS.

69. *The Ranch Teacher,* [Box Butte and Cheyenne Counties, published in
Hemingford, Nebraska] 1:2 (May 1908): 31, 14 NSHS.

70. *The Nemaha County Teacher* 2:7 (March 1906): 113, 122, NSHS.

71. Ibid., 112–13.

72. Henry Sabin, *Common Sense Didactics for the Common School
Teacher,* 296–98.

73. Agnes Samuelson quoted in Dorothy Ashby Pownall, "Living in the
Present," *Palimpsest* 43:11 (November 1962): 544. Agnes Samuelson is the
subject of this issue of *Palimpsest,* 497–546.

74. Kenneth Wiggins Porter, ed., "Country Schoolteacher, 1898–1902,
Rice County, Kansas," *Kansas Magazine* (1961): 44.

75. Mary O. Jones, "My Ideal Rural (Country) School," paper presented
at the Rural Section, Iowa State Teachers Association, 1910, 2, Huftalen

Collection. Huftalen used the terms *school-home* and *school family* in her scrapbook, "Personal—No. 2, Sarah L. Gillespie Huftalen, Manchester, Iowa, I Remember this and that," 86, 91–93, Huftalen Collection.

76. Esther Scott or Lillie M. Reeder, "Primary Reading," Esther Ruth Scott Collection, NSHS.

77. Emma Pospisil [non-teacher], "A Teacher of The Willow Creek School," *Nebraska History* 24 (January–March 1943): 18–19, 23.

78. Bessie Tucker Gilmer, "Journey through Life," September 18–20, 1918.

79. Ibid.

80. Huftalen, "Close Supervision of Schools in Bennington Township, Blackhawk County, Iowa," in "Personal—No. 2, I Remember This & That," 91–92, Huftalen Collection.

81. Evelyn Bolte Hurlbut, [non-teacher] oral family reminiscence, related to Mary Hurlbut Cordier, Muscatine, Iowa.

82. Townsley, Journal 1885, 109.

83. Townsley, Journal 1880–81, 80–85.

84. Huftalen, "Personal No. 2, I Remember This & That, " 64–65, Huftalen Collection.

85. Mabel Carney cites the "three incurable defects" as the multiple recitations, classes of one or two students, and the lack of high schools; other needs of the country schools were better supervision, trained teachers, and sufficient revenue. Carney, *Country Life and the Country School*, 143, 139, and chapter 10, "The Country's Teacher's Problem and Its Attack."

86. Bayne, "Reminiscences," 2.

Part II. Seeing the Context, Hearing the Voice: Introduction to Five Lives

1. Throughout Part II, "Seeing the Context, Hearing the Voice," the following sources have been indispensable in shaping the selection and interpretation of the schoolwomen's personal writings: Mary Catherine Bateson, *Composing a Life* (New York: Atlantic Monthly Press, 1989), chapter 1, "Emergent Visions"; the writings of Elizabeth Hampsten, in particular, *Read This Only to Yourself: The Private Writings of Midwestern Women, 1880–1910* (Bloomington: Indiana University Press, 1982); Carolyn G. Heilbrun, *Writing a Woman's Life* (New York: W. W. Norton, 1988); Nancy Hoffman, *Women's "True" Profession: Voice from the History of Teaching* (Old Westbury, New York: The Feminist Press; New York: McGraw-Hill, 1981); Personal Narratives Group, eds., *Interpreting Women's Lives: Feminist Theory and Personal Narratives* (Bloomington: Indiana University Press, 1989); and Lillian Schlissel, Vicki L. Ruiz, and Janice Monk, eds., *Western Women: Their Land, Their Lives* (Albuquerque, University of New Mexico Press, 1988).

2. Sherrill F. Daniels, "An Index to and Bibliography of Reminiscences

in the Nebraska State Historical Society Library" (Ph.D. diss., University of Nebraska, 1986), xxxvi.

3. Examples of beginning teachers' diaries are: Susan Ophelia Carter, Diary, 1887, NSHS; Clara S. Conron, Diary, October 3, 1884–July 1, 1885, KSHS; Bessie Tucker Gilmer, "Journey Through Life," Diaries 1918–1920, NSHS; Sarah Gillespie Huftalen, Diaries, 1883–1885, Huftalen Collection, ISHD-HS.

4. For examples of reminiscences, see: Ainsworth Area Retired Teachers, *The Sway of the School Bell, Schools and Histories of Brown, Keya Paha, and Rock Counties, Nebraska* (Ainsworth, Nebraska: Ainsworth Area Retired Teachers, 1976); Enid Bern, "Memoirs of a Prairie Schoolteacher," *North Dakota History* 42 (Summer 1975): 5–16; E. Mary Lacy Crowder, "Pioneer Life in Palo Alto County," *Iowa Journal of History and Politics* 46 (April 1948): 156–98; Iowa Retired Teachers Association, *Readin' 'Ritin' 'Rithmetic, and 'Reminiscin'* (Newton, Iowa: Iowa Retired Teachers Association, 1976); James Smallwood, ed., *And Gladly Teach: Reminiscences of Teachers from Frontier Dugout to Modern Module* (Norman: University of Oklahoma Press, 1976); Mary Ward Smith, "Autobiographical Reminiscences, 1856–1860," KSHS.

5. Daniels, "Index to and Bibliography of Reminiscences," xxv–xxvi.

6. For examples, see: Louise W. Mears, "Miss Eliza Morgan—A Short Biography," *Nebraska History* 17 (April–June 1936): 132–35; Cornelia Mallett Barnhart, "Phoebe Sudlow," *Palimpsest* 38:4 (April 1957): 169–76; Delta Kappa Gamma, typescript articles on Susan Frazier, Eliza Morgan, and Genevieve Giddings, Richmond, Nebraska educational leaders, NSHS; Dorothy Ashby Pownall, "Agnes Samuelson—a Dedicated Educator," *Palimpsest* 43:11 (November 1962): 497–544.

7. Courtney Ann Vaughn-Roberson, "Having a Purpose in Life: Western Women Teachers in the Twentieth Century," *Great Plains Quarterly* 5 (Spring 1982): 107–24.

Chapter 5 "A Sense of Unity": Nancy Rebecca Higgins Gaddis, Missouri, 1862–1875; Nebraska, 1875–1942

1. Unless specifically cited, the events of the life of Nancy Higgins Gaddis are documented by the family history, written by Nancy's youngest daughter, Ruth Gaddis Wilson, *"There is no place like Nebraska"* (by the author, 1984), unpaged. Additional information was obtained through interviews with Nancy's granddaughter, Eleanor McKinney.

2. All documents cited are the private collection of Eleanor R. McKinney, Kalamazoo, Michigan. Many of these documents were deposited at the Nebraska State Historical Society in 1988 by Eleanor R. McKinney.

3. All photographs concerning Nancy Higgins Gaddis are the private collection of Eleanor R. McKinney, Kalamazoo, Michigan; however, some

of the photographs were deposited at the Nebraska State Historical Society in 1988 by Eleanor R. McKinney.

4. For similar accounts of settler families, see Lillian Schlissel, "Family on the Western Frontier," in Lillian Schlissel, Vicki Ruiz, and Janice Monk, eds., *Western Women: Their Land, Their Lives* (Albuquerque: University of New Mexico, 1988), with commentaries, 77–112; Elliott West, *Growing Up with the Country: Childhood on the Far Western Frontier* (Albuquerque: University of New Mexico, 1989); and Hampsten, *Settlers' Children.*

5. Elsie Gaddis McKinney, *Make Mine Blue, a story of one family's home-steading in Nebraska* (Kalamazoo, Mich.: privately printed by Eleanor R. McKinney, 1987), ii.

6. Lawrence O. Christensen, "Missouri: The Heart of the Nation," in James H. Madison, *Heartland: Comparative Histories of the Midwestern States* (Bloomington: Indiana University Press, 1988), 99.

7. Solomon D. Butcher, *Pioneer History of Custer County, Nebraska with which is combined Sod Houses of the Great American Plains*, 2d ed. (Denver: Sage Books, 1965, reprint of original, ca. 1900), 232.

8. Ibid.

9. H. M. Sullivan, "Cattle Industry in Ranch Days," in Butcher, *Pioneer History of Custer Country*, 17.

10. Wilson, *Nebraska;* and "History of Religious Movement in Comstock Community," undated, typescript, McKinney Collection.

11. Porter Lemuel Gaddis (Nancy Gaddis's son) letter to his daughters, February 1, 1962, marking the 100th anniversary (January 31, 1862), of Nancy Gaddis's birth.

12. Wilson, *Nebraska.*

13. Birney H. Gaddis letter to Elsie Gaddis McKinney, undated.

14. William Porter Higgins, University Place, Nebraska, letter to Honorable S. C. Bassett, Gibbon, Nebraska, January 29, 1918.

15. Richard Crabb, *Empire on the Platte*, Cleveland and New York: World, 1967), 219–35.

16. William Porter Higgins to Bassett, January 29, 1918.

17. Hatch's photographs cited in Crabb, *Empire on the Platte*, 298. The Solomon D. Butcher Photograph Collection, Nebraska State Historical Society; and Butcher, *Pioneer History of Custer County.* Butcher's history contains numerous accounts of the range wars between cattlemen and farmers. The Solomon Butcher photographs in *Pioneer History of Custer County* and in the Butcher Collection, NSHS, include portrayals of the lynching of Mitchell and Ketchum.

18. Ibid.

19. Wilson, *Nebraska.*

20. Elliott West, *Growing Up with the Country*, chapter 4, "Child's Work," 73–100.

21. Porter Gaddis to his daughters, February 1, 1962.

22. Ibid.

23. "Wescott School Has Anniversary program Friday," undated newspaper clipping, ca. 1934.

24. Wilson, *Nebraska.*

25. T. C. Robert, letter to Nancy Higgins, March 26, 1876.

26. Carrie Callen, letter to Nancy Higgins, October 18, 1879.

27. "Wescott School has Anniversary Program Friday."

28. Frania Albert, letter to Nancy Higgins, September 28, 1881.

29. Frania Albert, letter to Nancy Higgins, November 6, 1881.

30. Metta Dungan, letter to Nancy Higgins, March 28, 1882.

31. Metta Dungan, letter to Nancy Higgins, May 6, 1882.

32. McKinney Collection.

33. Nancy Higgins Gaddis, Attendance Book.

34. Wilson, *Nebraska.*

35. Information about the Timber Culture Act from John M. Blum, et al., *The National Experience: A History of the United States,* 6th ed. (San Diego and New York: Harcourt Brace Jovanovich, Publishers, 1985), 445. The dimensions of the sod house and planting ten acres in trees from Porter Gaddis, letter to his daughters, February 1, 1962.

36. Nancy Higgins Gaddis, Attendance Book.

37. Wilson, *Nebraska.*

38. Sullivan, "Cattle Industry in Ranch Days," in Butcher, *Pioneer History of Custer County,* 27.

39. Wilson, *Nebraska.*

40. Porter L. Gaddis to daughters.

41. Ibid.

42. Carl F. Kaestle, "Literacy and Diversity: Themes from a Social History of the American Reading Public," *History of Education Quarterly* 28:4 (Winter 1988): 528.

43. Eleanor McKinney interview with author, Kalamazoo, Michigan, 1986.

44. Wilson, *Nebraska.*

45. "Wescott School Has Anniversary Program Friday."

Chapter 6 "Greater Usefulness in My Calling": Sarah Jane Price, Ohio, 1841/1843; Indiana, 1843–1873; Iowa, 1873–1876; Nebraska, 1876–1920.

1. Jessie Bernard, *Women, Wives, Mothers: Values and Options.* (Chicago: Aldine Publishing Company, 1975), 43.

2. Punctuation and capitalization have been added throughout the quotes from Sarah Jane Price's journals. Complete dates have been added where necessary in order to give an accurate chronology of the entries in-

cluded. The grammar and spelling are generally accurate and have not been changed. Sarah Jane Price Collection, NSHS.

3. Carol Gilligan, *In a Different Voice: Psychological Theory and Women's Development* (Cambridge: Harvard University Press, 1982), 100.

4. Ibid., 19, 173.

5. A. L. Gary and E. B. Thomas, eds., *Centennial History of Rush County, Indiana*, vol. 1 (Indianapolis: Historical Publishing Company, 1921) 375.

6. Ibid., 370–371.

7. Ibid., 374.

8. Ibid., 371.

9. DeRoss Andrews, grandnephew of Jane Price, and his daughter, Jan Pintcke, interview with author, Bridgman, Michigan, 13 October 1991. Also, Betty Merrill, niece of Sarah Jane Price, letter to Mary H. Cordier, undated [October 1991].

10. Andrews and Pintcke interview.

11. Sarah Jane Price, "A Dream," undated poem. Christy probably studied divinity at DePauw University while living in Greencastle, Indiana, in 1863, as his letter of September 30, 1863, to the family indicates he hopes to get used to studying. Private collection, DeRoss Andrews, Bridgman, Michigan.

12. De Ross Andrews, grandson of John T. Price, interview with author, 13 October 1991. John T. Price's teaching position and residence in Hamilton County is documented in Dale P. Stough, ed., *History of Hamilton and Clay Counties, Nebraska* , vol. 1 (Chicago: S. J. Clarke Publishing Company, 1921), 41.

13. *History of the State of Nebraska*, vol. 2 (Chicago: Western Historical Company, 1882), 945. The farm products are cited in Stough, 1:346; 342–347.

14. *Biographical and Historical Memoirs of Adams, Clay, Hall and Hamilton Counties, Nebraska* (Chicago: Goodspeed Publishing Co., 1890), 732; and, *History of the State of Nebraska*, 2:949.

15. *Biographical and Historical Memoirs*, 732.

16. Betty Merrill letter [October 1991].

17. Stough, 1:401.

18. Ibid., 218.

19. Gilligan, *In a Different Voice*, 7–9, identifies these aspects of femininity.

20. Essay titles are "Easter Thoughts," "Consider the Lilies," and "Standing Point of Life." Private collection, DeRoss Andrews.

21. Some of Jane Price's poetry appears in her journals of May 1882. The rhyming poems are religious in tone and deal with overcoming one's troubles through faith and God's guidance.

22. Bertha G. Bremer with James M. Kirk, *Centennial History of Hamilton County* (Aurora, Nebraska: Hamilton County Centennial Association, 1976), 216.

23. Andrews interview.

24. Price, "A Dream."

25. Andrews interview.

26. Merrill letter.

27. Lora I. Russel, "Where are the Old Settlers? Interesting Facts About Early Days Compiled by One Who is Familiar with the Subject," published in *Aurora Republican* 1918, and reprinted in Stough, 1:389, cites Mrs. Charlotte Ward as a homesteader and Jane Price as "another lady land owner."

28. John T. Price was described as "schoolma'am" in Russel in Stough, 1:390, 383–391; Illinois college attendance and teaching, from Dale P. Stough, ed., *History of Hamilton and Clay Counties, Nebraska* , vol. 2 (Chicago: S. J. Clarke Publishing Company, 1921), 41. Dates of his superintendency, *Biographical and Historical Memoirs of Adams, Clay, Hall and Hamilton Counties, Nebraska,* 749.

29. Eva Jane Price, *China Journal 1889–1900: An American Missionary Family During the Boxer Rebellion: with the letters and diaries of Eva Jane Price and her family,* foreward by Harrison E. Salisbury; introductory notes and annotations by Robert H. Felsing. Letters compiled by Virginia Phipps, Lucille Wilson, and Arlene Caruth (New York: Collier Books, 1989; originally published: New York: Scribner, 1989), xxi, 123.

30. Ibid.

31. Ibid., 133.

32. *Biographical and Historical Memoirs,* 581.

33. Carl F. Kaestle, "Literacy and Diversity: Themes from a Social History of the American Reading Public," *History of Education Quarterly* 28:4 (Winter 1988), 526.

34. Ibid., 528.

35. Sarah Jane Price, "Recollections of my mother," Diaries, vol. 5, September 1884–December 1885, pages 91–97, NSHS.

36. The changes in settlements can be seen in the shifts of the post offices in rural Nebraska. The post office of Lincoln Valley was discontinued and moved to the new village of St. Joe in 1881. In 1884, the Burlington and Missouri River Railroad was built and the town of Phillips was established. The post office of St. Joe was then moved to Phillips. *Biographical and Historical Memoirs,* 770.

37. Bremer, *Centennial History of Hamilton County,* 168–169.

38. It is difficult to determine in this context whether Lon is Susie's brother, or Jane's brother. The U. S. Census of 1880 of Hamilton County lists Elizabeth Lutz, 45, widow, keeping house, and her son, Alonzo W.,

eleven, at school. At this time, Jane's brother, Alonzo W. Price, a farm laborer, was 26.

39. There are eleven letters extant from William Ell to Sarah Jane Price from August 1862 to January 1864. Punctuation and capitalization has been added for clarity. Private collection, DeRoss Andrews.

40. According to the Indiana Commission on Public Records, Benjamin Bear was discharged in June 1865; and William Ell deserted in February 1864. Archivist Wayne Mann, RHC-WMU, indicates that soldiers who disappeared were frequently listed as having deserted even when they may have been missing in action, wounded, or taken prisoner.

41. Personal Narratives Group, *Interpreting Women's Lives* (Bloomington: Indiana University Press, 1989, 6–7.

42. Jane Price does not give Lizzie's surname in these diary entries. There were apparently several women named Lizzie among her circle of friends, relatives, and neighbors.

43. Price, Diary, April 4 and 15, 1882.

44. *History of Nebraska*, 1:548–549.

45. Elizabeth [Price] Babbitt, letter to Sarah Jane Price, January 17, 1875, indicates sending plants, "a bagful from my yard," including scented geraniums. Private collection, DeRoss Andrews.

46. The manuscript, describing Sarah Jane Price's trip to the International Sunday School Convention, housed at NSHS, is undated. However, Jane stated events as taking place on "Saturday, May 18th," and attended a reception given by Lloyd Griscom, American Ambassador to Italy. From these two indicators, her trip can be dated as 1907, according to the Reference Librarians, Kalamazoo Public Library, Kalamazoo, Michigan.

47. Price, International Sunday School Convention.

48. Ibid.

49. Ibid.

50. Price, "The Convention," undated.

51. Ibid.

Chapter 7 "To Be a Teacher": Sarah Gillespie Huftalen, Iowa 1885–1955.

1. Sarah Gillespie Huftalen, Arbor Vitae Summit School Record Book, 1904–1909, box 10, vol. 3, unpaged. Unless otherwise indicated, all documents are from the Sarah Gillespie Huftalen Collection, MS 10, ISHD-HS, Iowa City, Iowa. Because the Huftalen Collection is large and some information is duplicated in several notebooks and scrapbooks with similar titles, the box and volume numbers are cited for some documents.

2. Ibid.

3. Sarah Gillespie Huftalen, Diary, 1883–1889, 426–27, box 7, vol. 5.

4. Carol Gilligan, *In a Different Voice: Psychological Theory and Women's Development* (Cambridge: Harvard University Press, 1982), 139.

5. Ibid.

6. Sarah Gillespie Huftalen, "Normal Training Department, Muscatine High School, Muscatine, Iowa," in "Personal No. 2, Sarah L. Gillespie Huftalen, Manchester, Iowa, I Remember This & That," 102, box 8, vol. 11.

7. Ibid., "Personal Reminiscences," 1.

8. Judy Nolte Lensink, Christine M. Kirkham, and Karen Pauba Witzke, "'My Only Confidant': The Life and Diary of Emily Hawley Gillespie," *Annals of Iowa* 45:4 (Spring 1980): 288–312.

9. "Personal No. 2," 68.

10. Sarah Huftalen, "The Use of the Hand Book in Rural Schools," *Midland Schools* (1910–1911): 300–302.

11. Sarah Gillespie Huftalen, "School Days of the Seventies." *Palimpsest* 28:4 (April 1947): 123.

12. Lensink, Kirkham, and Witzke, "'My Only Confidant'", 302–3.

13. Ibid., 304.

14. Ibid.

15. Huftalen Diary, June 30, 1948, 383. Emily Hawley Gillespie's diaries and memorabilia are deposited in the Emily Hawley Gillespie Collection, Michigan Department of State, Michigan History Division, Lansing, Mich. Additional papers including diaries are included with the Huftalen Collection, ISHD-HS.

16. Emily Gillespie's relationship with her husband was similar to those described in Melody Graulich, "Violence Against Women: Power Dynamics in Literature of the Western Family," in Susan Armitage and Elizabeth Jameson, *The Women's West* (Norman: University of Oklahoma Press, 1987), 111–25.

17. Lensink, Kirkham, and Witzke, "'My Only Confidant,'" 309–10.

18. Sarah Gillespie Huftalen, "The Manchester Academy Normal School and Commercial Institute: 1879–1882," scrapbook, 26–27, box 12, vol. 12.

19. Huftalen, "School Days," 123.

20. Huftalen, "Personal No. 2," 2.

21. Diary, 1883–1889, 15.

22. Ibid., 14.

23. Ibid., 43.

24. Ibid., August 1884.

25. Ibid., 39–40.

26. Ibid., 75–76.

27. Ibid., 1914–1917, 381.

28. Ibid., 381–82.

29. Lensink, Kirkham, and Witzke, "'My Only Confidant,'" 311.

30. Diary, 1914–1917, 381–82. When Sarah Huftalen wrote the history of the Rural Section of the Iowa State Teachers Association, she recalled living in Des Moines and referred to "the Insurance office in the Hubbell Building where I had been book-keeper & cashier during a summer vacation." Huftalen, "How the Rural Section Became an Integral Unit of I.S. T. A. in 1909," 2.

31. Sarah Gillespie Huftalen, "Woman's Sphere," newspaper clipping, Manchester, Iowa, Wednesday, August 10, 1898, in "Personal No. 1, Sarah L. Gillespie Huftalen, Manchester, Iowa, I Rember[sic] This & That," 20, box 8, vol. 10

32. Ibid., 21.

33. Diary, June 28, 1914, 357.

34. Ibid., 358–59.

35. Ibid., 364.

36. "Personal No. 2," 75.

37. Ibid., 71.

38. Printed letter to rural teachers in Iowa, from Sarah Huftalen, Leader, Rural Teachers Round Table, Iowa State Education Association, 1910, 88, box 8, vol. 11,

39. "Personal No. 2," 64.

40. Ibid.

41. Ibid., 71.

42. Ibid., 79.

43. Ibid., 74.

45. Ibid., 79.

45. Ibid., 78.

46. Postscript written April 17, 1949, when organizing the school notes for deposit at the Iowa State Historical Department-Historical Society, in "Arbor Vitae Summit, Oneida, Iowa, 1904–1909," last page.

47. Arbor Vitae Summit School Record Book, 1904–1909, box 10, vol. 3.

48. Sarah Gillespie Huftalen, Arbor Vitae Summit School notes, 1906–1909, 11, box 10, vol. 2.

49. "Personal No. 2," 79.

50. Ibid.

51. "Arbor Vitae Summit Notes. Edited by Mrs. Sarah Huftalen— School Libraries and Notes," undated newspaper clipping, unpaged, box 10, vol. 5.

52. "Personal No. 2," 74.

53. Ibid., 69.

54. Arbor Vitae Summit School Notes, 1906–1909, box 10, vol. 2, 29.

55. Ibid., 12.

56. Sarah Gillespie, Huftalen, "How the Rural Section Became an Integral Unit of I. S. T. A in 1909," 2–3.

57. Ibid., 12.

58. "Personal No. 2," 88.

59. Ibid., 89.

60. Ibid., 41.

61. Ibid., 53.

62. Ibid., 75.

63. Ibid., index and 87.

64. Diary, June 28, 1914, 356–428.

65. Billie's age at his death is stated as eighty-six years old, however, in this entry, it appears that he was eighty-nine. Sarah indicated that Billie had not told his true age.

66. Diary, 1883–1889; 1914–1917, 384.

67. Lensink, Kirkham, and Witzke, "'My Only Confidant," 312; Obituary, *Manchester Press*, July 15, 1954.

68. Diary, June 28, 1914, 384–85, 387–88.

69. Ibid., 425.

70. Ibid., 427.

71. Ibid.

72. William C. Lang, *A Century of Leadership and Service: A Centennial History of the University of Northern Iowa*, vol. 1, *1876–1928* (Cedar Falls: University of Northern Iowa, UNI Alumni Association, 1990), 323–24.

73. Sarah G. Huftalen, "Close Supervision of Schools in Bennington Township, Blackhawk County, Iowa," in "Personal No. 2," 91–92.

74. Ibid., 8–9.

75. Ibid., 94–95.

76. Ibid., 99.

77. The forms to be filled out before and after every class included the following: A. Subject: Date; Assignment; Topic; Aim; Reference; Directions; Suggestions; Problems; Results; Memoranda. B. Recitation: Test [including questions]; Aim; Points to be developed; Drills; Method of instruction; Devices to be used; Time division of period; Results—What did you accomplish? What mistakes for improvement? "Personal No. 2," 99–104.

78. Ibid., typed copy of portion of letter from Sarah G. Huftalen to Forest Ensign, undated, 99.

79. Ibid., "Normal Training Department, Muscatine High School, Muscatine, Iowa," 102.

80. Ibid., 103.

81. Ibid., 102.

82. Ibid.

83. Ibid., Sarah Gillespie Huftalen, "Why a Teacher," 104.

84. Obituary, *Manchester Press* July 15, 1954.
85. "Why a Teacher," 104–5.

Chapter 8 "Attaining My Lifelong Ambition": Bessie M. Tucker Gilmer, Nebraska 1898–,

1. Bessie Tucker Gilmer, "Journey Through Life," diaries. NSHS. All dated quotes are from this source. Additional information from Bessie Tucker Gilmer, interviews with author, Lincoln, Nebraska, 12 and 13 July 1983, oral history tape recording, NSHS.
2. Thomas Dekker quoted in Bessie Tucker Gilmer, "The End of an Era," an overview of her life, sent with a letter to Mary Hurlbut Cordier, June 4, 1985.
3. James H. Madison, *Heartland: Comparative Histories of the Midwestern States* (Bloomington: Indiana University Press, 1988), 4.
4. James R. Shortridge, "The Heart of the Prairie: Culture Areas in the Central and Northern Great Plains," *Great Plains Quarterly* 8:4 (Fall 1988): 217.
5. Gilmer, "Journey Through Life," January 12, 1919.
6. Bessie M. Gilmer, "Pioneering in Nebraska," in University of Nebraska, Division of Continuing Studies with the Nebraska Commission on Aging, *A Flowering: A Festival*, vol. 3, *Writing and Storytelling for Older Nebraskans* (Lincoln: University of Nebraska, Division of Continuing Studies with the Nebraska Commission on Aging, 1983), 190.
7. Gilmer, interview.
8. Gilmer, "Journey Through Life," 30.
9. Ibid., 30–31.
10. Ibid., 37.
11. James C. Olson, *History of Nebraska*, 2d ed., (Lincoln: University of Nebraska, 1966), 258–60.
12. Gilmer, "Pioneering in Nebraska," 190.
13. Ibid., 191.
14. Gilmer, "Journey Through Life," 32.
15. Ibid.
16. Ibid.
17. Ibid.
18. Ibid.
19. Ibid., 4.
20. Ibid., March 18, 1918, 2.
21. In the 1970s, Bessie Gilmer again met the Clems at church meetings. Gilmer's son, Donald roomed with the Tiltons when he went to college.
22. Gilmer, "Journey Through Life," February 22, 1918.
23. Gilmer, "Journey Through Life," May 18, 1918.

24. Margaret Connell Szasz, *Education and the American Indian: The Road to Self-Determination Since 1928* (Albuquerque: University of New Mexico Press, 1977), 11.

25. Gilmer, "Journey Through Life," October 10, 1918.

26. Ibid.

27. Ibid.

28. Ibid., April 16, 1919.

29. Ibid., April 22, 1919.

30. Ibid., October 2, 1919, 28.

31. Ibid., 32.

32. Ibid., 41–42.

33. Gilmer, "End of an Era," 1.

34. Gilmer, "Journey Through Life," February 13, 1921.

35. Ibid., 2. While recording Bessie's oral history, we held hands and quietly wept together as she told me about her twin daughters. I shared pictures and experiences of my healthy twin daughters.

36. Ibid.

37. Ibid., 61.

38. Gilmer, "End of an Era," 4.

39. Bessie Tucker Gilmer, letter to Mary H. Cordier, May 27, 1985.

Chapter 9 "Teachers are Leaders": Ethel Hale Russel, Nebraska, 1895–1916; Idaho, 1916–1917; Utah, 1917–1919; Iowa, 1919–1922; and Michigan, 1922–

1. Ethel Hale Russel, interview with author, Kalamazoo, Michigan, 10 June 1982, oral history tape recording, RHC/WMU and NSHS.

2. Ethel Hale Russel to Mary H. Cordier, 11 November, 1982.

3. Ethel Hale Russel, interview with author, Kalamazoo, Michigan, 23 August 1985.

4. John C. Gerber, *A Pictorial History of the University of Iowa* (Iowa City: University of Iowa Press, 1988), 113.

5. Earl M. Rogers, Curator of Archives, University of Iowa, to Mary H. Cordier, October 12, 1990. Gerber, *University of Iowa*, 113. See also, *Pioneering in Child Welfare: A History of the Iowa Child Welfare Research Station, 1917–1933* (Iowa City: State University of Iowa, 1933).

6. Gerber, *University of Iowa*, 134.

7. Ethel Hale Russel, interview, 23 August 1985.

8. Ibid.

9. All salary data are from *The Minutes of the Meetings of the Michigan State Board of Education* for the fiscal years cited, RHC-WMU.

10. Russel interview, 23 August 1985.

11. Ibid.

12. "Western State Abnormal School Bullet, Shriekers Prevailable, Pub-

lished when necessary to maintain proper Esprit de Corps," 1925, RHC-WMU.

13. James O. Knauss, *The First Fifty Years: A History of Western Michigan College of Education, 1903–1953* (Kalamazoo, Michigan: Western Michigan College of Education, 1953), 164.

14. Christine Ferreira, "Robert Russel: Still teaching us things we need to know," *Graduate College Report,* (Winter 1986): The Graduate College, Western Michigan University, 4.

15. Ethel Hale Russel, television interview with Mary H. Cordier, "Making a Difference: Contributions of a Woman Leader, Ethel Hale Russel." Produced by Mary Appelhof for Public Access Television, Women's History Week, March 1985, Kalamazoo, Michigan.

16. Jon Cummings, "Nine decades into life, their fascination with world events keeps the Russels young," *Kalamazoo (Michigan) Gazette,* January 15, 1986, D1–D2.

17. Ibid., D2.

18. Ethel Hale Russel, interview with author, Kalamazoo, Michigan, 16 August 1985.

Epilogue

1. "Resolutions of the Teachers' Class of Osceola, Clark Co.," *Iowa Instructor—An Educational Journal* 1:4 (May 1869, 238–41.

2. Jessie Bernard, *Women, Wives, Mothers: Values and Options* (Chicago: Aldine Publishing Company, 1975), 43.

3. Cass G. Barns, *The Sod House* (Lincoln: University of Nebraska Press, 1970), 116.

Selected Bibliography

I. About and by Schoolwomen and Schoolmen, Including Primary Documents, Published and Unpublished

Ainsworth Area Retired Teachers. *The Sway of the School Bell, Schools and Histories of Brown, Keya Paha, and Rock Counties, Nebraska.* Ainsworth, Nebraska: Ainsworth Area Retired Teachers, 1976.

Barnhart, Cornelia Mallett. "Phoebe Sudlow." *Palimpsest* 38:4 (April 1957): 169–76.

Bayne, Martha. "Reminiscences of Mrs. Martha Bayne, a Teacher in the Country Schools of Russell, Lincoln and Osborn Counties in the '80s." KSHS.

Beall, Loulie Ayer. "Early School Experiences in Nebraska, A Webster County School."*Nebraska History* 23 (July–September 1942): 195–218.

Bern, Enid. "Memoirs of a Prairie Schoolteacher." *North Dakota History* 42 (Summer 1975): 5–16.

Bruner, Amelia Phoneta. Recollections of Childhood in 1860s and Early 70s. Bruner Family Collection. NSHS.

———. School papers, December 18, 1872. Bruner Family Collection. NSHS.

Carter, Susan Ophelia. Diary, 1887. NSHS.

Christie, Jean. " 'An earnest enthusiasm for education': Sarah Christie Stevens, Schoolwoman."*Minnesota History* 48:6 (Summer 1983): 245–54.

Clark, Ann Nolan. *Journey to the People.* New York: Viking Press, 1969.

Clarkson, Anna Howell. "A Beautiful Life: A Biographical Sketch [Drucilla Allen Stoddard]."*Annals of Iowa* 3:11 (July–October 1913): 188–99.

Clary, Irene, retired teacher. Interview with Betty Rowan. Fredonia, Kansas, 9 August 1983.

Coleman, Alice Cowan. "Miss Jacoby: 20th Century Educator, 20th Century Guardian of Excellence."*Montana: The Magazine of History* (Spring 1978): 37–49.

Conron, Clara S. Diary, October 1884–July 1885. KSHS.

Cordier, Mary Hurlbut. "Prairie Schoolwomen, Mid 1850s to 1920s, in Iowa, Kansas, and Nebraska."*Great Plains Quarterly* 8:2 (Spring 1988): 102–19.

———. "Teaching at home on the prairie."*Plainswoman* 10:6 (March 1987): 3–5.

Crowder, E. Mary Lacy. "Pioneer Life in Palo Alto County." *Iowa Journal of History and Politics* 46 (1948): 156–98.

Delta Kappa Gamma. Typescript articles on Susan Frazier, Eliza Morgan, and Genevieve Giddings Richmond. NSHS.

Delta Kappa Gamma, Alpha Chapter. "Pioneer Women in Education—A Study of Seven Women Who Each Taught 50 Years or More." Davenport, Iowa: Alpha Chapter, Delta Kappa Gamma. Typescript articles in author's possession.

Eastman, Elaine Goodale. *Sister to the Sioux: The Memoirs of Elaine Goodale Eastman, 1885–91.* Edited by Kay Graber. Lincoln: University of Nebraska Press, 1978.

Elder, Julia, retired teacher. Interview with Betty Rowan. Benedict, Kansas. 9 August 1983.

Farseth, Pauline, and Theodore C. Blegan, trans. and ed. *Frontier Mother: The Letters of Gro Svendsen.* Northfield, Minn.: The Norwegian-American Historical Association, 1950.

Fuller, Rosalie Trail, ed. "A Nebraska High School Teacher in the 1890s: The Letters of Sadie B. Smith."*Nebraska History* 58:4 (Fall 1977): 447–73.

Gaddis, Nancy Higgins. Collection of letters to Gaddis from teenaged girlfriends; attendance records; expense accounts, photographs, and other family papers. Private collection of E. McKinney, Kalamazoo, Mich., and Nancy Higgins Gaddis Collection. NSHS.

Gillespie, Emily Elizabeth Hawley. Diaries, 1858–1865. Huftalen Collection, ISHD-HS, and Emily Gillespie Collection, Michigan State Historical Society.

Gilmer, Bessie Tucker. Interviews with Mary H. Cordier, July 12 and 13, 1983. Oral history tape recording, NSHS.

———. "Journey Through Life," Diaries, 1918–1979, with notes and additions through December 1984. NSHS.

———. "Pioneering in Nebraska." In *A Flowering: A Festival.* Vol. 3, *Writing and Storytelling Festival for Older Nebraskans,* 190–92. Lincoln, Nebr.: Commission on Aging, 1983.

Gregory, George Albert. "The Gregory Trail," autobiography edited by Annadora Foss Gregory. NSHS.

Hampsten, Elizabeth, comp. *To All Inquiring Friends: Letters, Diaries and Es-*

says in North Dakota. Fargo: Department of English, University of North Dakota, 1979.

———. *Read This Only to Yourself: The Private Writing of Midwestern Women, 1880–1910.* Bloomington: Indiana University Press, 1982.

———. *Settlers' Children: Growing Up on the Great Plains.* Norman: University of Oklahoma Press, 1991.

Heller, Elizabeth Wright. "A Young Woman in Iowa." *Palimpsest* 54 (March–April 1973): 18–31.

Hiller, Gertrude. "An Apostle of Free Education [C. C. Nestlerode]." *Palimpsest* 29:2 (February 1948): 49–63.

Hoffman, Nancy. *Woman's "True" Profession: Voices from the History of Education.* Old Westbury, N.Y.: The Feminist Press, and New York: McGraw-Hill, 1981.

Hotze, W. H. "Pioneer School Days in Southwest Nebraska: A Reminiscence." *Nebraska History* 33 (March 1952): 41–53.

Huftalen, Sarah Gillespie. Diaries, 1877–1952; school notebooks, scrapbooks, photographs. Huftalen Collection. ISHD-HS.

Hull, Alta, retired teacher. Interview with Betty Rowan. Fredonia, Kansas. 2 April 1983.

Iowa Retired Teachers Association. *Readin', 'Ritin', 'Rithmetic, and 'Reminiscin'.* Newton, Iowa: Iowa Retired Teachers Association, 1976.

Jackson, Jane, retired teacher. Interview with Betty Rowan. Chanute, Kansas. 3 April 1983.

Jennings, Rosa Schreurs. "The Country Teacher." *Annals of Iowa* 31 (July 1951): 41–62.

Johnson, Anna. "Recollections of a Country School Teacher." *Annals of Iowa* 42 (Winter 1975): 485–505.

Kaufman, Polly Welts. *Women Teachers on the Frontier.* New Haven: Yale University Press, 1984.

Lawrence, Alice Money. "A Pioneer School Teacher in Central Iowa." *Iowa Journal of History and Politics* 33:4 (October 1953): 376–95.

Lensink, Judy Nolte, Christine M. Kirkham, and Karen Pauba Witzke. "'My Only Confidant': The Life and Diary of Emily Hawley Gillespie." *Annals of Iowa* 45:4 (Spring 1980): 288–312.

Lewis, Faye C. *Nothing to Make a Shadow.* Ames: Iowa State University Press, 1971.

Manning, Diane. *Hill Country Teacher: Oral Histories from the One-Room School and Beyond.* Boston: Twayne Publishers, 1990.

Mears, Louis W. "Miss Eliza Morgan—A Short Biography." *Nebraska History* 17 (April–June 1936): 132–35.

Mercer, Eliza Adaline. Reminiscences of childhood in Highland, Kansas Territory. KSHS.

Olmstead, Agnes Briggs. "Recollections of a Pioneer Teacher of Hamilton County." *Annals of Iowa* 18 (October 1946): 93–115.

Patton, Ora. Letters to Delbert Mann, 1913–1918, Oklahoma and Kansas. Mann Family Collection. RHC-WMU.

Paullin, Ellen Payne, ed. "Etta's Journal: January 2, 1874 to July 25, 1875," *Kansas History—A Journal of the Central Plains* 3:3 (Autumn 1980): 201–19; and 3:4 (Winter 1980): 255–78.

Porter, Kenneth Wiggins, ed. "Building a Kansas 'Soddy'—1885." *Kansas Magazine* 7 (1942): 17–18.

———, ed. "By Covered Wagon to Kansas." *Kansas Magazine* 7 (1941): 76–80.

———, ed. "Catharine Emma Wiggins, Pupil and Teacher in Northwest Kansas, 1888–1895." *Kansas History* 1:1 (Spring 1978): 16–38.

———, ed. "College Days at Cooper Memorial, 1895–1898." *Kansas Historical Quarterly* 26:4 (Winter 1960): 383–409.

———, ed. " 'Holding Down' a Northwest Kansas Claim, 1885–1888." *Kansas Historical Quarterly* 22 (Autumn 1956): 220–35.

———, ed. "A Little Girl on an Iowa Forty, 1873-1880—Catharine Wiggins Porter." *Iowa Journal of History and Politics* 51:2 (April 1953): 131–35.

———, ed. "School Days in Coin, Iowa, 1880–1885—Catharine Wiggins Porter." *Iowa Journal of History and Politics* 51 (October 1953): 310–28.

Pospisil, Emma. "A Teacher of the Willow Creek School." *Nebraska History* 24 (January–March 1943): 13–24.

Pownall, Dorothy Ashby. "Agnes Samuelson: a Dedicated Educator." *Palimpsest* 43:11 (November 1962): 497–544.

Price, Sarah Jane. Diaries, 1878–1895, and miscellaneous papers. NSHS.

Quick, Herbert. *One Man's Life: An Autobiography.* Indianapolis: Bobbs, 1925.

Rankin, Charles E. "Teaching: Opportunity and Limitation for Wyoming Women." *Western Historical Quarterly* (May 1990): 147–70.

Russel, Ethel Hale, retired teacher and community leader. Interview with author, 10 June 1982. Oral history tape recording, RHC-WMU and NSHS.

Russel, Robert R. Interview with author, 10 June 1982. Oral history tape recording, RHC-WMU and NSHS.

Sanford, Mollie Dorsey. *Mollie: The Journal of Mollie Dorsey Sanford in Nebraska and Colorado Territories, 1857–1866.* Lincoln: University of Nebraska Press, 1959.

Sawyer, R. McLaran. "Samuel DeWitt Beals, Frontier Educator." *Nebraska History* 50:2 (Summer 1969); 173–83.

Scrimsher, Lila Gravatt, ed. "The Diary of Anna Webber: Early Day Teacher of Mitchell County." *Kansas Historical Quarterly* 38 (October 1972): 320–37.

Slafter, Rebecca Bullard. Diary, 1849–1850. Rebecca Bullard Slafter Collection. RHC-WMU.

Smallwood, James, ed. *And Gladly Teach: Reminiscences of Teachers from Frontier Dugout to Modern Module.* Norman: University of Oklahoma Press, 1976.

Smith, Mary Ward. "Autobiographical Reminiscences, 1856–1860," KSHS.

Stewart, Isabelle Simmons. Isabelle Simmons Stewart Manuscript Collection. NSHS.

"Story of Routt County's Early Schools is Story of Emma Peck." *The Steamboat Pilot,* 75th Anniversary Edition, 8B. Steamboat Springs, Colo.: 1959.

Townsley, Frank S. Diaries, 1877–1894. ISHD-HS.

Underwood, Kathleen. "The Pace of Their Own Lives: Teacher Training and the Life Course of Western Women." *Pacific Historical Review* 55:4 (November 1986): 513–30.

Vaughn-Roberson, Courtney Ann. "Having a Purpose in Life: Western Women Teachers in the Twentieth Century." *Great Plains Quarterly* 5 (Spring 1982): 107–24.

———. "Sometimes Independent But Never Equal—Women Teachers, 1900–1950: The Oklahoma Example." *Pacific Historical Review* 53 (February 1984): 39–58.

Wyman, Walker D. *Frontier Woman: The Life of a Woman Homesteader on the Dakota Frontier.* River Falls: University of Wisconsin, River Falls Press, 1972.

II. The Historical Setting

Atherton, Lewis. *Main Street on the Middle Border.* Bloomington: Indiana University Press, 1984.

Armitage, Susan. "Through Women's Eyes: A New View of the West." In Susan Armitage and Elizabeth Jameson, eds., *The Women's West,* 9–18. Norman: University of Oklahoma Press, 1987.

Armitage, Susan, and Elizabeth Jameson, eds. *The Women's West.* Norman: University of Oklahoma Press, 1987.

Arthur, T. S., ed. *Our Homes: Their Care and Duties, Joys and Sorrows.* New York: John W,. Lovell Co., 1888.

Barns, Cass S. *The Sod House.* Lincoln: University of Nebraska Press, 1970.

Beeton, Beverly, and G. Thomas Edwards. "Susan B. Anthony's Woman Suffrage Crusade in the American West." *Journal of the West* 21:5 (April 1982): 5–15.

Biographical and Historical Memoirs of Adams, Clay, Hall, and Hamilton Counties, Nebraska. Chicago: Goodspeed Publishing Co., 1890.

Blum, John M., William S. McFeely, Edmund S. Morgan, Arthur Schlesinger Jr., Kenneth M. Stampp and C. Vann Woodward. *The National Experience: A History of the United States.* 6th ed. San Diego and New York: Harcourt, Brace Jovanovich, Publishers, 1985.

Brownlee, W. Elliot, and Mary M. Brownlee. *Women in the American Economy: A Documentary History, 1675–1929.* New Haven: Yale University Press, 1976.

Butchart, Ronald E. "The Frontier Teacher: Arizona, 1875–1925." *Journal of the West* 16 (March 1977): 545–66.

Butcher, Solomon D. *Pioneer History of Custer County, Nebraska with which is combined Sod Houses of the Great American Plains,* 2d ed. Denver: Sage Books, 1965, reprint of original, ca. 1900.

Carlson, Avis. *Small World, Long Gone.* Evanston, Ill.: Schori Press, 1975.

Christensen, Lawrence O. "Missouri: The Heart of the Nation." In Madison, James, ed., *Heartland: Comparative Histories of the Midwestern States,* 86–106. Bloomington: Indiana University Press, 1988.

Clement, Ora A. "Fort Hartsuff and the Local Pioneer Life." *Nebraska History Magazine* 12 (January–March 1929): 140–57.

Cordier, Mary Hurlbut, and María Pérez-Stable. *Peoples of the American West: Historical Perspectives Through Children's Literature.* Metuchen, N.J.: Scarecrow Press, 1989.

Crowder, E. Mary Lacy. "Pioneer Life in Palo Alto County." *Iowa Journal of History and Politics* 46 (1948): 156–98.

Degler, Carl. *At Odds: Women and the Family in America from the Revolution to the Present.* New York: Oxford University Press, 1980.

de Graff, Lawrence B. "Race, Sex, and Region: Black Women in the American West." *Pacific Historical Quarterly* 49:2 (May 1980): 285–314.

Fairbanks, Carolyn. *Prairie Women Images in American and Canadian Fiction.* New Haven: Yale University Press, 1986.

Gary, A. L., and E. B. Thomas, eds. *Centennial History of Rush County, Indiana.* Vol. 1. Indianapolis: Historical Publishing Company, 1921.

Graulich, Melody. "Violence Against Women: Power Dynamics in Literature of the Western Family." In Susan Armitage and Elizabeth Jameson, eds., *The Women's West,* 111–25. Norman: University of Oklahoma Press, 1987.

Griswold, Richard L. "Anglo Women and Domestic Ideology in the American West in the Nineteenth and Early Twentieth Centuries." In Lillian Schlissel, Vicki L. Ruiz, and Janice Monk, eds., *Western Women, Their Land, Their Lives,* 15–34. Albuquerque: University of New Mexico Press, 1988.

Ise, John. *Sod and Stubble: The Story of a Kansas Homestead.* Lincoln: University of Nebraska, 1936.

Jameson, Elizabeth. "Women as Workers, Women as Civilizers: True Womanhood in the American West." In Susan Armitage and Elizabeth Jameson, eds., *The Women's West*, 145–64. Norman: University of Oklahoma Press, 1987.

Jeffrey, Julie Roy. *Frontier Women: The Trans-Mississippi West, 1840–1880*. New York: Hill and Wang, 1979.

———. " 'There is Some Splendid Scenery,' Women's Responses to the Great Plains Landscape." *Great Plains Quarterly* 8:2 (Spring 1988): 69–78.

Jensen, Joan M. *With These Hands*. Old Westbury, N.Y.: Feminist Press, 1981.

Jensen, Joan M., and Darlis A. Miller. "The Gentle Tamers Revisited: New Approaches to the History of Women in the American West." *Pacific Historical Review* 49 (May 1980): 173–213.

Lowenthal, David. "The Pioneer Landscape: An American Dream." *Great Plains Quarterly* 2:1 (Winter 1982): 5–19.

Luebke, Frederick C. "Nebraska: Time, Place, and Culture." In James Madison, ed., *Heartland: Comparative Histories of the Midwestern States*, 226–47. Bloomington: Indiana University Press, 1988.

Madison, James, ed. *Heartland: Comparative Histories of the Midwestern States*. Bloomington: Indiana University Press, 1988.

Malone, Michael P., and Richard W. Etulain. *The American West: A Twentieth-Century History*. Lincoln: University of Nebraska Press, 1989.

Mattes, Merrill J. *The Great Platte River Road*. Lincoln: Nebraska Historical Society, 1969.

Matthaei, Julie A. *An Economic History of Women in America, Women's Work, the Sexual Division of Labor, and the Development of Capitalism*. New York: Schocken Books, 1982.

Moynihan, Ruth B., Susan Armitage, and Christianne Fischer Dichamp. *So Much To Be Done: Women Settlers on the Mining and Ranching Frontier*. Lincoln: University of Nebraska Press, 1990.

Myres, Sandra. *Westering Women and the Frontier Experience, 1800–1915*. Albuquerque: University of New Mexico Press, 1982.

National Archives and Records Service Catalog. "Federal Population Censuses, 1790–1890." Washington: U. S. Government Printing Office.

———. "1900 Federal Population Census." Washington: U. S. Government Printing Office.

———. "The 1910 Population Census." Washington: U. S. Government Printing Office.

Norton, Justin. *So Sweet to Labor: Rural Women in America, 1865-1895*. New York: Viking Press, 1979.

Noun, Louise R. *Strong-Minded Women: The Emergence of the Woman-Suffrage Movement in Iowa*. Ames: Iowa State University Press, 1969.

Opie, John. "Learning to Read the Pioneer Landscape: Braudel, Eliade, Turner, and Benton." *Great Plains Quarterly* 2:1 (Winter 1982): 20–30.

Oliva, Leo E. "Kansas: A Hard Land in the Heartland." In James Madison, ed., *Heartland: Comparative Histories of the Midwestern States*, 248–75. Bloomington: Indiana University Press, 1988.

Pomeroy, Earl. "Toward a Reorientation of Western History: Continuity and Environment." *Mississippi Valley Historical Review* 41:4 (March 1955): 579–600.

Rathge, Richard W. "Women's Contribution to the Family Farm." *Great Plains Quarterly* 9:1 (Winter 1989): 36–47.

Riley, Glenda, ed. "Eighty-Six Years in Iowa: The Memoir of Ada Brown Brinton." *Annals of Iowa* 45 (Winter 1981): 552–67.

———. *The Female Frontier: A Comparative View of Women on the Prairie and the Plains.* Lawrence: University Press of Kansas, 1988.

———. *Frontierswomen: The Iowa Experience.* Ames: Iowa State University Press, 1981.

———. *Inventing the American Woman: a Perspective on Woman's History, 1607–1877.* Vol. 1. Arlington Heights, Ill.: Harlan Davidson, 1986.

Sandoz, Mari. *Old Jules.* Boston: Little, Brown, 1935.

Schlissel, Lillian. *Women's Diaries on the Westward Journey.* New York: Schocken Books, 1982.

Schlissel, Lillian, Byrd Gibbens, and Elizabeth Hampsten. *Far From Home: Families of the Westward Journey.* New York: Schocken Books, 1989.

Schlissel, Lillian, Vicki L. Ruiz, and Janice Monk, eds. *Western Women, Their Land, Their Lives.* Albuquerque: University of New Mexico Press, 1988.

Schwieder, Dorothy. "Iowa: The Middle Land," In James Madison, ed., *Heartland: Comparative Histories of the Midwestern States*, 276–96. Bloomington: Indiana University Press, 1988.

Schwieder, Dorothy, and Deborah Fink. "Plains Women: Rural Life in the 1930s." *Great Plains Quarterly* 8:2 (Spring 1988): 79–88.

Shortridge, James R. "The Heart of the Prairie: Culture Areas in the Central and Northern Great Plains." *Great Plains Quarterly* 8:4 (Fall 1988): 206–21.

Sklar, Kathryn Kish. *Catherine Beecher: A Study in American Domesticity.* New York: Norton, 1973.

Stough, Dale P., ed. *History of Hamilton and Clay Counties, Nebraska.* Vol 1. Chicago: S. J. Clarke Publishing Company, 1921.

Stratton, Joanna L. *Pioneer Women, Voices from the Kansas Frontier.* New York: Simon and Schuster, 1981.

Turner, Frederick Jackson. *Frontier and Section: Selected Essays of Frederick Jackson Turner,* with introduction and notes by Ray Allen Billington. Englewood Cliffs, N.J.: Prentice-Hall, 1966.

U.S. Government Printing Office. *8th Census 1860, Population of the United States in 1860.* Washington, D.C.: U.S. Government Printing Office.

——. *11th Census, 1890, Report on the Population of the United States; and Abstract of the 12th Census of the United States, 1900.* Washington, D.C.: U.S. Government Printing Office.

Unruh, John D., Jr. *The Plains Across: The Overland Emigrants and the Trans-Mississippi West, 1840–60.* Urbana: University of Illinois Press, 1979.

Welter, Barbara. "The Cult of True Womanhood: 1820–1860." *American Quarterly* 18 (Summer 1966): 151–74.

West, Elliott. *Growing Up with the Country: Childhood on the Far Western Frontier.* Albuquerque: University of New Mexico Press, 1989.

Wheeler, Wayne. *An Almanac of Nebraska: Nationality, Ethnic, and Racial Groups.* Omaha: Park Bromwell Press, 1975.

Wilson, Ruth Gaddis. *"There is no place like Nebraska."* By the author: 1984.

III. The Educational Setting

Acker, Sandra. "Women and Teaching: A Semi-Detached Sociology of a Semi-Profession." In Stephen Walker and Len Barton, eds., *Gender, Class and Education,* 123–40. Falmer House, Barcombe, Lewes, Sussex, England: The Falmer Press, 1983.

Aurner, Clarence Ray. *History of Education in Iowa.* Vols. 1 and 2. Iowa City: State Historical Society, 1914.

Belding, Robert E. "Iowa's Brave Model for Women's Education." *Annals of Iowa* 43 (May 1976): 342–48.

Burnham, Ernest. *Two Types of Rural Schools: With Some Facts Showing Economic and Social Conditions.* Teachers College, Columbia University Contribution to Education Number 51. New York: Teachers College, Columbia University, 1912.

Caldwell, Howard W. *Education in Nebraska.* United States Bureau of Education, Circular of Information No. 3, 1902. Contributions to American Educational History, No. 32. Washington, D.C.: Government Printing Office, 1902.

Carney, Mabel. *Country Life and the Country School.* Chicago: Row, Peterson, 1917.

Carter, Susan B. "Incentive and Rewards to Teaching." In Donald Warren, ed., *American Teachers: Histories of a Profession at Work,* 49–62. New York: Macmillan, 1989.

Catalogue of the Delaware County Teachers Normal Institute, Delhi, Iowa 1876. ISDH-HS.

Catalogue of Instructors, Lecturers, and Members of the Teacher Institutes, Tipton, Iowa, December 29, 1856–January 3, 1857. ISDH-HS.

Clifford, Geraldine Jonçinch. *Lone Voyagers: Academic Women in Coeducational Universities 1870–1937.* New York: The Feminist Press at City University of New York, 1989.

———. "Man/Woman/Teacher: Gender, Family, and Career in American Educational History." In Donald E. Warren, ed., *American Teachers: Histories of a Profession at Work*, 293–343. New York: Macmillan, 1989.

Cohen, David K. "Practice and Policy: Notes on the History of Instruction." In Donald Warren, ed., *American Teachers: Histories of a Profession at Work*. 393–407. New York: Macmillan, 1989.

Colgrove, Chauncey P. *The Teacher and the School*. New York: Charles Scribner's Sons, 1910.

Conaway, Roscoe. "Van Huss Versus Turkey Creek." KSHS.

County Teachers Examination Papers, 1907. Nebraska Department of Education File. NSHS.

Cuban, Larry. *How Teachers Taught: Constancy and Change in American Classrooms, 1890–1980*. New York: Longman, 1984.

Daniels, Sherrill F. "An Index to and Bibliography of Reminiscences in the Nebraska State Historical Society Library." Ph.D diss., University of Nebraska, 1986.

Davis, Horace. "Collegiate Education of Women." *Overland Monthly II* 16 (October 1890): 337–44.

Donovan, Josephine. "Schoolbooks of Sarah Gillespie." *Palimpsest* 28:4 (April 1947): 113–21.

Elson, Ruth Miller. *Guardians of Tradition: American Schoolbooks of the Nineteenth Century*. Lincoln: University of Nebraska Press, 1964.

England, J. Merton. "The Democratic Faith in American Schoolbooks, 1783–1860." *American Quarterly* 15 (Summer 1963): 191–99.

Examination Papers, Davenport [Teacher] Training School, Davenport, Iowa, 1884. Davenport Community School Museum.

Frink, Eunice E. *Course of Study for the Public Schools of Cedar County*. Tipton, Iowa: Longley and Peet Printers, 1879. ISHD-HS.

Fuller, Wayne E. "Country Schoolteaching on the Sod-House Frontier." *Arizona and the West* 17 (Summer 1075): 121–40.

———. *The Old Country School: The Story of Rural Education in the Middle West*. Chicago: University of Chicago Press, 1982.

———. "School District 37: Prairie Community." *Western Historical Quarterly* (October 1981): 418–32.

———. "The Teacher in the Country School." In Donald Warren, ed., *American Teachers: Histories of a Profession at Work*, 98–117. New York: Macmillan, 1989.

Gerber, John C. *A Pictorial History of the University of Iowa*. Iowa City: University of Iowa Press, 1988.

Griffin, Clifford W. *The University of Kansas: A History*. Lawrence: The University Press of Kansas, 1974.

Guenther, Richard L. "The Santee Normal Training School." *Nebraska History* 5:3 (Fall 1970): 359–78.

Gulliford, Andrew. *America's Country Schools*. Washington, D.C.: Preservation Press, 1984.

Hargreaves, Mary W. M. "Rural Education on the Northern Plains Frontier," *Journal of the West* 18:4 (October 1979): 23–32.

Herbst, Jurgen. "Teacher Preparation in the Nineteenth Century." In Donald Warren, ed., *American Teachers: Histories of a Profession at Work*, 213–36. New York: Macmillan, 1989.

Hinsdale, B. A. *Horace Mann and the Common School Revival in the United States*. New York: Charles Scribner's Sons, 1900.

Hollis, Andrew P. *The Contributions of the Oswego Normal School to Educational Progress in the United States*. Boston: D. C. Health, 1898.

Huftalen, Sarah Gillespie. "School Days in the Seventies." *Palimpsest* 28:4 (April 1947): 122–28.

Iowa Instructor: an Education Journal 1 (October 1859–September 1860). Tipton, Iowa: Iowa State Teachers Association.

Johnson, William R. "Teachers and Teacher Training in the Twentieth Century." In Donald Warren, ed., *American Teachers: Histories of a Profession at Work*, 237–56. New York: Macmillan, 1989.

Johnson County Teacher 8:1, 8:2, 8:4 (January, March, and May 1896). Johnson County Iowa, Public Schools. ISHD-HS.

Jones, Vernon F., and Louise S. Jones. *Comprehensive Classroom Management: Motivating and Managing Students*, 3d ed. Boston: Allyn and Bacon, 1990.

Kaestle, Carl F. "Literacy and Diversity: Themes from a Social History of the American Reading Public." *History of Education Quarterly* 28:4 (Winter 1988): 523–49.

———. *Pillars of the Republic: Common Schools and American Society*. New York: Hill and Wang, 1983.

Kindley, Mark M. "Little schools on the prairie still teach a big lesson." *Smithsonian* 16:7 (October 1985): 118–28.

Lang, William E. *A Century of Leadership and Service: A Centennial History of the University of Northern Iowa*. Vol. 1, *1876–1928*. Cedar Falls: University of Northern Iowa, UNI Alumni Association, UNI Foundation, 1990.

———. "Higher Education in Cedar Falls: Town and Gown, in the First Hundred Years." *Palimpsest* 64:3 (May/June 1983): 70–84.

Lund, Doniver A. "Educational Experience in America: Immigrant and Native Born." *Swedish Historical Quarterly* 18 (January 1967): 13–31.

McArdle, Gladys. "An 1878 Model Kansas School, Lebanon, Smith County." KSHS.

McGrew, Charles H. *Institute Manual; or, Graded Courses of Study, and Note Book, for Normal Institutes*. 2d ed. Ottumwa, Iowa: Press of J. J. Bowles, 1884.

Manley, Robert N. *Centennial History of the University of Nebraska.* Lincoln: University of Nebraska Press, 1969.

Morain, Thomas. "The Departure of Males from the Teaching Profession in Nineteenth Century Iowa." *Civil War History* 26:2 (1980): 161–70.

Mott, Frank L. "Teachers' Journals." *Palimpsest* 44 (August 1963): 328–33.

Mountain Plains Library Association. *Country School Legacy: Humanities on the Frontier.* Silt, Colo.: Country School Legacy, 1981.

Murphy, Anna Marie, and Cullen Murphy. "Onward, upward with McGuffey and those Readers." *Smithsonian* 15:8 (November 1984): 182–208.

National Education Association. *Report of the Committee of Twelve on Rural Schools, July 9, 1895.* Chicago: University of Chicago Press, 1897.

"Nebraska Teachers' Reading Circle, 1904–1905." NSHS.

The Nemaha County Teacher [periodical] (1906–1907). Nemaha (Nebraska) County Public Schools. NSHS.

Nestlerode, C. C. "Theory and Practice of Teaching, No. 6, Opening School." *The Iowa Instructor: an Education Journal* 1 (April 1860): 207–10.

Pangburn, Jessie M. *The Evolution of the American Teachers College.* Teachers College, Columbia University, No. 500. New York: Teachers College, Columbia University, 1932.

Parkhurst, Charles, H. "Collegiate Training for Women." *Ladies Home Journal* 12 (May 1895): 15.

Paskewitz, Frank. "Box Stove, Cipher Downs, Sleigh Rides: Memories of a Rural School." *Ramsey [Minnesota] County History* 3:1 (Spring 1966): 11–13.

Petersen, William J. "Education for All." *Palimpsest* 39:2 (December 1959): 545–55.

The Ranch Teacher: Box Butte and Cheyenne Counties [periodical] 1907–1908. Box Butte and Cheyenne Counties (Nebraska) Public Schools. NSHS.

"Reading Circle Work and Teachers' Certificates:" Bulletin No. 3 (1907). NSHS.

Reports of the Superintendent of Public Instruction of the State of Iowa, 1864–1906. Des Moines, Iowa.

Reports of the Superintendent of Public Instruction of the State of Kansas, 1866–1906. Leavenworth and Topeka, Kansas.

Reports of the Superintendent of Public Instruction of the State of Nebraska, 1865–1902. Lincoln, Nebraska.

Rury, John L. "Who Became Teachers? The Social Characteristics of Teachers in American History." In Donald Warren, ed., *American Teachers: Histories of a Profession at Work,* 9–48. New York: Macmillan, 1989.

Sabin, Henry. *Common Sense Didactics for the Common School Teacher.* New York: Rand, McNally, 1903.

Sawyer, R. McLaran. "No Teacher for the School: The Nebraska Junior

Normal School Movement." *Nebraska History* 52:2 (Summer 1971): 191–203.

Saylor, J. Galen. *Who Planned the Curriculum? A Curriculum Plans Reservoir Model with Historical Examples*. West Lafayette, Ind.: Kappa Delta Pi, 1982.

[*School work and*] *Literary Notes* (1883). Official Journal of the State Board of Education, Nebraska. NSHS.

Scott, Esther, or Lillie M. Reeder. "Primary Reading." Esther Ruth Scott Collection. NSHS.

Second Annual Catalogue of the Eastern-Iowa Normal School 1875–1876. ISHD-HS.

[Shinn, Miss M. W.]. "Etc. [Marriage statistics of women collegiate alumnae to 1889]." *Overland Monthly II* 13 (May 1889): 556–57.

Siampos, Helen. "Early Education in Nebraska." *Nebraska History* 29 (June 1948): 113–33.

Solomon, Barbara Miller. *In the Company of Educated Women: A History of Women and Higher Education in America*. New Haven: Yale University Press, 1985.

Szasz, Margaret Connell. *Education and the American Indian: The Road to Self-Determination Since 1928*. 2d ed. Albuquerque: University of New Mexico Press, 1977.

Thompson, Thomas, ed. *The Schooling of Native America*. Washington, D.C.: American Association of College for Teacher Education in collaboration with the Teacher Corps, U.S. Office of Education, 1978.

Tyack, David. "The Future of the Past: What do We Need to Know About the History of Teaching?" In Donald Warren, ed., *American Teachers: Histories of a Profession at Work*, 408–22. New York: Macmillan, 1989.

———. "The Tribe and the Common School: Community Control in Rural Education." *American Quarterly* 24 (1972): 3–19.

Tyack, David, and Elisabeth Hansot. *Learning Together: A History of Co-education in American Public Schools*. New Haven: Yale University Press, 1990.

———. *Managers of Virtue: Public School Leadership in America, 1820–1980*. New York: Basic Books, 1982.

———. "Silence and Policy Talk: Historical Puzzles About Gender and Education." *Educational Researcher* 17:3 (April 1988): 34–36.

U.S. Department of Interior, Bureau of Education. *Report of the Commissioner of Education*. Vols. 1 and 2. 1902.

Warren, Donald, ed. *American Teachers: Histories of a Profession at Work*. American Educational Research Association. New York: Macmillan; London: Collier Mcmillan, 1989.

Welch, W. M. *How to Organize, Classify and Teach a Country School*. Chicago: W. M. Welch, 1886.

Wesley, Edgar B. *National Education Association: The First Hundred Years: The Building of the Profession*. New York: Harper and Brothers, 1957.

Westerhoff, John H. *McGuffey and His Readers: Piety, Morality, and Education in Nineteenth Century America*. Nashville: Abington Press, 1978.

Wray, Angelina. *Jean Mitchell's School*. Bloomington, Ill.: Public School Publishing Company, 1901.

Wright, David Sands. *Fifty Years at the Teachers College: Historical and Personal Reminiscences, 1876-1926*. Cedar Falls: Iowa State Teachers College, 1926.

IV. Perceiving Women's Lives

Bateson, Mary Catherine. *Composing a Life*. New York: Atlantic Monthly Press, 1989.

Bernard, Jessie. *Women, Wives, Mothers: Values and Options*. Chicago: Aldine Publishing Company, 1975.

Flynn, Elizabeth. "Composing as a Woman." In Susan L. Gabriel and Isaiah Smithson, eds., *Gender in the Classroom: Power and Pedagogy*, 112–26. Urbana and Chicago: University of Illinois Press, 1990.

Gilligan, Carol. *In a Different Voice: Psychological Theory and Women's Development*. Cambridge: Harvard University Press, 1982.

Grumet, Madeleine R. *Bitter Milk: Women and Teaching*. Amherst: University of Massachusetts Press, 1988.

Heilbrun, Carolyn G. *Writing a Woman's Life*. New York: W. W. Norton, 1988.

Personal Narratives Group. *Interpreting Women's Lives: Feminist Theory and Personal Narratives*. Bloomington: Indiana University Press, 1989.

Ribbens, Jane. "Interviewing: An 'Unnatural Situation'?" *Women's Studies International Forum* 12:6 (1989): 579–92.

Index